MW00575547

BIM
IN SMALL-SCALE SUSTAINABLE DESIGN

BIM

IN SMALL-SCALE SUSTAINABLE DESIGN

FRANÇOIS LÉVY

John Wiley & Sons, Inc.

Pour Milo. Tu serais fière.

This book is printed on acid-free paper. ∞

Published by John Wiley & Sons, Inc., Hoboken, New Jersey.
Published simultaneously in Canada.

For general information on our other products and services, or technical support, please contact our Customer Care Department within the United States at 800-762-2974, outside the United States at 317-572-3993 or fax 317-572-4002.

Wiley also publishes its books in a variety of electronic formats. Some content that appears in print may not be available in electronic books.

For more information about Wiley products, visit our Web site at *http://www.wiley.com.*

Library of Congress Cataloging-in-Publication Data:

Levy, Francois, 1966-
BIM in small-scale sustainable design / Francois Levy.
p. cm.
Includes index.
ISBN 978-0-470-59089-8 (hardback); ISBN 978-1-11810385-2 (ebk); ISBN 978-1-118-10386-9 (ebk);
ISBN 978-1-118-10681-5 (ebk); ISBN 978-1-118-10682-2 (ebk); ISBN 978-1-118-15342-0
1. Building information modeling. 2. Sustainable construction. I. Title.
TH438.13.L48 2011
628—dc23 2011010957

Printed in the United States of America

10 9 8 7 6 5 4 3 2 1

Contents

Acknowledgments

I would like to thank the many firms and individuals who have supplied materials for this book. Every caption that bears a credit is a testament to their generosity and contribution, and they have my heartfelt thanks. The firms who contributed case studies have added a depth and richness that would have been sorely missed. My thanks especially to James Anwyl, Marianne Bellino, Robin Clewley, jv DeSousa, Lindsay Dutton, David Light, David Marlatt, Tim McDonald, Olivier Pennetier, Mariko Reed, Carol Richard, David Scheer, Ted Singer, Brian Skripac, Lane Smith, Chikako Terada, Joseph Vigil, and Carin Whitney.

Dr. Mark Nelson graciously contributed important material on Wastewater Gardens. My special thanks to Veronika Szabo at Graphisoft, Wes Gardner and Jeff Ouellette of Nemetschek Vectorworks, Ralph Wessel of Encina, Carol Lettieri of Autodesk, Jeff Kelly of Bentley, and Per Sahlin and his colleagues at EQUA. Thanks to Ann Armstrong for reading early chapters and providing helpful comments. Rebecca Moss of the Digital Content Library at the University of Minnesota helped me track down a tricky image, for which I am grateful. I also would like to extend my appreciation to Andy Alpin, Gordon Bohmfalk, Dr. Muniram Budhu, Laura Burnett, Alexa Carson and Sarah Talkington of Austin Energy, Kelly Cone, Emma Cross, Tim Eian, Christopher Frederick Jones, Mimi Kwan, Betsy Pettit of Building Science Corporation, Mary Petrovich and Pliny Fisk III at CMBPS, Thomas McConnell, Andrew McAlla of Meridian Solar, Mariko Reed, Eleanor Reynolds, Marc Schulte, and Deborah Snyder. Paul Bardagjy has been very generous with his photographs of Moonrise Ranch and CMBPS, which he shot in the best possible light.

Architectural colleagues and friends have provided encouragement, images, and constructive commentary. I'd like to thank Al Godfrey and Mell Lawrence, as well as all members of our software users group. Also my thanks go to Ben Allee, James Austin, Stephen DuPont, Frank Gomillion, Michael Heacock, Nathan Kipnis, Laurie Limbacher, Dwayne Mann, Kelly Mann, Dr. Steven Moore, Andrew Nance, Adam Pyrek, Keith Ragsdale, Don Seidel, Marshall Swearingen, Charles Thompson, Dason Whitsett, Krista Whitson, and Mandy Winford. Gregory Brooks collaborated with me on a project that makes a few appearances between these pages. Mark Winford deserves special mention for being my architectural partner and collaborator on many projects. Daniel Jansenson provided invaluable rendering advice (and has for years); any deficiencies in my images are due to my not listening to him.

We learn by teaching. Colleagues and students in academia have particularly enriched my understanding and practice of architecture. Kevin Alter and Dean Fritz Steiner of the University of Texas at Austin have generously provided me teaching opportunities which have prepared me to write this book, and for that I am very grateful. Other colleagues, some of whom are specifically named above, have contributed to my academic career. Finally, I have learned a great deal from my students and teaching assistants; if they have gotten from me half of what I gained from them, then I count myself a successful educator.

My clients, past and current, deserve a great measure of appreciation. Their projects have been the proving grounds for much of what has emerged as this book, and I owe them all a debt of gratitude for their tremendous patronage, trust, and friendship.

Justin Dowhower deserves particular recognition for his extraordinary assistance with many of the images in this book, as well as the creation of several of them. Justin's knowledge of BIM and sustainability were tremendous assets to this project.

Finally, and hardly least, I now know how insufficient an author's acknowledgment of his spouse is. To Julie I give a profound measure of gratitude for her generosity, love, and stalwart support of my academic, professional, and creative career. My words fall far short of their mark.

Building Information Models and Modeling

Rapid developments in building design and analysis software over the last decade, coupled with advances in desktop and laptop computational power, have led to the emergence of new digital models for the design and documentation of buildings: virtual buildings or building information models (BIM). Thanks to these advances, BIM-authoring software applications combine three- or four-dimensional models with imbedded, intelligent building objects related in a contextual database. An inescapable buzzword these days in the practice of architecture (and among other building professionals), BIM may commonly mean both *building information modeling* (the process) and *building information model* (the digital artifact). In this book, I use *BIM* (alone) to refer to the modeling process, whereas the model itself I call somewhat redundantly the *BIM model* or ArchiCAD's *virtual building*.

For example, a BIM column is not merely depicted as a two-dimensional representation or three-dimensional extrusion, but exists in the model as an intelligent object that "knows" that it is a column. Contrast this with a column drawn conventionally in plan: increased line weight and perhaps poché allow the user, thanks to established graphic conventions, to *infer* the meaning of four lines which are themselves "dumb" (both in the sense of unintelligent and mute).

As a result of BIM's data-rich 3D modeling, various design disciplines can extract and manipulate relevant tabular or graphical building views such as reports and drawings. Such an approach can improve building construction and operational performance, increase design efficiencies, and foster an integrated design workflow, among other benefits.

The cost of buildings

Trends in global climate change are correlated with carbon emissions, in that the cost of hydrocarbon fuels upon which world economies are largely dependent is trending upwards, and geopolitical instabilities abound in oil-rich regions of the world. Reducing our carbon emissions sufficiently to slow global warming will require far more radical changes in energy use than most political and corporate leaders will acknowledge; reversing it in the near term is probably impossible. At the time of this writing, the catastrophic and anguishing deep-sea oil spill in the Gulf of Mexico has once again drawn the world's attention to the true costs of our society's dependence on hydrocarbon fuels. And startlingly, 48 percent of US energy expenditure today is devoted to the building sector—it is roughly evenly divided between commercial and residential structures, including energy costs of materials. Given the above, there is a real and meaningful environmental impact that building design professionals will have on the state of the world in the coming decades.

Like BIM, sustainable design is also often seen as an approach more appropriate to large projects, again where design fees can absorb the requisite additional research and design innovation. This perception disregards that residences represent over 20 percent of American energy consumption; our houses therefore make a considerable contribution to our societal carbon footprint and the depletion of our energy resources. Energy efficiency in housing is thus ignored at our peril.

Furthermore, large buildings are typically internally load dominated, whereas small projects are envelope or skin-load dominated. That is, climate and how we design for it has a much larger impact on a small building's energy consumption than it does for a large building's. Therefore, having good quantitative data is essential for architects to make more intelligent choices about how they design all projects—even small ones.

See, change

BIM is a *design environment* that requires that the designer reevaluate the practice of architecture. Distinguishing "design environment" from "design tool" underscores the reality that BIM represents more than a single tool or software application. Rather, BIM requires a complete shift in the way one goes about the design process.

At the very least, with BIM, buildings are modeled rather than drawn. This may seem very obvious, but the implications are profound. Modeling represents a radical departure from the way we architects have traditionally undertaken the work of our profession for centuries. This not only represents a change in the mechanics of our work, but I contend it is a shift in the cognitive processes that accompany and ultimately drive that work. We work differently, and as a result, probably think differently, too. Furthermore, while modeling decisions may be deferred (a floor, for example, may be represented as an undifferentiated slab), it is difficult to ignore conditions entirely ("the model doesn't lie").

As a result, *design decisions are evaluated based on 3D model views as well as from 2D projections of that model.* The former take the form of perspectives, isometrics, orbital flyovers, fly-throughs, perspective sections, exploded views, and so on. The latter are "drawing" views that may appear to conform to the graphic conventions of traditional plans, sections, and elevations, but in fact are just that—views of the ubiquitous model.

Because of the completeness of the virtual building, extracting views (such as elevations and sections) is nearly trivial—generally a matter of a few clicks of the mouse. As a result, *design development and construction documents are produced far more rapidly* than in the traditional architectural process of constructed drawings. This production efficiency has significant effects. As discussed in greater depth in Chapter 1, by necessity more design decisions are taken earlier in the project. This so-called front-loading (or left-shift in the design phases timeline) of the design process requires that all major geometrical relationships in three dimensions be established earlier. However, the resolution of the details of those relationships may be deferred, as noted above. The practice of architecture is necessarily affected. Workloads and fee structures must be reevaluated in light of a new paradigm of more time spent in schematic design (SD), and less time spent in the construction documents (CD) phase.

With the possibility to explicitly model structural and mechanical components (and ready-made tools for doing so with relative ease), there are *greater opportunities for coordination and collaboration* between architects and engineers. For the architect, an intelligent model helps ensure better coordination of other disciplines. Automatic clash detection—inspecting, analyzing, and alerting the user to undesired interference between model elements—is a BIM feature that originated in automotive and aerospace design software. Clash detection requires a data-rich model to distinguish colliding supply and return air ducts, for example, from a branching supply duct; or to properly identify a column and beam connection as a desirable "interference" rather than as a "clash." Further, common data exchange formats like buildingSMART International's industry foundation classes (IFC) create opportunities for more open exchange of models between architect and structural and mechanical engineers. Conversely, this has given rise to as-yet unresolved issues such as those of model ownership. Nevertheless, BIM and integrated project delivery (IPD) facilitate a more collaborative approach to design that admits structural and mechanical issues as potential design influences rather than mere afterthoughts.

Finally, and the brunt of this book's objective, BIM creates opportunities for the *quantitative assessment of design options*. That is, the data bound to the virtual building model can be defined, analyzed, and parameterized by the designer, with the ultimate goal of positively influencing building performance. As a practicing architect aspiring to produce work of relevance and beauty, I have a vested interest in finding forms that support high performance buildings and are expressive of that performance.

BIM for the rest of us

For these reasons, I am advocating the somewhat contrarian position that BIM is appropriate as a *design environment*. Architectural design is, after all, a process of proposing and evaluating alternative spatial, geometrical, and material solutions to a stated problem of the built environment. Traditionally qualitative evaluation has been performed in real time, whereas quantitative analysis is often deferred. BIM, if used as I propose in this book, potentially allows quantitative analysis in real time.

I must emphasize that in spite of popular perception, BIM methodology—and the shifts it entails—are applicable to projects of all scales. Small-scaled projects are no less prone to erroneous quantitative analysis. As small buildings are skin-load dominated rather than internally load dominated, their morphology is most impacted by climate. Indeed, thanks to the greater influence of climate on such buildings, they may benefit all the more from "climate indexing," whereby building massing, geometry, fenestration, envelope and interior materials, and passive strategies are specifically tailored to the building's region and site.

Largely seen as a design and documentation methodology (and ultimately a social convention) rather than a specific technology, BIM promises to allow building designers and stakeholders to leverage greater efficiencies from digital files through the use of such data-rich building models. Almost universally assumed to be appropriate to large projects with fees to support the "left-shift" in the design process, BIM is often ignored in the context of small projects by many practitioners and software developers. In most instances the BIM workflow is promulgated for large firms and large projects, the supposition being that small firms and projects can't sustain the presumed up-front labor costs that BIM implies.

Yet the production benefits that large firms realize from BIM are also translatable to small firms and projects. Most BIM applications include parametric objects that are suitable to building technologies appropriate to buildings of a variety of scales. From personal experience I can vouch that production efficiencies that I have consistently realized—even on tiny projects of a few hundred square feet—have paid for more time spent on other aspects of design, or allowed me to deliver projects at lower fees, or both. The "left-shift" that I refer to elsewhere is very much real.

According to the Boston Society of Architects, 80 percent of US architecture firms are comprised of six or fewer architects. Increasing the penetration of BIM and sustainable design practices into small firms will be helpful in counteracting the schism between small-firm and large-firm practice. As a practicing architect and university lecturer, I have taught building technology, BIM, and design courses. In my experience, BIM in the context of small architectural projects is a much-neglected topic. I know from personal experience that the assumption that BIM is only appropriate to large projects is false, and that small firms can reap tremendous benefits in sustainable design and production efficiency from a properly integrated BIM work process.

Historically, architects in a variety of firm types all adhered to a similar set of work and documentation conventions; this has been true even to the extent that architects from different regions or countries could understand each other's documents, variations in building technologies notwithstanding. Indeed, the profession is practiced universally to the extent that it is quite common for architects to gain their architectural education in one country but develop their early career in another, and, at times, practice in a third. As both BIM and sustainable design gain a greater foothold in the architectural community, cultural and technological differences in the practice of architecture in large and small firms may only increase, undermining the universality of architectural training. Such a schism in the architectural practice is undesirable as it further fractures the profession into increasingly specialized niches.

I further contend that BIM is appropriate for sustainable design. There are currently two general approaches to designing for sustainable projects, each with distinct advantages and drawbacks. A *prescriptive* approach, taken by some aspects of Leadership in Energy and Environmental Design (LEED) for example, dictates the measures to be taken to achieve sustainability. Such prescriptive measures serve as proxies for actual building and occupant performance.

Performance design guidelines, on the other hand, require that an aspect of building operation be modeled as a prediction of actual behavior. (LEED also has performance guidelines.) The detailed modeling required is well beyond the scope of BIM applications, requiring building energy performance analysis using dedicated energy simulation software. The BIM model may be exported to the energy modeler, however (See Chapters 1 and 11). Some of the benefits of both prescriptive and performance measures can be attained within BIM, however, through the quantitative analysis techniques that I describe in this book. The benefit of early analysis—even as early as conceptual design—is that it allows the most influence on building performance with the least effort. BIM's adaptability is compatible with performance-driven (sustainable) design. BIM becomes a sustainable design environment, then, as it potentially integrates quantitative analysis in the design decision-making process.

What this book is, and isn't

My challenge has been to pen a book that is a useful guide to small- and medium-sized firms that hold a commitment to sustainable design and are contemplating or undertaking the transition to BIM. As such, I've had to walk a fine line between being too general and too specific. A book that is too broad might give an interesting, even thought-provoking, overview of the relationship between BIM, skin-load dominated buildings, and small-design practices. But without a highly practical perspective on the topic, it might be of little useful relevance to the practitioner and remain a largely academic exercise. While a theory of BIM is of enormous interest (and essential on some level), it may have little application for most users.

On the other hand, a text that is too detailed, with step-by-step instructions, screenshots, and itemizing particular tasks, might seem attractive, but ultimately would be too limited. Such a book would be more or less a software manual. While this might suit some BIM users, this approach has several shortcomings. Aside from many software users' disinclination to read them, "software manuals" are not relevant to users across a spectrum of proficiencies or at various stages of BIM implementation. By their very nature, manuals must address a certain level of user with certain skills. Second, manuals naturally must address users of a particular software platform. While it's true that Revit, for example, enjoys a large market share, it may not be the software of choice for all users, and there are several other viable alternatives (see Chapter 2). Third, a software manual is quickly outdated. BIM is a rapidly evolving environment, so even a book that is not tethered to a particular release will need to be updated. But a manual is reference for one release cycle (about a year), after which it just takes up shelf (or disk) space. Finally, a manual focuses on tasks, not principles. These tend to be limited to a particular application of the technology, rather than leading to a deeper understanding of the appropriateness of that technology.

Fundamentally, then, this book is meant as a guide. You should be able to read the relevant chapter(s) and then apply the material to actual design projects using the content as a model. Naturally, this will require that you refer to your software's documentation for the particular tasks required to implement these strategies. I have made efforts to be as comprehensive as possible; a scan of the table of contents will reveal a broad range of sustainable design topics. It will be the rare project indeed that makes use of all aspects of this book. Certain topics will be more or less relevant to a given building given climate, program, site, and so forth. The designer using this book should, as always, use professional and practical judgment in determining the applicability of a topic or technique. Don't expect that in order to design sustainably or design with BIM all aspects addressed here must be applied.

Finally, I should emphasize that in spite of the pervasive discussion of quantitative analysis, the host of other criteria that form the basis of design do not thereby go away. Your training, experience, aesthetic, and qualitative judgment are all still in play. It is not a matter of either BIM and sustainability or purely architectural design; it is a "both and" relationship. You are adding a tool, albeit a powerful one, to your repertoire. Your trusted old tools are not going away, and indeed they must not be neglected.

A word on the case studies

Each chapter concludes with a case study of an architecturally notable project whose designers have used BIM as a parametric design tool for sustainability. Given the complexity of building performance and variety of software applications available, the methods suggested in this book are by no means exhaustive; many other approaches for performance-based design informed by quantitative analysis are possible. I have attempted to draw from a variety of case studies representative of a wide range of climatic, geographic, and architectural responses to design. As a result, the methods used in the case studies do not necessarily perfectly follow the methodologies outlined in the chapter. This only further demonstrates the vast flexibility and usefulness of BIM, and an evolution of "best practices" for this emerging design environment.

Chapter 1

BIM and Sustainable Design

Having established in the broadest terms the purpose and goals of this book in the Introduction, later chapters will discuss in detail the specific strategies the designer may employ to effectively use building information modeling (BIM) in the design of sustainable, skin-load dominated buildings. Beforehand, however, it is important to define BIM in greater depth, while considering its advantages and limitations (both perceived and real). We will also discuss BIM in the context of the design process, as well as consider its various other roles presented in later chapters. Finally, this chapter, like all others, will conclude with a relevant case study project.

The emergence of Building Information Modeling

Historical context

For centuries, master builders and architects have relied on drawings as an inventive and analytical medium, and to convey instructions to building trades. Vitruvius mentions drafting in *De Architectura*: through geometry the architect's "delineations of buildings on plane surfaces are greatly facilitated." While little medieval construction documentation is extant, it is known that drawing was used to work out and illustrate the proportional system of cathedrals of the day. Models were apparently also not unknown: building models are depicted in medieval ecclesiastical art, and Brunelleschi had a 1/12th-scale model of the Florence Cathedral constructed prior to the construction of the actual building. The extensive technical expertise of historical craftsmen and tradesmen, combined with established and fairly static vernacular building practices, reduced the need for extensive construction documents. Generations of buildings were constructed with little more than a few drawings and a pattern book of carpentry and masonry details. By the eighteenth century, drafting with specialized steel nibs on prepared surfaces, more or less as it had come to be practiced in my lifetime, had come into being. Such technical documents consisted of precisely constructed drawings executed on vellum, at times watercolored for aesthetic and communicative effect. Examine a Beaux-Arts elevation and marvel both at the beauty of its rendering and the remarkable paucity, by modern standards, of separate details.

The advent of computer-assisted drafting (CAD) did little to change the nature of drawing. It may seem surprising to claim that CAD is similar to eighteenth-century drafting, but consider that CAD drawings are, for the most part, manually assembled. The gestural tasks involved in their construction may be vastly different from those associated with inking vellum, but the cognitive and social processes remain largely the same. In both cases, the architect must manually construct and coordinate various orthographic views—plans, sections, elevations, and details—of a hypothetical building (Fig. 1.2).

Moreover, over a century ago, buildings had none of their construction budgets devoted to mechanical and electrical systems, simply because those systems did not exist; today it is common for about a fifth to a quarter of a building's construction

FIGURE 1.1 A late nineteenth- or early twentieth-century elevation is both extremely expressive of design intent and carries very little detailed constructible information. This type of drawing embodies several social factors from a highly artisanal labor pool to a lack of pervasive litigiousness. Note the minimal dimensions.

Albert Simon, architect, from the author's private collection.

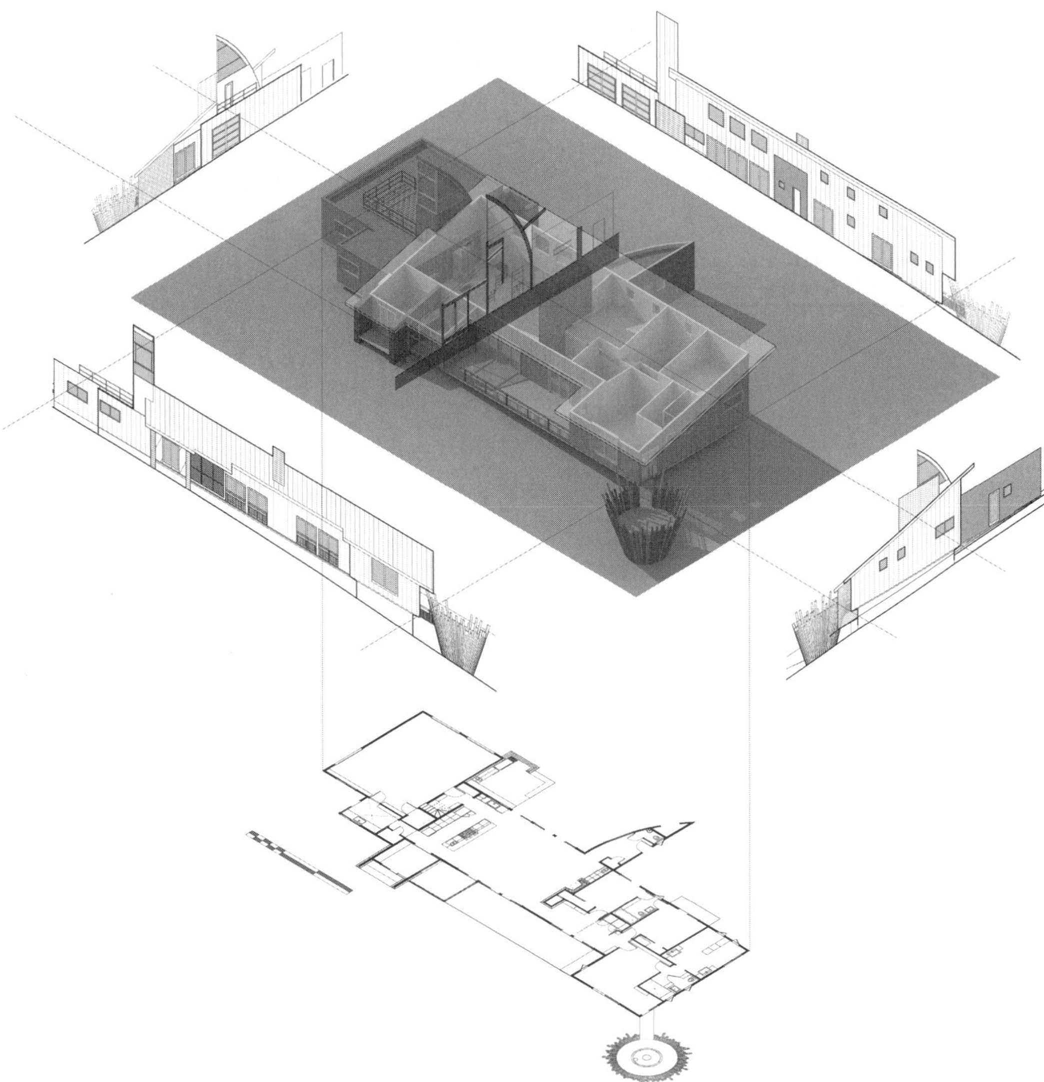

FIGURE 1.2 In traditional construction drawings, a comprehensive "model" of the building is a composite of a variety of 2D views, which are commonly called drawings. If a view is missing, there is a gap in the model.

cost to be for such systems. Specialized projects like laboratories or medical buildings may have as much as 60 percent of construction costs dedicated to mechanical, electrical, and plumbing (MEP) systems (Fig. 1.3). Furthermore, building materials and techniques are by now constantly and rapidly evolving. This, coupled with a tendency to mitigate risk through litigation, has contributed to the trend toward more extensive, complex, and detailed architectural drawing sets. It is in this technological climate that BIM has emerged.

Defining BIM

Over the last decade, *building information modeling* has gained currency among growing numbers of building professionals and stakeholders, emerging

	pre-1900	since 1970	since 2000
Foundation	15%	15%	15%
Architectural	70%	35%	30%
Structural	15%	15%	15%
HVAC	0%	25%	25%
Electrical	0%	10%	15%

FIGURE 1.3 A greater portion of building cost over time has been dedicated to mechanical and electrical systems. Since structural costs remain somewhat fixed, architectural expenditures have proportionately decreased. These figures are approximated averages based on unpublished research by Steven A. Moore of the University of Texas at Austin School of Architecture in 1999, updated by Dason Whitsett, also of UT SOA.

from arcane obscurity to inescapable buzzword. Developments in building design and analysis software in recent years, coupled with advances in desktop and portable computational power, have engendered effective virtual buildings, or building information models. Gradually, use of BIM is replacing traditional two-dimensional drawing as an architectural design and documentation methodology. Such an approach can increase design efficiencies, foster an integrated design workflow, speed construction documentation and reduce errors, improve building construction and scheduling, and optimize operational performance.

Along the way, BIM has been variously defined, according to the user's profession, perspective, or agenda. In their *BIM Handbook*, Eastman et al. (2008) define BIM as "a modeling technology and associated set of processes to produce, communicate, and analyze building models." They go on to distinguish building models as possessing contextual data-rich building components, whose data are consistent and non-redundant, and have coordinated views. While it is beyond the scope of this book to frame an exhaustive debate of BIM that will satisfy all practitioners, it's essential to clearly define the term in the context of sustainable design for small projects.

Building information modeling: an architectural software environment in which graphic and tabular views are extracted from data-rich building models composed of intelligent, contextual building objects.

Thus, a BIM column is not merely depicted as a two-dimensional drawing or a three-dimensional extrusion, but as an intelligent object that "knows" that it is a column. As a result, various design disciplines can extract and manipulate relevant graphical or tabular building views. *Views* does not mean drawings only (in the form of plans, elevations, sections, isometrics, and perspectives). The term also includes reports: door, window, fixture, and finish schedules, for example, as well as various performance reports (Fig. 1.4).

BIM is a substantial departure from the traditional design methodology that architects have followed for millennia, thanks to both 3D digital modeling capabilities and the critical feature of view extraction. Heretofore, designers constructed multiple 2D drawings that, when viewed together, composed an implicit 3D representation of the building being designed. With BIM, the intelligent model is developed first, and drawings (views) are the result. This not only offers opportunities for greater production efficiencies, but also helps assure greater coordination between deliverables (again, drawings, schedules, and reports) and avoidance of conflicts and collisions. On the other hand, this methodology is to a large extent an inversion of the traditional workflow, with its emphasis on designing by drawing.

Of critical interest to designers is the opportunity to spend relatively more time on design, design more effectively, and capitalize on performance feedback from the virtual building to design for greater sustainability. Patrick MacLeamy, CEO of HOK, is credited with popularizing this graph

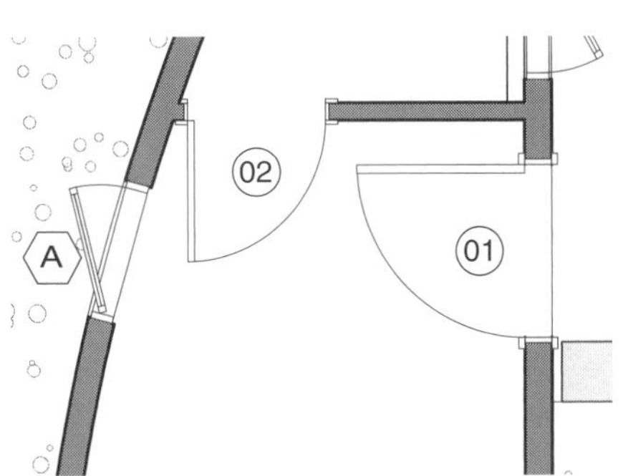

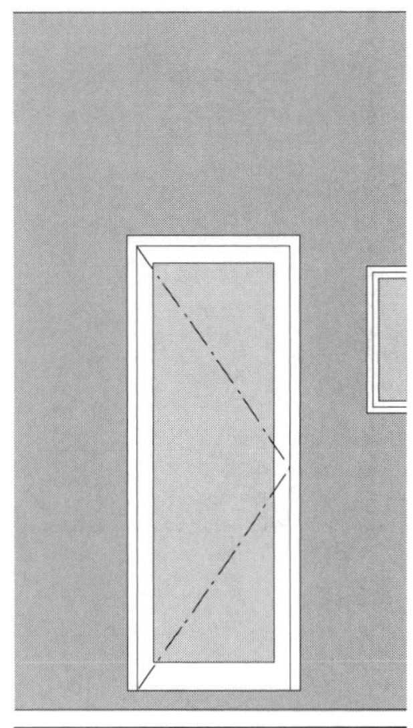

Door Schedule

Key	Width	Height	R.O. Width	R.O. Height	Operation	Leaf	Thickness	Manufact
01	2'10 1/4"	7'10 1/2"	3'1 3/8"	8'0"	Swing Simple	Glass	1 3/4"	Marvin Inte
02	2'4"	6'8"	2'6"	6'9"	Swing Simple	Panel	1 3/8"	Supado
03	2'0"	6'8"	2'2"	6'9"	Swing Simple	Panel	1 3/8"	Supado

FIGURE 1.4 A BIM object resides in a relational database, and is subject to a variety of views. In this case, the same door object can be viewed in plan with or without its identifier key, in an elevation, or in a door schedule. None of these is any more the "real" door than any other, and all are editable. Changes to one view affect all other views.

comparing the design team's diminishing ability to control project costs and the increasing cost of making design changes over time, against the traditional architectural fee allocation (Fig. 1.5). Initially intended as an argument for integrated project delivery (IPD), the concept is equally applicable to BIM and sustainable design.

BIM among building professionals

BIM has a broad appeal to a wide variety of building professions throughout the planning, design, bidding and procurement, fabrication, construction, and operation phases of buildings. For many large projects, sophisticated building owners drive the adoption of BIM, perceiving it as an opportunity to reap greater value from Instruments of Service. In such cases, the owner may be motivated by opportunities for faster design and documentation processes with the expectation of fewer errors, in addition to the benefits of coordinated, interoperable documentation for building operations.

Large construction firms also have been aggressively adopting BIM, finding benefits in faster and more accurate quantity surveying and cost estimating, a reduction in errors through improved 3D collision or clash detection, and more efficient construction scheduling thanks to 4D (sequence) modeling. Anecdotally, it seems to be commonplace for such builders to have in-house staff, who are often recent architecture school graduates and intern architects, to rebuild the architect's CAD or BIM design documentation.

Architects, however, have met BIM with a certain degree of skepticism:

- Who pays for more service? There is the perception that with BIM the architect is providing

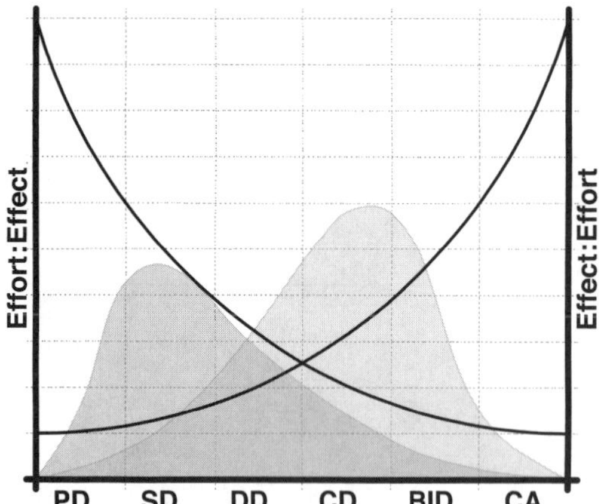

FIGURE 1.5 A version of the so-called MacLeamy curve, originally attributed to HOK's Patrick MacLeamy. As time progresses in the design process, it takes more and more effort to make changes that have a diminishing effect; the least effort will have the most significant impact early in the project. Typical project phases are listed left to right on the *x*-axis in chronological order: predesign (PD), schematic design (SD), design development (DD), contract or construction documents (CD), bid phase (BID), and construction administration (CA). The right-hand "camel hump" represents the traditional design process, with the bulk of work occurring in the CD phase. Note that a substantial portion of that effort lies outside the Effort:Effect curve. With BIM (and IPD), however, more work is "left-shifted" (the left "camel hump") and occurs when it is most effective—earlier in design. The shaded area lies under the Effort:Effect curve, which suggests that most work occurs when it has the most effect, and less work occurs when it has less effect on the design outcome.

a higher level of service and more useful Instruments of Service without commensurately increased compensation.

- Who is liable? There is a concern for increased liability. If a data-rich BIM model allows fewer construction errors and greater building performance, there might be the expectation that buildings designed with BIM would adhere to a higher professional standard, potentially increasing the architect's legal exposure.
- Who owns the Instruments of Service? In a world of document interoperability, some architects are uneasy with the potentially blurred line of intellectual property, and the questions arising from a potentially collective ownership of building documents. There is a substantial difference between an MEP supplier basing shop drawings on prints or electronic backgrounds provided by the architect, and that same subcontractor accessing and editing files which originated with the architect and design team.
- Who pays for re-training? There are substantial retooling issues in making the transition to BIM. As a consultant, I'm acutely aware of the hardware, software, and, most significantly, the staff re-training and initial productivity losses involved in transitioning from CAD to a new way of working.
- How can the firm handle collaboration? BIM implies not just a different work methodology within a firm, but also a change in the nature of relationships with consultants and other project team members. Not all firms are ready to jump into the world of integrated project delivery (IPD) and design-build (DB).

It will be obvious from this brief discussion that many of the hurdles that confront a firm transitioning to BIM are fundamentally social, not technological, in nature (as is often the case with technology).

On the other hand, most *small*-project owners tend to be less concerned than their large-project counterparts with building operational opportunities due to data interoperability or longevity. At present, most have never heard of BIM. Similarly, small project contractors operate far more informally, and do not have the staff to leverage BIM models, mine them for data, or perform collision detection—much less implement 4D model scheduling. Many of the BIM features that are attractive to large organizations are barriers to entry for their smaller counterparts.

BIM for design

This book emphasizes the use of BIM as an architectural design methodology. It is, therefore, aimed squarely at architects and designers. Gallagher's oft-cited 2004 NIST report on CAD identified economic opportunities for the implementation of BIM. Such projected savings result in part from construction scheduling efficiencies and reduced errors. In other words, BIM is potentially beneficial for documentation efficiencies. Indeed, the productivity gains due to automatically coordinated views of the virtual model are the most obvious benefit of BIM. But of the benefits ascribed to BIM, design is typically not the highest on the list. Indeed, many architects view BIM primarily as a documentation tool, rather than a design tool. This is a missed opportunity.

Design is a parametric process

Architectural design is both a forensic and a dialectic process. What could I mean by that? In architecture schools, it is not uncommon for instructors and students to refer to the design process, particularly in its early stages, as an *investigation.* This is not an inapt description, and is equally applicable to practice. Architects often begin a project by coming to an understanding of three overlapping realms: client, site, and program. In fact, in my first or second meeting with a client, I often sketch a little Venn diagram (Fig. 1.6), explaining that architecture occurs in the common conceptual space mutually captured by these three diverse agendas.

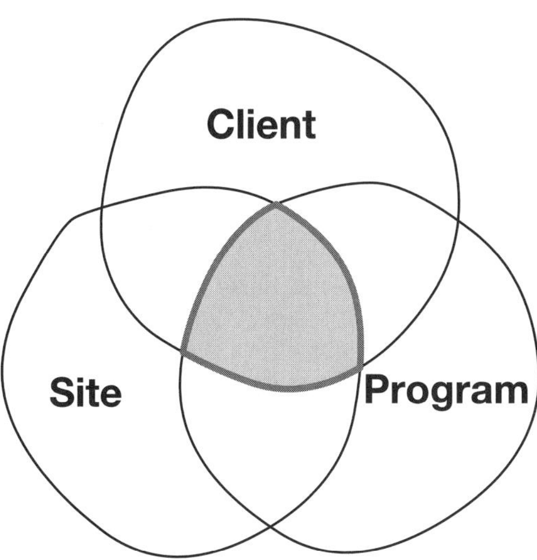

FIGURE 1.6 One way to frame a discussion of design is to think of it as the intersection of a particular client, a unique site, and a program. It might be drawn on the client's napkin, but the architect holds the pen.

An architect might ask, *Where do I fit in this diagram?* The architect profoundly affects the outcome of the project by influencing the framing of the issues. In other words, the architect "draws" the diagram, and thereby defines the boundary lines. Before we can get answers to our questions, we determine which questions to ask in the first place. Obviously, our choice of questions profoundly affects the answers we get (or don't). Will climate be considered, and if so, to what extent? Given inevitable conflicts in the client's program, how will they be prioritized? How much will we play to our client's aesthetic, functional, and financial expectations, and to what degree will we take it upon ourselves to challenge those expectations and educate the client? Will we argue for cost, or value? And so on.

This is why I claim that design is forensic in nature: we investigate and uncover a project's constraints. But there is perhaps another way in which designing is a forensic process. Constraints give life to the project itself, or as Nadia Boulanger said: "*Great art likes chains.*" In this act of uncovering constraints, we effectively uncover the building itself. Michelangelo's famous quote, too, is apt: "*Every block of stone has a statue inside it and it is the task of the sculptor to discover it.*"

What about my second assertion, that design is dialectic, or put another way, that architecture occurs in a conversation? Superficially, this may seem to contradict the inherent monumentality of our work. I expect that most of my work will outlast me, and I'm probably not the only architect who at times indulges the conceit of buildings as enduring testaments. This seeming permanence of our work, then, would tend to suggest that buildings are like monologues, impervious to their inhabitants. Yet I contend that buildings carry on lively conversations with us, on several levels. A good building exists as a variety of spatial and temporal expressions, creating for the occupant a correspondingly rich range of experiences. But more to my point, the *process* of designing consists of engaging in an almost Socratic inquiry. We ask the site about its topography and the flora that inhabits it, how the sun dances across it throughout the day and in the course of the seasons, and which way the wind caresses it. We engage our clients in long conversations about their aspirations, hopes, and needs, teasing from them (and from ourselves) what is appropriate for this client, this site, and this project. We push and pull volumes and strain materials, probing their limits.

And why is this relevant? BIM, it turns out, follows a similar Socratic and dialectic logic. A BIM model is assembled and populated with data, from which views are extracted. Architectural relationships and conditions that might not have been obvious, or emphasized, come to the fore. The model is queried; data are organized to tell a meaningful story; the model is changed to tell a different story, or one with a different ending. We ask, *What if . . . ?* and then ask it again. And again. The process of critically examining alternate design options, preferably balancing subjective and objective criteria, is *parametric design*.

It is precisely this parametric design ability to ask, *What if . . . ?* that makes BIM such a powerful *design* tool. This may come as a surprise to those who assume that BIM is only good for documentation once all high-impact decisions have been made, or that it forces premature project decisions due to over-specificity, or that it is an inappropriate medium to address architectural details. We've already looked at BIM's capability beyond mere documentation; let's challenge these other assumptions.

"BIM forces premature project decisions due to over-specificity"

The Government Services Agency (GSA), the United States' largest single landlord, has been a driving force in the adoption of BIM. This has in part been a reaction to the potential for reduction of inefficiencies outlined in the NIST report. Of greater concern to the GSA, however, are the advantages accruing to building owners who have at their disposal intelligent 3D models of their properties. The GSA has therefore required that BIM files contain Space objects, which are intelligent volumes that represent not a particular building component, but the spaces within the building. Occupancy type, code characteristics, internal energy loads, and other parameters are attributed to the Space object. Occupancy can be more easily planned and scheduled using such components, a clear benefit to the GSA and other building owner/occupants.

As a result of the GSA requirement, Space objects exist in every major BIM application. In some cases, as with Revit, the standard procedure is to "fill" a modeled volume bounded by floors, walls, and ceilings with a Space object. (In energy modeling, it is important that the Space object be exported to an energy modeler, as it contains critical energy load data. Such programs can also often ignore some of the BIM's more complex geometries for the sake of computational economy.) In other BIM workflows, the Space object can also be created first, and then "skinned" with walls, floors, ceilings, and roof components. This is the case, for example, with Vectorworks.

This seemingly innocent GSA-mandated component can become a powerful tool in conceptual and schematic design. Occupancies, room sizes, and other program-driven criteria constitute some of the earliest information gleaned or developed in the design process, and an early requirement of the conceptual design phase is the determination of spatial adjacencies and the development of building massing. Space objects are a useful tool in the BIM arsenal when used as intelligent building masses, providing quantitative data in support of design analysis and decisions. Here are a few early design operations involving Space objects that will be covered in greater detail in later chapters:

- Adjacency matrices that score spatial configurations in real time can help the designer develop more efficient building arrangements. Vectorworks and others have such tools built in.
- Since Space objects are intelligent volumes, competing concepts' ratios of envelope to effective floor area can be readily analyzed, providing preliminary material and cost optimization of early massing models.

- BIM Spaces combined with a topographical model and a 3D maximum building envelope can be visually or automatically analyzed for clash detection, depending on the BIM software used. Even in small projects, there are often complex zoning and solar rights codes that demand a 3D analysis of setback planes and terrain topography as they interact with the building mass. In Austin, where I practice, the so-called McMansion ordinance stipulates a building "tent" whose geometry is site-dependant and beyond which building elements, with some exceptions, cannot penetrate (Fig. 1.7). This tent can have a complex shape depending on topography and metes and bounds geometry, and an early envelope check is critical to avoid catastrophic problems later in the project.
- Site-indexed massing models can be analyzed for solar exposure and solar rights. In developing massing models for skin-load dominated buildings, early attention must be paid to sun angles for solar exposure and shading, and solar rights impacts on adjacent properties. A massing model that is informed by correct orientation, the site's global position, and the massing of adjacent structures, can be analyzed for solar optimization through automatic surface analysis or the creation of sun studies and solar animations (Fig. 1.8).

In addition to Space objects, most BIM applications allow the user to create generic walls (Fig. 1.9) and slabs (floors and roofs). Such components can be deployed early in schematic design when materials and perhaps even structural systems are as yet undetermined. The designer can specify wall thickness, for example, without concern for the exact particulars of the wall's components:

- Characteristics such as cost per linear foot or overall thermal resistance factor (U-factor) can be assigned to such a generic wall for preliminary cost estimating or thermal envelope performance evaluation.

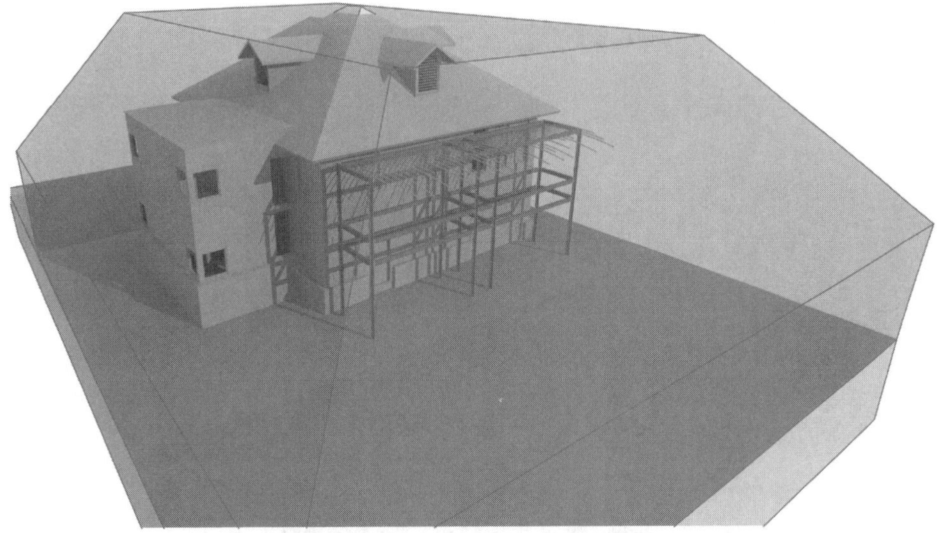

FIGURE 1.7 Form-based codes have been in existence for at least as long as New York stipulated solar access rights, but they are becoming increasingly popular tools for municipalities to govern growth and development. Sites may be straightforward, but even so, careful modeling can be a useful tool in verifying compliance. When sites are challenging with irregular metes and bounds, a model may be the only way to validate an allowable maximum design envelope (see also 3.19).

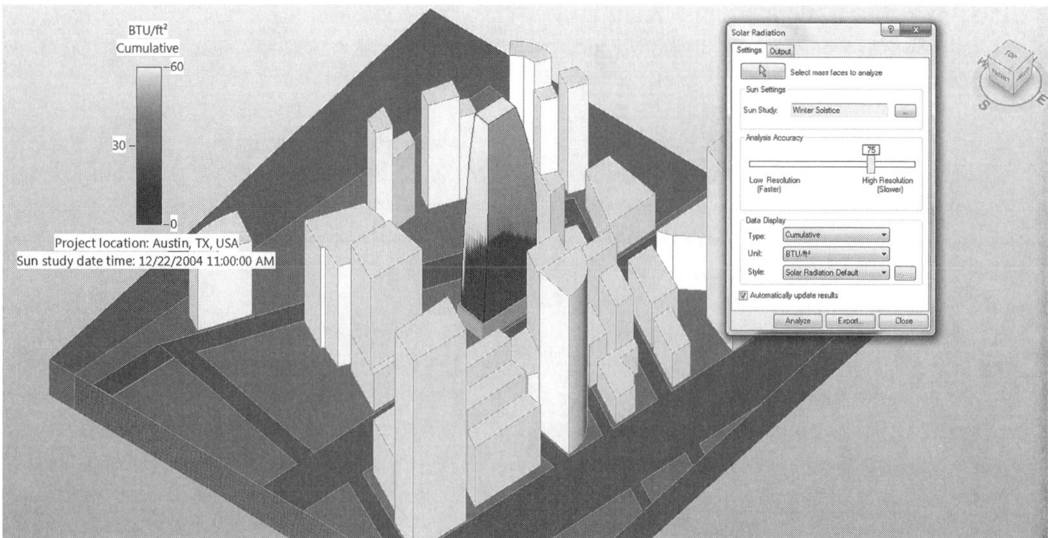

FIGURE 1.8 There are a growing number of BIM or BIM-compatible energy tools targeted for the conceptual design phase. Autodesk's Project Vasari, for example, allows preliminary energy performance analysis at the massing model stage.

Image courtesy of Justin Firuz Dowhower, LEED AP.

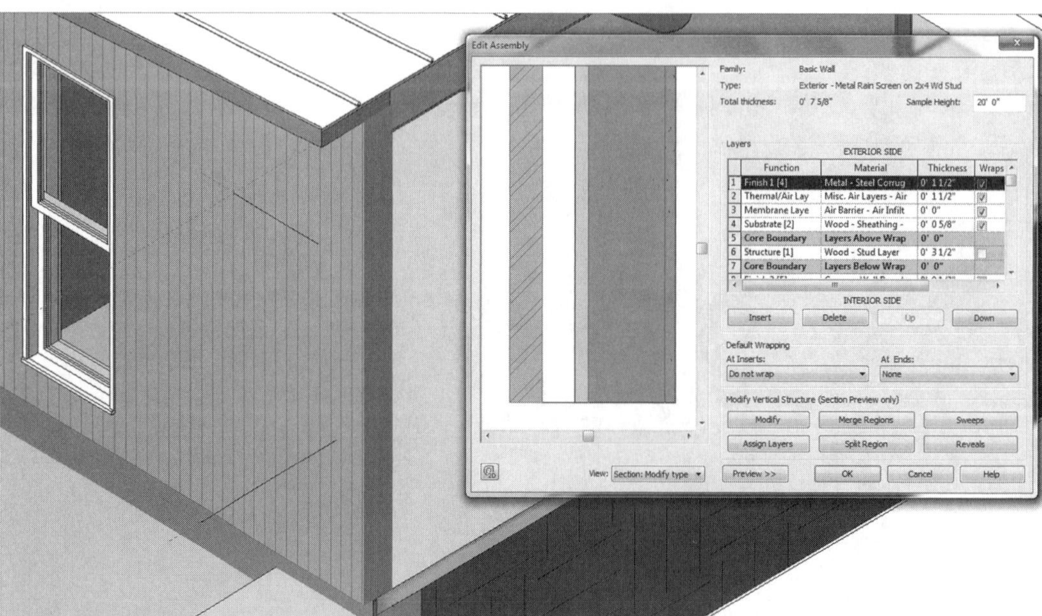

FIGURE 1.9 BIM walls are more than mere extrusions with penetrations for windows and doors; they are potentially composed of components with individually assigned characteristics (data and geometry).

Image courtesy of Justin Firuz Dowhower, LEED AP.

- Doors and windows may initially be modeled with little or no detail, to the point of being represented as simple openings. Optionally, the designer may assign code-specified minimum performance standards (U-factor and SHGC) or cost assumptions.
- BIM software can calculate percentage glazing, to optimize thermal performance based on rules of thumb. The model can be queried for total glazing area, which may be compared to gross or net exterior wall area, even when no specific window system has been selected.
- A total U·A limit (U-factor, times exterior wall assembly area) can be calculated for the BIM model in real time as the design progresses, beginning in schematic design. Commonly, projects are verified for energy code compliance through the use of applications such as the US Department of Energy's free ResCheck and ComCheck software. For thermal envelope performance, a total U·A must not be exceeded. If such code compliance is verified late in Design Development or, worse yet, just prior to permitting, design changes to insure compliance in the event of failure are time consuming and expensive—and undermine the designer's credibility.
- For projects where architectural controls govern, such as in deed-restricted subdivisions, calculating compliance with exterior material percentages is readily accomplished when the exact nature of wall materials is unknown. A homeowner's association might stipulate 75 percent masonry for exterior walls, for example; as the schematic design progresses, walls may be assigned generically as masonry or nonmasonry, to assure compliance throughout the design process.

It should be clear from the above examples and discussion that BIM does not inherently require the designer to make final material or design decisions early in the design process. In fact, the opposite is true: BIM allows the designer to quantitatively and qualitatively test design assumptions about the project from an early stage, without being constrained regarding design-decision outcomes.

"BIM doesn't address designing details"

BIM relies on standard construction components (e.g., open web bar joists, standard steel profiles, conventional window sash configurations and profiles). As software applications develop, they tend to add larger libraries of standard building components. While such ever-growing libraries of building elements streamline design and documentation, they do not necessarily contribute to fully custom design. This is most evident in architectural detailing, where the designer may require an extremely flexible software environment in order to model conditions where standard components and connections may not be appropriate (Fig. 1.10).

While it's true that conventional components may not lend themselves to unconventional applications, most BIM software permits custom or free-form modeling (Fig. 1.11). Revit allows the creation of families: user-defined parametric objects whose geometries can be controlled by relational algorithms governed by spreadsheets. Vectorworks includes robust 3D modeling, including non-uniform rational Bézier splines (NURBS), curves and surfaces with variable curvature, and potentially few vertices for computational efficiency. With some scripting, Vectorworks users can create their own custom parametric tools. And ArchiCAD, too, readily permits custom-created parametric objects.

Such user-defined elements can be assigned data, and exported for analysis and collaboration in buildingSMART's, the International Alliance for Interoperability, neutral and open Industry Foundation Classes (IFC) format. With IFC, components can be created in one BIM application, assigned a taxonomical label and data, and exported to another IFC-compliant BIM application, even if the receiving application does not natively support the object type (Fig. 1.12).

Drawing the line

Architects who are new to BIM understand the necessary abstraction of architectural communication

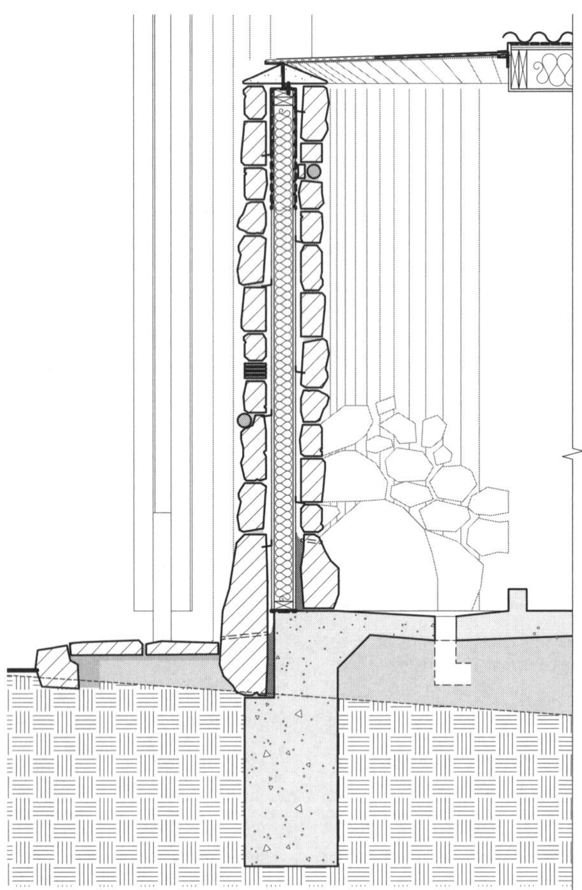

FIGURE 1.10 A wall section detail drafted over the geometry of a BIM model. While certain components (steel sections, dimensional lumber, repetitive materials, and conventional hatches) are quite typical and are considered "standard" 2D or 3D BIM elements, others are custom modeled, or drafted.

and may be concerned by BIM's potential specificity. Architectural drawings specifically but representations generally have always entailed a certain level of abstraction. This is not only necessary, but also desirable. Take for example the case of architectural scale. There is a certain level of information that is presented on a 1/4" (or roughly 1:50) scale plan that is omitted on a site plan or is inadequate for a plan detail at 1" (1:10) scale. In part this convention evolved from necessity: one could not realistically draft every stud, every piece of trim, and every wall component on an architectural layout plan. More importantly, however, architectural documents must communicate, and do so appropriately. The architectural floor plan is not intended for the trim carpenter except in the most general terms; the finish carpenter is particularly interested in interior elevations and millwork details, whereas the carpenter in wood-frame construction is keenest to understand the 1/4" (1:50) plans and attendant elevations and sections. We omit information from the architectural floor plan in part because it is not feasible to show it there, but also because we are directing the drawing toward a particular trade, or trades, who will execute their portion of the work from it.

Indeed, with the advent of CAD, it has become possible to draw every building component, regardless of size, limited only by the resolution of current

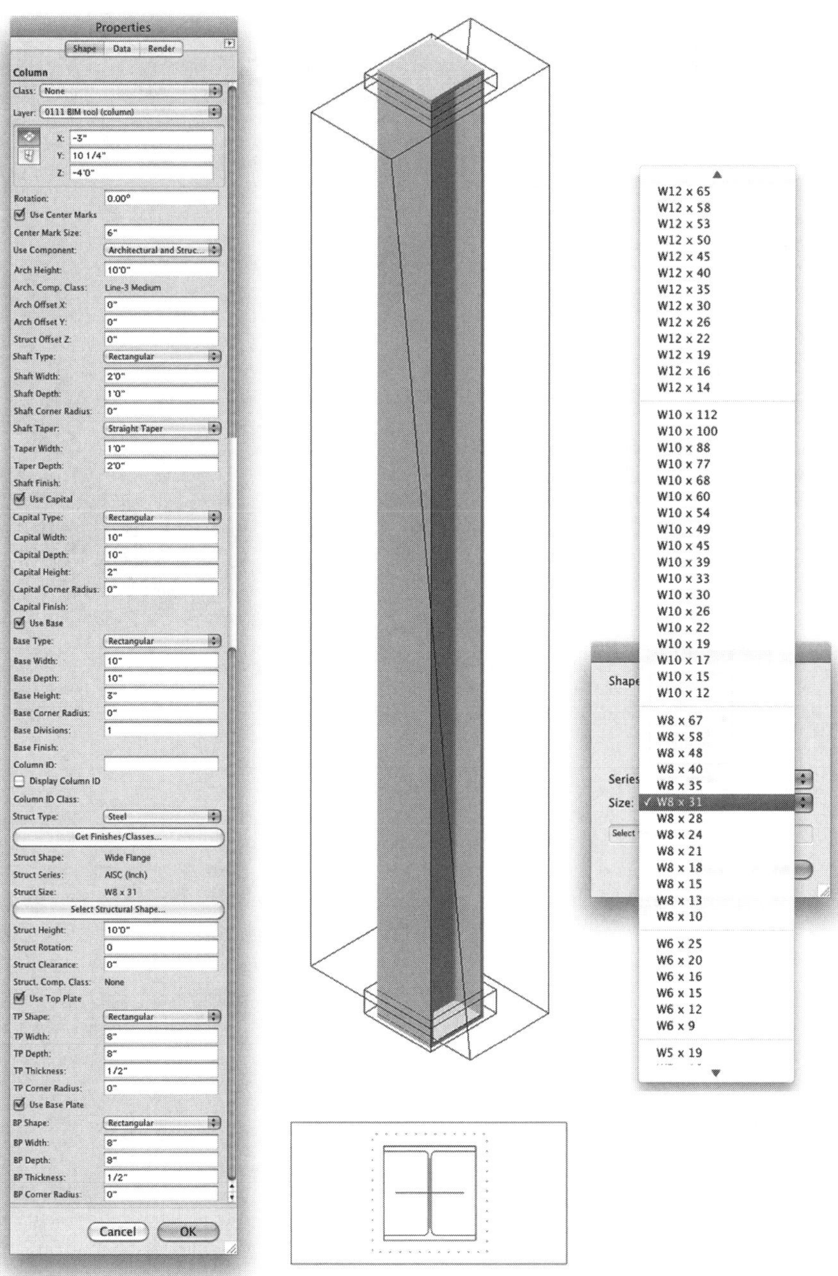

FIGURE 1.11 A BIM column—like walls, doors, windows, beams, roofs, and foundations—is controlled by a variety of settings that are germane to its nature. Columns may contain structural and/or architectural graphical and numeric data.

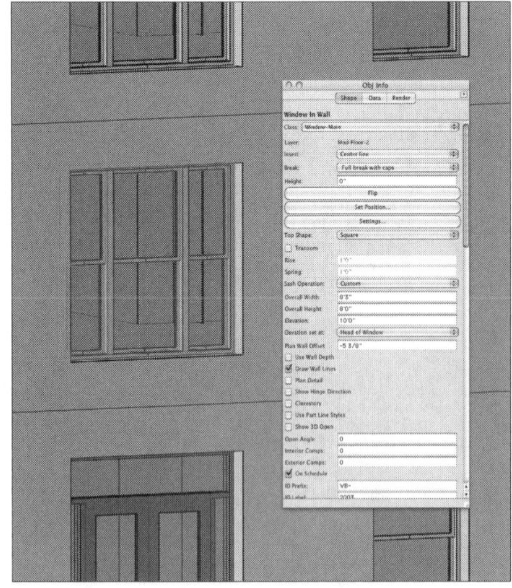

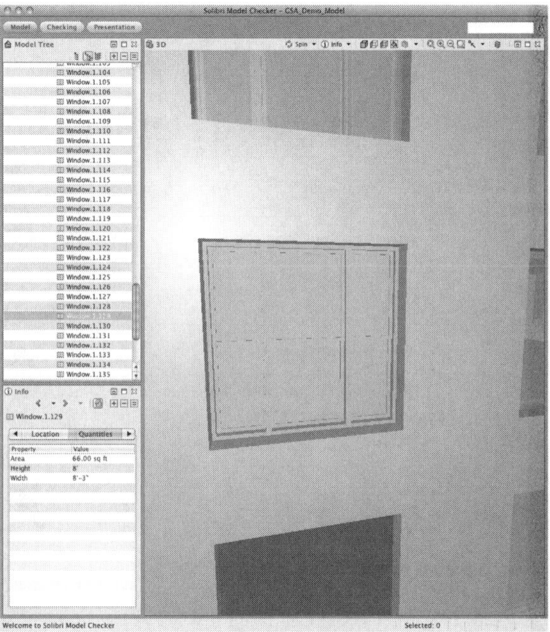

FIGURE 1.12 Two views of the same BIM object: the window at left is in its native Vectorworks format, and is a fully editable parametric and data-rich object. At right, the same model exported as IFC 2x3 is inspected in Solibri Model Checker. The geometry and IFC data are preserved ensuring interoperability, but the window is no longer an easily editable parametric object.

printing technology and by the visual acuity of the user. Yet abstract drawing conventions are still observed (Fig. 1.13). For example, at a 1/4" (1:50) scale plan:

- Walls are shown poché. Studs are not delineated, and only major components (structural core, veneers on the order of 4" [100 mm]) are shown, with thinner materials (plaster, wallboard, sheathing, vapor barriers, flashing, air spaces) typically omitted;
- Doors are generally shown as rectangles open 90°, with swings indicated by arcs, and sometimes trim is indicated (the prevalence of the latter is a more recent development). Hardware is never shown at this scale;
- Handrails are often depicted as double lines, and brackets and connection details are omitted.

We still deliver drawings at set scales with certain abstract drawing conventions, in order to clearly and appropriately communicate the particular intent of a given drawing. To that end, it is at least as significant which information a particular drawing omits as which information it includes (Fig. 1.14). In fact, this process of abstraction is the foundation of the craft of architectural documentation, a craft whose fruits are no less necessary now: the trades at present still need drawings, even if this may someday change.

In architectural detailing, the abstraction of graphic information is taken a step further. Details often depict typical conditions (from which similar conditions are to be inferred), special conditions, or critical conditions (Fig. 1.15). Details are not intended to represent all conditions, for several reasons. First, even in a modest project it would be unfeasible to do so. Further, many conditions may be commonplace, whether industry-wide or regionally.

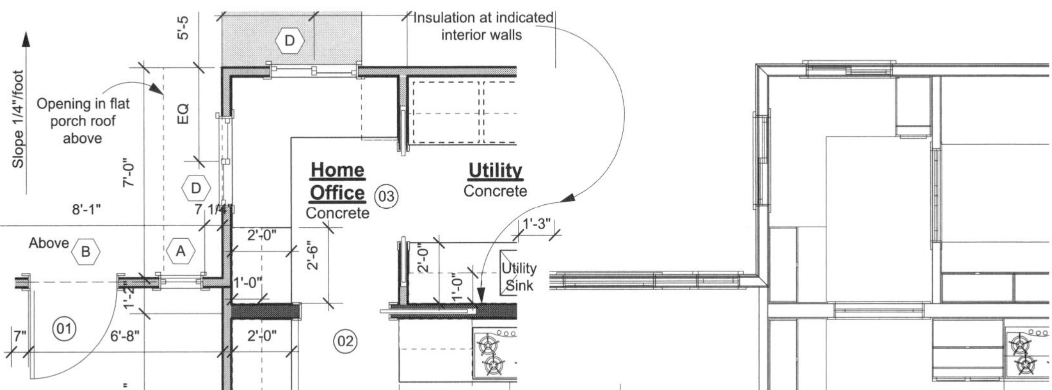

FIGURE 1.13 Compare a portion of a traditional plan view at 1/4" scale (1:50; left) with a model view from above of the same file (right). The usual plan view is an abstraction, intended to convey only the requisite information and nothing more. The model view dispenses with the graphic conventions that building professionals expect from a plan drawing—door swings, abstract window representations, depth-cued line weights, and so on.

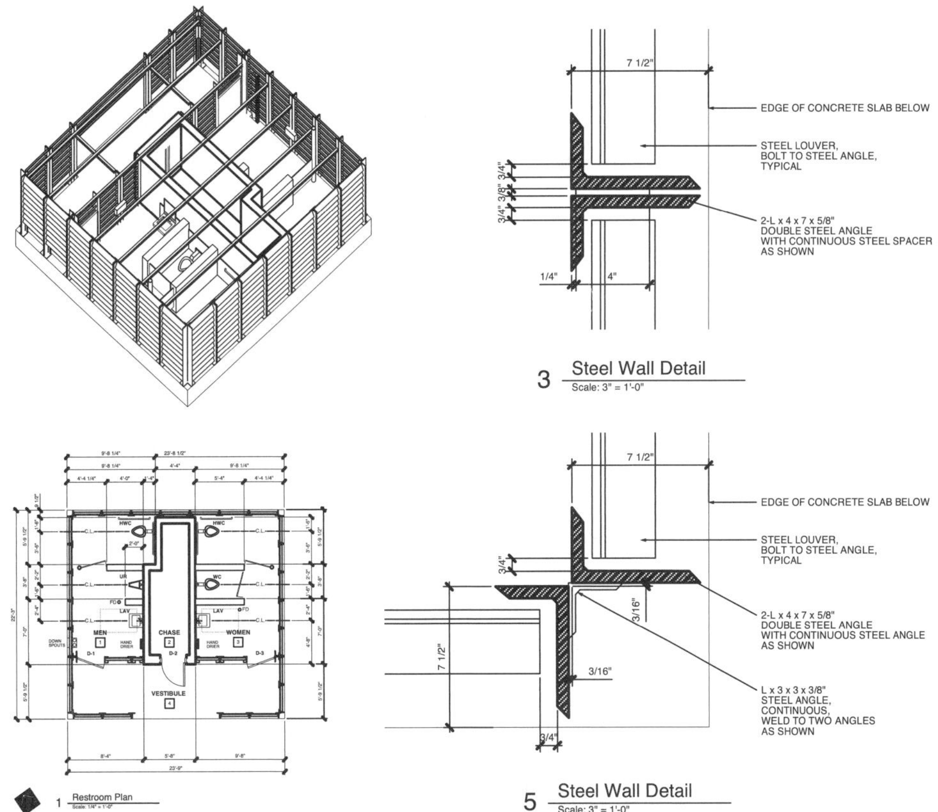

FIGURE 1.14 In this small BIM project, every deliverable drawing is a view of the model; nothing is drawn in the conventional 2D, CAD sense.

Image courtesy Limbacher & Godfrey Architects.

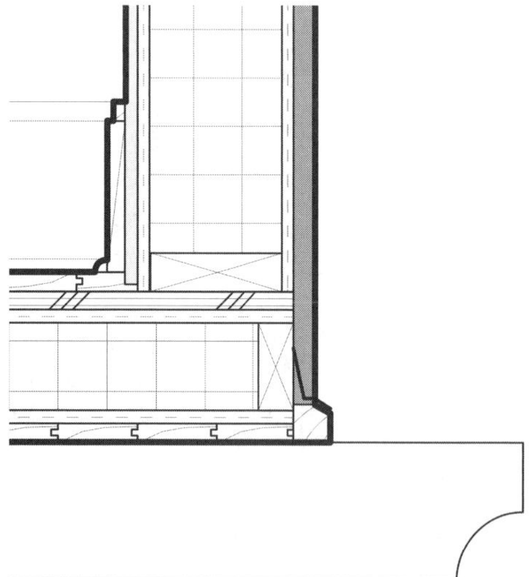

FIGURE 1.15 A flashing detail is a common condition depicted in a set of construction documents that would not usually be modeled in BIM. This case is one of many where the abstraction of a 2D drawing representing a typical condition is appropriate, but not every variation is necessarily drawn, nor modeled.

Finally and perhaps most importantly, there are often conditions where the trades' expertise and experience may exceed that of the architect, and a good construction set should allow some latitude in those conditions.

In BIM as in CAD, however, there is the potential to model building components beyond the needs of the deliverables, or extracted views. While it may be *possible* to include every fastener and length of flashing in a building model, it is hardly desirable, if only for computational economy. The question therefore arises: What should be modeled, and what should be omitted in a building model? Three tests can be applied to answer that question:

- Is the feature represented in more than one view? Arguably, features that occur only once might be drawn (as opposed to modeled) for the sake of economy. A foundation footing, for example, will appear in a foundation plan, but will appear in building sections as well. Light fixtures may only appear in a single graphic view, the lighting plan, but they also populate lighting fixture schedules and a variety of performance reports (power budgets, general illumination calculations). Generally, building components that populate more than one view should be modeled. Consider, too, that the number of views that a component may populate may increase as the project progresses.
- Is the designer responsible for designing or coordinating the component? A building component that the architect is neither designing *nor* coordinating may be omitted from the model. The assumption is that another discipline may later contribute to the overall project model as required.
- Is it more appropriate to model the component, or specify it? The model indicates the location, placement, quantity, and extent of any given portion of the project; specifications define the standards of installation and specific materials and products, in addition to referencing portions of applicable building codes. By this standard, for example, drywall fasteners are covered by the specifications (their kind and spacing is governed by code), but a handrail bracket may not be (Fig. 1.16). The latter might therefore be modeled.

Components that fulfill all three of the above criteria should be modeled.

High-performance architecture

Architectural design for performance necessarily requires quantitative building data, and therefore BIM is a natural and appropriate methodology to support performance architecture. For architects who aspire to have the form of their work informed by and expressive of performance, BIM may be particularly apt. Conceptually, the underlying methodology proposed seeks to dynamically link building geometry with data, in order to satisfy performance criteria according to sound design practices.

Most BIM applications are not, per se, performance analysis software, except in specialized instances. The software may detect for collisions

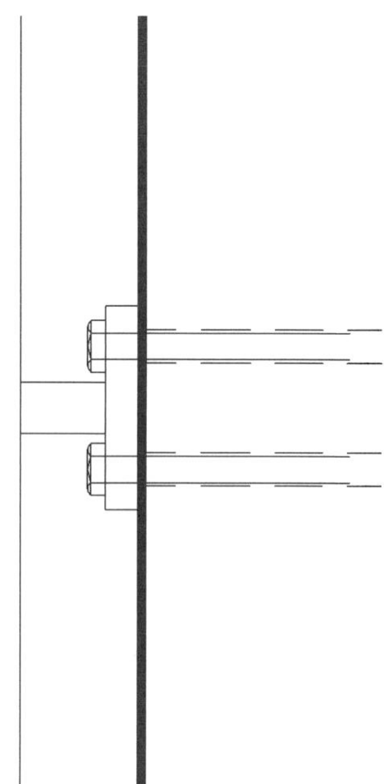

FIGURE 1.16 Where to draw the line? The ability to draw or model every component of the building is hardly an excuse to do so. One could model every fastener in this handrail, but it may be sufficient to model the rail and supporting brackets and leave the bolted connection to a detail drawing.

Image courtesy of Justin Firuz Dowhower, LEED AP.

(clash detection), or verify basic code compliance (alerting the user, for example, when a 20-minute fire-rated door is placed in a one-hour fire-rated wall assembly), but in general BIM applications are not energy modelers, for example. On the other hand, BIM modelers can and routinely do produce user-specified reports (tabular views) of the virtual building.

The designer is therefore faced with a decision. In reductionist terms, the architect may either apply proven geometric relationships ("rules of thumb" and approximations) in real time early in the design process, or perform more precise modeling based on more refined data later in the design process. The first is a "parametric design," and the other is "design validation." In reality, the architect is free to choose both methods; the dichotomy is an artificial one for argument's sake.

Design validation has distinct advantages, the most obvious of which is that it is presumably more accurate. In addition, it is the required method for demonstrating compliance with applicable building or energy codes. On the other hand, validation requires detailed data to be meaningful. Any experienced energy modeling specialist will attest that without accurate data—accounting for specific internal loads, climate data, and building parameters—an energy model is extremely prone to error. Much of that data cannot be provided until the building has largely been designed. Exporting BIM data to specialized modelers certainly yields more accurate results, but once design is well underway it may be too late to make a substantial difference. Referring to the MacLeamy curve above, it's clear that by mid to late design development, the designer has reached a point where significant changes come with significant expenditures of effort (read: scheduling delays, work hours, and money). *Round-tripping* is a term that describes exporting a building information model to a performance modeler (such as an energy modeler or computational fluid dynamics modeler), analyzing performance, and then making design changes based on the results of the detailed analysis. Even with round-tripping, however, there may be significant effort required to prepare a model for export—in some cases involving data re-entry in the performance modeler due to translation data loss. As a result of the potentially labor-intensive nature of round-tripping, as well as file format translation pitfalls, this process has nontrivial barriers to entry. Finally, most small projects will not have provision in the design fee for intensive performance modeling, and clients may be reluctant to pay additional fees for what they may perceive, rightly or wrongly, as a basic service. In short, as necessary as design validation may be in many cases, detailed performance modeling may be too much, too late.

On the other hand, *parametric design* is intended to inform decisions as they are being made. This requires that assumptions be made about building characteristics from the onset. Those assumptions are then tested and refined based on direct feedback from the model. Building performance thereby potentially becomes an architectural form-giver, insofar as the designer allows it to be so. Parametric design is advocated as a means to empower the architect, and therefore by extension the client, to make informed tests of building technology choices before becoming committed to those choices.

> Thermal design of the building must fit into the design process that evolves from the general to the specific as an integral part of the process. In recent history, thermal design usually has been relegated to the final construction documents phase . . . By then it is too late to mold a passive building—the commitment to passive design must be made in . . . schematic design . . .

Many times I have said something to the above effect to students, clients, or fellow architects. Unwittingly I was quoting Doug Balcomb and his colleagues (1980), authors of the *Passive Solar Design Handbook,* who wrote the above passage three decades ago. While the building design professions have made many advances, the relevance of this quote even today is a clear admonition that as a profession we must further evolve our early design work practices to incorporate sustainable design. Below is a cursory listing describing some specific BIM parametric design strategies for sustainable performance architecture. The reader is referred to the relevant chapters for more detailed discussions.

Site indexing (Chapter 3)

BIM can produce dynamic data-driven site models with editable 2D contours and 3D topography (Fig. 1.17). Such models are parametric in that they may be regraded and recontoured either through

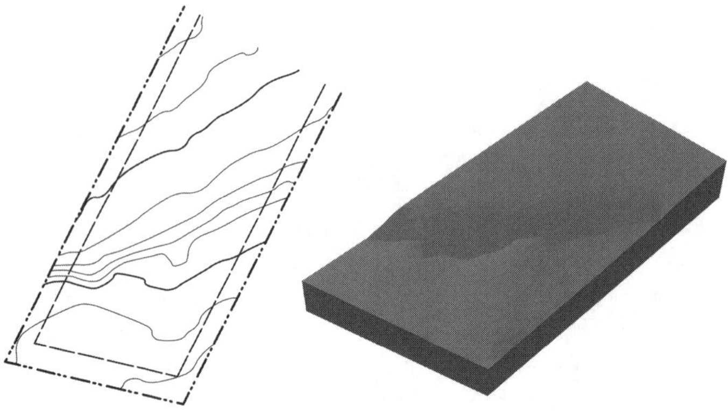

FIGURE 1.17 Two views of a dynamically editable BIM site model. Both the 2D topography and the 3D solid model (in this case rendered with smoothing) are different views of the same object.

the use of area tools (imagine a level building pad or paved area with a user-defined slope) or contour lines (similar to the traditional manual method of site design). Once created, such a site model can report (and dynamically update) site conditions for either existing or proposed conditions:

- Net cut and fill volumes. This is highly useful for reducing project costs and limiting environmental impact. In some jurisdictions or sensitive areas, soil may not be removed from the site.
- Buildable envelope. Most jurisdictions impose building setback limits. In an increasing number of cases, a maximum building envelope or tent will also be imposed by ordinance, in addition to floor area ratio (FAR) limitations. Such form-based code restrictions may be quite complex depending on the boundaries and topography of the site, and cannot be feasibly analyzed without the use of 3D site models. A BIM site model can greatly streamline such analyses.
- Slope analysis. Net buildable area is sometimes jurisdictionally limited by excessive slopes, such as when water quality ordinances reduce FAR for steep portions of a site. In addition, excessively steep portions of a site may not be legally or feasibly buildable. Some BIM applications color-code portions of the site by slope value, to obviously signal buildable and unbuildable areas.
- "Viewsheds." Some BIM software, such as Vectorworks, can automate the process of determining those portions of a site visible from a given point. Even in cases when such analysis is performed manually (the user sets the location and direction of a particular view), perspectives establishing viewsheds are critical to design programs with desirable or undesirable views, or for refining solar orientation.

Climate indexing (Chapters 3–5)

Consideration of climate and orientation is obviously critical to the design of any sustainable skin-load dominated building. Not only do general climatic conditions (or climate zone) profoundly affect the appropriate design response, but also building orientation, with respect to solar geometry and prevailing winds, will determine the effectiveness of a host of passive cooling and heating strategies. Building information models can be analyzed for these conditions to a large extent, even before exporting for further analysis in software like Ecotect and Green Building Studio.

- Sun studies. These may range from fixed shade and shadow renderings (Fig. 1.18), to interactive renderings depicting shadows at different times of day or year, to solar animations exported as separate files. It is also possible to set views to "what the sun sees."
- Determining daylight factor. Reducing electric lighting increases a project's sustainability for two reasons: less energy is consumed directly by electric lighting, and cooling loads are reduced due to (inefficient) heat generated by such lighting. Daylight factor, a ratio of interior illumination to exterior illumination, can indicate when adequate natural light is provided, and is directly related to room geometry. It is thus another opportunity to use the intelligent modeling of BIM.
- Capturing prevailing winds. Wind roses are available for major locations, and informal surveys of prevailing breezes can be graphically represented in the BIM file and appropriate responses designed.

Energy efficiency (Chapters 5–8)

Well before the energy modeler stage of design (design validation), the designer will make critical decisions that will irrevocably affect the building's overall energy performance (Fig. 1.19). The building's aspect ratio and orientation will largely be determined at the massing model stage, and can have a profound affect on building performance. Obviously, not every building can be optimally oriented due to limitations of site and zoning ordinances. Nevertheless, the architect has a great deal

FIGURE 1.18 Sun shading models are invaluable BIM tools. In this case, glass, color, and material textures have been selectively turned off; the parametric site model is displayed as extruded contours; diffuse ambient lighting supplements the virtual sun. At first glance, the resulting rendering could be mistaken for a photo of a physical museum-board model. More importantly, it clearly communicates the degree to which the design's shading devices are effective.

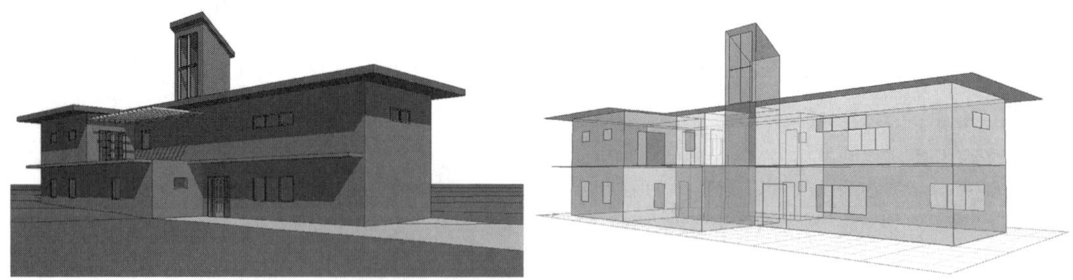

FIGURE 1.19 A BIM model (left) is divided into zones (right) in preparation for energy modeling analysis.

Image courtesy of Justin Firuz Dowhower, LEED AP.

of latitude in making early decisions, which, if well informed, will result in better buildings.

- Heat gain and loss. Envelope energy code compliance for buildings in the United States in many jurisdictions can be verified with the DOE's ResCheck and ComCheck. These free applications calculate total heat loss through the envelope, as well as lighting power density and mechanical systems compliance. Unfortunately, there is currently no common file format that allows direct exporting of BIM data to these applications. However, calculating total building thermal conductivity, U·A, is possible within the BIM modeler itself. This allows the designer to make rapid global changes to envelope systems and determine their effectiveness in meeting or exceeding energy codes in real time.
- Passive cooling (ventilation, thermal mass). Depending on the climate zone of the project, various passive cooling strategies are appropriate. For hot, humid climates, natural ventilation is most effective, whereas projects in hot, dry climates respond more favorably to adiabatic

cooling and thermal mass. The effectiveness of these strategies can be determined directly from the building geometry and certain basic climate assumptions, such as ambient temperature. BIM allows those geometric relationships to be linked to calculations that return dynamic information to report the relative effectiveness of design configurations.

- Passive heating (solar orientation, net glazing area, and thermal mass). As with passive cooling, factors determining the effectiveness of passive heating strategies are largely orientation- and geometry-driven. How much south-facing glazing is present in the current design? What is the area of available thermal mass? How much sun does the building face receive over the year? BIM can readily answer these questions, supporting the optimization of the building design for improved thermal performance.

Effective building hydrology (Chapter 9)
For a variety of reasons, ranging from water conservation, water quality, and erosion control, a building's response to water is critical. BIM allows several approaches to designing for these issues:

- Rainwater harvesting. Growing in popularity despite the lag in recognition by local jurisdictions for potable water, rainwater harvesting is a viable alternative to wasteful residential irrigation with treated (potable) water, as well as a potential source of safe drinking water. In many municipalities, the water department is the largest single consumer of electricity, as massive pumps are employed to provide pressurized water supply throughout the community. Increasing reliance on site-generated water supplies supports sustainable communities. Correctly sizing major system components, the roof catchment area and the cistern, is possible using established formulas and dynamically linking them to the appropriate roof area and cistern geometry.
- Site grading for proper surface water flow. Site model analysis of the triangulated irregular network (TIN), just as with slope analysis, can determine direction and intensity of surface water flow. Such surface flow studies not only help confirm positive drainage at building perimeters, but also guard against inadvertently shedding water onto adjacent properties.
- Roof, gutter, and downspout sizing. Similarly, gutter sizes and the number and sectional areas of downspouts are determinable from basic climate data and roof areas. The drawn or modeled roof elements are sized according to those relationships as reported by the building model.

Waste stream (Chapter 10)
Generally, over a building's useful life, operating costs will exceed construction costs by roughly a factor of ten. Reducing the operational environmental impact of buildings is therefore logical and should be a priority for any sustainable design. Whenever possible, materials use (and therefore cost) should also be reduced, particularly when such reduction leads to improved operational efficiency.

- Reducing waste through alternate building techniques. Dimensional lumber framing enjoys widespread use in the United States (although rare elsewhere). Forest Stewardship Council (FSC)–certified forests are sustainable, and wood is a renewable resource. Even so, embodied energy, represented by transportation and processing costs, can be reduced if materials are used wisely. Framing techniques like advanced framing not only use less material, but avoid "wall washing" and other mold-encouraging conditions. BIM can be used to quantitatively compare conventional and advanced framing in order to better determine cost benefits of the latter for a particular project. While some BIM modelers may model unit takeoffs, even gross quantity surveys can help the architect make appropriate decisions.

FIGURE 1.20 A BIM model after having been decomposed and the walls' continuous structural core converted to discrete studs, headers, and blocking. The roof has likewise been framed according to user parameters for framing member size and spacing.

- Accurate, dynamic quantity surveys. BIM software does not necessarily model every individual component of a wall (individual CMU, length of lumber, sheet of plywood, etc.), but tends to represent assemblies more abstractly (wythes of masonry, depth of stud wall, layer of sheathing, and so on). Some applications allow modeling and reporting of every individual length of framing lumber (Vectorworks's Wall Framer and Roof Framer modules do so, for example). It is often sufficient for takeoffs to be more abstract, limited to area takeoffs of a particular material, rather than unit takeoffs. Such reports are possible with BIM, with or without specialized modules (Fig. 1.20).

■ Case study: Moonrise Ranch, Hill Country, Texas

By François Lévy

Design Firm: Mark Winford and François Lévy (Studio Mosaic)

Client: Jan Gauvain and Stanley Tartakov

FIGURE 1.21 The project seen from the south. The roof's curved ridge and level perimeter created a complex curved surface that was more readily analyzed and represented with BIM. Note a portion of the original cabin visible behind the ladder, well-protected by the generous roof overhang.

© Paul Bardagjy.

Several years ago, my design partner at the time and I were approached to design a private residence on a ten-acre riverfront site in the rural Hill Country of central Texas—near the town of Wimberley, a 40-mile drive from Austin. Our client had a highly artistic sensibility and had been hiking and camping in the area for years before acquiring the property a year prior to commissioning us. As a result of her experiences, she desired an idiomatic home strongly connected to the site that would heighten the experience of the land's natural beauty. Eight years prior, the previous owner had moved a nineteenth-century two-room dogtrot cabin onto the site (Fig. 1.22). This building, with its remarkable mud plaster interior, was gradually succumbing to the elements.

(Continued)

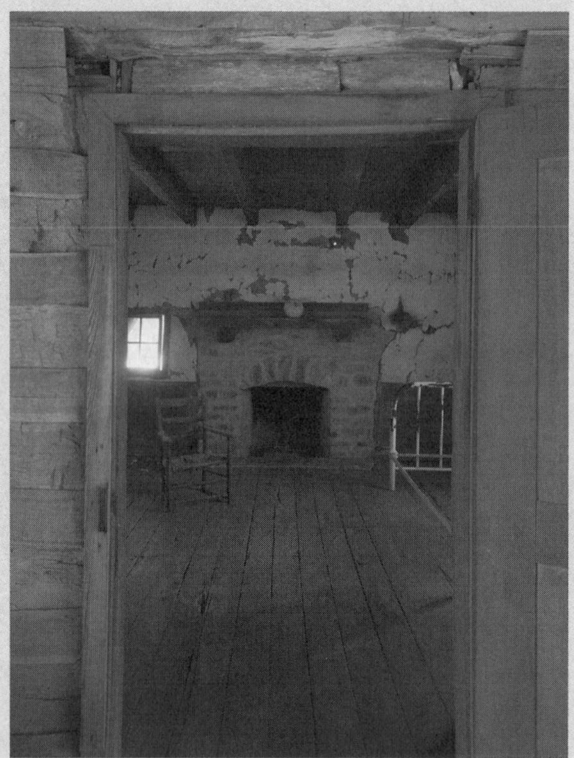

FIGURE 1.22 The original cabin structure as it was prior to being relocated and integrated into the new house.
© Paul Bardagjy.

Design Intent

We suggested to our client that the cabin be relocated on the house site to a bluff line just within earshot of the Blanco River. The historical cabin would constitute two rooms of the new house, with the rest of the structure designed around and cradling it. At that location, the new house would capture prevailing breezes and command a view over the riparian meadow below—future site of her gardens.

We developed this idea into two competing design themes. On the one hand, we conceived the project as a "village of spaces," each room articulated by form and material to distinguish it from the others (Fig. 1.23). As a result of this articulation, most of the house would be "one room deep," and most rooms would have access to natural light from three sides. In addition, we designed a corrugated metal, parasol roof both metaphorically and literally sheltering the historic cabin and the assembled spaces. The form of the boat-like roof invoked the gurgling Blanco River, and also the nearby rounded central Texas hills. Tree trunk columns would support the roof's gently arched spine, inspired by the tall cypresses growing in the Blanco and on its banks.

FIGURE 1.23 The precinct plan of the project indicating the relationship of the covered cistern to the site topography and internal arrangement of spaces.

Drawing by the author and Mark Winford, AIA.

We included a tall tower to create a dramatic viewing platform. Prevailing breezes, tempered by the deep shade porches, would be naturally exhausted through the dual-purpose observatory and thermal chimney. Harvested rainwater would be stored in a covered cistern dug into the bluff just below the house. Our architectural approach maximized the building's exposure to appropriate natural light, views of the extended site, and opportunities for natural ventilation. The design exposed and celebrated these natural passive systems, making them didactic and legible.

BIM Solutions

There were several challenges that a BIM approach helped address, not all of which were strictly technical. At the outset of conceptual design, the project had an indeterminate budget. As the conceptual design evolved—beginning as early as our conversations on-site with the

(*Continued*)

FIGURE 1.24 A sketch rendering of the BIM model. Completed a decade ago, the project's early use of BIM was key to resolving qualitative and quantitative design decisions.

Model by the author and Mark Winford, AIA.

client, and even before the development of preliminary sketches—it became clear that the design goals of client and architects might prove unusual and outside the experience of many local builders in this remote area. From the beginning, therefore, we negotiated a fee structure that was weighted more heavily toward construction administration (CA) than is typical, and correspondingly tilted away from construction documents, reducing our fee sans CA by 20 percent. (In the end, our final total fee was lower than typical for our firm.) As designers, our expectation was that we would produce a more forgiving drawing set that had built-in design tolerances such that construction inaccuracies, if any, would be less noticeable. This fee arrangement was fortuitous, as it encouraged us to leverage the design and production advantages of BIM without sacrificing design and documentation quality (Fig. 1.24).

The non-orthogonal and compound geometry of the project was a form that would have been challenging to construct as a series of two-dimensional drawings. The roof's shape was particularly challenging: the curved ridge beam and level parallel perimeter beams created a hyperbolic paraboloid surface; each pair of straight rafters was set at a different pitch than adjacent rafters. Modeling the structure allowed us to verify its constructability, as well as to rationalize the rafter spacing and symmetry to simplify construction for the framers as much as possible.

Given such a roof shape, and that the walls were arranged non-orthogonally to the column grid, constructing interior elevations as 2D drawings would likewise have been time-consuming and prone to error. In this case, fitting the BIM walls to the roof model in 3D was relatively simple. The interior elevations could then be readily derived from the fitted walls. The same held true of other elevated and sectional views: building elevations and sections were more easily and accurately derived from the 3D model than constructed as 2D drawings.

As might be expected from her deep connection to the site, our client was interested that the project emphasize sustainable systems as much as practicable. This emphasis on

FIGURE 1.25 The curved roof shelters conditioned, enclosed, and open spaces, and is peeled back to admit mature live oak trees. 3D modeling the complex geometry resulting from the interaction of curved forms was more direct and accurate than constructing 2D drawings.

© Paul Bardagjy.

sustainable systems suggested an analysis of an intelligent 3D model to help derive and validate our design decisions (Fig. 1.25). In this case, there were several opportunities for a BIM design process to advance our green agenda.

Water wells in developed areas a few miles away were gradually being drilled deeper and deeper as consumption pressures were lowering the tenuous water table, and we were all acutely aware of the water problems that future, neighboring development might bring. We therefore elected to incorporate a rainwater harvesting system in the project, and offered perspective renderings for a variety of different cistern designs, from a single low tank some distance from the house to a scalable array of smaller tanks. In our research, we had determined that cistern costs were roughly comparable regardless of the size and number of tanks; all solutions were about a $1 per gallon of storage. We thus decided to use the cistern as an architectural feature, setting it into the hillside and covering it with a walkable surface. We were able to dynamically calculate the cistern size as our roof design evolved, thanks to

(Continued)

our ability to quickly query the roof plan area and use it to inform the cistern geometry. As a result, we could readily determine which roof areas should be guttered for drainage and which for catchment. (Chapter 9 discusses BIM and building hydrology: roof catchment sizing and rainwater harvesting design.)

For sun studies, our model allowed us to verify the shading of certain windows at various times of the year, and we could adjust their placement and size accordingly (for an in-depth discussion of solar modeling with BIM, see Chapter 5). Even with coarse tree models, we could establish shading patterns on exposed windows, such as the southwest-facing dining room windows. Similarly, diagonal views through the model from a high elevation sighting to a lower one could be mapped out in three dimensions, helping to refine our window placement in some instances.

Passive cooling of the house was best achieved through natural ventilation, given the climate (see Chapter 6). The observation tower doubled as a solar chimney, and we used open bar grate for the upper flooring to allow upward air movement and light penetration down into the tower. Due to the stack effect, in a thermal chimney, the rate of air movement is predicated on air inlet and outlet sizes, the difference between their respective heights, and inlet and outlet air temperatures. All the geometric information in this relationship, including window elevations and aperture sizes, was readily and dynamically determined from the BIM model as the design evolved. Inlet and outlet temperatures were estimated based on experience and climatological data. The owner currently reports that the thermal chimney is highly effective, and cools the house well on all but the very hottest Texas summer days.

Nationally published and a popular destination on the 2001 Austin AIA Homes Tour, Moonrise was successful, in large part, thanks to an extraordinary client. Given the design intent, sustainable program, and constructability constraints, I am convinced that this project would have not been feasible for our firm at the time without the use of a BIM design process.

Chapter 2

Design Software

Some readers of this book are likely to be evaluating the transition from a drawing-oriented architectural practice—and here CAD drawing is included—to a BIM-oriented one. In Chapter 1, we visited the compelling arguments for BIM as a design environment, particularly in support of sustainable design. This runs counter to the general expectation that BIM is a mere production tool, divorced from design and therefore having little or no impact on architecture. It is a common conceit among architects that the tool or methods of working are independent of the resulting building. To confirm that nothing could be further from the truth one has only to look at the architectural landscape of London over the past decade or more, for example, to see that there the digital means of production have very much influenced the architectural outcome (Fig. 2.1).

In this chapter, we'll examine some of the architectural issues that arise or may be addressed as a result of software choices. Some of these issues will have a direct bearing on sustainable design practices. Others are more general to the practice of architecture, but are either so important that they cannot escape mention, or are oft-neglected topics that nevertheless are worth considering. In Chapter 11, we'll return to some of these issues, such as the teamwork coordination capabilities of BIM, as we consider collaborating with other architects and consultants, who may be using other software applications either for design, analysis, production, or all three.

BIM applications

Accepting the premise for the moment that "the tool matters" begs the question: *What is the right tool for your practice?* While a software vendor's marketing department might construct a one-size-fits-all table demonstrating the superiority of their particular products for all design firms, objectively, all BIM applications have relative strengths and limitations. The prospective adopter may consider how those advantages and drawbacks marry with the firm's size, project types, design approach, information technology aptitude, legacy hardware and software, and even culture. The following discussion of some common BIM applications is not intended as a "feature list face-off." Rather, it is meant to illustrate some of the issues that prospective BIM users may consider in selecting a software platform. Given the significant investment in software and training, this decision should not be taken lightly. Once an office establishes a software standard, technological inertia makes changing that standard challenging (Fig. 2.2).

Throughout this book, strategies and work approaches common to all or most BIM applications are discussed. In order to be relevant to all BIM practitioners, regardless of the software application they may use, detailed reference to specific tools and commands have been avoided. Most BIM programs share critical traits (Fig. 2.3), and while the specific methods of achieving them vary, the tasks remain largely the same:

- **create** a building model that:
  - addresses common building technologies and conditions, using libraries of customizable (parametric), preset tools
  - incorporates, as needed, nonstandard or uncommon conditions or building technologies, with a corresponding potential loss of automation

FIGURE 2.1 The architecture of recent years in cities like London is a clear demonstration of the relationship between the nature of design tools and the buildings produced with them. Arguably Rogers's Lloyd's of London was the first major architectural project that would not have been feasible without computer-assisted design technology. Today, projects like Foster's London City Hall are likewise unimaginable without sophisticated BIM and structural analysis software.

Image courtesy of Gregory L. Brooks.

- **embed** or attach default or user-defined data to components of the model to represent a variety of performance factors, such as:
  - unit cost
  - thermal characteristics
  - orientation and relative and absolute position in space
- **extract** views from the model, including:
  - orthographic views such as plans, sections, and elevations
  - planographic views (like isometric and axonometric drawings) and perspectives, in a variety of rendering styles from hidden line to shade and shadow, color, and in some cases photorealistic renderings
  - tabular views including default and custom schedules and reports, tables of values, and material take-offs

BIM is rapidly evolving and expanding, both as a social phenomenon and a technological space. Software developers both respond and drive that evolution. Most vendors are on annual revision

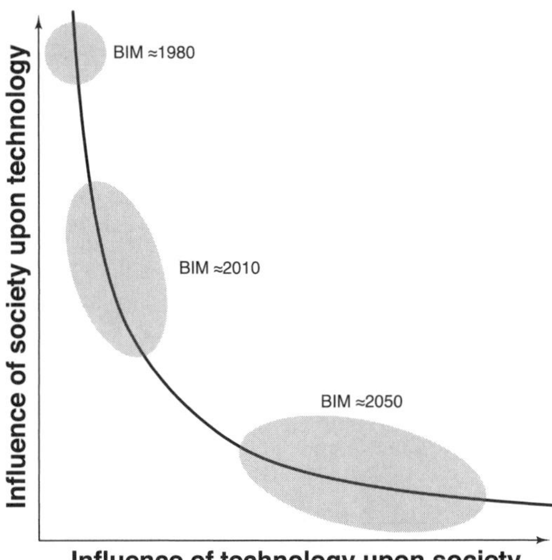

FIGURE 2.2 Thomas Hughes is credited with coining the term "technological inertia" to describe the process by which innovations become entrenched in the social fabric. This concept has been reframed in the context of BIM.

Redrawn by the author from a graphic by Justin Firuz Dowhower, LEED AP.

cycles, and they react to market and user pressures by rapidly implementing improvements and adding new features or improving existing ones. Such rapid changes in the technology of BIM enforce a very short shelf life for software manuals; each edition is generally only relevant for a year or so. A strategic handbook has to take a higher-level view.

In those few instances when referring to a process specific to only one or a few BIM products, the discussion is deliberately kept somewhat limited and the BIM application in question is identified. Efforts have also been made to select case study projects produced in a variety of BIM applications, in order to represent and emphasize the work flow, rather than a particular product or software-specific tools and commands. In the interests of full disclosure, the author's primary BIM application is Vectorworks Architect.

The reader is referred to Eastman et al. (2008) for its analyses of many key BIM authoring tools, several of which are oriented to larger firms and

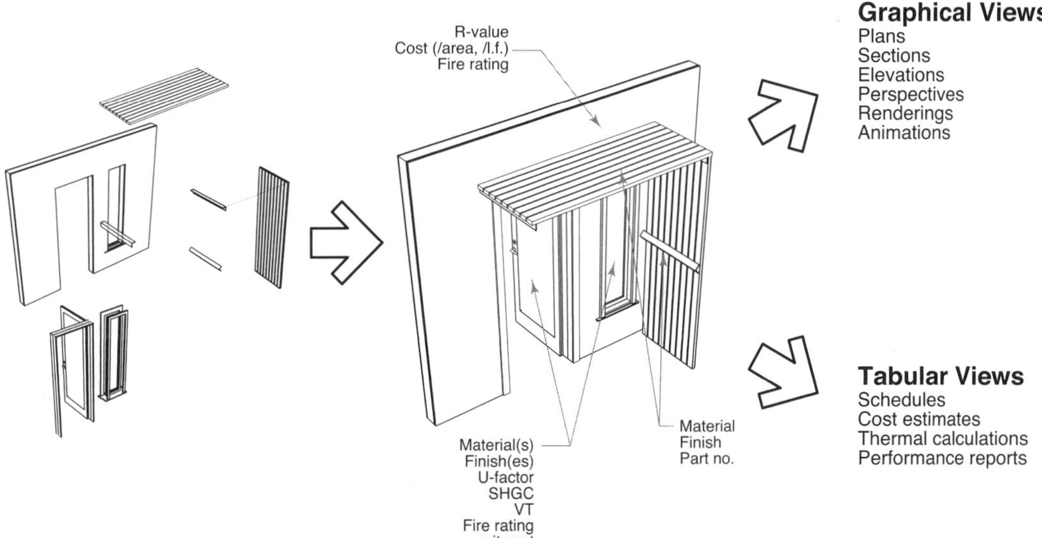

FIGURE 2.3 At its simplest, BIM is a process by which contextual virtual building components are assembled to create a cohesive model; those components have default or user-defined data embedded within them, and useful graphical and tabular views are extracted.

projects. Two applications that are relevant to this book, ArchiCAD and Revit Architecture, are briefly revisited here. Vectorworks Architect, a popular BIM application for small- to medium-sized firms that is omitted by Eastman et al., is discussed in greater detail below.

ArchiCAD

Arguably the first BIM application (before the term was coined or widely circulated), ArchiCAD (Fig. 2.4) has long been available on both Macintosh and Windows platforms. Exact numbers are difficult to calculate, but there may be 100,000 active users worldwide. Like all other BIM programs, ArchiCAD files consist of models—"virtual buildings" in ArchiCAD parlance—from which views are extracted. A long-standing feature with appeal to designers is dynamic live sectioning, by which a plane can be dragged through the model to section it in real time. Within the last few versions it has become possible to cut a live section through a section (for example, vertically sectioning a plan section in real time).

As of this writing the current version is ArchiCAD 15, but beginning with version 13, a first-of-its-kind BIM server became available. This centralized-database approach to file management facilitates teamwork by efficiently apportioning parts of the project to those teammates that need authorship access. Only those parts of the database that have been changed are transmitted over the network, greatly speeding model updates and avoiding data bottlenecks.

Of particular relevance to readers of this book is the inclusion of EcoDesigner, an additional plug-in module for ArchiCAD that became available with version 12. Like some of the methods described in this book, EcoDesigner applies rules of thumb to

FIGURE 2.4 The Vörösmarty tér 1 project in Budapest, Hungary, was developed in Graphisoft's ArchiCAD. Architect: György Fazakas; consulting architect: Jean Paul Viguier.

Image courtesy of Graphisoft.

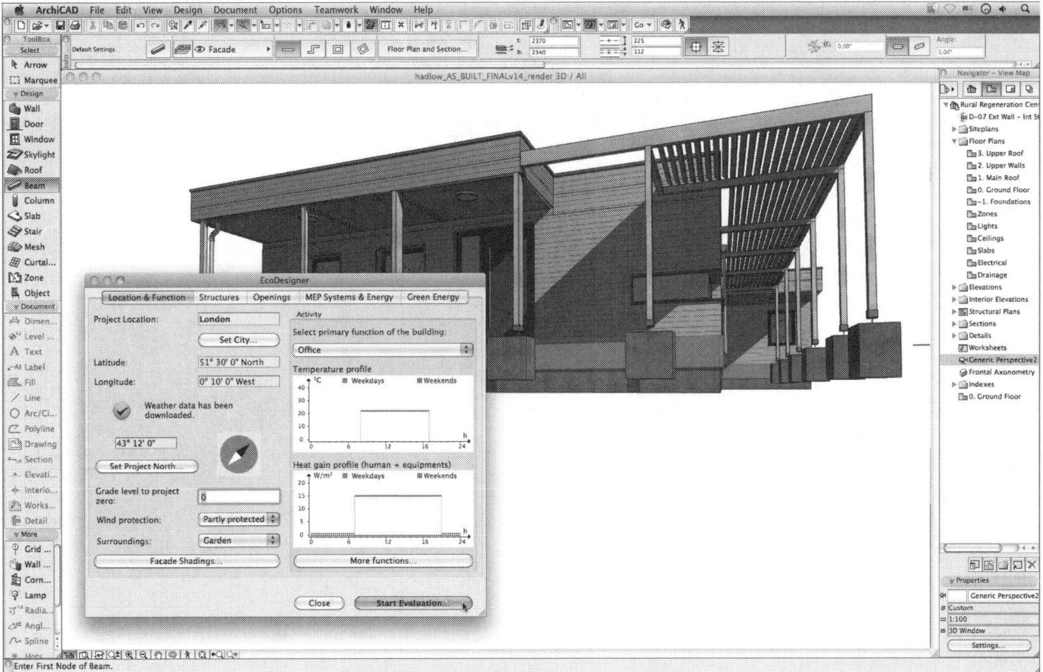

FIGURE 2.5 ArchiCAD's optional EcoDesigner add-on allows basic building energy analysis from within ArchiCAD. While not as fully-featured as standalone energy simulation programs, EcoDesigner allows the architect to make informed quantitative decisions earlier in the design process, when such decisions have the greatest impact. Here the Hadlow College Rural Regeneration Centre case study from Chapter 6 is being set up for analysis, establishing its location, use, and occupancy schedules.

Image courtesy of James Anwyl.

some data extracted from the ArchiCAD virtual building to provide the designer with important design feedback on building performance (Fig. 2.5). While not a full-blown energy modeler, it does provide early design information useful in energy performance decision making (Fig. 2.6). Several comprehensive reviews of the program are available on the Web.[1]

Revit Architecture

Thanks to the prevalence of AutoCAD in the automated drafting world, Autodesk's Revit offering has enjoyed the widespread reputation as the most commonly used BIM application. Often the words *BIM* and *Revit* are carelessly used interchangeably, just as students and laymen seem to use the terms *CAD* and *AutoCAD* interchangeably. Some market research seems to tell a different story; Gartner's (2007) market survey report shows 7 percent of CAD users are on Revit, compared to 55 percent on AutoCAD (presumably including AutoCAD LT), and 15 percent on Vectorworks (also presumably all industry versions). Of the estimated 400,000 Revit users, a fraction are presumably in small firms designing skin-load dominated projects.

As a production tool, Revit undisputedly has a broad range of robust features and tools (Fig. 2.7). Like many BIM applications, it is rarely considered as a design environment. However, as a few of my colleagues in architectural research have demonstrated, there are very interesting design

[1] Software reviews are available at: http://www.aecbytes.com/review/2010/ArchiCAD14.html; http://www.aecbytes.com/review/2010/EcoDesigner.html; and http://architosh.com/2008/12/product-review-graphisoft-archicad-12/.

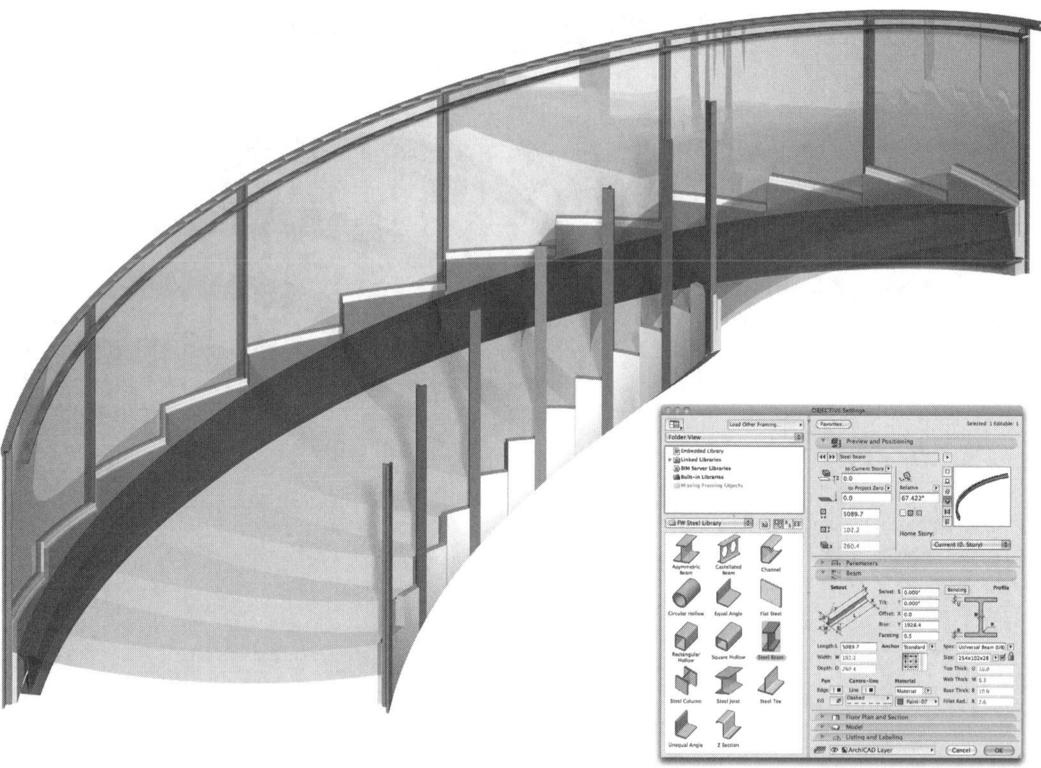

FIGURE 2.6 The OBJECTiVE add-on to ArchiCAD allows a tremendous range of parametric control over 3D building components.
Image courtesy of Ralph Wessel, Encina Ltd.

possibilities inherent in some seemingly innocuous Revit tools. Two that are particularly compelling include:

- **Custom Families.** Revit families are parametric objects, that is, they are 3D models whose various dimensions are numerically controlled and reshaped based on user input. The ArchiCAD analog of families includes Graphic Design Language (GDL) objects; Vectorworks has Plug-In Objects (PIOs). Revit ships with hundreds of families, from columns to windows. Of greater interest to this discussion, however, is the relative ease with which users can build their own parametric objects. For example, a vertical shading device could be designed as an extruded profile whose depth was proportional to its height.

- **Curtain Wall Tool.** As its name implies, this tool is for the design, modeling, and documentation of curtain wall systems, and is typically used to represent extruded aluminum storefront systems. However, in the interest of giving designers tremendous flexibility in the number, spacing, and profiles of mullions, Autodesk has created a tool whose possibilities far exceed the humble storefront. A few designers are using this tool to parametrically study shading walls with adjustable repeating elements. David Light, for example, has blogged about creating curtain walls inspired by the work of architectural sculptor Erwin Hauer using this technique (see the case study at the end of this chapter). The ability to (relatively) easily parameterize the subcomponents of a "curtain" wall in Revit opens exciting architectural possibilities for

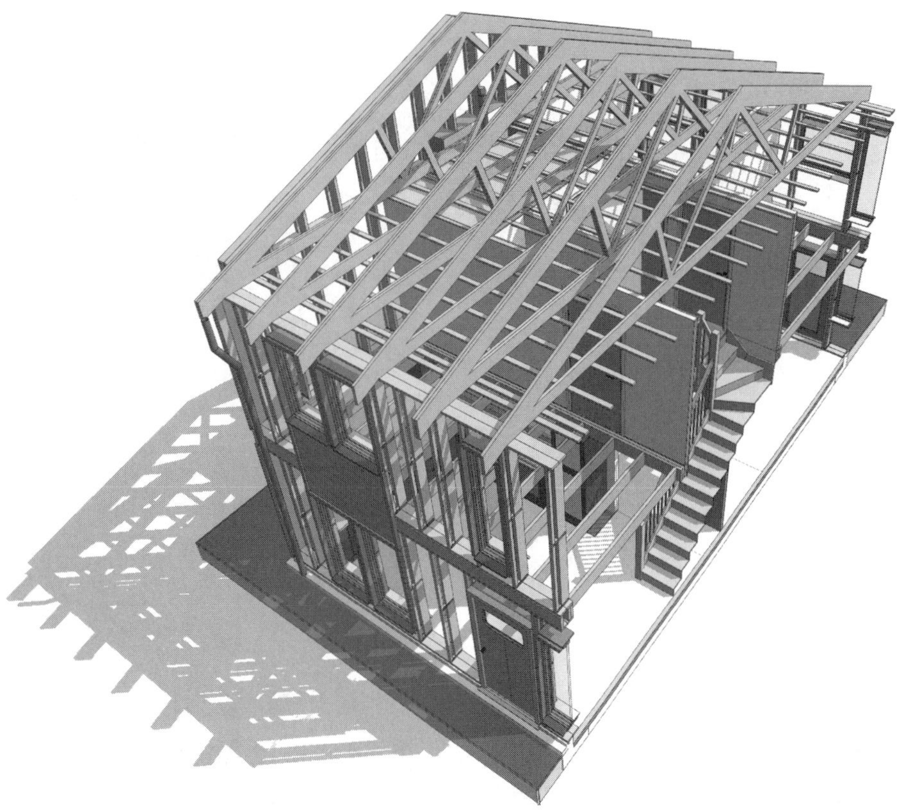

FIGURE 2.7 The Spacehus is a single-family dwelling meeting the UK "Code for Sustainable Homes." It was constructed in four weeks and cost less than £150k. The project was entirely modeled in Revit, and the model was used for fabrication and assembly through Navisworks.

Image courtesy of _space architecture, UK

designing and testing, for example, double-skin envelopes or shading screens that eliminate glare and heat gain but maximize diffuse daylight.

Anecdotally, very few Revit users fully exploit these tools in practice, which is a real missed opportunity.

Like ArchiCAD, Revit now has a server-based file structure available for better teamwork, and has recently introduced Conceptual Energy Analysis (CEA). In a vein similar to the premise of this book, CEA performs basic energy analysis of buildings at the massing model stage to allow the designer to make quantitative assessments along an iterative design process.

Vectorworks

Vectorworks 2012 is currently available both for the Mac OS and Windows (Fig. 2.9). This application was initially introduced in 1985 as a Mac-based CAD application, MiniCad. By MiniCAD+ 4, which was released in 1993, the application had incorporated 2D/3D walls, roofs, and slabs, satisfying the basic definition of a BIM application. Of the over 450,000 users worldwide, approximately 11,000 are estimated to be BIM users working in US firms of six or

FIGURE 2.8 The Washington Park Custom Home by West Standard Design Build is a residential project designed with Revit. BIM played an important role in design, development, and project visualization.

Image courtesy of West Standard Design Build.

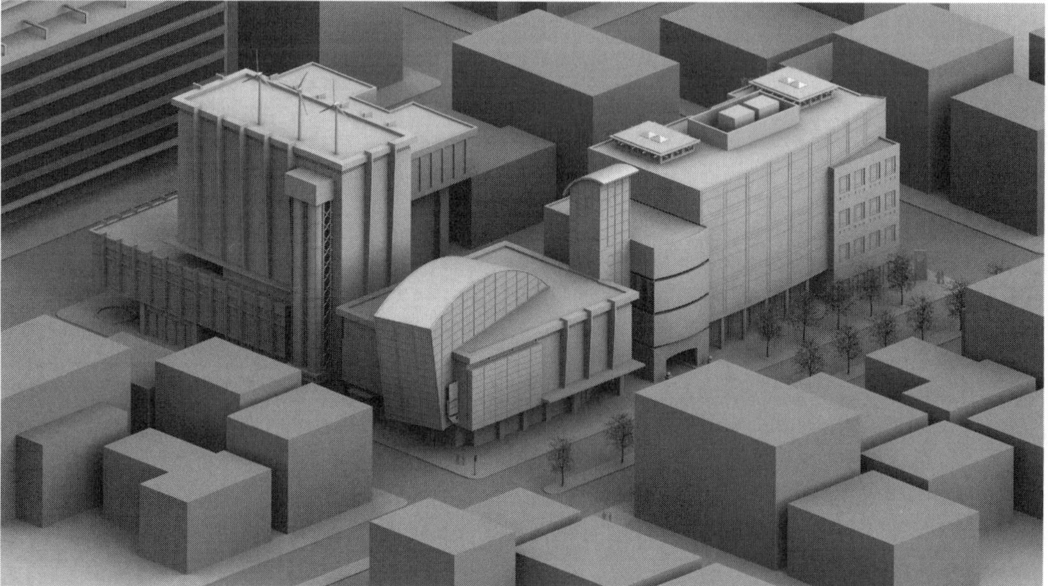

FIGURE 2.9 Vectorworks with Renderworks is capable of a variety of high-quality rendering styles, from sketching to photorealistic. In this image the building model was deliberately stripped of material textures and colors and lit with a diffuse high definition range imaging (HDRI) background to achieve a "museum board" effect.

Image courtesy of Wes Gardner.

fewer licenses. Vectorworks is a robust 2D drawing and 3D modeling application and has several industry-specific versions:

- Architect (architecture, engineering, and construction, or AEC)
- Landmark (landscape and site design)
- Spotlight (theatrical and exhibit design)
- Machine Design
- Fundamentals (nonindustry specific version)
- Designer (includes all industry tools, commands, and objects)

All are available with or without Renderworks, an extended rendering engine based on Cinema 4D.

Vectorworks Architect is a full-feature BIM authoring environment. All versions contain industry-relevant parametric objects, as well as allow free-form Boolean and *non-uniform rational Bézier splines* (NURBS) modeling using the Siemens product lifecycle management (PLM) parasolid kernel. User-defined data can be attached to any object and manipulated via built-in spreadsheets; most built-in parametric objects are by default populated with data. One can model anything using Vectorworks's flexible geometric tools, attach a complete BIM data set to it, and export the BIM model to an open IFC standard. This gives Vectorworks a high degree of design flexibility among BIM authoring tools (Fig. 2.10). A built-in Pascal-like programming language, VectorScript, allows advanced users to create custom parametric 2D and 3D tools. There is also an SDK (C++ based) available for third-party developers. Vectorworks contains extensive data-rich object libraries for the various industry products. Export formats include comma- and tab-delimited worksheets, DXF/DWG, EPix/Piranesi, EPSF, image

FIGURE 2.10 Vectorworks is a general CAD platform; the Vectorworks Architect product is a BIM authoring tool popular with small- and medium-sized firms, as it runs on both Mac and Windows operating systems.

Image courtesy of Wes Gardner.

files (such as JPEG and PNG), PDF, Windows Metafile, QuickTime, VR Object and VR Panorama, VectorScript, DIF, SYLK, Parasolid X_T, IGES, SAT (ACIS 3D solids), Strata, STL, KML, SketchUp, DOE-2 and, critically, IFC 2x3. Vectorworks Architect is GSA BIM compliant.

Strengths

Vectorworks Architect is one of two available BIM applications for Mac. While it originated as a CAD application, it has for years incorporated a unique 2D/3D hybrid environment that allows for both data-rich modeling and traditional drafting and 2D presentation capabilities. It is therefore a "one-stop shop," providing full drawing, drafting, modeling, data, and rendering capabilities in a single application. It is less than half the cost of competitor applications, and does not follow a subscription model (users are not required to upgrade annually, although recently Nemetschek Vectorworks, the application's developer, has offered a subscription service to the United States and some European users). Its 3D Boolean and NURBS capabilities allow modeling of virtually any object. Vectorworks symbols offer a flexible "on the fly" custom object creation solution.

Limitations

There is no industry version aimed specifically at structural or mechanical design; while Vectorworks Architect has some structural and mechanical modeling tools available, structural analysis is limited. On the other hand, IFC interoperability allows such analysis in other applications. Vectorworks's intentionally flexible design environment does not enforce a strict BIM workflow; this must be provided by the designer, which may be problematic for inexperienced users. Vectorworks workgroup solutions are file-based as opposed to server-based. While this does not pose a real problem for smaller offices, the new and ever-expanding BIM paradigm will impose scalability requirements that will make this increasingly problematic for larger projects and firms. The application suffers from the misperception that it is not a full-fledged BIM application. It enjoys a minority, but noticeable and growing, market share in the United States.[2]

Complementary software

While certain BIM applications strive to provide a "one-stop shop," incorporating a broad range of features beyond those strictly found in BIM, most avoid the Swiss-army-knife approach and adopt a narrow focus, choosing to limit application scope to 3D and information modeling. Moreover, in spite of the usefulness of BIM, architects are ultimately concerned with the design of buildings. Those concerns may exceed the capacity of a single application to satisfy, although the application may be within the scope of BIM. Given that architectural design needs may exceed the breadth of tools offered in BIM applications, there are some supplementary software programs that complement the BIM workflow.

Complementing BIM

There is a legitimate role in a BIM workflow for non-BIM applications that may compensate for certain limitations of building information modeling, per se. While some of the functions described immediately below may be incorporated in some BIM applications, they are not in and of themselves BIM features.

Advanced modeling

BIM applications are by their very nature intended to model building components and conditions—walls, doors, windows, roofs, stairs, and so on. As such, they are required to model common building elements, albeit typically in a parametric format that accounts for a wide range of permutations. Earlier software versions required the user to create many of these components on their own as compound

[2] Software reviews are available at: http://www.laiserin.com/features/issue26/feature01.pdf; http://www.macworld.com/reviews/product/412823/review/vectorworks_2009; http://architosh.com/2009/02/product-review-nemetschek-vectorworks-architect-2009/; and http://www.cadalyst.com/aec/vectorworks-2008-cadalyst-labs-review-3701.

models of 3D extrusions, sweeps, and Boolean (additive and subtracted) solids. Over time, BIM applications have included a growing number of parametric building objects. For example, doors may be resizable to any dimension while maintaining consistent user-defined leaf stile and rail dimensions; door objects must also account for common operations (such as swing, pocket, bi-pass, overhead). However, even the most comprehensive parametric door tool may not account for every conceivable configuration or allow unusual door types. Such limitations are understandable, but the user will in some cases need to circumvent them. It should be added that there is a strong trend for BIM applications to include more building component objects and for them to be increasingly flexible.

Free-form modeling

For those cases, formerly quite common but now less so, the designer may wish—or even need—to model geometries not readily available as a standard BIM object tool. Free-form objects include

- Primitive solids like rectangular prisms, spheres, cones (Fig. 2.11);
- Extrusions of lines or polylines (called profiles):
  - Simple extrusions, whether or not perpendicular to the plane of the profile;
  - Tapered, multiple extrusions, or blends—the latter two lofting solid geometry between profiles; these profiles are, in essence, ordered sections through the resulting 3D geometry;
- Revolving solids like sweeps and spirals;
- Solid additions, subtractions, and intersections (Fig. 2.12).

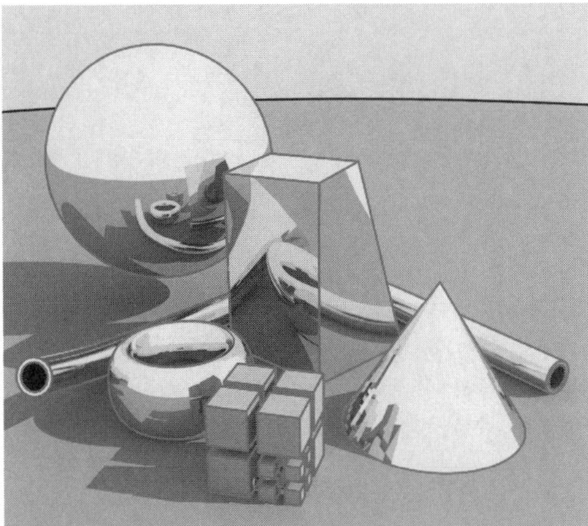

FIGURE 2.11 Some 3D solid geometry, ranging from simple prisms to NURBS surfaces, can be produced in BIM.

Non-uniform rational Bézier splines (NURBS)

Pierre Bézier was an engineer for Renault who furthered the mathematics for describing compound curves with relatively simple algorithms. As the French auto manufacturer investigated and then developed computer-driven fabrication processes for auto bodies, Bézier was put in charge of their efforts. Bézier curves (his contributions to geometry) are well known to graphic and type designers, having been adopted as part of the Postscript language. Indeed Bézier himself developed UNISURF, a 3D modeling application, and today many 3D modeling applications now employ his work as the underlying math behind NURBS. These compound 3D curves and surfaces can be used to describe or approximate everything from tensile structures to the compound curve of a piece of furniture to the 3D path of a handrail. In contrast with geometry based on a mesh of 3D polygons (like a triangulated irregular network, or TIN, as discussed in Chapter 3), NURBS achieve smooth curvature with minimal computational overhead (Fig. 2.13).

BIM modelers like Revit and ArchiCAD currently do not allow for NURBS, although they do permit creation of their 2D cousins, Bézier splines. Some non-BIM modelers like SketchUp also don't support NURBS or Béziers, although certain third-party (and free) add-ons permit the approximation of the latter. It may look like SketchUp and Revit are creating smooth curved surfaces, but, in fact, this is due to smoothing algorithms in the rendering engine; the underlying geometry is polygonal (Fig. 2.14).

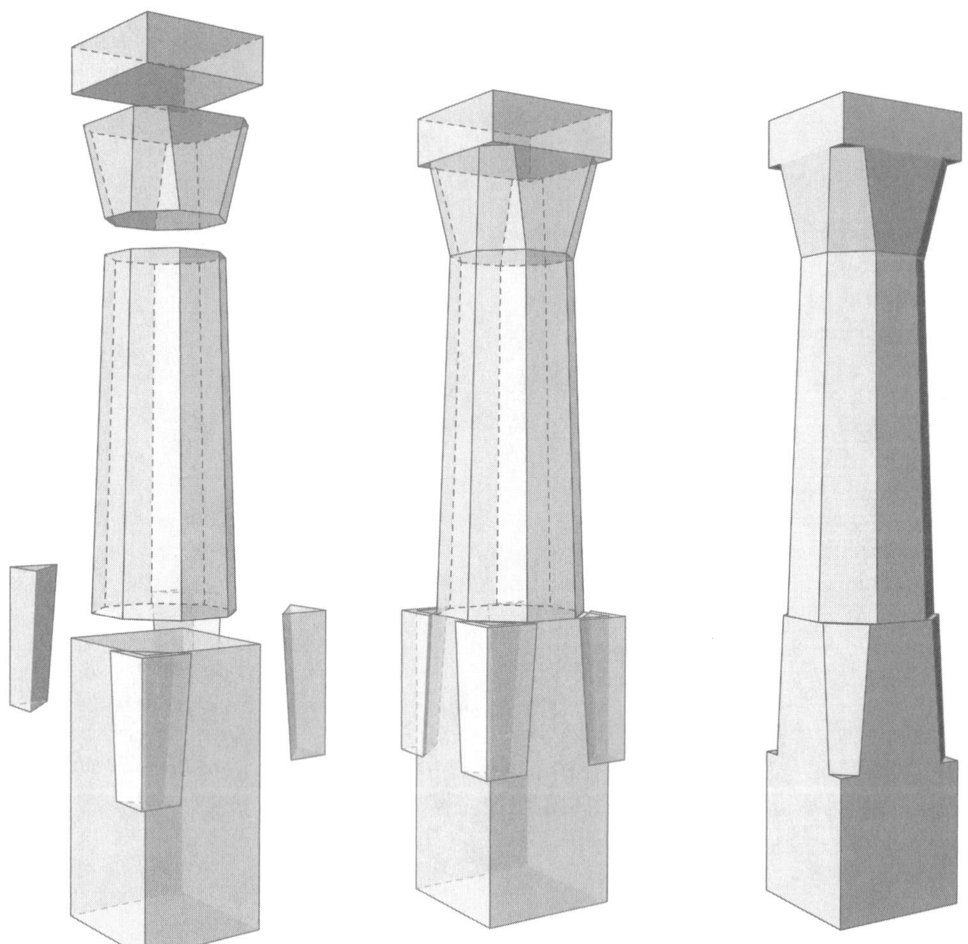

FIGURE 2.12 As flexible as they are, there are times when a desired building component cannot be fully modeled using standard parametric BIM object models. All BIM applications to varying degrees allow the user to create custom models and assign data to them. The final column at right is developed from a series of Boolean operations performed on simple solids (simple extrusions, tapered extrusions, multiple extrusions).

And in many cases a polygonal geometry is perfectly adequate. Provided the polygon count is not so high as to be computationally expensive (resulting in long calculation and rendering times), or so coarse as to be too heavily faceted (resulting in unacceptable representation or noticeably faceted sections), then the approximation of curved surfaces by triangulated polygons is acceptable. However, there are some geometries that can far more easily be modeled using NURBS than with the solid objects and operations depicted in Figure 2.10. A simple example is a plumbing fixture (Fig. 2.15). Sufficient instances of manufacturers' models with high polygon counts (for accurate approximations of a vessel form) may significantly slow a BIM file. Rebuilding the model as a shelled NURBS fillet may be straightforward yet it produces faster, more attractive, and more accurate models.

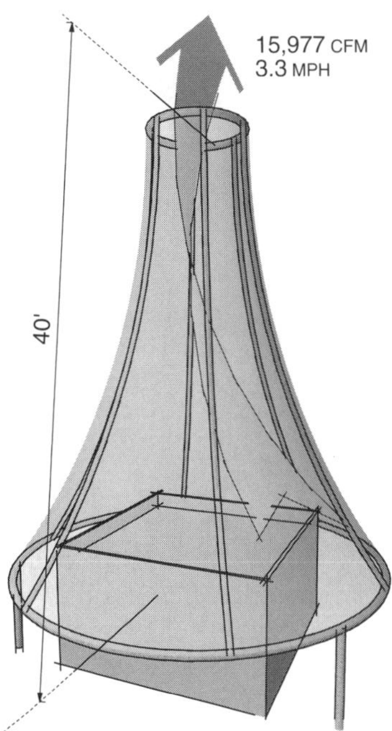

FIGURE 2.13 One of a series of models developed to study the feasibility of retrofitting small buildings with shading devices to reduce solar heat gain while site-generating energy from the stack effect. Curved surfaces and the conceptual structure were modeled with NURBS.

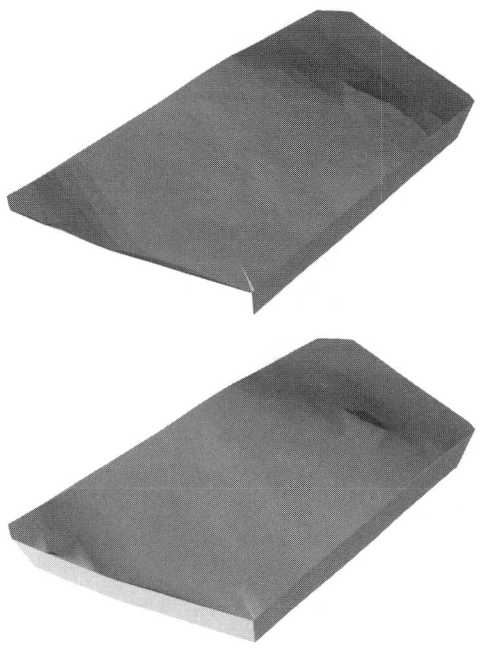

FIGURE 2.14 A site model showing noticeable polygon triangulation is shown at top. The exact same site model is below, except that rendering settings have been adjusted to smooth faceting. This is purely a display smoothing; the geometry of the site has not actually been altered. Both site models would produce the exact same profile if a section were taken.

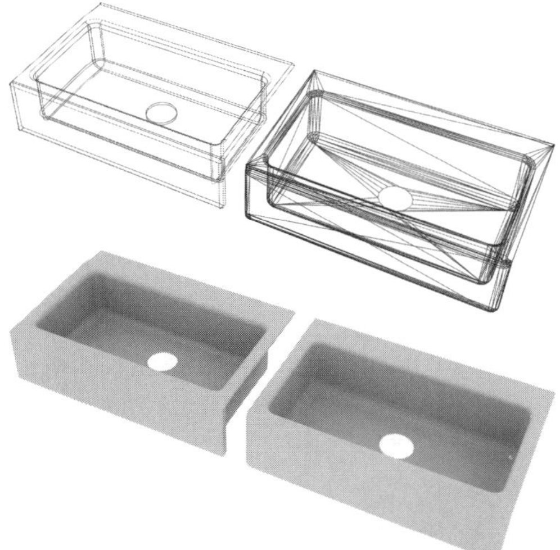

FIGURE 2.15 A sink modeled as NURBS (left) compared to the original polygon model (right) in both wireframe (above) and rendered views (below). The polygonal model is composed of over 600 triangular facets, which produces slower, poorer renderings that may appear faceted in section views.

Pure modelers like Rhino and BIM applications like Vectorworks support NURBS. However, if the object is to render models more efficiently, then creating NURBS objects in Rhino to import them into Revit, for example, will be of limited usefulness—as the NURBS object will become polygonal in the target application if it does not support NURBS. On the other hand, if the end of modeling a NURBS object is to create geometry not easily produced otherwise (as a massing model, or to shape a special roof form, or to represent certain fixtures), then it may well be worthwhile to create a NURBS-based object in another application and import it (albeit as polygons) into the BIM applications. Common modelers that support NURBS creation include:

- 3ds Max
- Blender (free)

- bonzai3d
- Cheetah3D (Mac OS only)
- Cinema 4D
- Cobalt
- form•Z
- Maya
- Rhinoceros 3D
- solidThinking
- Vectorworks (all industry versions)

Ready manipulation of massing models

Software developers focusing exclusively on BIM may have limited or challenging tools for developing massing models. It is commonly recommended, for example, that Revit users develop massing models in applications (like SketchUp) with more robust or accessible 3D modeling tools, then import the model into the BIM modeler when the architect is ready to proceed beyond the massing stage. This workflow is supported by Revit's excellent Wall by Face, Curtain by Face, and Curtain System by Face tools, which as their names imply quickly "skin" a mass object with the appropriate BIM object. If the underlying mass is changed, the dependent walls and curtain components can be updated as a user action.

However, if the massing model originated outside the BIM model, was edited and updated elsewhere, and then reimported and re-placed in the BIM model, updating all dependent components may be tedious and may discourage iterative design. In my experience, it's unusual for design to be a purely linear process; cycling through iterations of the building is not only necessary but also desirable. This is especially true when the model becomes a source of quantitatively informed performance decisions. *Create workflows that support and encourage iterative design.*

Graphic communication

Architects may well transition to a mode of exclusively delivering their instruments of service—for centuries primarily the drawing—that does not involve paper, or even virtual "sheets" (in Chapter 11's case study, Workshop8 describes sharing a building model with a contractor). But architectural deliverables now include drawings, even if much of our coordination work with other disciplines is now paperless and consists of comparative analysis of computer files.

A common (and not always justified) complaint about BIM is that the quality of the printed drawing—the deliverable—may leave something to be desired. It has been my observation that in some cases the transition away from manually prepared drawings, beginning with CAD, has led to drawing sets that are less graphically communicative and clear than they used to be. On the other hand, there is no shortage of old drawings that are poorly drafted. It may be that we are witnessing a gradual cultural shift in the design professions away from emphasizing clarity and the loss of a certain graphic quality to our instruments of service.

Nevertheless, it is quite possible to produce clear and communicative—and handsome —drawings in BIM. The following are key points to consider, regardless of the BIM application used.

Line weight matters

Experienced draftspersons with an understanding of visual communication recognize that variation in line weight is the key to legible drawings. Without sufficient line weight differentiation, the eye wanders; information may be on the page, but meaning is lost. A broad range of line weights in the drawing are not sufficient; line weights must also be distinguishable. My first studio professor—an exquisite draftsman—admonished us to throw out every other pen when we first got our rapidograph sets of ten technical pens, so as to have a clear differentiation between lines of differing weights. To this day my "drawings" still include the five weights Richard Dodge urged me to adopt.

Typically, BIM line weights are set as a function of object type (walls, doors, plumbing) or view. In the former case, line weights are typically set to values that are appropriate for object types in plan views. However, those same object-based line weights are not necessarily ideal for elevations, sections, details, or perspectives. Typically, therefore, line weights are overridden in other views such that all objects have a uniform weight. This avoids, for example, all walls having a heavy line weight, even distant ones, but it creates drawings that are flat and read poorly (Fig. 2.16).

The solution for legible drawings is no different now than it was in the Beaux Arts period: rendering. In this case I mean the process of increasing drawing legibility by manipulating line weights. There are a variety of methods for achieving this, but they typically involve annotating the underlying view of the BIM model with traditional CAD drafting tools: lines, polylines, arcs. In Revit, for example, the Silhouette Edge and Linework tools permit this type of line weight work. ArchiCAD, Vectorworks, and others have similar procedures. This methodology is applicable to building and interior elevations, building and wall sections, and details. Plans are the drawings that are most automatically handled by BIM and tend to require little or no *ex post facto* rendering.

Users of all BIM applications have oft requested the capability of the model to automatically detect distance between receding planes in an elevation, and automatically adjust line weights according to a user's preferences. Sketchup, incidentally, has a depth cue feature that performs similarly, although it is usually applied to perspectives.

Hatches, fills, and shades

In addition to appropriate use of line weights, orthographic-drawing legibility benefits greatly from the use of simple BIM rendering techniques (Fig. 2.17). There are several options available, depending on the software and the user's needs.

- ArchiCAD views may be attributed a shade and shadow rendering, in addition to the line work referenced earlier. For example, portions of a building visible beyond a section plane may be line rendered and shaded.
- Revit, like ArchiCAD, allows the application of dynamic vector hatches to 3D as well as 2D surfaces.
- In Vectorworks, viewports can be given two superimposed rendering styles, combining for example shade and shadow Final Quality background, over which a hidden line rendering mode may be overlaid. This is true of any view, whether orthographic or perspective. Recently, Vectorworks users gained the ability to add vector (2D) hatches to 3D surfaces, although the process is not yet as automated as it is with ArchiCAD and Revit.

Scale is a function of appropriate information, not paper size

A student just learning to draft (by hand) in architecture school may assume that drawing scale is a function of desired or available paper size, or perhaps a function of the building size and the width of the parallel bar. But as the experienced draftsperson has learned, it is the intended level of information to be communicated that determines the appropriate scale of a drawing. Drawing scale is far less about paper size and far more about appropriate information. Indeed, a drawing's scale has always determined what information should be omitted. When the medium contains information as rich as BIM, deciding what to omit is as critical as deciding what to include in a particular view (Fig. 2.18).

BIM applications address the issue of scale and the automated display of appropriate information in a simplified, progressive but effective manner. Revit users, for example, may choose among three view options—coarse, medium, and fine—and the application automatically adjusts the level of detail of objects. Window mullions, muntins, and jambs for example may be shown in full, or simplified, or omitted. As another example, Vectorworks settings can be adjusted to hide wall components globally within a file at any scale smaller than a user-defined threshold, or on a viewport-by-viewport basis.

Test your assumptions—and your settings

Like CAD, BIM allows the user to define several standard pen weights—usually on the order of 15 or 16 standard weights. Before changing the default standards, it may be best to first test the preset lines in a few trial views and print them out. Generally, software developers have set defaults with care and

FIGURE 2.16 Two views of the same BIM model demonstrate the importance of implementing good line weight control. The top image uses line weights to provide depth cues and to render surface materials; the result is a legible drawing that communicates effectively. The view below has had all its lines forced to the same weight and rendering line work is suppressed. The result is confusing and unclear.

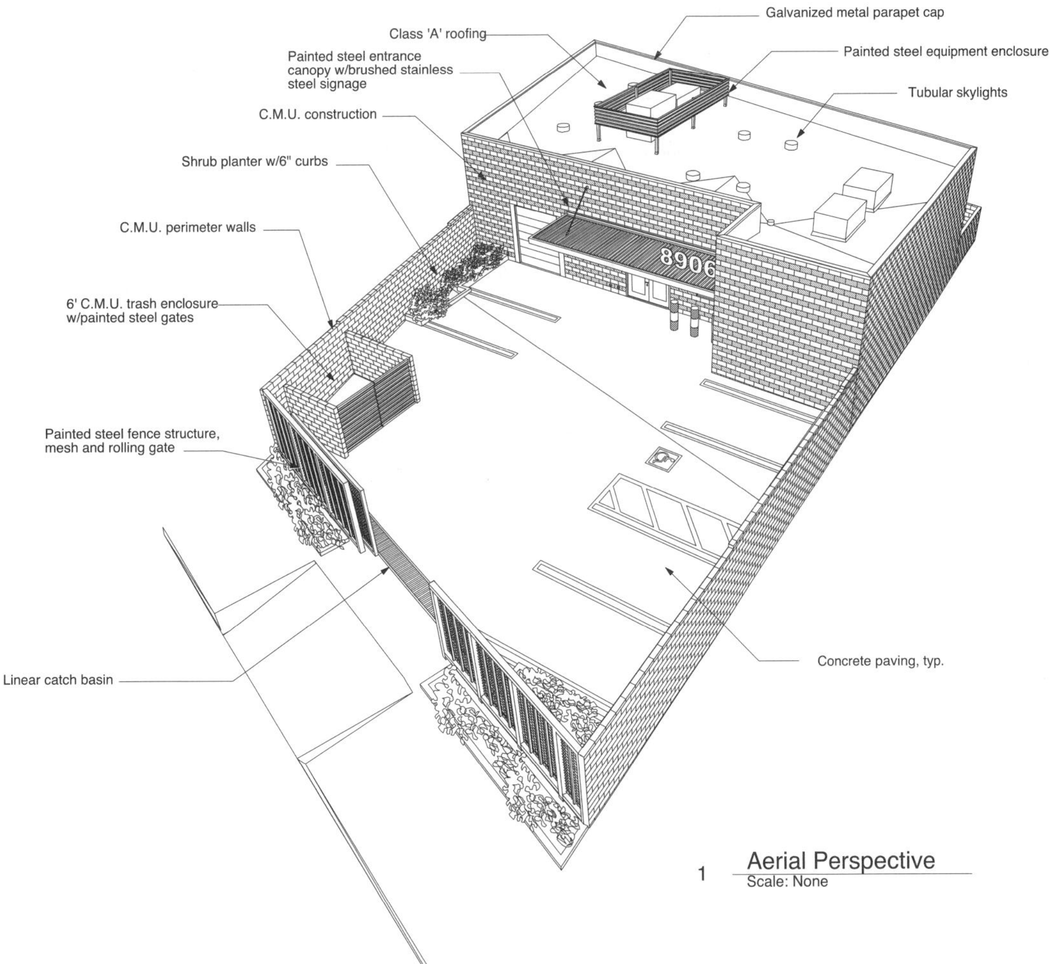

FIGURE 2.17 Line work need not be limited to 2D elevation projects; here hatches have been applied to the building model to effectively communicate the structural system and architectural intent of the project.

Image courtesy of Daniel Jansenson, Architect.

the resulting values are optimized for the typical user. If default line weights are changed from the default settings, once again the new line weights should be evaluated by printing a few representative views: a plan, elevation, building section, interior elevation, and a few details.

There is also some slight variation in line quality from one printer to another. Two different models of printers may output the same drawings with somewhat different line weights. For the discerning architect who takes care and pride in line work, it's important to test-print on the printer(s) likely to be used before establishing office-wide line weight standards.

Detailing

The conventional approach to detailing is to produce a 2D drawing of a particular condition, to scale and annotated, following familiar and established graphic conventions that have little literal relationship to the materials they describe. Rigid insulation may be shown as having a rectangular or triangular

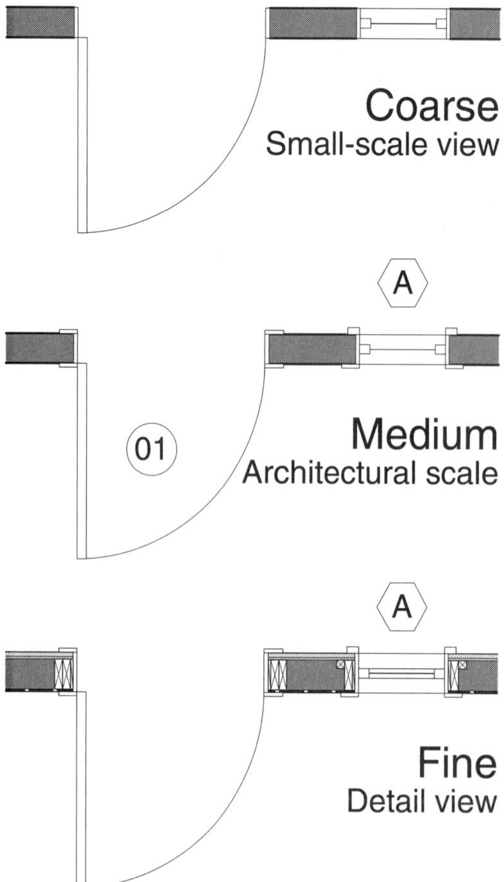

FIGURE 2.18 Three views of the same condition with different view settings applied. Depending on the phase of the design or communication intent, the BIM user may selectively filter out certain components.

hatch, steel in section detail is depicted as two diagonal lines spaced closely together, plywood as three diagonal lines intersecting lines parallel to the plies, and so on. Such details may be drawn in plan, elevation, or section, although most often they are the latter (Fig. 2.19). These details are *abstractions* in important ways:

- They often represent typical conditions, from which similar conditions may be extrapolated;
- They convey a design intent, but are not shop drawings *per se*;
- They may not capture every single condition, and the owner and architect may rely on the expertise of the general contractor (and the trades) to apply their skill and knowledge to other conditions that may arise.

For BIM to include such detailed conditions throughout the virtual building would be problematic at best. One might naively imagine that a BIM model would include every stud, every fastener, every piece of flashing, every length of caulk, and every seal. But a model is just that—a model. It too, like the detail, is an abstraction. This is not only a necessary limitation of finite computational resources (and the extensive but finite expertise and time of the designer), but it is even desirable. The architect is not the contractor usually nor (except by accident) a member of the trades—much less all the trades. Abstraction gives those who build the project room to exercise their craft, accumulated experience, knowledge, and even imagination.

In short, even BIM models need abstract details, and those details are not usually entirely extracted from the model. The current best practice—regardless of particular software application—consists of extracting a general condition from the model and using it as the background or guide for construction a conventional 2D detail. The latter is an overlay partly or completely masking or replacing the underlying model geometry.

Lest the reader cry foul and object to drafting within a BIM model, some would argue that a parametric 2D element is a legitimate instance of a "smart object" within a "model," even if this does not follow the commonly accepted assumption that a model must be three dimensional. Nevertheless, BIM applications contain libraries of parametric 2D objects used as detailing elements. These include repetitive linear elements like brick, siding profiles, decking, insulation, and so forth.

BIM libraries of detailing elements are not limited to 2D components, of course—appropriate 3D parametric elements that can be used at a detailed scale are also included in the BIM repertoire. Standard steel sections, from angles to W-sections, timber or lumber framing elements, trusses,

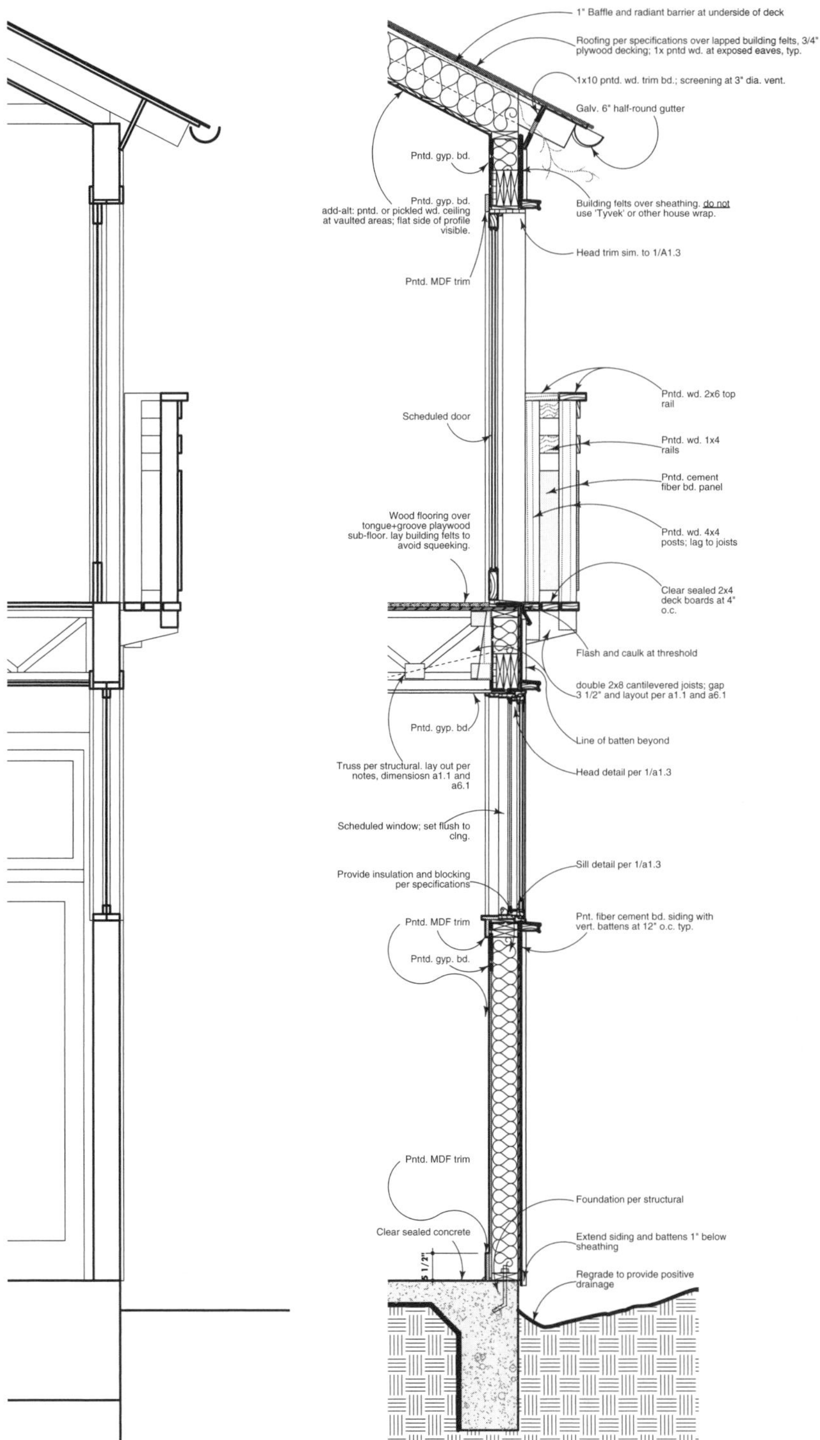

FIGURE 2.19 To an ever-increasing degree, BIM applications are able to produce "detail ready" views of the model. Nevertheless, it is often desirable, if not necessary, to overlay drawn information for complete wall sections and details.

fasteners such as bolts and clevises, mechanical system components like ducts and registers, and so on are commonly seen in BIM software. And of course, families, GDL objects, symbols, or custom parametric objects can be created to fulfill the users' particular needs (Fig. 2.20).

Thanks to these and other small-scale BIM objects, there are underexploited opportunities for isometric, exploded, or perspective detail views. These may illustrate conditions that may not be clearest from conventional 2D details, or may be used to complement such traditional details. Any efforts that make design information clearer and more accessible to consultants, contractors, subcontractors—and owners—lead to improved communication, trust, fewer errors, and a better project. Even the designer can learn something unexpected from a three-dimensional detail, so these are valid exploration tools as well.

In my own practice, I find that the nature of my drawing sets has evolved over time with my use of BIM. Whereas early in my career I relied heavily on elevations in addition to sections and plans, I find nowadays that I use the model as a design tool far more than I do elevations. While useful for composition and proportional studies, for example, the elevation has become relegated to a deliverable. That is, its primary uses are explaining the project to a contractor, and providing the basis for material takeoffs. The model is a better vehicle

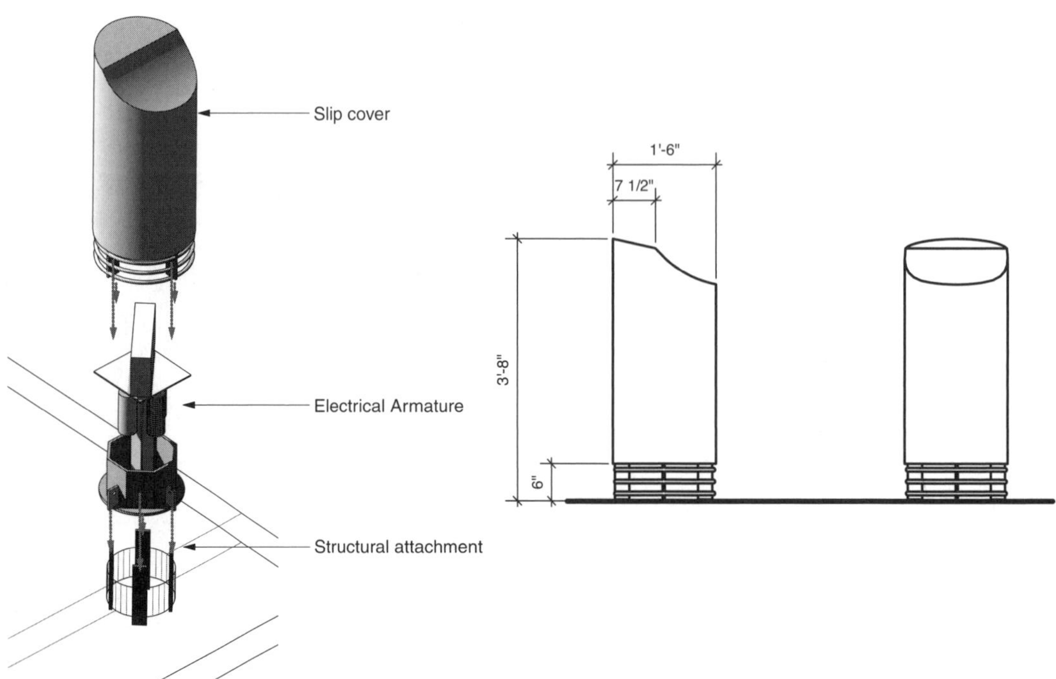

FIGURE 2.20 A completely custom lighting bollard is modeled and detailed in BIM. The exploded isometric and elevations are different views of the same BIM components.

Image courtesy of Limbacher & Godfrey Architects.

for the former, and BIM's takeoff capabilities are more accurate than the latter. Similarly, my drawing sets now always include views of the model. For certain details, such as millwork, for example, a hidden line perspective or isometric is highly valuable. As a result, my interior elevation and detail sheets routinely contain 3D details.

Annotations and callouts

As my late professor Richard Dodge would say, a word is worth a thousand pictures. Just as not all modeling is inherently three-dimensional, in BIM not all information need be innate in a modeled object. Historically, the annotation of drawings (whether by hand lettering or CAD text blocks) was decoupled from the drawing. That is, the "information" (annotations, even dimensions) was not inherent to the "model" (the drawing), but instead essentially an overlay. In the days of the pin bar Mylar drafting system, in fact, notes and dimensions were on an overlaid sheet, separate from the drawing itself.

It is possible to follow this approach within BIM, treating individual text blocks as unique objects disassociated from the geometry they refer to. There are many instances when this is appropriate and useful. However, similarly to model objects, BIM callout annotations are parametric instances (in this case, of text strings) linked to a database. That is, changing one instance of the text changes all instances; the notes may be edited from the database itself.

In their least intelligent form, dimension strings may also be independent from the geometry they nominate—"reading" the geometry at the moment of its creation but thereafter independent of it—this is the hallmark of the CAD paradigm. On the other hand, dimension strings in BIM may be used both to report geometry and control it. Revit's temporary dimensions allow this, for example, as do associative dimensions in Vectorworks when the appropriate document preference is selected.

Further reading

In Chapter 11 we will discuss exporting the BIM model to other formats in order to facilitate collaboration with consultants, including supplemental computation for:

- Energy modeling
- Structural analysis
- Sequencing (4D modeling)
- Cost estimating

▪ Case Study: Parameterized Hauer Curtain Wall

By David Light
Designer: David Light

The significance of parametric design tools in BIM authoring software such as Revit cannot be underestimated. Whilst parametric functionality is not, per se, essential to Building Information Models, it does offer greater design leverage, and allows rapid evaluation of multiple iterations of design concepts. The application of a minimal set of parametric rules to an initial design idea may lead to unexpected results. Advanced math is hardly required to start applying rules to digital components, although a good grasp of trigonometry is helpful. The current crop of BIM tools allows the user to apply very simple rules such as dimension length or angle to components in context. Some of more complex parametric design tools do require a programming background to script or code the rules.

(*Continued*)

Inspired by the work of Austrian sculptor Erin Hauer, who designed sculptural forms suggesting infinitely repeating geometric surfaces, Light wondered if Hauer's technique could be applied to modern day parametric BIM tools. Revit's Curtain Wall is a parametric tool that creates repeatable 3D geometries (Fig. 2.21). Whether this application is architecture or art, the ability to create a parametric form and quickly push design changes through multiple iterations to achieve a numerous variations is a design capability.

FIGURE 2.21 This rendered perspective of the Hauer-inspired Curtain Wall is the result of a custom Revit Family applied as a component of the Curtain Wall. A far cry from the kind of storefront assemblies often associated with the Curtain Wall tool, this application is a fascinating application of parametric design to derive new and potentially unexpected architectural forms.

Image courtesy of David Light, Revit Specialist, HOK London

A parametric approach is particularly applicable to the design of buildings that meet growing sustainability requirements. For example, a complex façade for a building in a hot climate may need to be tested to determine its shading. Applying geometric relationship rules to the BIM components constituting the façade allows the designer to evaluate variations of the façade quickly and flexibly. Each iteration of the façade can then be tested, using sun study functionality built into to the software, allowing the architect or designer to review how the façade may influence the shadowing of the building surface. Having applied parametric rules to the components, if amendments or changes need to be made quickly, the parameters can be varied as required to make specific changes to the components. The sun study can then be quickly run again to see the impact of changes the design. As a final step, linking the parametric geometric output from the BIM model to rapid prototyping tools creates a true design-to-fabrication workflow.

In this particular case, the initial component of the Curtain Wall array is a 3D model object to which various parametric rules are applied, allowing variations in form as required.

Of interest in this particular form is that it contains various solids and voids which constitute the component as a whole, with parametric constraints to control the initial cube form in the centre. This in turn controls various other extrusions and sweeps, which make up the component; note that the cube is hollow in the centre.

To prevent the component from breaking, a check parameter was included in its definition. This is reasonably straightforward to achieve. A parameter called "length_outer" controlled the overall size of the cube within the component. Another parameter was created as a check parameter, called "length_outer_check" and contained an "if" statement:

if(length_outer > 5,000 mm, 5,000 mm, length_outer)

This expression effectively prevents the user from creating lengths greater than five meters, the limiting value beyond which the Revit Family would break. This component is then nested into a curtain panel component (Fig. 2.22). The logic here involves the application of a process of nesting components into one another like Russian dolls and connecting the rules between the various elements. As one parameter is changed at the top level, it alters the related subcomponents.

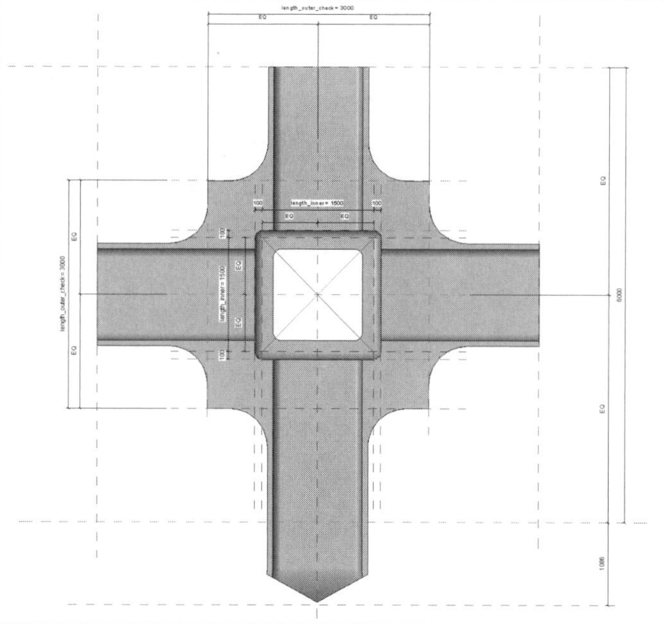

FIGURE 2.22 A dimensioned elevation view of the Revit Family that forms the core component of the Curtain Wall array. The dimension strings do not merely nominate the geometry of the object, but control it, a common feature of many BIM applications.

Image courtesy of David Light, Revit Specialist, HOK London.

(*Continued*)

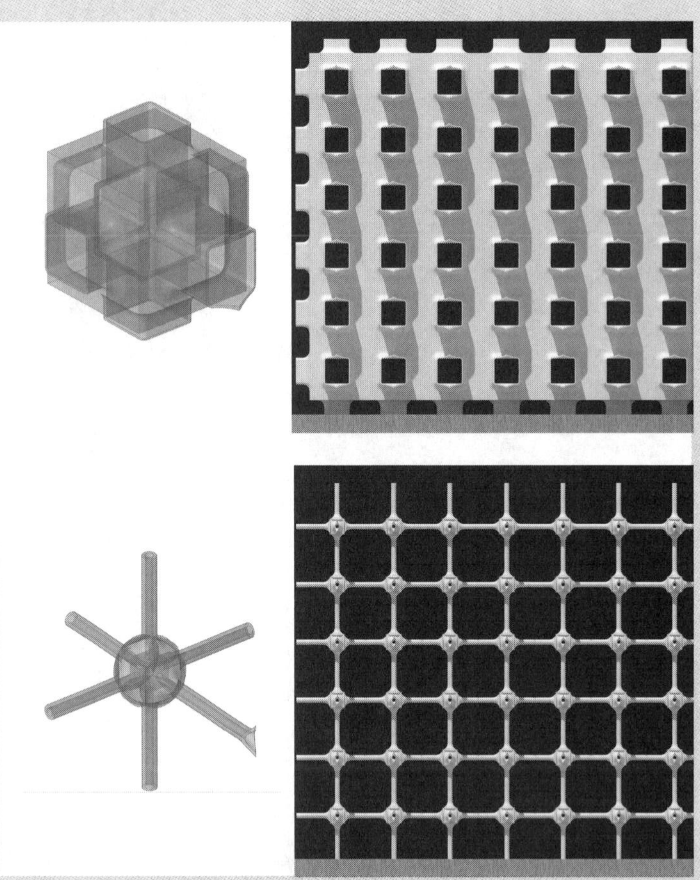

FIGURE 2.23 The Curtain Wall in two extreme configurations: above, the outer length has been set to 1,050 mm (component at left, Curtain Wall at right). Below, the outer length has been set to its maximum of 5,000 mm.

Image courtesy of David Light, Revit Specialist HOK London.

The nested curtain wall panel component was then loaded into a Revit Curtain Wall system. By nature, the Curtain Wall has various other parameters that control the number, size, and rotation angle of panels (Fig. 2.23).

The Hauer Curtain Wall (Fig. 2.24) may simply be an exercise in parametric design and the outcome abstract or academic. However, novel applications like these of seemingly innocuous BIM tools point to the underlying power of BIM software that few users capitalize upon. Some applications, like the Grasshopper extension of Rhino and Bentley's Generative Components, rely on relational geometries for much of their modeling power. As BIM grows in sophistication and user interfaces are streamlined, the computational power to design new expressions of high-performance architecture will hopefully be in the hands of more and more users.

David Light, Revit Specialist and buildingSMART Implementation Leader for HOK London, is one of the leading UK experts in Revit and is a popular speaker and blogger (autodesk-revit.blogspot.com).

FIGURE 2.24 In another perspective of the Hauer Curtain Wall, the geometry of the governing component can be clearly seen. Such a repetitive and parametrically controlled array has enormous potential for, among other things, optimization of novel shading device geometries.

Image courtesy of David Light, Revit Specialist HOK London.

Chapter 3

Site Analysis

With the exception of the International Space Station, no building exists without a site. Experienced architectural practitioners intimately understand that building design is lacking an important dimension without careful consideration of the site (Fig. 3.1). Buildings are not objectified artifacts that are isolated from experience (that is, inhabitation) or divorced from context (or site). Further, proper sustainable site design requires a quantitative understanding of site conditions: topography, solar orientation, prevailing winds, and so on. This is nothing new, of course, but BIM presents an opportunity to integrate manipulable site data into the design process in an immediate and recursive way (Fig. 3.2). This chapter frames the discussion of the role of BIM in the analysis and design of sustainable sites.

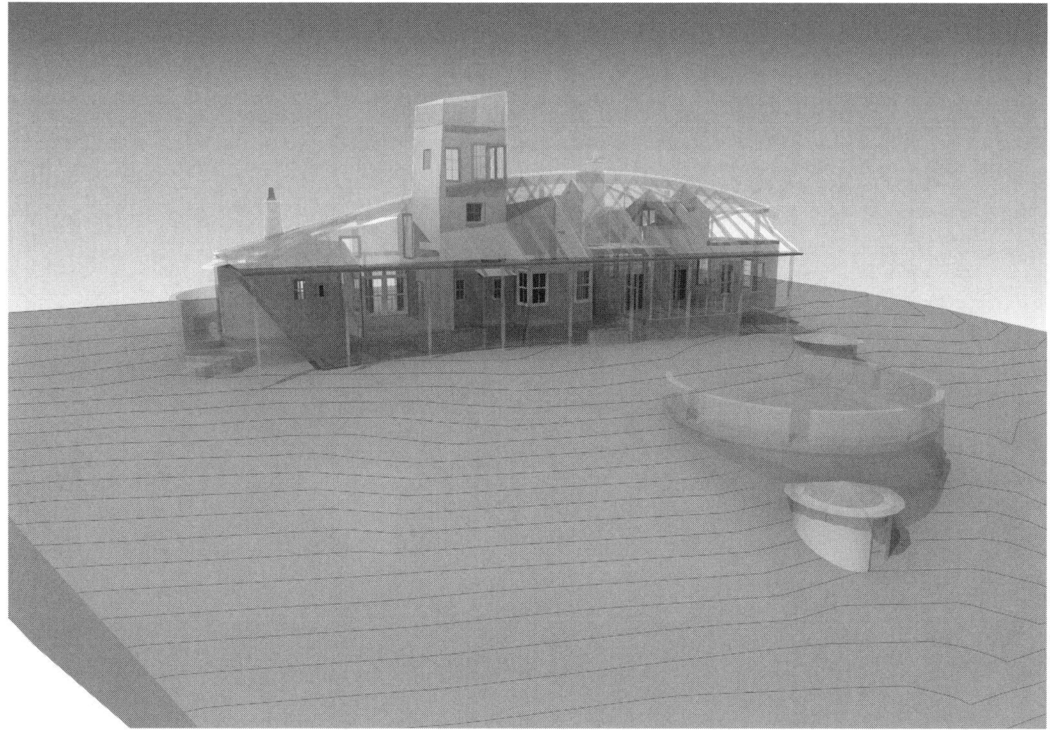

FIGURE 3.1 Addressing steep or difficult topography is one obvious way in which a robust site model is an important dimension of BIM.

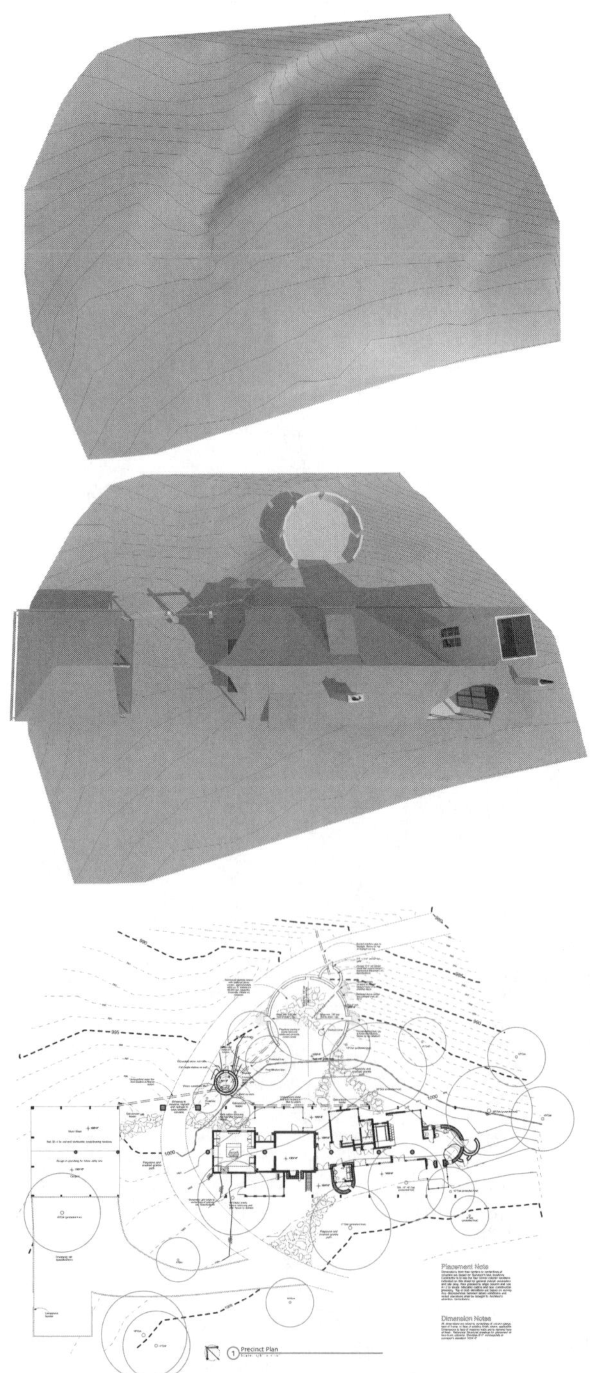

FIGURE 3.2 Three plan views of site models: a rendered mesh, a 3D view including the building, and drawing from the construction documents. All three views are of the same site model.

Developing a site model

Traditionally, architects have documented, analyzed, designed, and communicated site information in one of two ways: through drawings or physical models. Of the two, the former has traditionally been a more flexible and powerful tool in large part due to its graphic abstractness and the convention of topography lines. Site plans and their topographies can readily be manipulated with a pencil and quantified with a scale. With these simple tools and a little arithmetic, grades, slopes, and elevations can be drawn, studied, analyzed, changed, and finalized. Physical site models have until recently been extremely time-consuming to make, particularly for large and complex sites. The advent of digital fabrication technologies (laser cutters, computer controlled routers, and to a growing extent 3D printers) has facilitated physical site model production, but the process is still time consuming, and at the time of this writing few firms, particularly small ones, have digital fabrication capabilities in-house. Most physical site models are thus still cut and glued by hand. As useful as they are for visualization and presentation, for most projects, only a handful of iterations of the site at most are constructed (Fig. 3.3).

But as with all drawings, coordination can be problematic. Agreement between site plan, ground floor plan, building elevations, and building sections can be tedious, time consuming, at times complex, and prone to error. This is particularly the case as the designer regrades the site to accommodate the building, and adjusts the building to better fit the site; a well-sited building may require several design iterations to best fit its location. With views extracted from a building model that includes digital

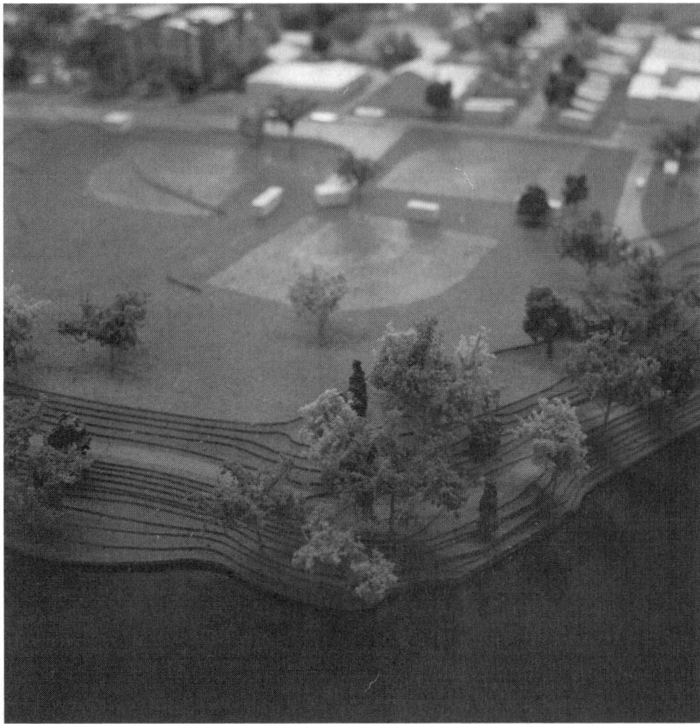

FIGURE 3.3 Digital fabrication does not exclude hand modeling. Here the contours were digitally fabricated directly from CAD contours, and formed the base for a hand-made site model.

Image courtesy of Flying Fish Designs and Studio Maquette. Photograph by Veronica Winford.

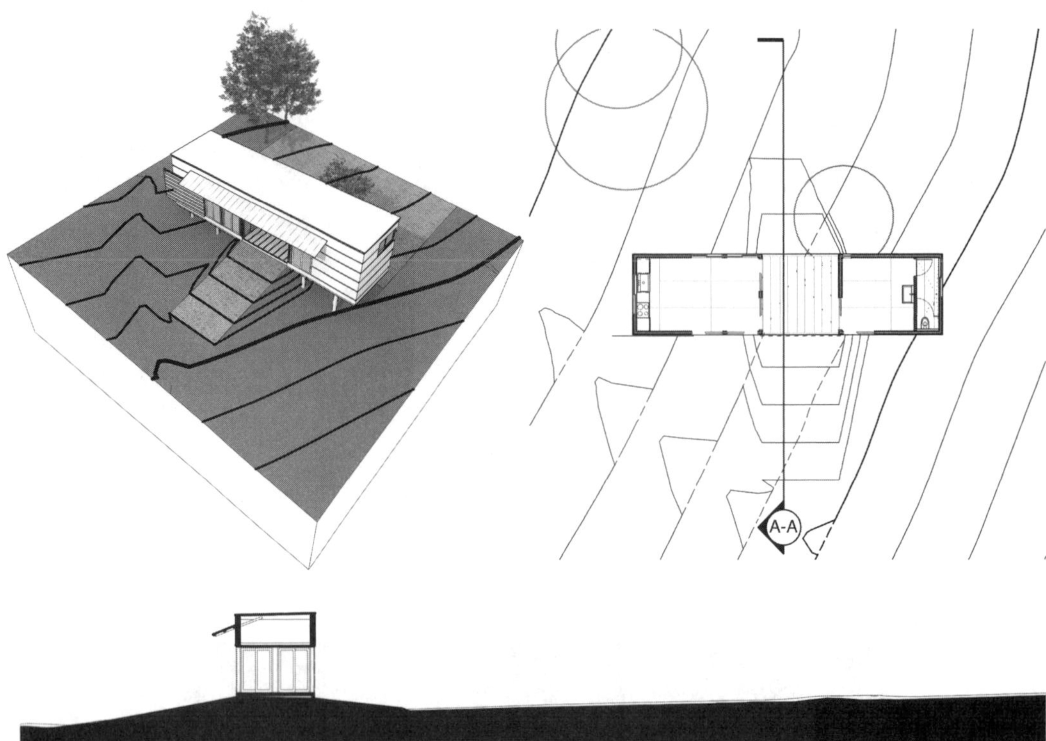

FIGURE 3.4 As in reality, in BIM the building model may interact with the site. Here, the site model has been regraded to meet the building, coordinating the ground floor plan and site conditions.

terrain, however, coordination of building and site can be automated (Fig. 3.4). Most site models consist of meshes of triangular 3D polygons, or triangulated irregular networks (TINs) (Fig. 3.5). There are several possible approaches to the preparation of a digital terrain model (DTM), depending on the needs of the designer, software tools employed, and the nature of available site or survey data.

Generally, inexperienced users tend to err on the side of providing too much detail in a model rather than not enough. (A model is, after all, just that: an abstraction, as opposed to a miniature, which seeks to faithfully represent every aspect of the original.) This is true for site models as well, where the novice is often apt to create or reproduce as "faithful" or nuanced a contour as possible. This tendency may lead to terrain models whose resolution is far too high. For example, given a sinuous Bézier contour in Figure 3.6, one might be tempted to reproduce it as a polygonal approximation of several thousand points (top left). However, as can be seen, even a rough approximation may lead to an acceptable terrain model, provided it preserves the inflections of the original (right).

There are four views that one might expect from a site model:

- A traditional site plan view, with equal-interval contours;
- An analytical plan view, for example color-coded to slope or indicating flow arrows;
- A rendered 3D view, such as a perspective;
- A site section (and, by extension, a building elevation that shows existing and/or finished grade relative to the building).

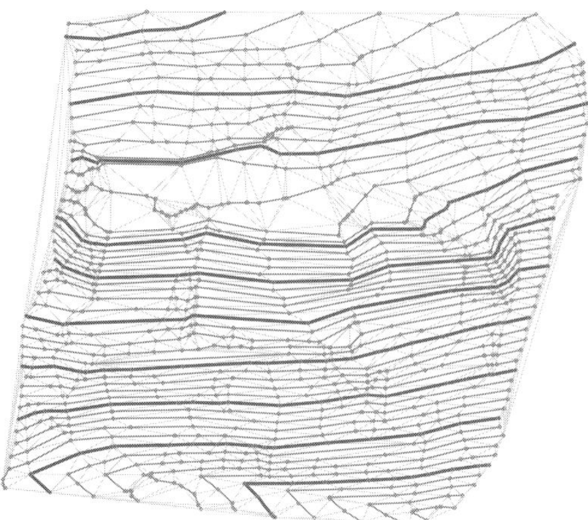

FIGURE 3.5 A triangulated irregular network (TIN) site model. The *x, y, z* coordinate vertices that constitute the actual data points generating the TIN have been highlighted with dots.

In the case of the first, it happens that TIN models may be acceptable at a lower resolution (that is, possessing fewer data points, or 3D vertices) than one might expect, for several reasons. Many applications, from BIM modelers like Revit and Vectorworks, to surface modelers like SketchUp, are able to use rendering algorithms to make faceted site models appear smooth in 3D rendered views. This has the significant benefit of drastically reducing rendering times, as a smoothed, faceted model may be calculated and rendered much faster than one that owes its smoothness to having significantly more data points (what has been termed here "higher resolution"). Hence smooth, high-vertex-count contours may safely be reduced in resolution with little loss in quality. The designer should take care to maintain each contour's general shape (inflection). If the number of vertices is reduced by means of an automated script or command, inspect the simplified contours to insure that highly inflected, close-set contours do not end up crossing nearby contours. Most TINs do not allow perfectly shear faces (contours stacked on top of one another), nor "caves" (crossed contours).

It may also bear mentioning that most survey contours are themselves interpolations and approximations based on a few data points. Reducing a contour to a more faceted polygon does not necessarily represent a loss of true data (Fig. 3.6, top and lower right).

As most site sections have little dramatic inflection in the finished or existing grade line, a lower resolution TIN once again may produce very satisfactory results. Site sections and building elevations may realize little benefit from high-resolution TINs, yet the user may pay for the high number of data points with a high computational penalty: slow calculations, regenerations, and renderings.

It may be difficult to make a blanket assessment of what constitutes too high a resolution for a TIN and what is an appropriate low (but not too low) resolution of data. Variables such as the size and scale of the project, the relative uniformity of site grade, the capabilities of the software, and the computational power available to the designer are all significant factors. Unfortunately, some trial and error may be necessary for a particular designer to determine an ideal minimum and maximum number of 3D vertices for a "typical" model. As a point of departure, I have produced very convincing site models of far less than 50,000 3D vertices; 100,000 3D vertices is probably an upper limit at the time of this writing for most software and hardware to handle without excessive sluggishness.

If the designer needs an extended site model that may have only one or a few areas of particular interest, one useful technique is to "nest" site models (Fig. 3.7). Using this method, a large area (over which little or no construction is to take place, but which is to serve as site context) is modeled at a relatively low resolution (and smoothly rendered). Smaller areas of interest are modeled at a much higher resolution, and inset into the larger site context model. In this way, one benefits from having a large model expanse, which is more highly detailed only in needed portions in order to reduce computational cost, or rendering times.

From rough field surveys

The designer may wish to perform an informal field survey in order to establish preliminary site

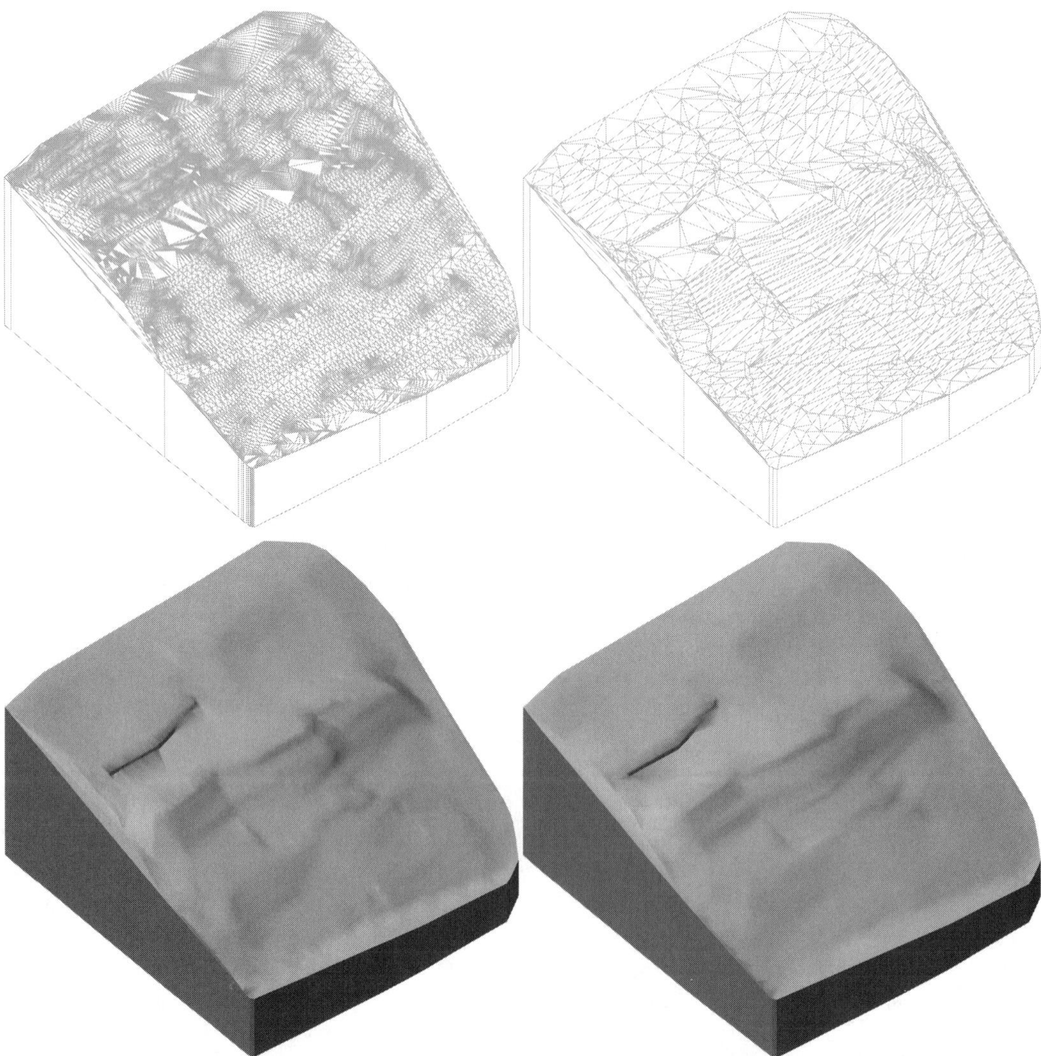

FIGURE 3.6 The site model at left is derived from smooth cubic spline polylines that, when converted to 3D polygons, yields almost 8,000 vertices. The one at left is composed of more angular polygonal approximations with less than a thousand vertices. The rendered views below are of the same respective site models; thanks to smoothing algorithms, the coarser site model (with much faster computation and rendering times) appears just as smooth or smoother than its high-vertices-count counterpart.

conditions: a survey may not yet be available, or the project may be at a feasibility stage and not warrant a survey. With basic surveying techniques a few data points may be established (Fig. 3.8). This is particularly useful where the designer may possess a 2D site plan with no topographical information (such as a metes and bounds or plot plat) and can add elevation information. An arbitrary benchmark may be established and approximate or exact elevations can be taken relative to that benchmark: at tree locations, existing building corners, and so on. A simple surveyor's hand level may be used, or even a measuring tape can indicate existing finish floor above grade at building edges.

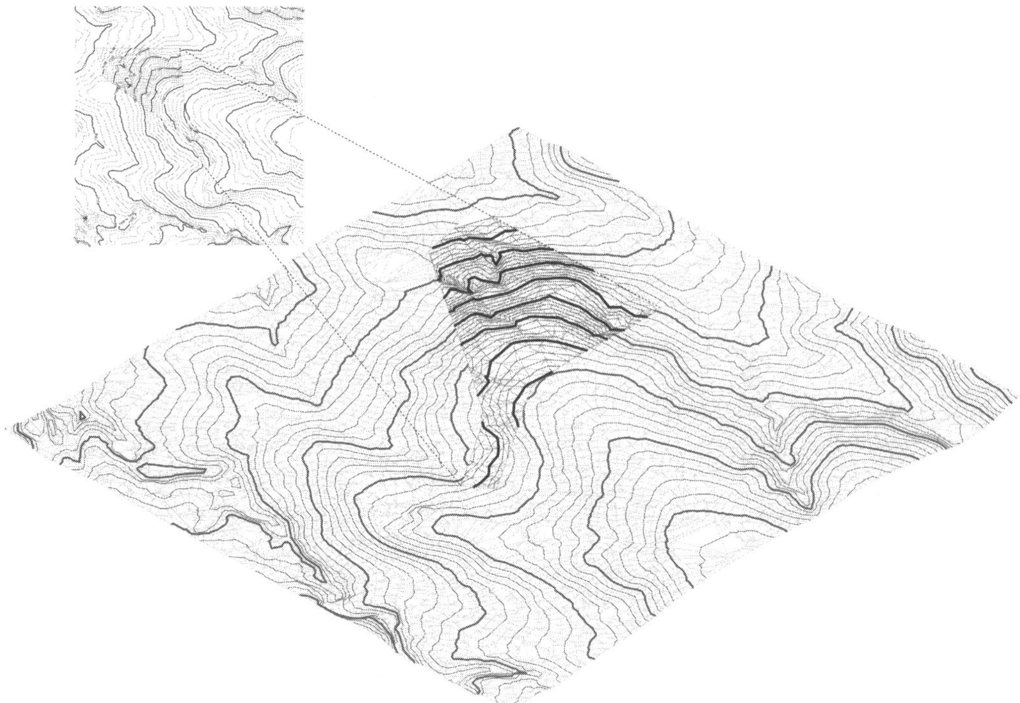

FIGURE 3.7 To reduce computational cost, it may be acceptable to have an extended site model generated at a coarser data resolution, within which a more precise site model is nested. Here a higher polygon count site model for a site of interest is inserted in a larger (and less precise) site model. The larger model is derived from aerial geographic information system (GIS) data; the inset site was surveyed on the ground by a licensed surveyor.

Once several points are established (with correct or approximate *x*, *y*, and *z* coordinates), there are several options for generating a survey. Most BIM software has an automated command or tool for doing so, such that site model creation can be somewhat automated. For example:

- ArchiCAD allows the importation of theodolite *x*, *y*, and *z* coordinates and their automatic conversion to a (static) site mesh model.
- Revit's *toposurface* command allows the automated surfacing of 3D contours to a static mesh surface. Site tools exist for adding roads and pads. The civil engineering version of Revit includes more robust tools for site creation and modification, but these are likely not in the scope of most architectural firms (see Chapter 11).
- Vectorworks Architect and Landmark can convert 3D loci (*xyz* coordinates) or 3D polygons to a dynamic site model. The Vectorworks site model may be modified with proposed contours, graders, pads, and roads; display existing or proposed conditions; and be analyzed for slope and cut-and-fill (Fig. 3.9).
- SketchUp's sandbox tools allow the creation of site models from contours; the site can be exported in a 3D format using SketchUp Pro, or imported directly from SketchUp to a BIM application with appropriate import function (SketchUp is so popular that most BIM software supports direct importing of SketchUp models).

As a last resort, the user can manually (and tediously) "stitch" a mesh as a series of triangular

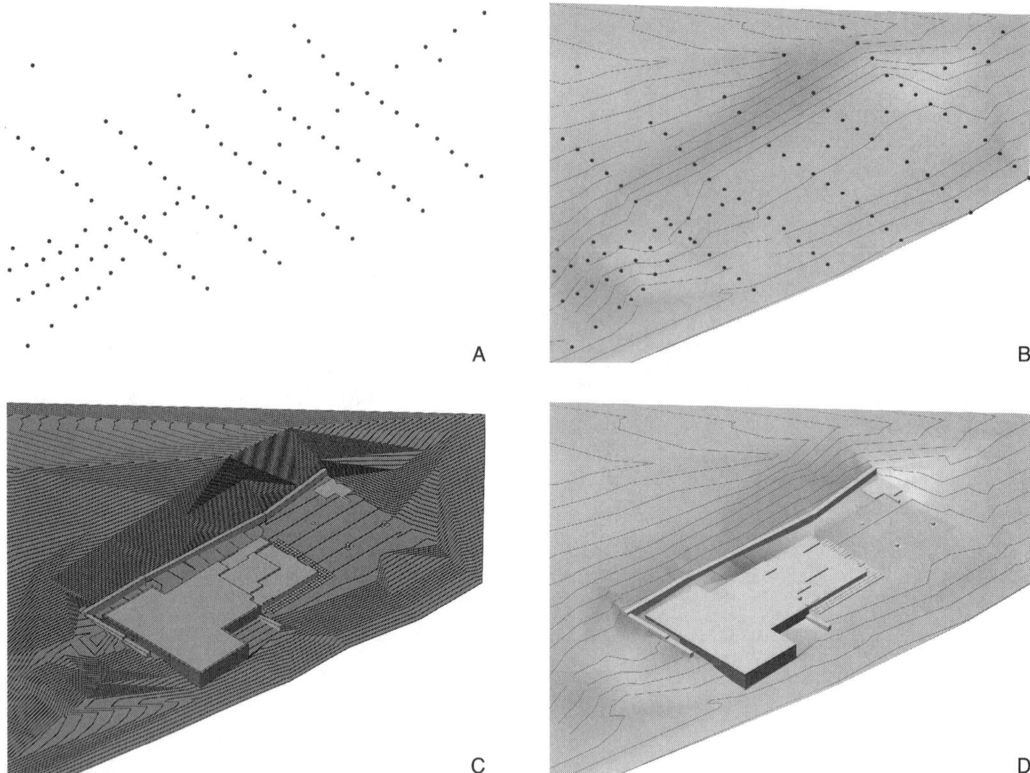

FIGURE 3.8 The development of a site model: the architect made field topography measurements (vertices, upper left, and superimposed over generated site TIN, upper right) and constructed the site model in Vectorworks. The bottom left view shows the preliminary site model regraded with the building slab modeled; at bottom right is the smoothed site. The previous owner had excavated a portion of an existing slope and the new owners wanted to use this area for placement of their home. The model and siting were so accurate that the foundation contractor confirmed the recommended removal of an additional 9 inches at the northwest corner of the existing excavation.

Rancho Encino Residence by Agruppo.

3D polygons (which is in essence what the automated tools do).

From surveyed contours

The most common form of imported site information is in the form of surveyor's files. These are commonly DWG files (Autodesk's AutoCAD native DraWingG format) that all BIM applications can import. Modern surveying techniques consist of data points collected at spot locations via GPS equipment. These points are stored as *xyz* coordinates in a database, from which civil engineering software can interpolate topographical elevation contours (among BIM applications, Vectorworks Architect includes this function and can derive both 2D contours and a mesh model from discrete *xyz* points or 3D polygon contours). When surveyors drew contours by hand, and technology did not enable the extensive sampling of data points, 2nd it seems that surveys were more irregular than they are today. The interpolation of contours from points may have contributed to more regular topographical site surveys. Archaic surveys, on the other hand, may have been less accurate, but perhaps more faithful to observed nuances of the land.

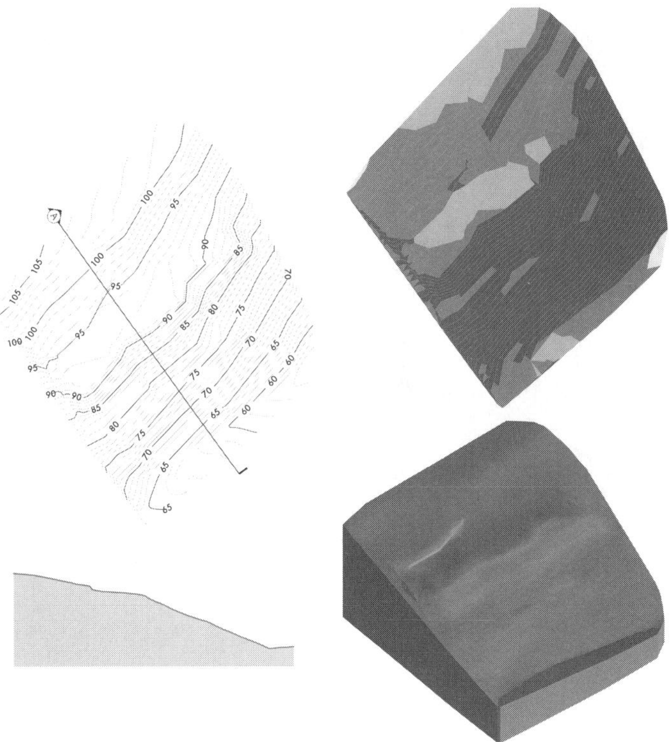

FIGURE 3.9 Four views of the same Vectorworks site model, demonstrating the flexibility of view representations. Counterclockwise, starting with top left: 2D plan view with dynamic site section marker; a 2D site section; triangulated site mesh rendered smoothly; and 2D site analysis with shaded polygons indicating slope ranges.

Surveyors provide either 2D or 3D contours, or both. If the contours are 2D only, they will need to be converted to 3D and each one given the appropriate elevation—which may be quite tedious for extensive site models with thousands of data points. In some software, the assignment of a *z* value (height) to contours may be automated, but this will still require some user involvement to assure correct elevations. Once the 3D data is complete, the site model itself may be "built" as described above, according to the particular BIM software used.

Care should be taken that the surveyed contours do not contain too many data points. This may particularly be the case if the contours originated as smooth splines, or curves. Such contours, while seemingly desirable for their apparent accuracy, may lead to 3D polygons that are computationally too intense (slow), as discussed above. In such cases, simplify the imported polygonal contours to a manageable number of points (Fig. 3.10). Again, consider the guides provided above for the total number of data points in the site model, adjusted for project requirements and hardware and software capabilities (Fig. 3.11).

In the United States, surveyors typically use decimal feet as their default unit of length, and this is reflected in their software. Architectural BIM software, however, usually uses imperial feet and inches as the default unit. Modern BIM software will often automatically negotiate the translation of units, but on occasion due to a missed setting or error the survey will be the wrong size. In every case that I've seen, the imported site too small by a factor of 12, as feet were read as inches. This is easily corrected,

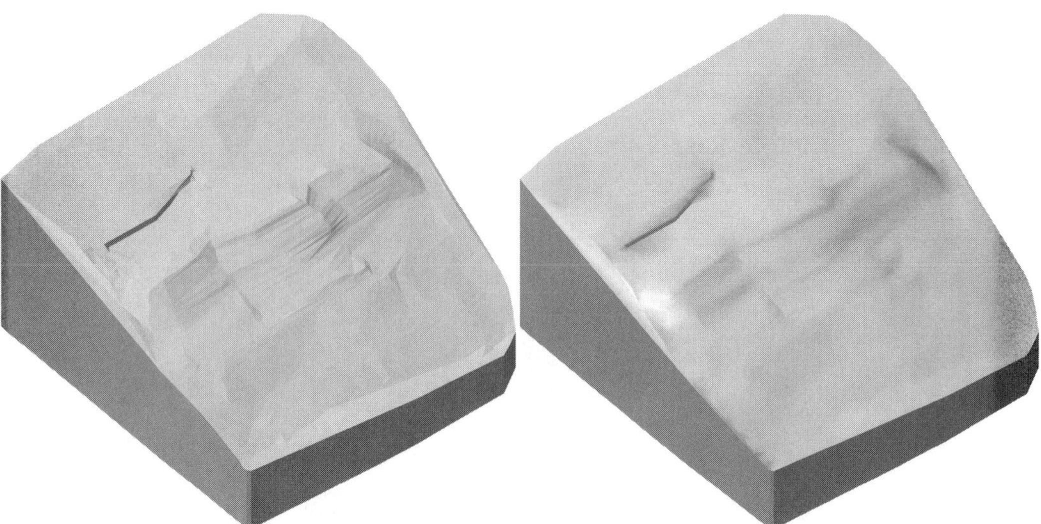

FIGURE 3.10 These are two views of the exact same (relatively low-polygon count) site models. At left is the actual geometry of the site; at right the file settings have been changed to visually smooth any angle over 70°. This smoothing is apparent only; the actual geometry does not change (hence computation times are not increased).

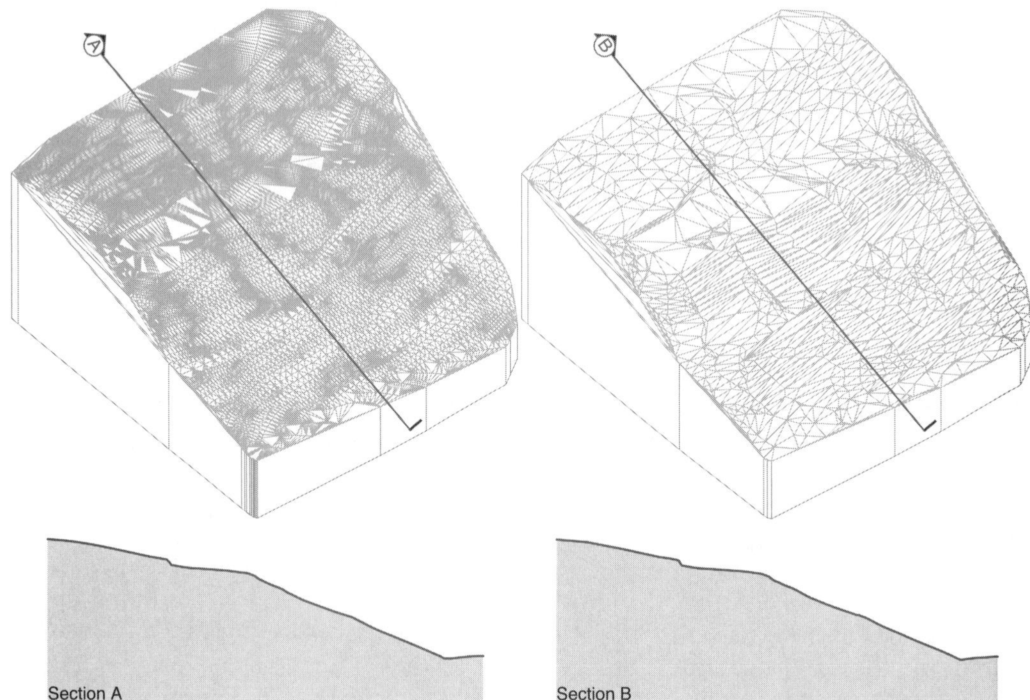

FIGURE 3.11 Two site models of the same site have very different polygon counts, with nearly 8,000 vertices at left, and under 1,000 vertices at right. Their respective site sections, however, are indistinguishable, suggesting that coarser site models are just as suitable for design and documentation, but come at a lower computational cost.

either by re-importing the survey correctly, or scaling the imported file up by a factor of 12.

From aerial and topographical surveys

With the prevalence of Google maps and Microsoft Research Maps (MSR; formerly TerraServer), users have free online access to aerial photography and in many cases topographical information, albeit in a raster (pixel) format. US Geological Survey map information is available from MSR, and many Google maps include a topographical view option, albeit at a fairly small scale. Scanned hard-copies of maps or digital raster files may be used as well.

Using GIS data

For over two decades now, geography, planning, and related fields have benefitted from access to geographic information system (GIS) data and software, the geographical equivalent of BIM. In GIS, discrete layers of information represent groupings of similar data, called overlays or layers. There may be a layer for topography, another for trees (further differentiated by type or species), another for zoning classification, several for economic activity, and so forth—all associated with their relative spatial positions. Municipalities and states often have GIS files accessible for online viewing or data download, or available via disk.

To produce a useable site model, vector data are required, whether 2D or 3D; as with surveyor's files, the later is obviously preferable for TIN as it eliminates the end user's need to input contour *z*-coordinates or elevations. In some cases, it may be possible to download or acquire the topographical layer (contour data) as 2D or 3D DXF (Drawing eXchange Format, a more universal and archaic format) files, which may then be directly imported into the BIM application. In the case of web-viewed GIS data, where a web page serves as the user's access to the GIS data, the designer may need to capture topography as raster images (screen captures), then trace contours manually or using a raster to vector conversion tool (Fig. 3.12). Adobe Illustrator, Vectorworks, and many other applications have this capability, resulting in vector data of varying degrees of accuracy and usability.

Once the site topographical information has been gathered and imported as 2D or 3D vector objects (such as lines, polylines, and polygons) it may be processed to create the site model (Fig. 3.13).

Analyzing the site

How can BIM help inform the designer of the design implications of existing and proposed grade? How can the site be treated to minimize disturbance while supporting the design objectives? What imposed limitations and revealed opportunities for the project can BIM uncover in the combination of site and zoning ordinances?

Topographical analysis

A primary function of a site model is to facilitate topographical analysis of the site. Grade obviously has a significant impact on building placement and design. Fortunately, there are a variety of ways in which a BIM site model can help the architect analyze the site for sustainable design.

Cut-and-fill analysis

In a growing number of jurisdictions, regulations aimed at promoting sustainable development prohibit the removal of soil from construction sites. Even when not a legal requirement, good stewardship of the land suggests that soil be as undisturbed as possible during construction. Removing or bringing soil to a site is also an added construction expense that may be avoided with careful design. Rather than leaving soil management to an afterthought handled during construction, the analysis of a site model in BIM can be a useful tool in designing for sustainable sites (Fig. 3.14).

A cut-and-fill analysis is one way of quantifying development impact. When the BIM application allows the automated comparison of existing and proposed sites (Vectorworks Architect, Landmark), performing cut-and-fill analysis to achieve a net zero fill design is a matter of a few commands or the click of a button. Usually, however, such an analysis is the

FIGURE 3.12 This set of two-foot contours is fairly typical of GIS data available from municipalities. In this case, over a million 3D vertices cover an area of over 636 acres; the two-acre site of interest is shown shaded, center-left.

function of civil engineering software, which may not be available for smaller projects. In such cases, however, there are still options for rapid and meaningful analysis of proposed topography changes.

The designer should prepare at least two site models: one representing existing, undisturbed conditions, and another for each proposed design solution, if competing designs are to be analyzed. Each model is queried for total volume, and compared to the existing site's volume as a reference baseline; the difference in respective volumes is the cut (if negative) or fill (if positive) of the design being considered (Fig. 3.15). Competing site models may thus be evaluated.

Such a method only compares net (total) cut-and-fill; for a more nuanced analysis, the designer should distinguish soil removed from that added; a site design could have a net cut-and-fill total of close

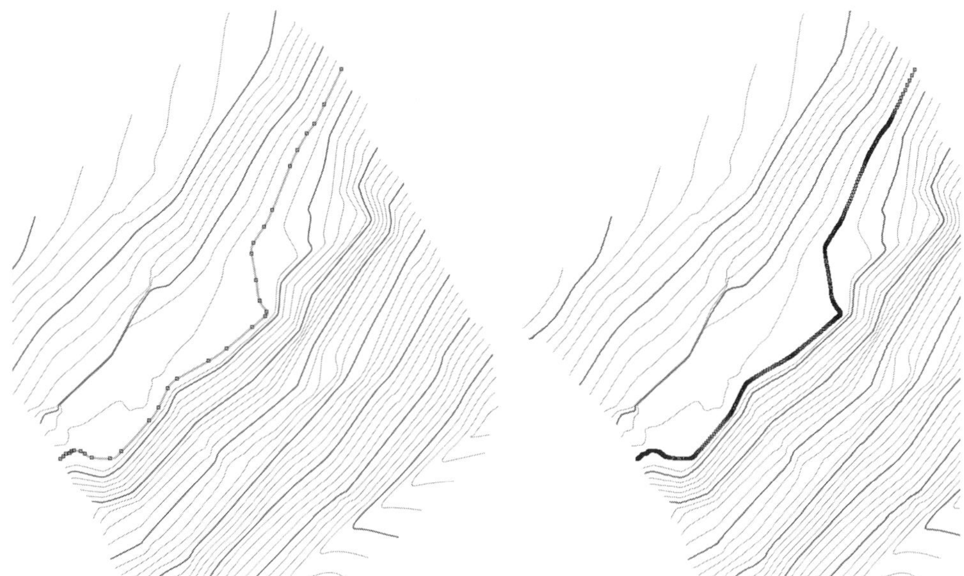

FIGURE 3.13 The contours generating the site models from Figure 3.11 appear similar to visual inspection. The contours at right are polygons converted from smooth splines; those at left are (angular) polygons. As can be seen from the number of vertices in the two corresponding and highlighted contours, the splines create many more vertices with little or no benefit.

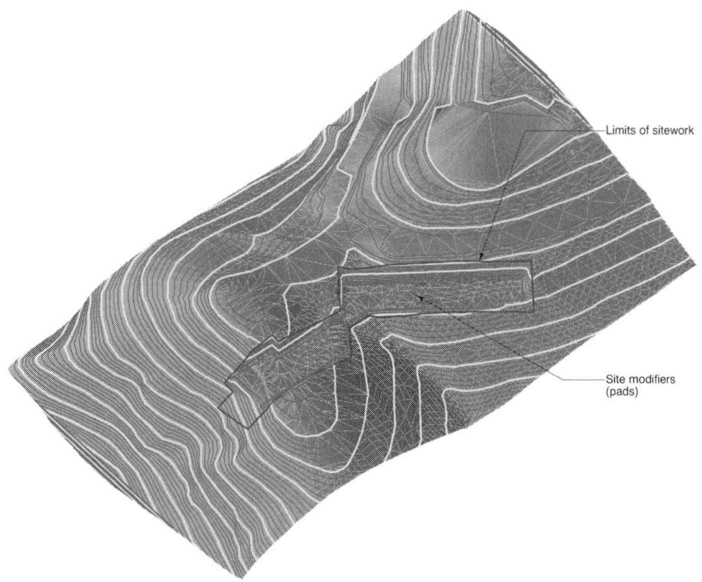

FIGURE 3.14 A site model that has been modified for a building pad.

Image courtesy of Keith Guiton Ragsdale.

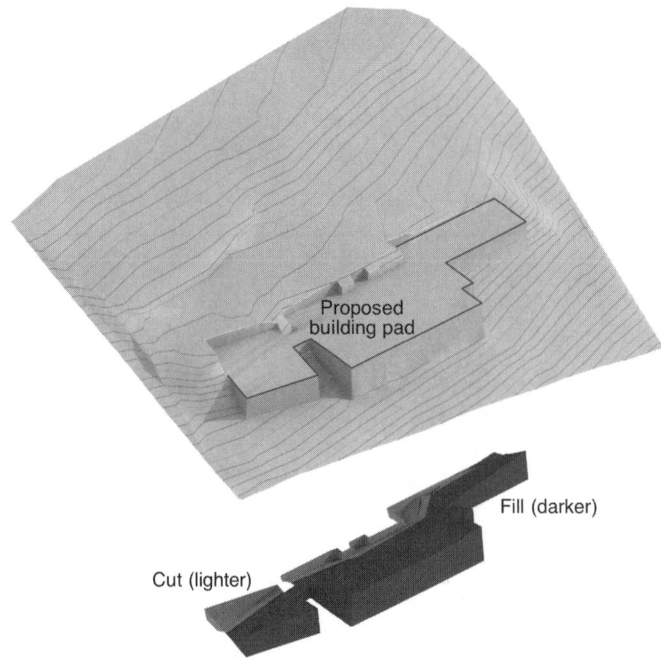

FIGURE 3.15 More advanced site modeling software may represent cut-and-fill volumes numerically as well as graphically, as in this rendering from Vectorworks Architect.

to zero, but might still represent a drastic amount of earth moved. For a more refined analysis, compare a site model representing fill (alone) with the undisturbed site, as well as cut (alone) with the existing site. Here again, civil engineering software potentially used by consultants (or among architecture BIM products, Vectorworks Architect) may allow separate calculation of cut-and-fill.

Drainage analysis

Traditionally, drainage on the site may graphically be represented in plan by drawing vectors (arrows) between two given contours, perpendicular to the higher contour; the length of the arrows may be scaled to the slope. In Vectorworks (Architect and Landmark), such flow arrows may be automatically placed on the 2D representation of the site model, albeit they are all of uniform length (they show direction, but not degree, of slope; Fig. 3.16). Site drainage is discussed more fully in Chapter 9.

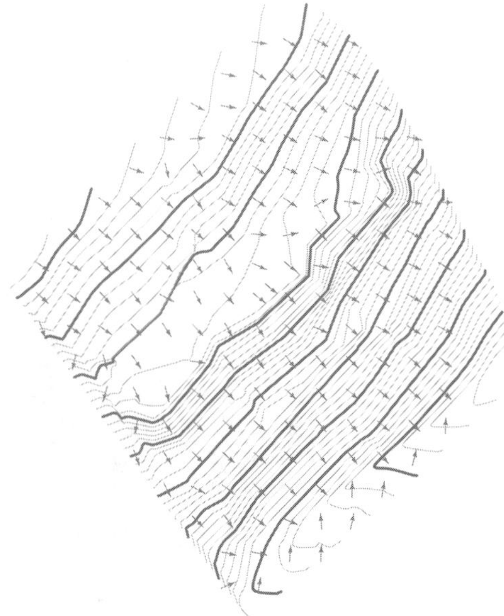

FIGURE 3.16 A site model analysis with flow arrows. The arrows in this case indicate direction, but not degree of slope (all arrows are the same length regardless of slope).

Site sections

Site sections are hardly new to BIM, and have always been an important site design tool. A section cut through the site model automates what otherwise would be a potentially laborious and error-prone drawing. For very large sites with little topography change relative to the length of the section, it may be useful to exaggerate the site section's height values (*y*) relative to its length values (*x*). Some BIM applications automate this process (Fig. 3.17).

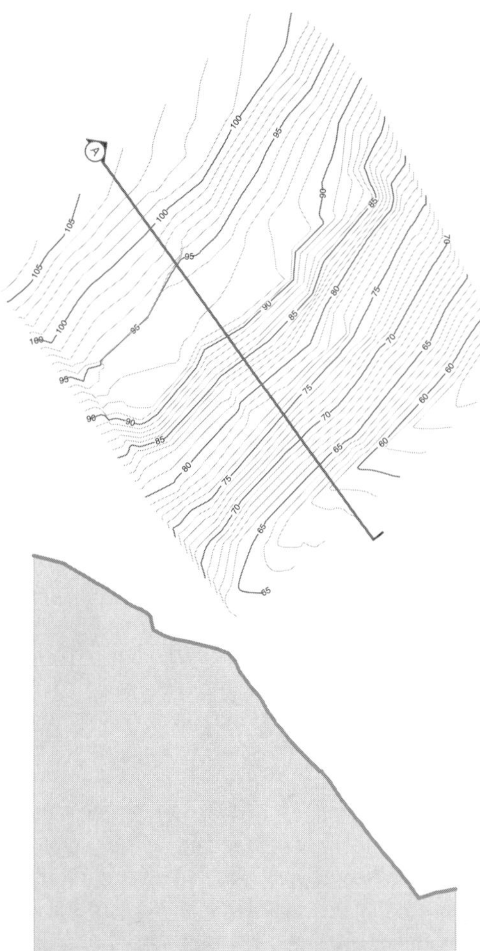

FIGURE 3.17 In a graphic convention common to civil engineering (with relatively slight elevation changes over long distances) the *y*-axis in this section has been uniformly exaggerated for clarity.

Float to surface/gravitate to mesh

A distinct advantage of an accurate 3D site model is the possibility of using it as a reference datum for existing as well as proposed site objects: trees, hardscape, street furniture, vehicles, entourage figures, and so on. "Floating" or "sending" objects to the surface of the site model is useful for such objects (Fig. 3.18). Various BIM applications automate this process (ArchiCAD's Gravitate to Mesh tool, or Vectorworks Architect's Float to Surface command, for example), saving time and helping to insure accuracy. There are some less obvious uses for this feature too:

- A series of 3D points can be sent to a mesh surface, with varying degrees of density, distributed over a limited area of the site as desired. Those points can then form the basis of a more detailed site model for the limited area.
- Similarly, a group of floated 3D points can serve as the basis for secondary mesh over a portion of the site to represent a distinct material, such as a walking path. While BIM software is increasingly able to produce site-specific objects like roads and parking areas, some of those tools have geometrical limitations. For example, roads made with a road tool may be limited to a constant width. Paved areas may require complex grading that cannot be easily achieved with a mono-sloped pad. More free-form shapes, therefore, may require a floated mesh.

Buildable envelope maxima and minima

Very early in the design process, the architect must research applicable building codes, zoning ordinances, deed restrictions and covenants, comparing them to the project brief to determine the maximum (and in some cases minimum) buildable floor area and/or volume. Often these restrictions originate from multiple and overlapping jurisdictions, and it is the designer's responsibility to properly apply them. Some of these restrictions may be fairly straightforward (e.g., vertical building setback planes) and easily applicable to a 2D drawing

FIGURE 3.18 Two views of the same Vectorworks site model; at left, trees have been placed at the appropriate ***x*** and ***y*** coordinates (they appear correct in plan) but "float" at a uniform and arbitrary height (*z* coordinate). At right, the trees have been sent to the surface—"gravitated to mesh," in ArchiCAD terms.

(lines in plan); others, such as solar access rights, building "tents," or floor area ratios (FAR) may be more complex and best resolved by an intelligent 3D massing model (Fig. 3.19). Obviously, errors in zoning and restriction application can lead to unviable designs. This is especially the case early in the design process when decisions are more easily made and errors can have catastrophic results.

Solar rights and setbacks

Many jurisdictions impose building setbacks for most zoning classifications; those setbacks may not always be vertical, but may be angled back:

- To help assure neighboring buildings access to the sun;
- To avoid blocking views or maintain view corridors of significant natural or urban landmarks;
- To control the scale of development or impose architectural controls that encourage certain styles and discourage others.

In 2006, Austin, Texas adopted a residential buildable envelope restriction to discourage new development within the urban core that was out of scale with existing housing stock. This so-called McMansion ordinance stipulates a "building tent" bound by three planes (at the side and rear property lines) angled back 45° from the building and a vertical front plane beyond which, with some exceptions, new construction may not protrude. Given that not all residential lots are rectangular in plan, nor are they all level, there is potentially some geometrical complexity in determining whether a proposed project violates the "tent," depending on the site.

As an example of a BIM component's usefulness in dealing with such geometries, a graduate student of mine developed a prototype of a Revit family to parametrically generate a McMansion tent for a site (Fig. 3.20). This custom Revit object allows a project to be quickly tested for conflicts with the tent, taking into account the geometry of the particular site. While obviously no BIM application can

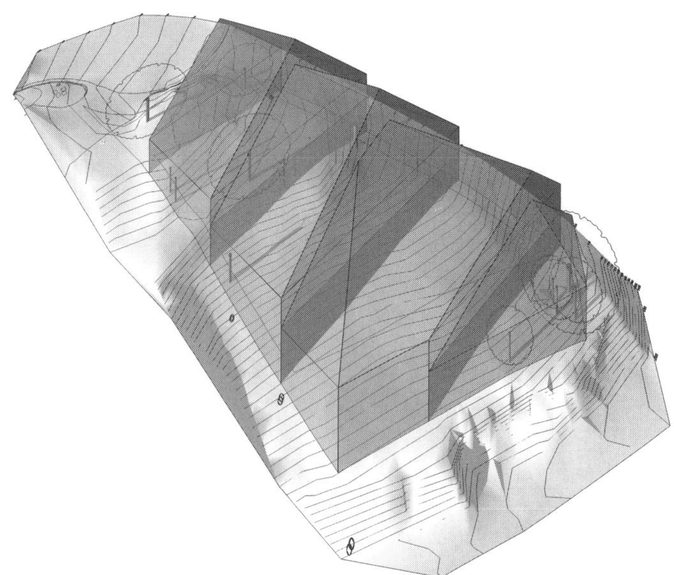

FIGURE 3.19 Form-based zoning codes are growing in popularity, but their application can sometimes be far more complex than their authors anticipate. Here, a site with a challenging topography and very irregular metes and bounds has a maximum buildable envelope that can only be understood and represented with a site model.

Image courtesy of Mell Lawrence Architects.

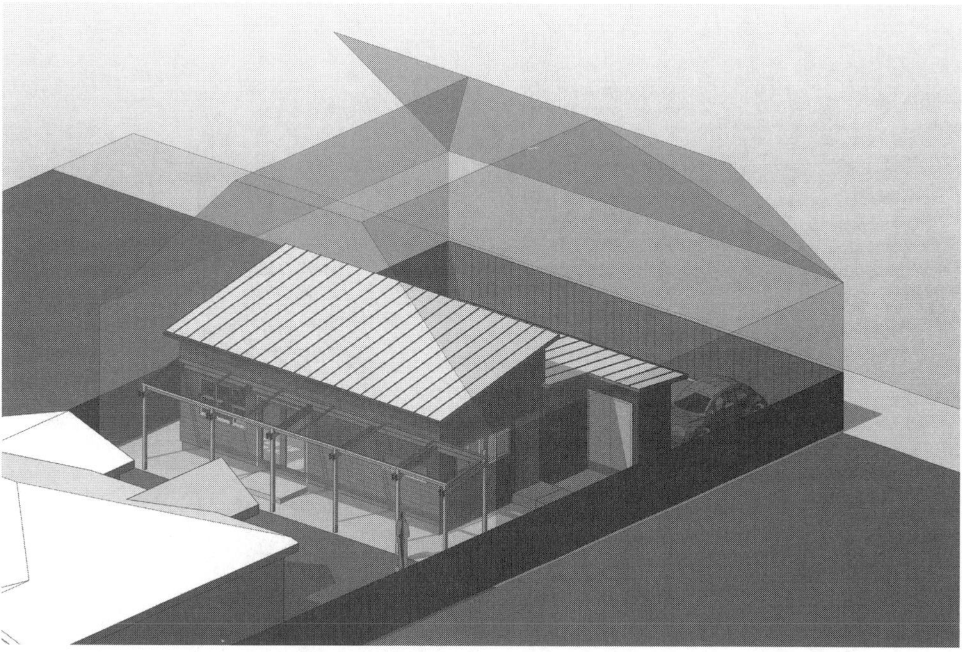

FIGURE 3.20 This custom Revit family of Austin's McMansion tent is parametrically reshaped depending on site metes and bounds.

Image courtesy of Justin Firuz Dowhower, LEED AP.

anticipate every ordinance in every jurisdiction, the ability of users to verify compliance even with custom 3D objects is of critical importance.

Floor area ratio calculations

Typically, zoning ordinances limit the project's floor area ratio (FAR). In these cases, the maximum total building area is some percentage of the site (less than, equal to, or greater than the site area depending on the nature of the zoning classification and ordinance). In some instances, the basis area of the site may be reduced for sensitive sites. Here, a quantitative analysis of a BIM site model based on grades may be very useful in determining the amount of reduced FAR site basis (see Chapter 3).

The tabulated gross or net building area derived from the BIM model can be dynamically linked to a report, thereby allowing the designer to make quantitatively driven design decisions from real-time data (Fig. 3.21). Incorporating FAR calculations into the BIM workflow creates very tight feedback loops. Such a work process is more efficient and effective than designing, checking the results of the design against project limitations, and then redesigning.

Viewsheds

An advantage of having a 3D site model that is integrated with the building model is the ability to accurately determine views of the extended site from within and around the building, in addition to the obvious benefit of evaluating the building's placement on the site. There are several techniques available, with varying degrees of complexity (and accuracy), depending on the particular features of the BIM software being used.

One such approach is to set up one or more perspective views from the point of view of the viewer. While the view may be set, the contents of that view (wall placement, window arrangement, built and natural features intervening between the viewer and the subject) may vary as the design progresses and be periodically checked from the preset view (Fig. 3.22). The subject and intervening features can be coarse, show little detail, and still be quite useful.

A raster image (e.g., PNG, JPEG) of a scene of interest may be accurately placed in 3D in the model. Some care must be taken; an incorrectly placed or scaled image will be misleading.

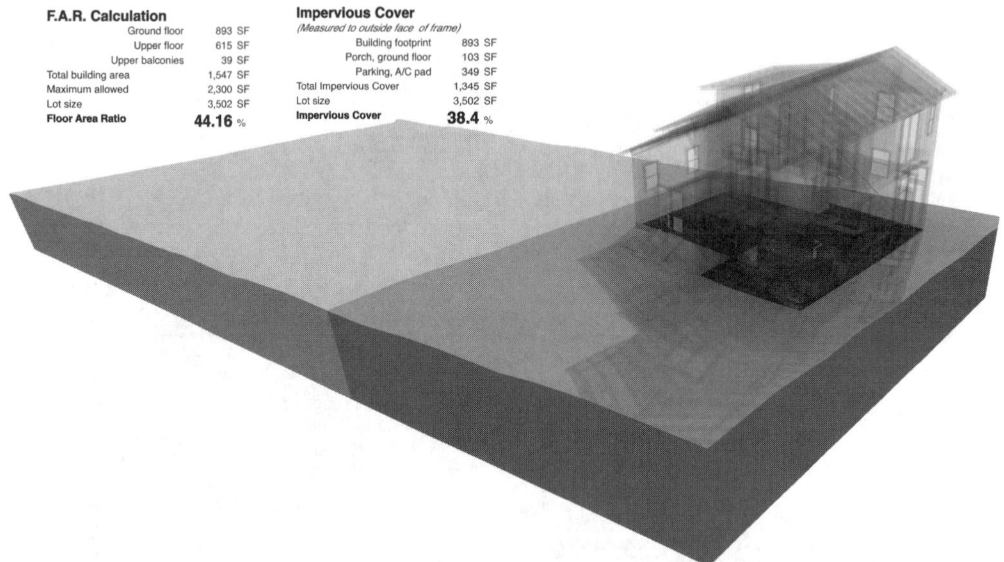

F.A.R. Calculation
Ground floor 893 SF
Upper floor 615 SF
Upper balconies 39 SF
Total building area 1,547 SF
Maximum allowed 2,300 SF
Lot size 3,502 SF
Floor Area Ratio 44.16 %
Impervious Cover
(Measured to outside face of frame)
Building footprint 893 SF
Porch, ground floor 103 SF
Parking, A/C pad 349 SF
Total Impervious Cover 1,345 SF
Lot size 3,502 SF
Impervious Cover 38.4 %

FIGURE 3.21 This BIM FAR worksheet links the site to building floor plates to accurately and dynamically report local zoning and water quality compliance as the design evolves.

FIGURE 3.22 At the conceptual design stage, a site photo is placed within the model at the correct size and location to help evaluate the impact of proposed structures (here rendered as translucent) on desirable and undesirable views.

As above, preset views are essential to effectively evaluating proposed design iterations.

A single scene or a short series of scenes are effective view determinants when the designer is concerned with a few isolated viewed subjects that are to be seen or avoided. However, this may not be a practical approach when the architect wants to assure that an entire area is to be viewed or concealed. In this case, a useful technique consists of placing a single point light in the BIM model at the viewer's location. Care should be taken to locate the light at the appropriate height, the elevation of a viewer's eyes. With the appropriate shadowed rendering option and an aerial view, the light source will illuminate all visible surfaces and objects, while those not visible to the viewer will be in shadow (Fig. 3.23). (Vectorworks uses this technique very effectively with its Zone of Visual Influence tool in its site design application, Vectorworks Landmark.) This technique may be used at any scale, for building interiors as well as for sites.

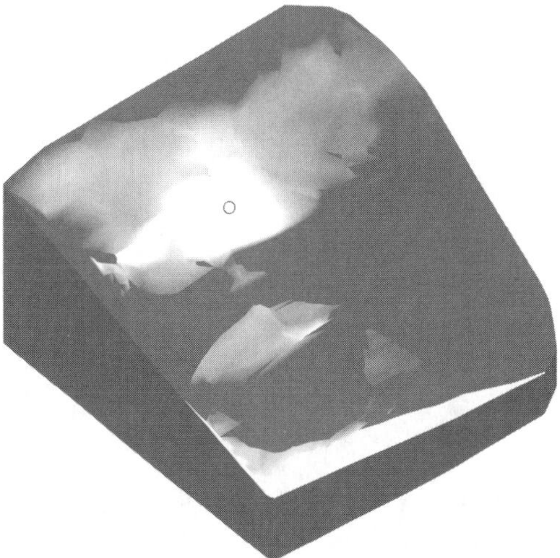

FIGURE 3.23 A simple but clever tool in Vectorworks is the Zone of Visual Influence, which can be reproduced in any model. A point light is placed at the viewer's exact *xyz* position; any surface in shadow is not visible to the viewer.

Case Study: House in Sonoma, California

By David Marlatt
Design firm: David Marlatt, DNM Architect
Client: Withheld

Approached from above and set on a nearly three-acre hillside overlooking the town of Sonoma, this 3,600 square foot (SF) two-bedroom house with a 650 SF garage breaks conventional notions of front yard and rear yard (Fig. 3.24). Its large overhangs protect the west-facing views from the morning sun and provide outdoor shelter adjacent to the trellis and lap pool. Located just below a ridge line, the house's long, low, north-south orientation follows existing contours, does not interrupt nearby views (Fig. 3.25), and optimizes cross ventilation in all rooms. The folded roof maximizes the surface available for photovoltaic and hot water solar collectors.

Completed in the spring of 2011, the house was designed to consume net-zero energy. Heat is provided through a radiant floor slab and heat pump powered by a roof-mounted solar array. In lieu of conventional air conditioning, summer air is drawn through an insulated, naturally cool plenum below the house and exhausted through clerestory windows and vents near the roof. Every aspect of the design plays a simultaneous role in the function, aesthetics, and livability of the overall project. The house's relatively shallow depth in the north-south direction maximizes the eastward views toward the town of Sonoma and encourages cross-ventilation from the cool Pacific air that rolls in from the west in the afternoons and pours down the hill.

FIGURE 3.24 The Sonoma house is sited in a sloped site, with both desirable views from the house and neighbor's views to be preserved. Accurate and quantitative site analysis was one of the key tools to help ensure a successful response to the program.

Image courtesy of DNM Architect.

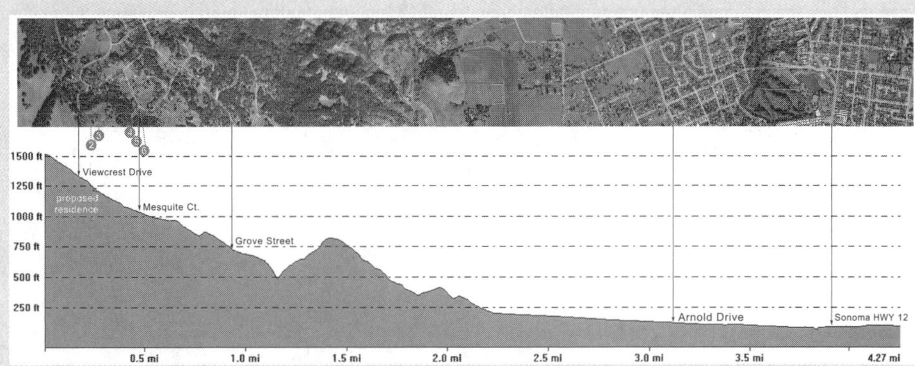

FIGURE 3.25 Long site sections taken of a comprehensive site model were used to evaluate the impact of the proposed design on neighboring viewsheds.

Image courtesy of DNM Architect.

The foundations were formed using insulated concrete forms (ICFs) and the exterior walls were constructed using a structural insulated panel system (SIPs), providing a tightly sealed and insulated shell as well as saving significant time and labor during framing. Although the house has an eastern exposure, overhangs were studied to optimize summer shading. The exposed polished concrete slab over a metal deck pan system provides even thermal mass throughout the house to modulate temperature swings. The exterior doors and windows are thermally broken aluminum with tinted dual glazing. Other key features include a 20,000-gallon rainwater harvesting system and semi-permeable driveway paving to minimize surface water run-off (Fig. 3.26).

BIM software (ArchiCAD) was critical to each step of the project's success, including:

- site analysis to understand view lines and topography
- 3D visualization for the client and the Planning Department
- sun shadow and ventilation studies
- preparation and verification of the SIPS shop drawings

Even as the project progressed on the ground, the Building Information Model was updated through all of the design changes and remained "alive" on the project's dedicated project Web site hosted by the architect.

Working from 2D survey data and publicly available topographic information, we constructed a 3D model of the site and surroundings and analyzed the view shed from a major road in the valley below. This helped establish that the house would not be within the Sonoma County view shed and therefore avoided a higher level of scrutiny by the county planning department. Understanding and controlling view corridors was equally important to the client, who desired to optimize the major view of the town of Sonoma to the east without

(*Continued*)

FIGURE 3.26 This view of the Sonoma house's entry illustrates the degree to which site topography influences and challenges the design. The driveway is semi-permeable pavement to reduce runoff.

Image courtesy of DNM Architect.

FIGURE 3.27 A site section through the Sonoma house reveals building volumes, as well as the balanced uphill cut and under-slab fill. An extensive site model helps evaluate sight lines.

Image courtesy of DNM Architect.

obstructing the neighbor's view uphill to the west. In addition to view analysis, the 3D site model helped us understand prevailing wind patterns and design the house for optimal cross ventilation (Fig. 3.27). Using the 3D model and Ecotect, the design was analyzed to insure that all major spaces received ventilation and dead spots or eddies were eliminated.

The 3D model was also used to approximate cut-and-fill calculations on the sloped site. However, a 3D terrain model will not capture subterranean conditions that can increase or decrease actual grading, nor the "fluff" that always occurs when tightly packed soil is excavated. Simply balancing cut-and-fill in the 3D model calculation does not mean that soil will not be hauled away or brought to the site, as the quality of the soil being excavated may not be suitable for the areas being filled. On this project, we balanced cut-and-fill in our calculations, but more excavation than anticipated was required due to loose rock formations under the topsoil, and the amount of fluff was not adequately anticipated. Fortunately, the three-acre site allowed us to redistribute all of the soil on site so that neither importing nor off-hauling were required.

Chapter 4

Massing Analysis

Frequently conceived as a documentation or production tool, BIM is rarely considered as a design tool in schematic or conceptual design. This is unfortunate, as the earliest design decisions potentially have the greatest impact on a project's sustainability—not to mention its architectural success (Fig. 4.1). Data-driven massing models can offer important insights into potential building performance that can provide huge benefits in sustainability. Moreover, ignoring quantitative information affecting critical massing factors like building orientation, aspect ratios, and maximum envelope may lead the architect to commit to decisions that may be expensive or impossible to reverse later. This chapter therefore frames the discussion of the role of BIM in conceptual design and the quantitative sustainable analysis of building massing.

Creating massing models

Inherent in any conceptual architectural design is the requirement to establish building massing. From establishing a proposed building's relationship to its site context, to compliance with the maximum buildable envelope, to optimizing a building's spatial use and thermal performance, massing models can be invaluable tools in incorporating sustainable design in a BIM process. There are several approaches to developing intelligent conceptual models; some are "data-ready," while others are truly "data-rich."

FIGURE 4.1 BIM need hardly be limited to documenting fully developed designs. While the skill of the render might give an initial impression of a fully developed design, this is a conceptual model intended to confirm general program and site limitations.

Image courtesy of Daniel Jansenson, Architect.

Import from SketchUp

Originally developed by Boulder, Colorado's @Last Software, SketchUp filled a need for simple, quick 3D conceptual modeling that many more powerful and fuller-featured CAD/CAM modelers did not meet. As such, it especially appealed to architects and designers who had little day-to-day contact with CAD operation. After @Last's acquisition by Google and SketchUp's availability as a free consumer version, its popularity only grew. One of SketchUp's great strengths is its limited tool palette; rather than trying to be all things to all users, it fills a specific niche—conceptual design—and does it well (Fig. 4.2).

Some have suggested that SketchUp is BIM authoring software. This is partially true, in the sense that third-party additions have enabled users to assign data to SketchUp models. In many ways, however, SketchUp does not fulfill the requirements for BIM:

- Components are not data-rich. With the exception of third party add-ons, SketchUp walls cannot be assigned an R-value, for example.
- Components are not contextual. Objects in SketchUp do not contain data or tags that functionally relate them to other objects in the model. Put another way, SketchUp walls don't "know" that they are walls.
- The model is not parametric. A SketchUp stair, for example, cannot be linked to building floor levels, such that as floor-to-floor heights are parametrically modified, the stair's run is automatically adjusted to preserve code-prescribed riser maxima and tread minima.

Multiple views of the same model are not supported. That is, while different rendering styles of a 3D model are possible, one cannot readily produce a plan view *from the same object* with 2D graphic conventions (doors open 90° with an arc shown) and 3D views (perspectives, elevations, sections).

Nevertheless, SketchUp can be very useful as a tool within a broader BIM workflow, particularly when deployed in tandem with a robust BIM modeler that may lack easy 3D conceptualizing tools.

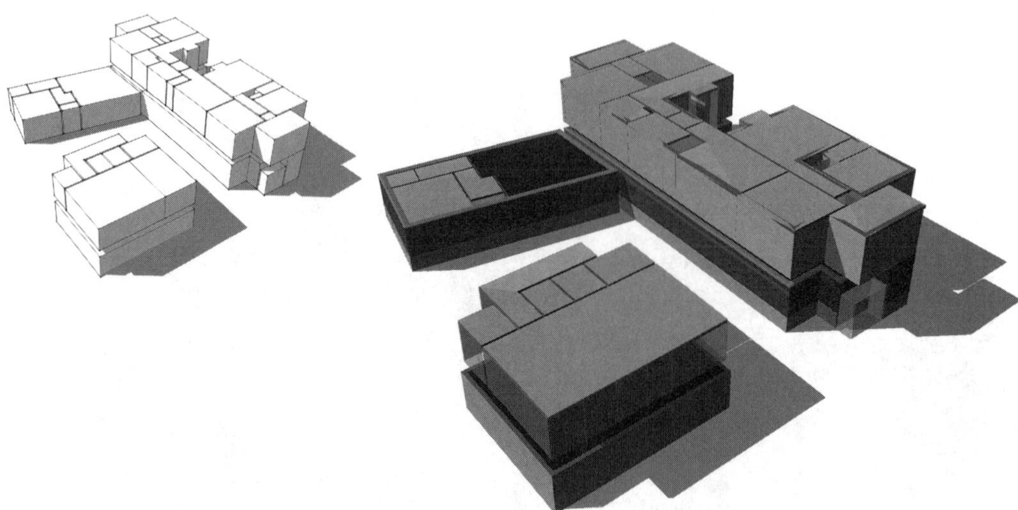

FIGURE 4.2 SketchUp extrusions (inset, left) can be the starting point for a BIM model. Here, a Revit in-place mass was populated by prepared SketchUp objects (under the Revit Insert tab, choose Import CAD, selecting the SKP file format and opening the desired SketchUp file). The system family (roof, wall, floor) to be applied to each mass surface is then applied via the Massing & Site tab.

Image courtesy of Justin Firuz Dowhower, LEED AP.

In such cases, easily developing a massing or conceptual model in SketchUp as a precursor to a true BIM model is a helpful, efficient strategy. In some cases, such as in Revit, a SketchUp model can be imported and then "skinned" with suitable walls, curtain walls, or roof elements. Even in applications that have full-featured free-form modeling tools, like Vectorworks, SketchUp's 3D geometry can be automatically and correctly interpreted upon import to correspond to the target application's parametric BIM objects: walls, floors, and roofs.

Free-form modeling

BIM applications support creation of native, generic 3D geometry with varying degrees of control, refinement, and parameterization (Fig. 4.3). As previously noted, it is a commonly held fallacy that BIM requires designers to make premature decisions about a project. In fact, unspecified components like generic walls, roofs, and slabs are common. The modeler is also free to construct completely free-form solids and 3D polygons, ranging from simple extrusions, sweeps, and polygonal planes to, in some cases, Boolean additions and subtractions. Some BIM tools allow nonuniform rational Bézier splines (NURBS), which are potentially complex curved 3D polylines and surfaces.

One advantage of generating the conceptual massing model within the BIM authoring tool is that iterative changes to the massing model can inform the BIM model, and vice-versa, with a minimal loss of data or need for repeating work (Fig. 4.4). If the massing model is developed outside of a BIM environment, then design development leaves the massing model behind. This may not seem to be a problem, except that even in later phases of design the massing model may serve some analytical purposes.

Space objects

Originally developed in response to the United States Government Services Agency's (GSA) requirement that building spaces in BIM models have occupancy data assigned to them, Space objects in building models are more than mere occupancy labels—they are 3D objects that carry a host of data, from finish schedule information to GSA project classifications. Properly formed GSA-compliant BIM models fill the entire model with

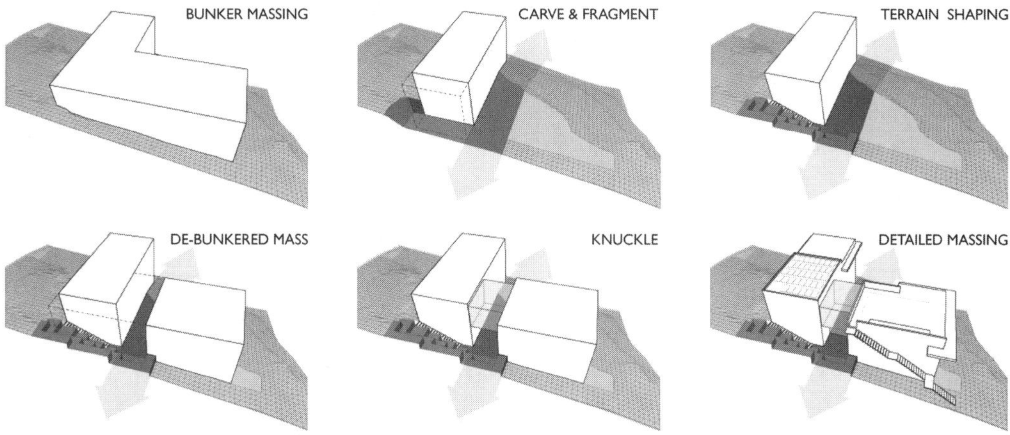

FIGURE 4.3 3D-modeled massing studies are an invaluable tool even in preconceptualization stages of the project. Here, a series of massing and terrain manipulations are documented for the Margarido House, A LEED for Homes project.

Architect: Plumbob LLC.

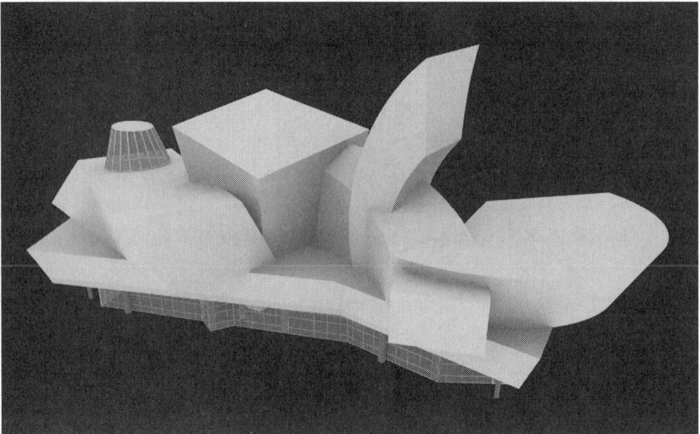

FIGURE 4.4 Even early in the design phase BIM can produce models that may be used to test basic design decisions. For example, how does the massing suggested by program and site fit maximum building envelope restrictions? These models may be simple solid prisms, the digital equivalent of hot-wire-cut blue foam, or may be quickly skinned to look like a developed building design.

Photo courtesy of Wes Gardner, NV.

Space objects; even vertical chases with floor penetrations greater than nine square feet are assigned Spaces. If an open area comprises two or more occupancy types, then the modeler must create an imaginary boundary between the Spaces with a specially classified wall; such a wall is conceptual only and is not actually built.

In a typical BIM work process, the Space object is applied to the model once virtual exterior and interior walls and slabs are in place, "filling" the resulting voids. Such an approach has merit, as it allows the creation of what amounts to data objects once the architectural parameters are established. In essence, the Space object is a rough casting or imprint of the architecture, lacking certain details. Unlike an actual casting, the Space object does not adopt the full geometry of the model—mullions and jambs, for example, are ignored. A Space object is therefore a means of abstracting the building model in a less-articulated form for those applications that do not require detailed physical modeling. This lack of detail has certain advantages. Energy modeling programs, like eQuest for example, provide perfectly valid analysis without such details, and function well (and perform faster) with such simplified modeling.

Certain BIM authoring applications, like Vectorworks, allow the typical workflow to be reversed. That is, Space objects can be created early in conceptual design and then later "skinned" with a proposed building envelope (Fig. 4.5). This approach has certain distinct advantages:

- The Space object is used as a dynamic, data-rich massing model component, consistent with the BIM paradigm of intelligent modeling;
- It can initially be generated as a polyline of any given shape and "extruded" by assigning net (ceiling) and gross (roof or overhead floor) heights;
- Proximities between Spaces can be quantified and scored to compare the relative space-planning merits of competing plans, as with Vectorworks' adjacency matrix;
- Comparisons of Space object perimeters (or surfaces) to floor area can be made to evaluate the envelope-to-area ratio efficacy of competing plans;
- Preliminary building aspect ratio assumptions can be tested for site indexing against solar geometry. With a massing model, sun and shading studies can yield very useful information with a minimum of modeling effort;

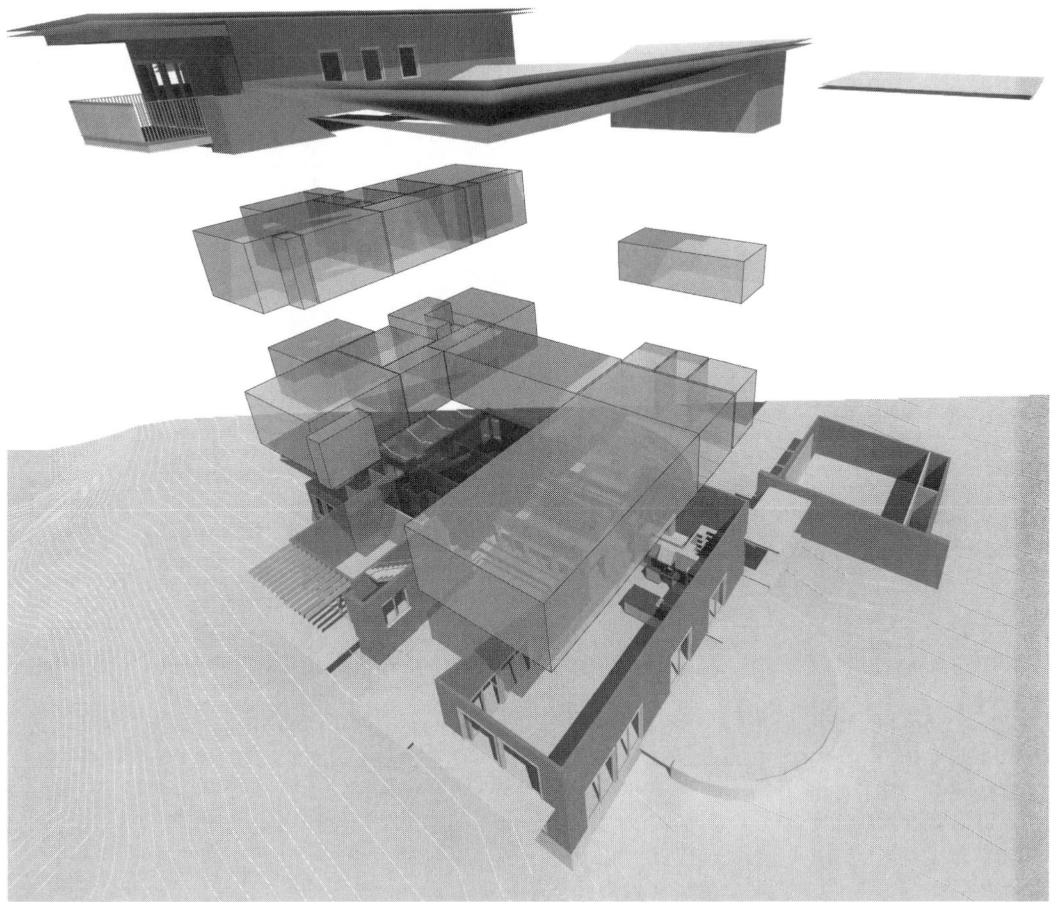

FIGURE 4.5 Space objects (rendered here as translucent blocks) may fill empty volumes defined by existing walls, or the walls may "skin" existing Spaces after the fact.

Author's image of a project designed with Gregory L. Brooks.

- Overall thermal conduction can be quickly tested to confirm a particular wall system's suitability or parametrically inform early envelope design decisions.

Later in this chapter, we'll look at these and other specific, quantitative uses for intelligent massing models.

Perimeter/volume ratios: optimizing for envelope quantity

Aside from designing for envelope restrictions imposed jurisdictionally, intelligent massing models may inform the designer's efforts to design economically or to optimize energy performance. In cases where construction budgets are restrictive, it may be desirable to evaluate the relative costs of two or more divergent designs, even at a very early stage. For example:

- Is a particular courtyard *parti* economically competitive with an H-shaped plan?
- What are the relative merits, in terms of respective envelope quantities, of a more compact two-story scheme versus a single-floor design?

- Is it cost effective to develop a more compact plan, but maintain a sense of architectural spaciousness by increasing ceiling heights?

These and similar questions can begin to be addressed by evaluating the ratio between the total envelope surface area and either building floor area or building volume, net or gross, as appropriate and with varying degrees of refinement:

- Compare the total exterior wall length to floor area (this assumes fairly consistent wall heights across competing schemes);
- Compare wall area to floor area (for evaluating designs with differing wall heights);
- Compare total envelope area (roof, wall, slab or ground floor, basement wall, and slab) to total useable volume (when evaluating designs with highly divergent massing and configuration).

The BIM model already includes within it values for exterior wall length, roof area, enclosed volume, and so forth (Fig. 4.6). These may be reported in worksheets, in a tabular form, or with basic arithmetical formulas to dynamically display the desired ratio(s). Care must be given to assign distinct wall types to differentiate interior from exterior walls, for example (if the design is even developed enough for interior wall placement), but those envelope components can be generic (a six-inch-thick wall, for example, of indeterminate material), as discussed previously.

With respect to energy performance, conductive heat loss or gain through the building envelope is determined by the total conductance of the building, measured by each individual building assembly's conductance, *U,* multiplied by the area, *A,* of the assembly. In the United States, buildings may not exceed a given U·A whose value is given by locally applicable energy codes and building type. Compliance can easily be determined by using simple (but at times tedious) software like the Department of Energy's free ComCheck and ResCheck applications. Unfortunately, all too often compliance is verified late in the design process, when many nearly irreversible decisions have already been made.

A far better approach is to begin with plausible assumptions about envelope assembly thermal performance early in the design process, and quantify the basic thermal conductance of competing schemes in order to make a better informed decision. One may go so far as to use the thermal conductance values of a project at a conceptual stage and refine the design by verifying the improvements afforded by a series of incremental modifications. Such a parametric approach to design can lead to

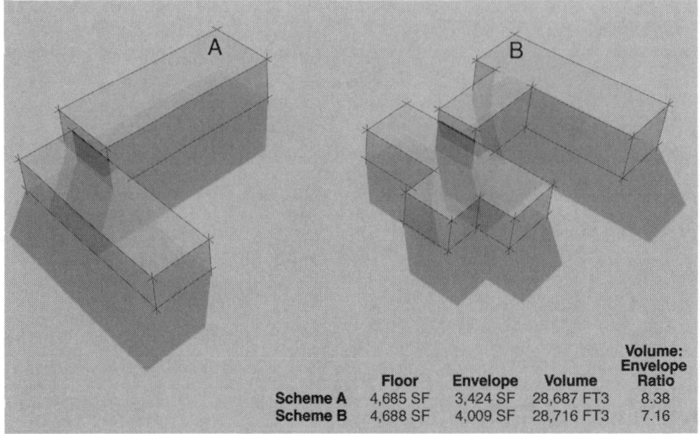

A
B
Floor
Envelope
Volume
Volume: Envelope Ratio
Scheme A 4,685 SF 3,424 SF 28,687 FT3 8.38
Scheme B 4,688 SF 4,009 SF 28,716 FT3 7.16

FIGURE 4.6 Space object geometry can be used to evaluate massing models even when little or no detailed design information has been determined. Here, a BIM worksheet reports basic quantitative information from the Spaces shown.

significant improvements in building performance, particularly if this methodology is applied at preliminary phases of design.

As an example, for a small, conventionally framed building, one might assume a U-factor of 0.07 for walls and 0.03 for roofs. A steeper roof would enclose more volume, some or most of which could be useable. What are the specific consequences on thermal performance of varying the roof pitch? Comparing total U·A for alternative proposals, even before exact materials are selected, could lead to a solution that was optimized for maximum volume and minimum U·A within a given envelope boundary and for a particular architectural program (Fig. 4.7).

Of course, there are far more factors than just optimization of envelope-to-area or envelope-to-volume ratios that influence the architect's selection of one *parti* over another. The design should naturally be informed by a host of other factors, from aesthetic considerations to potential solar collection. Many of those factors are qualitative and essential to the success or failure of the design (Fig 4.8). Nevertheless, weighing quantitative factors is an important task of conceptual design, too often ignored to the detriment of the project. "Front-loading" a quantitative analysis process and integrating it into design can vastly improve project performance.

Confirming desirable and undesirable views

While views may not, per se, seem to have an impact on building sustainability, their control is in fact important to high-performance buildings:

- Views may conflict with undesirable window orientation, size, and location for thermal performance (Fig. 4.9);
- Views will obviously impact daylighting, an important strategy to increase reliance on natural light, thereby decreasing lighting costs and their attendant cooling loads (see Chapter 5);
- Building occupants report higher satisfaction and exhibit higher job performance when they have a sense of connection to the natural world. The single most costly component of a building is its personnel.

There are a variety of methods the designer may employ to accurately determine the accessibility of views to a project. The most obvious, of course, is to draw in plan the angle subtending the view of interest, with the viewer as the vertex. The two lines of the angle will intersect the building envelope plane, defining the extent of the view as projected onto the building plane. However, this method, known to any architecture student, is only valid if there is

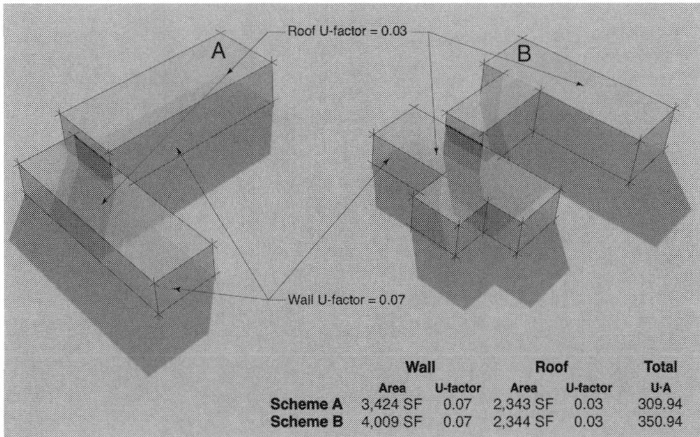

	Wall		Roof		Total
	Area	U-factor	Area	U-factor	U·A
Scheme A	3,424 SF	0.07	2,343 SF	0.03	309.94
Scheme B	4,009 SF	0.07	2,344 SF	0.03	350.94

FIGURE 4.7 By using the quantitative nature of Spaces, competing massing schemes can be evaluated for, among other factors, relative U·A or envelope area-to-volume ratios.

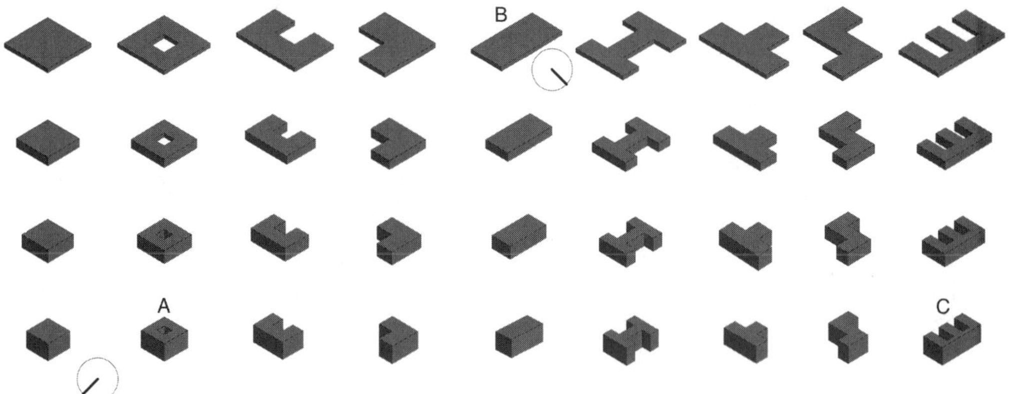

FIGURE 4.8 A systematic arrangement of building forms from one story to four stories constitutes a series of massing analyses undertaken by students and researchers at the University of Texas at Austin Department of Civil, Architectural, and Environmental Engineering. Each massing represents a 20,000 SF office building in Austin, Texas (hot humid climate), with all design variables held constant except for form. Models were built in Revit and analyses were performed using Green Building Studio. The analyses accounted for daylighting in the design, and all of the buildings were subsequently ranked in order from lowest annual energy cost to highest. The annual operating cost for the most expensive form was twice that of the least expensive one. When photovoltaic collection was factored into the analyses, the most expensive form in that scenario was 30 times more expensive per year. Energy analyses were performed for each model (except for the box and courtyard forms) oriented in two directions (north being the lower left face in one run, and the lower right face in another). In addition, each mass was studied as completely opaque building (no windows), then again with fully glazed walls. For an opaque building in Austin, the most expensive energy costs were incurred by the four-story courtyard massing (labeled A in the image). As might be expected, the most energy-efficient mass was the one-story, long rectangular form rotated such that the long axis ran east-west (labeled B). In the all-glass wall series, the rotated rectangular shape remained the least expensive, but the four-story E-shape (labeled C) was the most expensive to operate.

Image courtesy of Gregory L. Brooks and Eleanor Reynolds.

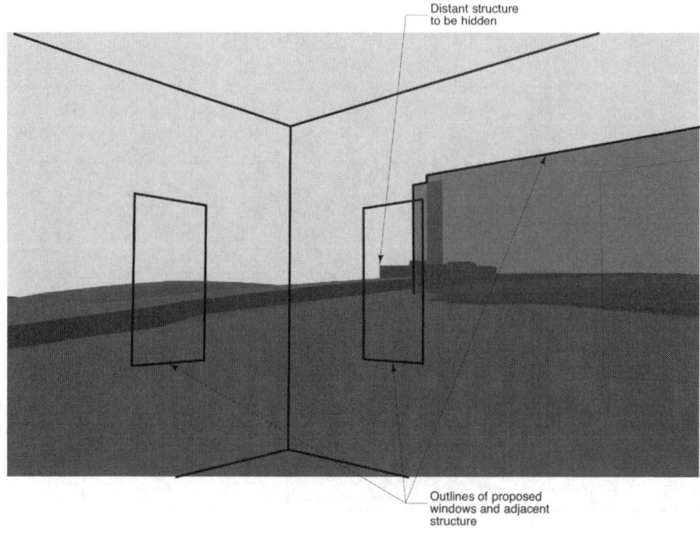

FIGURE 4.9 Even coarse massing models can be useful to verify that views of adjacent structures are excluded in three dimensions.

negligible elevation difference between the viewer and the subject(s); the site is relatively flat, or the view of interest is distant and near the horizon. In other cases, a perspective projection of the scene modeled in three dimensions may be useful. Here again, judicious use of even a simple BIM massing model can be quite useful, particularly if that model is integrated in an accurate 3D site model; there are a variety of massing model techniques to help determine appropriate views. For a complete discussion of BIM site models, review Chapter 3.

Preliminary cost and feasibility analysis

Very early in the design process the architect may be required to verify the project's feasibility with respect to land development codes (zoning or setback restrictions) or the client's budget.

Assigning costs on a massing basis

At its most fundamental, probable cost of construction can be estimated from building areas and volumes. It is quite common—even ubiquitous—to refer to cost per square foot based on historical data. Experienced design professionals (and contractors) understand that there are manifold shortcomings of such an approach to cost estimating. Several come to mind:

- Historic cost data is not necessarily a reliable predictor of current or future market prices;
- Especially among residential contractors, there is a wide variety of building costs (and quality). Cost numbers derived from one pool of builders will not necessarily be applicable to another contractor;
- Buildings are idiosyncratic, and the larger the historic data, the more cost idiosyncrasies will be "smoothed out." The smaller the statistical pool (number and size of referenced historic projects), the less likely historic values are to be accurate predictors of construction costs, as fewer total square feet of construction available for comparison will lead to less reliable estimates. Similarly, a historic review of residential costs will not serve to accurately predict, say, a branch library project construction cost;
- Projects vary significantly in level of finish, complexity, and materials, all of which affect cost. While a given firm may have a consistent design vocabulary and detailing sensibility which would tend to normalize construction costs over several projects, individual client choices may increase or decrease those costs;
- Site conditions vary from project to project, and these can have a significant impact on foundation complexity and therefore cost;
- Cost per square foot ignores the building in elevation. A project that is taller or squatter than the historic average may be under or over-estimated.

In spite of the above limitations and others, the designer can partially mitigate some of these factors with careful analysis. BIM has two roles here: analysis of past projects and analysis of dynamic data on the current project being estimated.

Past projects may be analyzed by any dimensional unit desired: average cost per square (plan) foot, cost per cubic foot (Fig. 4.10), or cost per square foot of envelope. The latter is likely the best choice, on the assumption that this measure better represents the materials and labor cost of construction. Costing by envelope area also indirectly accounts for building complexity, at least grossly: a more convoluted envelope will be greater in area than a simple mass, for the same floor plate area or volume. If detailed cost data by trade is available, then costs can be further broken down and differentiated by building space function (kitchens cost much more than garages). Projects may be further differentiated into three or so subjective (but informed by experience) buckets by level of finish. In this way the designer can compare the anticipated level of finish of the current project to similar past projects.

In order to simplify historical cost analysis and help insure accuracy, BIM massing models of past projects may be constructed using Space objects,

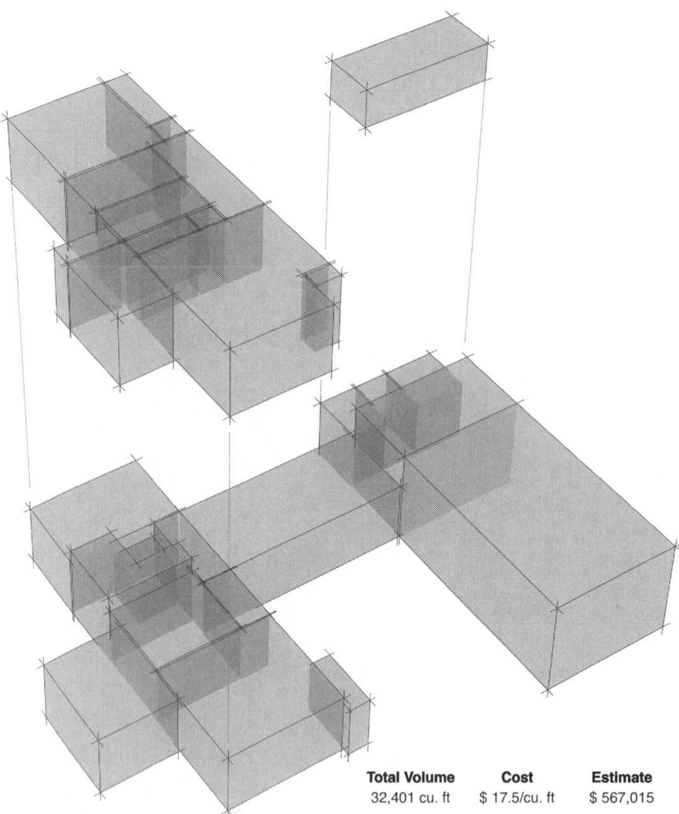

Total Volume
32,401 cu. ft
Cost
$ 17.5/cu. ft
Estimate
$ 567,015

FIGURE 4.10 A simple massing model composed of Space objects is analyzed for preliminary probable project cost on an average cost per volume basis.

3D primitives, Boolean solids, or even NURBS surfaces as appropriate (Fig. 4.11). Such models need not be highly detailed, simply dimensionally accurate such that values reported for surface area are correct within a tolerable margin of error.

To derive a cost per square foot of envelope, divide the total project cost by the massing area reported by the BIM model. If a more detailed cost analysis is desired, high-cost areas may be modeled separately, and the additional budget amounts associated with such areas (for special equipment or finishes) may be added to the base project cost assigned to the entire historic massing model.

Component-based cost analysis

The designer may wish to produce a more detailed analysis of the probable cost of construction at the massing model stage, and again this may be achieved without recourse to detailed modeling of, say, every framing member. Once again historic cost data is required, but in this case the designer should have access to detailed costs by building trade. If drawing upon cost breakdowns from several past projects from different contractors, it will probably be necessary to reconcile the cost data to common divisions, as individual contractors often categorize costs differently from one another. Alternately, a cost database like RS Means may be referenced.

Here again, the cost per envelope or floor area, as appropriate, is applied to the massing model, but on a trade or material basis. For example, a past project with a structural insulated panel (SIP) cost of $91,300 and an envelope surface area of 13,400 square feet would have a SIPs cost of $9.10 per square foot of

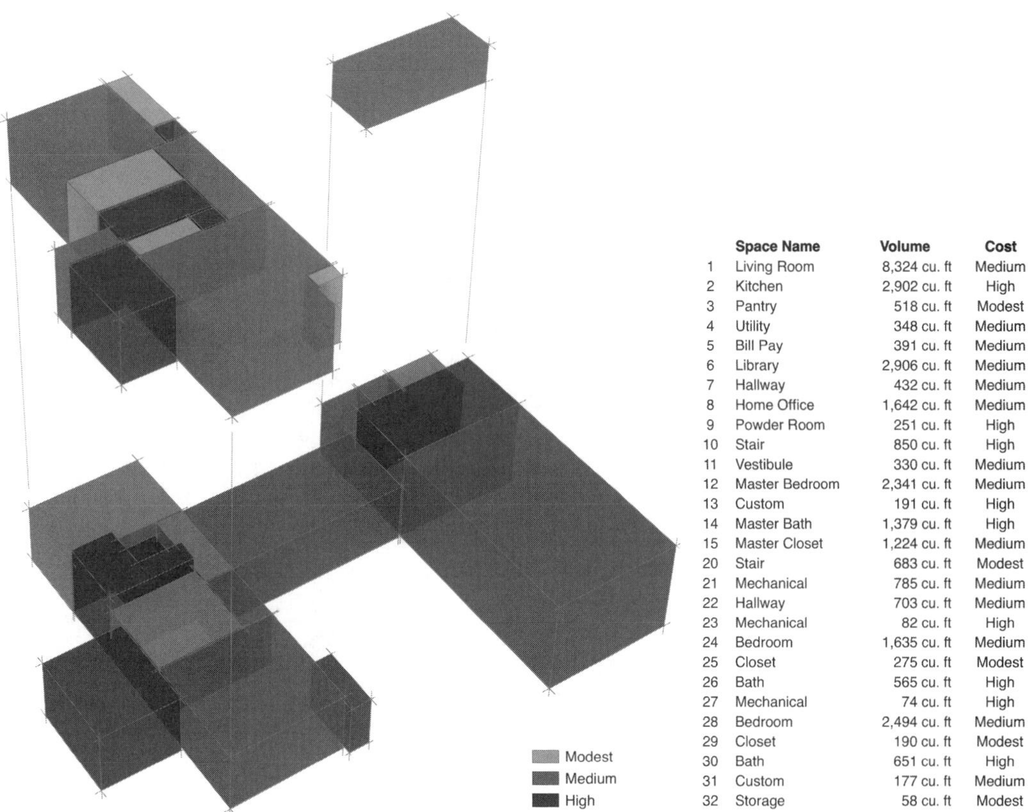

	Space Name	Volume	Cost
1	Living Room	8,324 cu. ft	Medium
2	Kitchen	2,902 cu. ft	High
3	Pantry	518 cu. ft	Modest
4	Utility	348 cu. ft	Medium
5	Bill Pay	391 cu. ft	Medium
6	Library	2,906 cu. ft	Medium
7	Hallway	432 cu. ft	Medium
8	Home Office	1,642 cu. ft	Medium
9	Powder Room	251 cu. ft	High
10	Stair	850 cu. ft	High
11	Vestibule	330 cu. ft	Medium
12	Master Bedroom	2,341 cu. ft	Medium
13	Custom	191 cu. ft	High
14	Master Bath	1,379 cu. ft	High
15	Master Closet	1,224 cu. ft	Medium
20	Stair	683 cu. ft	Modest
21	Mechanical	785 cu. ft	Medium
22	Hallway	703 cu. ft	Medium
23	Mechanical	82 cu. ft	High
24	Bedroom	1,635 cu. ft	Medium
25	Closet	275 cu. ft	Modest
26	Bath	565 cu. ft	High
27	Mechanical	74 cu. ft	High
28	Bedroom	2,494 cu. ft	Medium
29	Closet	190 cu. ft	Modest
30	Bath	651 cu. ft	High
31	Custom	177 cu. ft	Medium
32	Storage	58 cu. ft	Modest

FIGURE 4.11 A slightly more detailed cost analysis of the massing model is achieved by assigning categories of cost to the differentiated Space-object–based massing model.

envelope. Since the whole project is SIPs, then that unit cost would be applied to the entire envelope of a proposed project to be analyzed (assuming no inflation or other cost escalations). Moreover, the total cost of tile, plumbing, and counters (which occur only in the kitchen and baths) of the precedent project was $84,500, over a surface area of 795 square feet. Such spaces add over $110 per square foot of kitchen and bath only. If the project is still at a very preliminary massing stage and the exact disposition of its internal arrangement is unknown, it may be preferable to apply that budget line item to the overall floor area, in this case $14.80 per square foot when distributed over the entire area of the building.

These calculations are of course possible without a BIM model, but they quickly become tedious and require constant updating. If the data is attached to elements of the model, however, then calculations are automated. What is of greater interest, however, is that those calculations may be updated in real time as the design evolves, giving the architect immediate quantitative feedback on the implications of design decisions.

Preliminary passive heating and cooling design data

It is becoming increasingly popular to make use of energy modeling in architectural design. Such quantitative analysis of performance may occur at several stages of the design process. The following sections discuss these stages in reverse chronological order but listing most common first.

Energy compliance

At permitting, depending on the jurisdiction, the project is analyzed for mechanical, lighting, and thermal envelope compliance using the Department of Energy's COMcheck or REScheck. Since this is a common requirement for a growing number of jurisdictions, it is the most universal form of thermal performance "analysis." Unfortunately, by the time of permitting, at best such a compliance check will affect the selection of insulation type, window and door specifications, or induce the addition of slab perimeter insulation (Fig. 4.12). This is hardly capitalizing on the opportunity to consider energy use as an architectural formgiver. Furthermore,

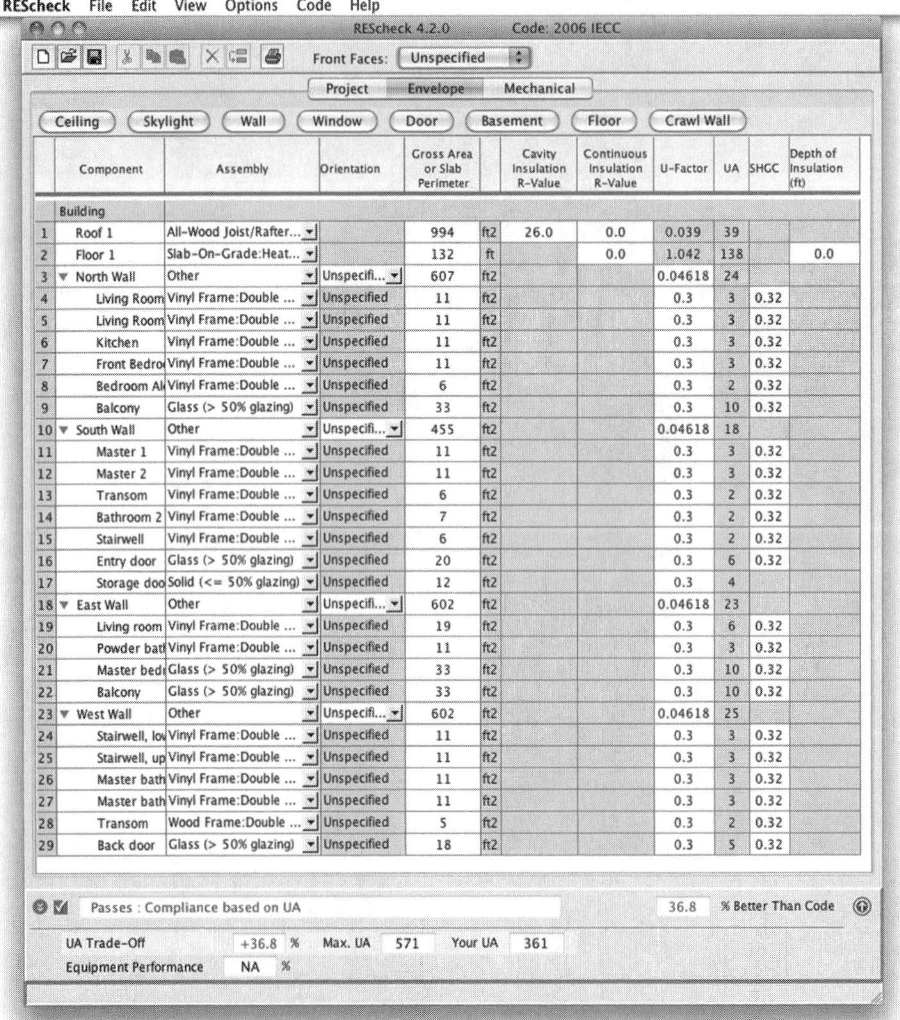

	Component	Assembly	Orientation	Gross Area or Slab Perimeter		Cavity Insulation R-Value	Continuous Insulation R-Value	U-Factor	UA	SHGC	Depth of Insulation (ft)
	Building										
1	Roof 1	All-Wood Joist/Rafter...		994	ft2	26.0	0.0	0.039	39		
2	Floor 1	Slab-On-Grade:Heat...		132	ft		0.0	1.042	138		0.0
3	▼ North Wall	Other	Unspecifi...	607	ft2			0.04618	24		
4	Living Room	Vinyl Frame:Double ...	Unspecified	11	ft2			0.3	3	0.32	
5	Living Room	Vinyl Frame:Double ...	Unspecified	11	ft2			0.3	3	0.32	
6	Kitchen	Vinyl Frame:Double ...	Unspecified	11	ft2			0.3	3	0.32	
7	Front Bedro	Vinyl Frame:Double ...	Unspecified	11	ft2			0.3	3	0.32	
8	Bedroom Al	Vinyl Frame:Double ...	Unspecified	6	ft2			0.3	2	0.32	
9	Balcony	Glass (> 50% glazing)	Unspecified	33	ft2			0.3	10	0.32	
10	▼ South Wall	Other	Unspecifi...	455	ft2			0.04618	18		
11	Master 1	Vinyl Frame:Double ...	Unspecified	11	ft2			0.3	3	0.32	
12	Master 2	Vinyl Frame:Double ...	Unspecified	11	ft2			0.3	3	0.32	
13	Transom	Vinyl Frame:Double ...	Unspecified	6	ft2			0.3	2	0.32	
14	Bathroom 2	Vinyl Frame:Double ...	Unspecified	7	ft2			0.3	2	0.32	
15	Stairwell	Vinyl Frame:Double ...	Unspecified	6	ft2			0.3	2	0.32	
16	Entry door	Glass (> 50% glazing)	Unspecified	20	ft2			0.3	6	0.32	
17	Storage doo	Solid (<= 50% glazing)	Unspecified	12	ft2			0.3	4		
18	▼ East Wall	Other	Unspecifi...	602	ft2			0.04618	23		
19	Living room	Vinyl Frame:Double ...	Unspecified	19	ft2			0.3	6	0.32	
20	Powder bat	Vinyl Frame:Double ...	Unspecified	11	ft2			0.3	3	0.32	
21	Master bed	Glass (> 50% glazing)	Unspecified	33	ft2			0.3	10	0.32	
22	Balcony	Glass (> 50% glazing)	Unspecified	33	ft2			0.3	10	0.32	
23	▼ West Wall	Other	Unspecifi...	602	ft2			0.04618	25		
24	Stairwell, lo	Vinyl Frame:Double ...	Unspecified	11	ft2			0.3	3	0.32	
25	Stairwell, up	Vinyl Frame:Double ...	Unspecified	11	ft2			0.3	3	0.32	
26	Master bath	Vinyl Frame:Double ...	Unspecified	11	ft2			0.3	3	0.32	
27	Master bath	Vinyl Frame:Double ...	Unspecified	11	ft2			0.3	3	0.32	
28	Transom	Wood Frame:Double ...	Unspecified	5	ft2			0.3	2	0.32	
29	Back door	Glass (> 50% glazing)	Unspecified	18	ft2			0.3	5	0.32	

FIGURE 4.12 COMcheck and REScheck require that building component areas and thermal properties be provided for energy code compliance validation. Users have limited choices of predefined options, which may be overridden to some extent (in this image "vinyl windows" were the closest approximation to fiberglass units). While no geometric modeling occurs in either software program, the data required can easily be pulled from BIM—the earlier, the better. COMcheck and REScheck are by the Office of Energy Efficiency and Renewable Energy (EERE) of the US Department of Energy (www.energycodes.gov).

compliance simply means the project meets the minimum standards for energy performance. We will find our world in a perilous state—as if it weren't precarious enough—if our buildings merely meet minimum standards of performance.

Energy simulation

In Design Development or later, a project may undergo a detailed energy modeling analysis using Ecotect, eQuest, EnergyPlus, Energy10, Green Building Studio, HEED, or SUNREL, to name a few.[1] Such an analysis is highly advisable, and required in a growing number of cases. However, there are limitations to detailed energy modeling or simulation.

First and foremost, a simulation requires accurate data in order to produce accurate results. The old programming term for this is GIGO: garbage in, garbage out. (Some wags have recently interpreted the acronym as garbage in, gospel out, alluding to a tendency to place too much trust in fallible computer models.) For building energy simulation, the underlying physics are well understood, and most simulation programs have been validated with experimental data. However, even a good modeling program based on accurate algorithms requires good data.

Envelope assemblies

Envelope assemblies must be accurately described in terms of U-factor, reflectance, emissivity, porosity, and orientation. Energy simulation software generally includes libraries of envelope components and equipment based on empirically tested values. This is extremely helpful, as even an expert user will not be able to realistically determine values for materials, assemblies, and equipment. However, such databases are at times localized (North American wall assemblies, for example) or limited (commonly found assemblies and equipment only). In cases when a designer is proposing an unusual component, some approximation may be required.

[1] A comprehensive list is available at http://apps1.eere.energy.gov/buildings/tools_directory.

Equipment

Equipment must include correct values for energy use, total heat generated, and, in some cases, pollutant output (including water vapor or CO_2).

Schedule

The building's seasonal and daily occupancy schedule must be accurate. The number of occupants in the building in any given hour will affect performance, as people contribute sensible and latent heat loads to a building, which raises temperatures and adds moisture.

Weather data

Typical meteorological year version 2 (TMY2) includes a large array of meteorological factors: dry- and wet-bulb temperature, rainfall amount and direction, wind speed and direction, overcast conditions, solar energy falling on a horizontal surface (insolation), and so forth. This free database developed by the US National Renewable Energy Laboratory (NREL) displays hourly weather data and represents average data over a 30-year period for 239 North American locations. For example, the data for 1:00 p.m. to 2:00 p.m. on May 24 includes the average temperatures for that hour over the past 30 years. Similar databases (WYEC2 in the United States and Canada and TRY in Europe) also are available. TMY2 and others do not forecast future weather data, obviously, and cannot account for exceptional weather patterns. As a measure of average weather it will not allow the software to predict actual building performance. Energy simulation software therefore does not tend to predict worst-case scenarios.

In short, a detailed energy modeling exercise is most useful when assembly and equipment selection is still being investigated, but after sufficient parameters have been established to provide meaningful data. In conceptual or schematic design, too many variables are unknown; by the construction documents phase, the energy model can at best help refine decisions, but is not likely to dramatically affect performance.

Schematic design: designing parametrically for energy use

Later chapters will examine in greater depth and detail the methods for applying BIM to specific passive strategies, such as heating or cooling. Such methods necessarily require more detailed models and imply a more mature design. As we are concerned with massing models in this chapter, however, we will focus the present discussion on relevant, coarser, modeling and information processing: those "back of the envelope" calculations that, while approximate, can be immensely useful.

The following detailed outline represents a comprehensive approach to parametric design for energy at a conceptual level. Much of the basis for the discussion below can be found in *Mechanical and Electrical Equipment for Buildings* (MEEB; Grondzik et al. 2010). The primary reference for the Building Systems section of the Architectural Registration Examination (ARE), MEEB is an indispensable volume for architect candidates and architects alike.

It bears repeating that these calculations are not intended, strictly speaking, as simulations. Rather, they represent quantitative data in an iterative procedure allowing the designer to evaluate the relative merits of competing conceptual designs or refine a design. As a convenience, a checklist is included at the end of this chapter.

Envelope U·A

Total conductance of an envelope with an *N* number of assemblies (wall types, roof types, glazing types, and so on) can be expressed as:

$$U_{\text{assembly 1}} \cdot A_{\text{assembly 1}} + U_{\text{assembly 2}} \cdot A_{\text{assembly 2}} + U_{\text{assembly 3}} \cdot A_{\text{assembly 3}} + \ldots + U_{\text{assembly N}} \cdot A_{\text{assembly N}}$$

Where *U* is the conductance of an assembly and *A* is the area of that assembly. The inverse of conductance is thermal resistance, *R,* the oft-cited R-value of a wall or building material:

$$U = 1/R \qquad \text{[Equation 4.1]}$$

R-values are cumulative, whereas U-factors are not. To determine the overall U-factor of an assembly, sum the R-values of all components, and then take the inverse (Fig. 4.13). (Note that conductivity, *k,* is distinct from conduct*ance*, *U.* The former is the degree to which a material conducts heat *per unit thickness*, and the latter is a measure of heat transfer for a given material or assembly's *overall* thickness.)

Total conductance through the building envelope is critical in determining building energy performance. The greater the temperature difference between the desired indoor dry-bulb temperature (the set point) and outdoor temperature, the more significant resistance to heat transfer (loss or gain) will be. Hence insulation is most important in cold climates, where the temperature difference may be 70°F or more. Conversely, very temperate climates, where outdoor temperatures are fairly constant and at or close to human comfort norms, may require little or no insulation. One has only to visit the Schindler House in West Hollywood, for example, to appreciate the relative indifference to thermal controls that early California modernism could afford.

Roof conductance

Even in a preliminary massing model, it is critical to differentiate the building's roof from other envelope components. There are key reasons for this:

- Roof assemblies typically have differing (higher) U-factors than walls, given greater available structural depth and exposure to the sky;
- Roofs may have a higher reflectance and/or emissivity than walls;
- On clear, cold nights, roofs may get colder than the air temperature, since they radiate energy to the near black-body of the cloudless night sky;
- Because of their greater exposure to solar *insolation,* roof *insulation* effectiveness is reduced. A roof's R-value expresses the assembly's thermal conductance, but does not fully account for radiation or convection, two other heat transfer mechanisms. The insulation actually functions just as well in a roof assembly as in a wall, but for calculation purposes its value is diminished

FIGURE 4.13 BIM walls are typically populated with data by the software vendor—in this case, Vectorworks Architect. Even "generic" walls (at right) employed at a conceptual design stage, before the envelope has been designed, may be assigned a probable R-value or U-factor.

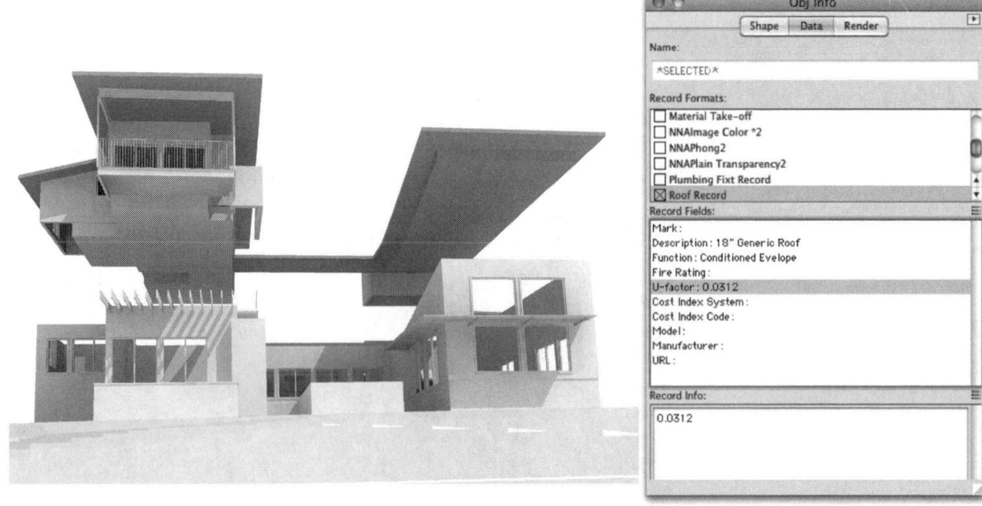

FIGURE 4.14 As with walls, BIM roofs may be assigned general characteristics even when modeled as generic slabs.

in order to account for increased roof thermal radiation and convection. For details, see Chapter 7.

In the BIM model, assign an *adjusted* appropriate U-factor ($1/R_{effective}$) to the distinct roof assembly (Fig. 4.14). Roof overhangs, while they will provide shade and contribute to energy performance, should not be counted, whether insulated or not.

Exterior opaque wall area

As with roof assemblies, it is not necessary to make precise decisions of exact envelope assemblies—a probable U-factor assigned to a generic wall will do. If the designer intends multiple wall types, then these should be differentiated by U-factor. However, as consequence of the above formula for total U·A of individual wall assemblies, a preliminary assumption of a single average U-factor for all walls will do if the architect is undecided on wall types. Obviously, changes in wall types may lead to variable U-factors, which may affect the overall envelope U·A.

Basements and slabs

Portions of buildings below grade do not lose heat through basement walls and slabs in the same way as walls above grade, because a wall contacting earth experiences different thermodynamic conditions and behavior than one in air. (Generally only heat loss is in issue, since soil temperatures are almost always below the human comfort zone.) Soil temperature varies with depth; as a result, a basement wall's U-factor is not uniform, but also varies with depth. For very preliminary design, typical wall U-factors can be used. An appropriate approach at the conceptual design stage would be to model the basement as a simple prism (such as an extruded rectangle, for example) and use the perimeter area of the solid to derive total basement U·A.

For a building in a predominantly warm climate with mild winters, a slab or basement may be used as a heat sink and in that case it should have as high a U-factor as possible, in order to encourage maximum heat transfer out of the building. Under certain conditions, however, when the air is warm and moist and the basement walls are cool, condensation could occur, encouraging mold growth and unhealthy air. The designer must therefore carefully consider relative humidity and dew point temperature in warm months.

Heat has a tendency to conduct far more from basement sides and far less from floors. When calculating heat loss through slabs, consider only the slab perimeter length in linear feet, rather than its area. For analysis at the conceptual stage, a

Comparative Thermal Analysis

	Wall		Roof		Glazing		Total U·A
	U-Factor	Area	U-Factor	Area	U-Factor	Area	
Scheme 1	0.043	657.0 SF	0.025	936.5 SF	0.280	315.3 SF	*140*
Scheme 2	0.048	734.1 SF	0.033	936.5 SF	0.300	238.2 SF	*137*

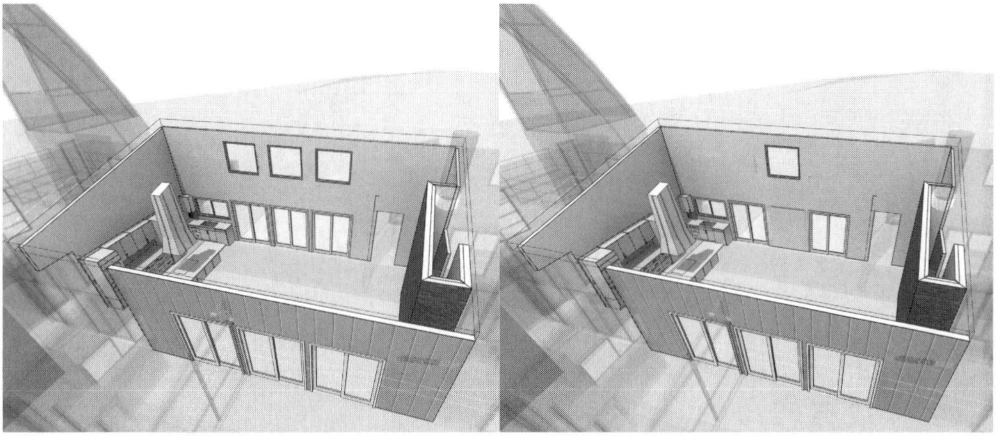

FIGURE 4.15 Two competing room designs are quickly analyzed for relative thermal performance. The room at left has more north glazing (for better diffuse daylighting) but must have lower envelope component U-factors to maintain the same overall U·A as the more opaque design at right. In both cases reports within the BIM model allow quick analysis and optimization of the design.

total U·L (length) for the slab (whether basement or at-grade) is sufficient to make a comparative analysis between competing schemes. Chapter 7 will discuss more detailed analysis for BIM parametric energy optimization of slab design.

Glazing

If possible, the amount of glazed envelope should be included in preliminary massing models. Even if the designer has not yet determined the exact distribution of windows, it is useful to model glazing as an approximate percentage of total envelope, if only to establish U·A for the envelope. Since U·A considers only conductance multiplied by total area, the size, placement, and number of windows and glazed doors is irrelevant to that calculation—only total area matters. However, considerations of appropriate shading and heat gain suggest the designer model rough glazing placement.

South-facing and non-south-facing window areas Orientation of glazing obviously affects undesirable heat gain in summer and desirable heat gain in winter. It also has an impact on daylighting and can be affected by shading devices (overhangs, awnings, vertical shading fins)—see Chapter 5. Even at the massing model stage, however, differentiating between south-facing and non-south-facing glass in the BIM model is crucial for passive heating design. Distinguishing between the two is helpful, and here again quantitative take-offs can help the designer decide between competing designs. Of course, properly speaking "south-facing" means "equatorial facing" (projects in the southern hemisphere should distinguish north-facing and non-north-facing glass).

Conductance When the total amount of glazing is to be determined, assign a U-factor to opaque assemblies (walls and roofs) as well as windows and calculate total U·A (Fig. 4.15). Rapid comparisons can be made to help the designer assess the impact of varying glazing quantity or quality:

- Increasing (or decreasing) total window area, and the corresponding decrease (or increase) in opaque assembly U-factor needed to maintain an overall U·A target;
- For a given area, selecting more or less conductive windows, and the subsequent offset required in the opaque assemblies to maintain desired U·A.

Operable areas There are three quantitative drivers that will determine minimum operable window sizes in skin-load dominated buildings:

- *Energy use.* As we'll see in Chapter 6, natural ventilation can be a successful cooling strategy for hot and humid climates. Both wind- and buoyancy-driven ventilation are strongly dependent on aperture (window) sizes.
- *IAQ.* Satisfactory indoor air quality requires adequate ventilation; for most skin-load dominated buildings, this is achievable with passive ventilation. It is a mistake, however, to assume that outdoor air is invariably healthier than indoor air.
- *Egress.* Building codes require minimum operable window openings for sleeping rooms to allow for emergency egress. In this case, operable area is a minimum value (in both area and width), rather than a percentage of total wall assembly area.

In all three of the above cases, it's useful for the designer to quantitatively evaluate operable window (and/or door) area. In the BIM model, differentiate operable window area and compare it to the total *floor* area. As a rough rule of thumb, assume 1 percent operable area as adequate for natural ventilation in residences, assuming moderate wind speeds. As the design develops, more detailed quantitative relationships such as those described in Chapter 6 can help the designer more precisely establish optimum minimum operable area.

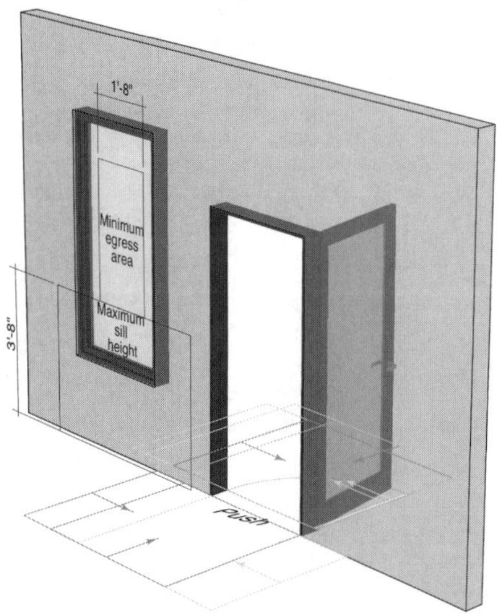

FIGURE 4.16 Simple "template" objects (custom families or symbols) can be quickly and effectively be used to visually check for code compliance.

For egress code compliance, verify minimum operable size:

- Minimum net clear opening height: 24 inches;
- Minimum net clear opening width: 20 inches;
- Minimum net clear opening: 5.7 square feet (some codes allow a 5-square-foot opening at the ground floor);
- Maximum sill height: 44 inches above finish floor.

It's critical to confirm the above with local building officials, as codes vary by jurisdiction, and changes may have been adopted within a community. The designer can use some simple techniques to quickly verify compliance in the BIM model with a minimum of effort (Fig. 4.16):

- Establish a 3D guide (whether a plane or solid) at minimum sill height; windows may thus be visually inspected for violations;
- Create a compliance guide in the form of a family (Revit) or symbol (ArchiCAD, Vectorworks). Such an object is as simple as a 3D polygon of the minimum width, height, and area, set at the maximum sill height. The guide object can be placed at all proposed window locations, then turned off or removed later as desired;
- Establish families or symbols of egress-compliant windows in a variety of sizes, including a distinguishing character in the name to readily identify them as compliant. This is possible even at a highly conceptual level, before actual window objects are used, as simple 3D polygons can be so used;
- If the design is sufficiently mature to include wall objects (even generic ones), use egress-compliant window manufacturer families or symbols. Most such library objects include data that designates whether the window in question

Thermal mass schematic estimate

K mass	A mass	A floor	% SG	A SG	SSF
0.137	732 SF	2,132 SF	11%	235 SF	**43 %**

SSF = K mass · A mass / A SG

Where:
SSF = Solar Savings Fraction
K mass = specific heat coefficient of material (masonry)
A mass = concrete and masonry surfaces exposed to winter sun, SF
% SG = Maximum recommended south-facing glass, as ratio of floor area
A SG = Assumed south-facing glazing area, SF (from % SG)

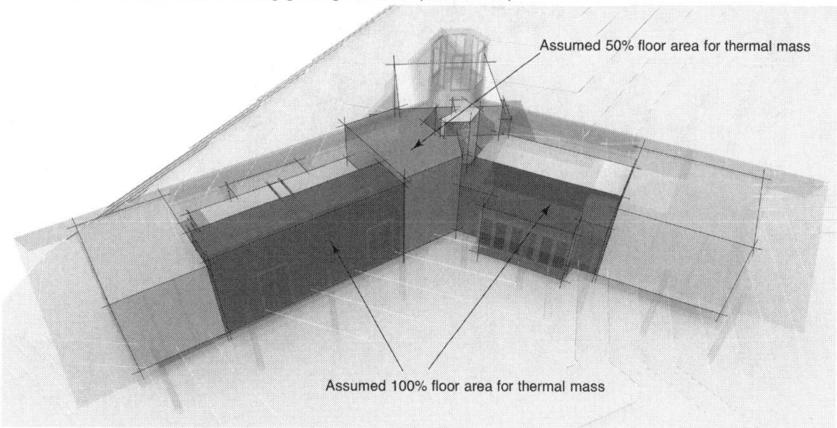

FIGURE 4.17 An early massing model comprised of rectangular prism Space objects may not offer detailed thermal massing information, but can provide rough approximations. Before the building has been designed, one might make certain assumptions: south-facing glass may be the maximum recommended (Equation 7.8, Figure 7.12), and that certain spaces contribute all, none, or some fraction of their floor area as useable thermal mass. Refer to Figure 7.16 for an illustration of a somewhat more detailed thermal massing analysis.

is compliant (for example, a TRUE or FALSE Boolean statement).

Thermal mass

For climates with modest humidity, and especially those with significant diurnal temperature swings, thermal mass may be an effective passive cooling strategy. The total area of exposed thermally massive materials (generally stone, concrete, or water) within a building interior can be optimized for the building (Fig. 4.17) by considering:

- Roof (underside) area for concrete roofs;
- Structural walls, columns, and beams;
- Slab area.

These building elements are best optimized beyond the massing model stage; the reader is referred to Chapters 6 and 7 for passive cooling and heating optimization.

Spatial dependencies

We've addressed in BIM the quantitative limits to the schematic design construction envelope imposed by zoning, first costs, and energy use, among other factors. In addition, building performance will be influenced by other spatial dependencies: occupancy and ventilation requirements.

Occupancy loads

For residential projects, the number of occupants will generally not impact design, except at a programming level and in determining water use and cooling loads. For other project types, however, the number of occupants will affect egress and ventilation requirements.

For egress, consult local codes in force and determine:

- Number of occupants from gross square footage
- Width of egress from number of occupants

Space Occupancy Calculations

Space	Net Area	Occupants (IBC)	Exit Width	Occupants (ASHRAE 62.1)	Ventilation
	SF	1 Occupant/100 SF	0.2"/Occ, 36" min.	1 Occupant/200 SF	5 CFM/Occ + 0.06 CMF/SF
A1	2264.2 SF	23	36"	12	316 CFM
A2	2342.0 SF	23	36"	12	321 CFM
B1	2264.2 SF	23	36"	12	316 CFM
B2	2342.0 SF	23	36"	12	321 CFM

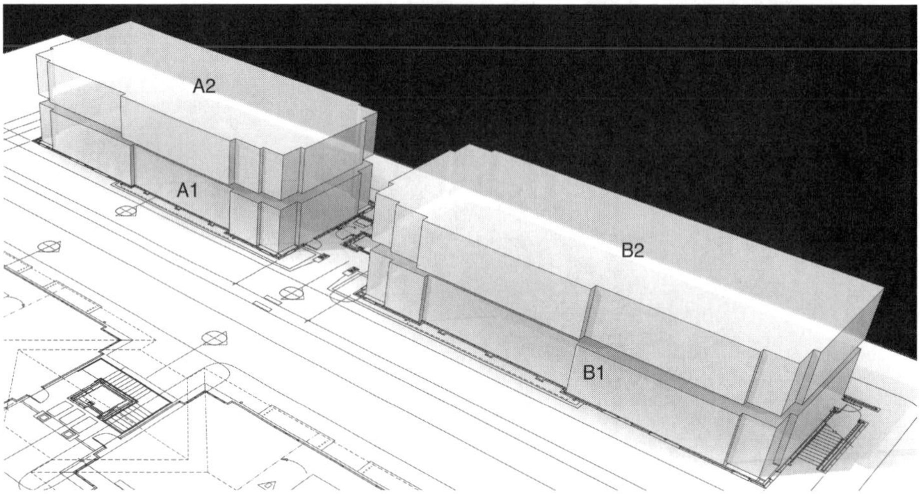

FIGURE 4.18 Data derived from Space objects, such as area-based occupancy loads, may have design implication—such as egress requirements.

The BIM model can readily report gross square footage, from which all other calculations may be derived and tabulated in a dynamic work sheet within the file (Fig. 4.18). The designer can thus get real-time occupancy feedback.

Ventilation

ASHRAE Standard 62.1 recommends ventilation requirements (in cubic feet per minute, or CFM) for all occupancy types except low-rise residential occupancies; Standard 62.2 covers detached and low-rise residential buildings.[2] Total required ventilation is given in 62.1 as the ventilation rate per person times the population plus the rate per area times the area.[3]

[2] Both ASHRAE standards are available at ASHRAE.org.

[3] The interested reader is referred to the full publication, with particular attention drawn to Equation 6-1 and Table 6-1.

[4] The reader is referred to Equation 4-1 (which establishes total ventilation in CFM as a function of floor area and number of bedrooms), or Table 4-1, which does the same.

Standard 62.2 is considerably shorter. For low-rise residential buildings,[4] the model can dynamically report total floor area and automatically count the number of bedrooms if these are assigned the correct data object (Space or named area polygon), with the appropriate formula incorporated in the BIM file (Fig. 4.19).

Conceptual design thermal performance BIM checklist

The following list may be used as a guide at the conceptual design stage.

ENVELOPE U · A

- ❑ Exterior opaque wall

  $Area_{wall1} \cdot U_{wall1} + Area_{wall2} \cdot U_{wall2} + Area_{wall3} \cdot U_{wall3} + \ldots + Area_{wallN} \cdot U_{wallN}$

- ❑ Roof conductance

  $Arearoof \cdot 1/(R\text{-}9)^{-0.1}$

- ❑ Basement wall

  Use total wall height for uniform insulation

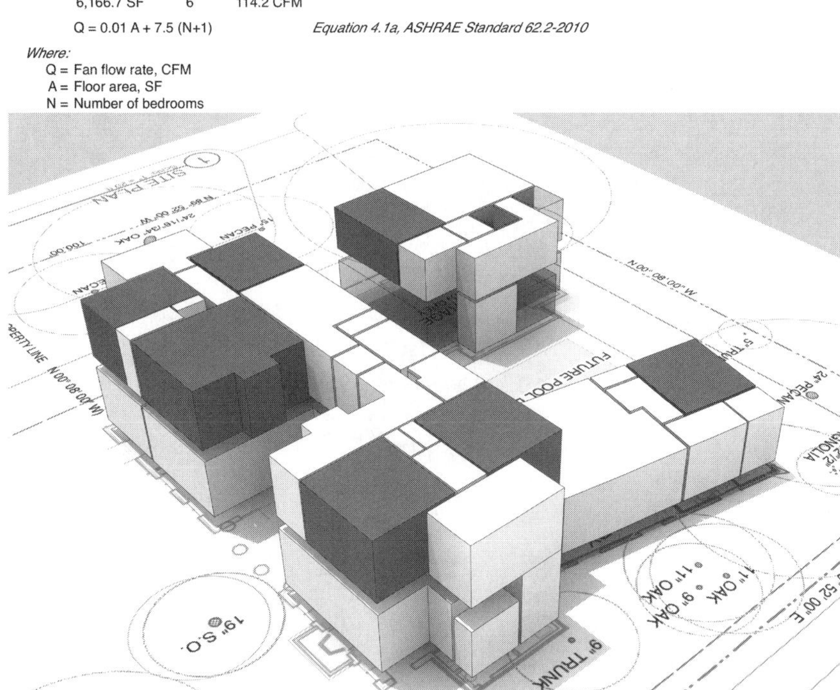

ASHRAE Standard 62.2
A N Q
6,166.7 SF 6 114.2 CFM
Q = 0.01 A + 7.5 (N+1)
Equation 4.1a, ASHRAE Standard 62.2-2010
Where:
Q = Fan flow rate, CFM
A = Floor area, SF
N = Number of bedrooms
FUTURE POOL
19" S.O.
9" TRUNK
11" OAK
9" OAK

FIGURE 4.19 ASHRAE Standard 62.1 and 62.2 ventilation requirements are by occupancy type, and are dependent on area and number of occupants. A BIM report can easily track these requirements based on the geometry of the spaces. While a BIM Standard 62.2 analysis for a single-family residence may be unnecessary, 62.1 ventilation requirements for even small commercial or civic projects are more laborious to calculate and may be conveniently calculated within BIM.

Use vertical segments of wall for variable insulation

Glazing

- ❏ Differentiate south-facing and non-south-facing area
- ❏ Conductance

  Use manufacturer's values, or parameterize in conjunction with total opaque U · A

- ❏ Operable area as percentage of total floor area; assume ≈1%
- ❏ Operable area to meet egress minima

  20" width, 24" height, 5.7 SF minimum

  44" sill height maximum

VOLUMETRIC DEPENDENCIES

- ❏ Occupancy

  Function of floor area

- ❏ Egress

  Width

  Minimum width by code; width function of number of occupants

- ❏ Egress number

  Minimum number by code; actual number function of number of occupants

- ❏ Ventilation

  ASHRAE Standard 62.1: per occupancy type, number of occupants, floor area

  Standard 62.2: per floor area, number of bedrooms

■ Case Study: New High School, Carlsbad, California

By Lane Smith
Design firm: Roesling Nakamura Terada Architects, Inc.
Client: Carlsbad Unified School District

Lane Smith of Roesling Nakamura Terada (RNT) Architects, Inc., in San Diego, California, discusses the use of BIM at the early schematic design stage in RNT's new high school project in Carlsbad, California (Fig. 4.20), to answer the question, "How does BIM make for better architecture?"

BIM was introduced to our office by building contractors, who have been utilizing BIM models developed from the design team and subcontractors' documents to detect and resolve conflicts prior to construction. Could the same tool that saves a contractor significant amounts of time and money also make better architecture?

The new high school at College and Cannon was the first project at RNT to explore the capabilities of BIM throughout all design phases. The site scheme and initial elevations for

FIGURE 4.20 Preliminary design sketches of the new high school project were developed freehand and informed development of early building modeling.

Image courtesy of Roesling Nakamura Terada Architects, Inc.

the topographically complex site were sketched by hand initially. These sketches, combined with bubble diagrams based upon the district's building program, were extrapolated into Revit models, and then incidental spaces such as restrooms, mechanical rooms, and stairs were added. Although the site design remained in 2D form, the utilization of BIM in this early stage was invaluable (Fig. 4.21). The sectional relationships between the upper and lower levels with a central promenade became apparent very early on (Fig. 4.22). Revit real-time room area calculations and schedules expedited the process of translating program into building forms that met the client's program.

FIGURE 4.21 The design development site plan for Roesling Nakamura Terada Architects' new high school project in Carlsbad, California integrated digital imaging with hand-drawing techniques.

Image courtesy of Wallace, Roberts & Todd.

(Continued)

FIGURE 4.22 Presentation elevations of the new high school project were based on the BIM model, which was used to establish correct massing and architectural relationships.

Image courtesy of Roesling Nakamura Terada Architects, Inc.

Perhaps the most powerful design method that BIM has brought to RNT is to interface BIM models with the traditional design method of hand sketching. BIM can generate any possible view of a structure. For the high school at College and Cannon, perspectives and views of prominent or important areas were printed and subsequently sketched over on trace paper. The ideas in sketch form were then incorporated into the model with the opportunity to see the direct effects and changes resulting from the suggestion, allowing design ideas to be quickly incorporated and evaluated from an unlimited number of views (plan, elevation, section, axonometric, perspective, and so on). Massing and forms for complex or important spaces, such as the campus entry, library, gym, and administration buildings were refined rapidly and effectively (Fig. 4.23).

While BIM, as a free-standing software platform, is not a complete formula for architecture superior to that generated in 2D or information-less formats, it does bring an additional and valuable tool to the practice of architecture (Fig. 4.24).

FIGURE 4.23 Rapid development of massing and forms were developed using BIM, so that key projects could be designed quickly, accurately, and efficiently.

Image courtesy of Roesling Nakamura Terada Architects, Inc.

FIGURE 4.24 The BIM model of the Carlsbad High School is part of an iterative design process that employs a wide range of visualization and design tools, from freehand sketching to 2D drafting to intelligent modeling.

Image courtesy of Roesling Nakamura Terada Architects, Inc.

Chapter 5

Solar Geometry and Daylighting

For almost all of human existence people have organized their lives around the diurnal cycle and seasonal variations of light and warmth. A relatively short time ago, evolutionarily speaking, we learned to artificially light our nighttime world with burning plant matter, followed by processed animal fat and oils. Then in the blink of an eye we created a 24-hour society thanks to industrially produced lighting—first gas, then electricity. But prior to those last innovations, most buildings made adequate use of *daylighting*—that is, they relied on natural light for functional average illuminance. Even if buildings' nocturnal use was limited, thanks to the difficulty of adequately illuminating them at night, they did not require much—if any—artificial lighting by day (Fig. 5.1).

Prior to the advent of electric lighting, architects and indigenous builders understood how to design for daylight, even if that knowledge was the result of empirical application of patterns rather than scientific development. Equally important, consciousness of daylighting was second nature, pervading the building vocabulary so thoroughly as to be almost unnoticeable by its users. But thanks to advances in materials and engineering, buildings grew ever

FIGURE 5.1 Edmond Paulin's 1880 section perspective, "Restitution of Diocletian Bath," underscores the importance of passive solar design in Roman architecture.

Image courtesy of the Digital Content Library of the University of Minnesota.

larger, and those advances paralleled the artificial lighting that was necessary to illuminate the deep spaces that long spans created, even by day. Daylighting became a neglected function of design, and for some designers fenestration has come to be more about composition or a design dogma than about views, much less light.

At the same time that long spans and artificial lighting became commonplace, buildings were increasingly being mechanically cooled and heated. As with daylighting, passive heating and cooling design was falling by the wayside. But more than any other source of illumination, natural light provides the greatest illuminance for the least amount of heat. Nevertheless, heat gains from insolation can be quite significant—enough to impose significant building cooling loads in summer. Inadequate winter sun, on the other hand, is a missed opportunity to provide significant passive heating under cold conditions.

This reliance on mechanical and electrical systems for illumination and thermal comfort has, among other things, obscured the relationship between daylighting and passive design for thermal comfort. These design agendas are at times in sympathy, and at others at odds. That tension is both a source of potential architectural richness, and its resolution in high-performance buildings requires the application of technical knowledge.

As is the case with energy modeling or structural analysis, architectural BIM software is not by itself a full-featured daylighting analysis tool or passive heating modeler. It can, however, be a powerful tool for supporting passive lighting and heating design goals (Fig. 5.2). This is particularly true early in the design process, when BIM can be highly effective for quantitative design. This and subsequent chapters will focus primarily on applying scientific principles and rules of thumb for daylighting, shading, and passive cooling and heating to BIM. In addition, we'll look at ways in which the BIM model may support more detailed daylighting and energy analysis performed by simulation software.

There are three primary objectives in applying solar geometry and sun studies to architecture:

- shading the building in general from unwanted (summertime) solar insolation;
- allowing desirable (winter) direct solar insolation for passive heat gain; and
- encouraging diffuse and denying glaring daylighting.

The astute designer will grasp that the second and third points above are potentially at odds and therefore require careful control of the amount of southern (or more generally equatorial) glass.

Shade from the sun

Studies of solar access to the building envelope are key to effective daylighting and passive heating and cooling. For the former, diffuse daylight is most desirable: direct beam solar radiation creates glare problems and increases heat gains. Moreover, a well-designed space can receive adequate illumination from diffuse skylight alone (overcast skies, or just light from the sky dome other than the sun). For thermal comfort, reducing direct gain in summer is obviously critical. On the other hand, optimizing solar heat gain in winter is desirable in cold and temperate climates. This poses a potential conflict between daylighting and winter heat gain agendas: the low winter sun that the architect invites into a space for winter warming can also present a glare problem.

Designing shading devices

Shading devices are not limited to awnings or light shelves. Partial overhangs, vertical shading fins, egg crating, brise-soleils, pergolas, and so forth may be investigated given the range of BIM modeling characteristics. The designer can use BIM to help evaluate the effectiveness of shading devices both to deny direct gain in warm months and to admit it in cold seasons. A frequent question is what time of year should shading devices admit sun, and when should they block it? One possible early design guideline is based on a comparison of heating and cooling degree days. Highly accessible, tabulated online weather data are available at several

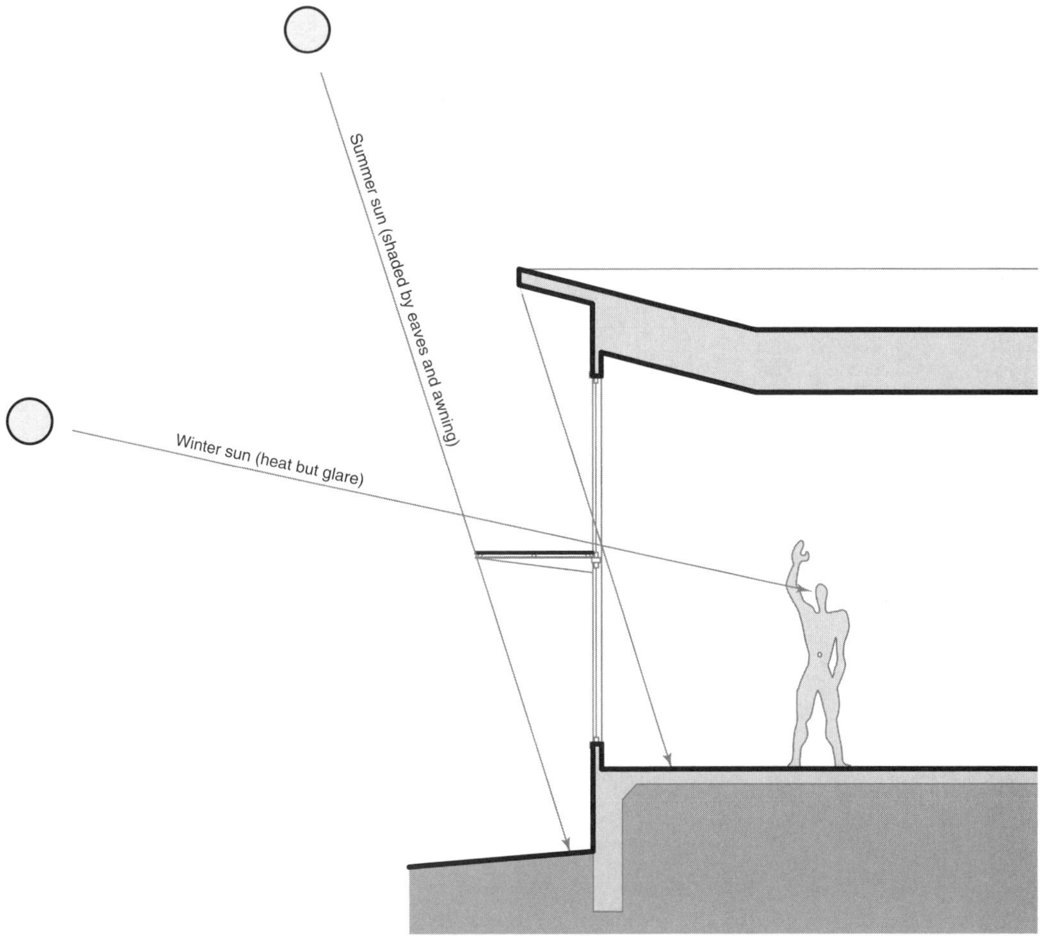

FIGURE 5.2 An appropriately designed south-oriented overhang or shading device can provide respite from the high summer sun while introducing low winter sun for better passive thermal controls. However, as can be seen in this section diagram, low winter sun can be a potential cause of glare and may be a concern when daylighting a space. Not all passive environmental controls work in sympathy; there may at times be competing agendas.

Web sites[1]. Compare monthly average heating degree days (HDD) and cooling degree days (CDD) for the building's site; shading devices may be designed to provide maximum protection from direct gain when CDD exceeds HDD (Fig. 5.3). For example, Austin, Texas' monthly HDD exceeds CDD from November through March; shading devices could be designed to maximize direct solar gain in those months, shade completely in May through September, and offer partial protection in between, in April and October. By contrast, Chicago, on the other hand, has a greater HDD from October through May, and so shade should be minimized in those months.

Of course, this is a preliminary design guide only, but one that can readily be applied in BIM. For a detailed analysis of the performance of shading and its effect on thermal performance, annual analysis using energy modeling software is recommended.

[1] The reader is referred to www.degreedays.net and www.wunderground.com.

	Chicago				Austin			
2009-10	HDD	CDD	Δ	Recommendation	HDD	CDD	Δ	Recommendation
Oct	482	2	-480	*Don't Shade*	112	204	92	*Shade*
Nov	562	3	-559	*Don't Shade*	259	63	-196	*Don't Shade*
Dec	1162	0	-1162	*Don't Shade*	584	8	-576	*Don't Shade*
Jan	1318	0	-1318	*Don't Shade*	590	18	-572	*Don't Shade*
Feb	1050	0	-1050	*Don't Shade*	534	6	-528	*Don't Shade*
Mar	694	3	-691	*Don't Shade*	312	53	-259	*Don't Shade*
Apr	328	48	-280	*Don't Shade*	88	162	74	*Shade*
May	195	119	-76	*Don't Shade*	23	417	394	*Shade*
Jun	21	218	197	*Shade*	0	557	557	*Shade*
Jul	4	411	407	*Shade*	0	597	597	*Shade*
Aug	3	375	372	*Shade*	1	685	684	*Shade*
Sep	91	124	33	*Shade*	14	471	457	*Shade*

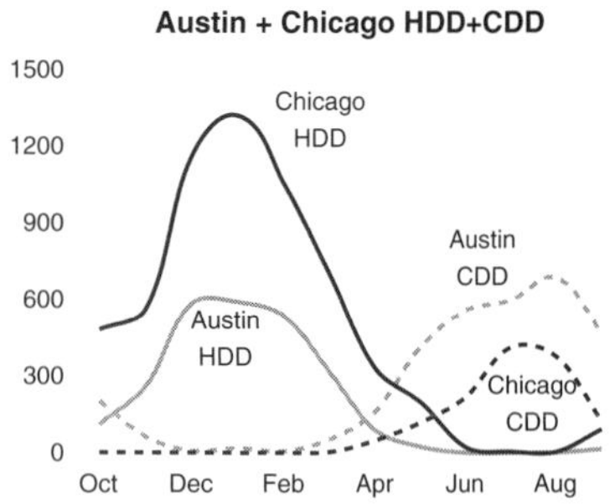

FIGURE 5.3 Monthly heating and cooling degree day data, rather than solar geometry, may govern appropriate times of year to shade windows and openings. Weather data for Austin, Texas, and Chicago, Illinois are compared and suggest that Austin windows should be shaded from April through October, whereas buildings in Chicago should have openings in shade from June through September to improve winter heat gain.

Optimizing for autumnal and vernal seasonal lag

Reconsider the example above, and note that in some cases the peaks in cooling load (highest cooling degree days) and heating load (highest heating degree days) do not necessarily fall on their respective solstices. For Austin, the greatest CCD is in August; the highest HDD is in January. Moreover, solar geometry is symmetrical about the solstices. That is, as far as sun angles are concerned, April and August are identical, but their respective HDD and CDD values couldn't be more different. This is due to the fact that earth, water, and air are heat sinks with (varying degrees of) thermal mass—and there's a lot of mass in the environment. As a result, weather "lags" behind solar geometry. Just as a thermally massive building redistributes daytime heat gain to nighttime, the environmental thermal mass shifts summer solar gains later into the year, and it takes a while in many regions for spring sun to take the chill off of winter.

The designer must therefore weigh whether to design fixed shading devices for warmer springs and therefore warmer autumns (less shade), or cooler autumns and therefore chillier springs (more shade). Here again, solar modeling in BIM used to test potential shading device designs, combined with consideration of simple HDD and CDD weather data, offers a potential design approach which can help to balance the asymmetry between solar geometry and annual weather patterns. An alternative is to design adaptive, polymorphic shading devices that are reconfigured (manually or automatically) to compensate for the weather-solar asymmetry.

Adjacent structures and vegetation

Whether designing for sun shading, access to solar rights, or daylighting, nearby obstruction may have a significant impact on lighting, either by blocking areas of sky dome illumination, or by diffusely (and even specularly) reflecting some light into the building. For design purposes it is not necessary to model adjacent buildings and other obstructions with a great deal of detail. The designer can ignore the fine points of adjacent building facades and fenestration; in most cases adjacent buildings may be modeled as simple masses, perhaps with approximations of their roof shapes. BIM applications typically include massing model tools that generate such adjacent structures quickly and easily (Fig. 5.4). Obstructions like trees should also be shown, especially for smaller projects, which may be significantly shaded by nearby large trees. Modeling all obstructions is especially critical when designing for on-site solar energy collectors, particularly photovoltaics (see Chapter 8).

Remember that these obstruction models are intended to aid in effective design and not to serve as rendering background or entourage. They should be included in the file if it is to be exported to an energy modeler or design aid for further analysis. For that reason, avoid modeling them with too much detail; trees with several hundred polygons

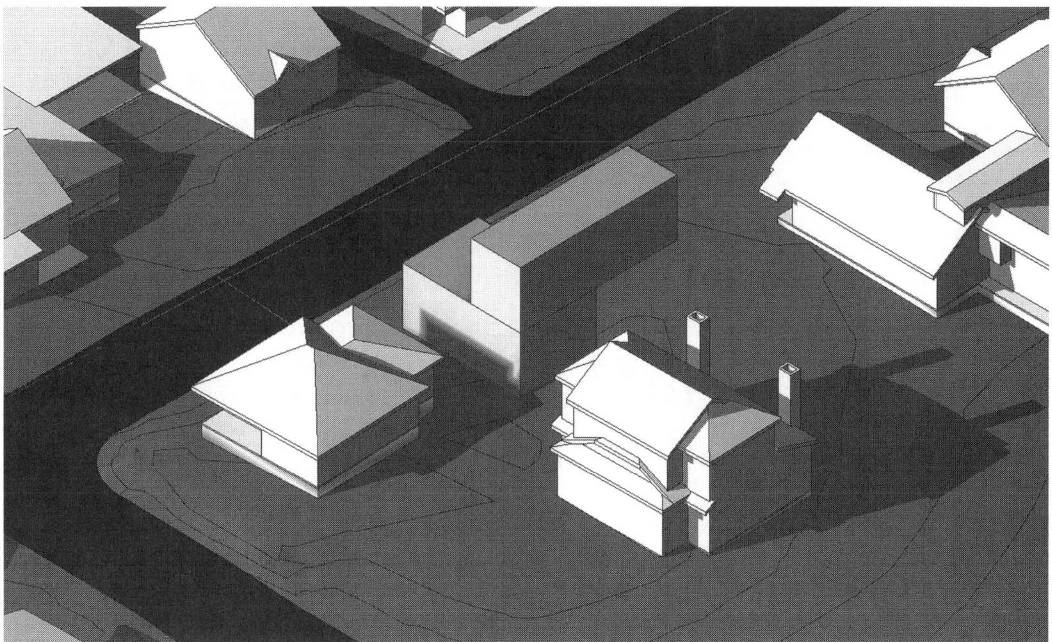

FIGURE 5.4 Autodesk's Project Vasari schematic design environment allows solar rights analysis. In this composite view of a massing analysis study, shadows from adjacent buildings have been superimposed with an insolation analysis of a massing model.

Image courtesy of Justin Firuz Dowhower.

to simulate leaves may be compelling in a rendering, but a high polygon count is counterproductive in analysis. Make tree canopies simple with low-polygon-count blobs (Fig. 5.5, left), or even spheres. It's more important to accurately represent a tree canopy's general shape and size than to model branches and leaves, which have little positive impact on analyzing building performance.

Static sun models

There are several types of sun or shade studies in which BIM can be extremely useful. These studies range from creating views that show sun shading for a single moment in the year (termed here as *static sun studies*; see Fig. 5.6), to animations showing the play of shadow on a building throughout a day, to fixed views that represent the total annual direct sun visible from a point.

The first are obviously the simplest to implement: set a scene, define the site's latitude or location from a menu, set the sun position based on time and date desired, and render for sun shadow. Two variations bear mentioning. To study sun shading throughout the year, when an animation is not feasible, and/or when a presentation sheet or board is desired, a matrix of renderings may be arrayed on a page view. Another possibility is to represent all the sun's possible location throughout the year as a sun *field*, rather than a single day's sun *path*.

Still images

By the earlier definition, solar "animations" might also include a series of static images that show sun shadows on a building on different days of the year and at different times of day, like cells in an animated film (Fig. 5.7). Primitive as they are, these have the advantage of informing the user at a glance how well shading devices generally perform over time.

- As with solar animations, it's best to establish a few views to serve as the basis for the sun study. Do not neglect views from the northwest and northeast.

FIGURE 5.5 A tree model with little detail other than a low-polygon-count canopy *(left)* is perfectly adequate for solar access studies; it will render faster than a highly detailed tree model, which is of particular concern if there are many plants in the model. For greater visual detail with a minimal rendering cost, use photos of trees with transparency masks *(right)* rather than high-polygon-count models.

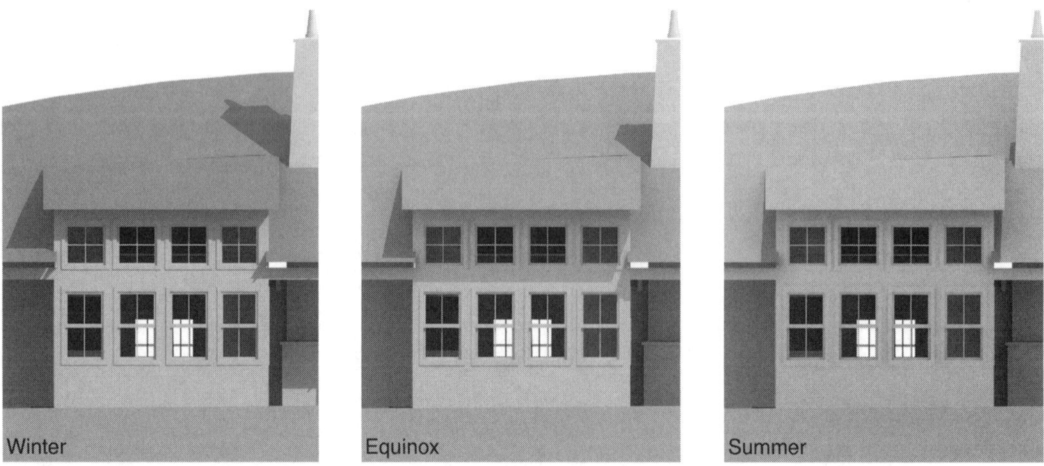

FIGURE 5.6 Three BIM sun shade studies at different times of year traditionally selected for winter solstice, equinox (spring and fall are identical), and summer solstice. Consider that the autumn lag that most locales experience would suggest that climate patterns, not solar geometry, should determine what dates to design shade for (see also Figs. 5.3 and 6.10).

- At minimum, select three dates: the summer and winter solstices, and either equinox (the solar geometry is identical for both equinoxes).
- If desired, select additional dates falling on about the 21st of each month. Both months in the pairs below have identical sun paths:
- January–November
- February–October
- April–August
- May–July

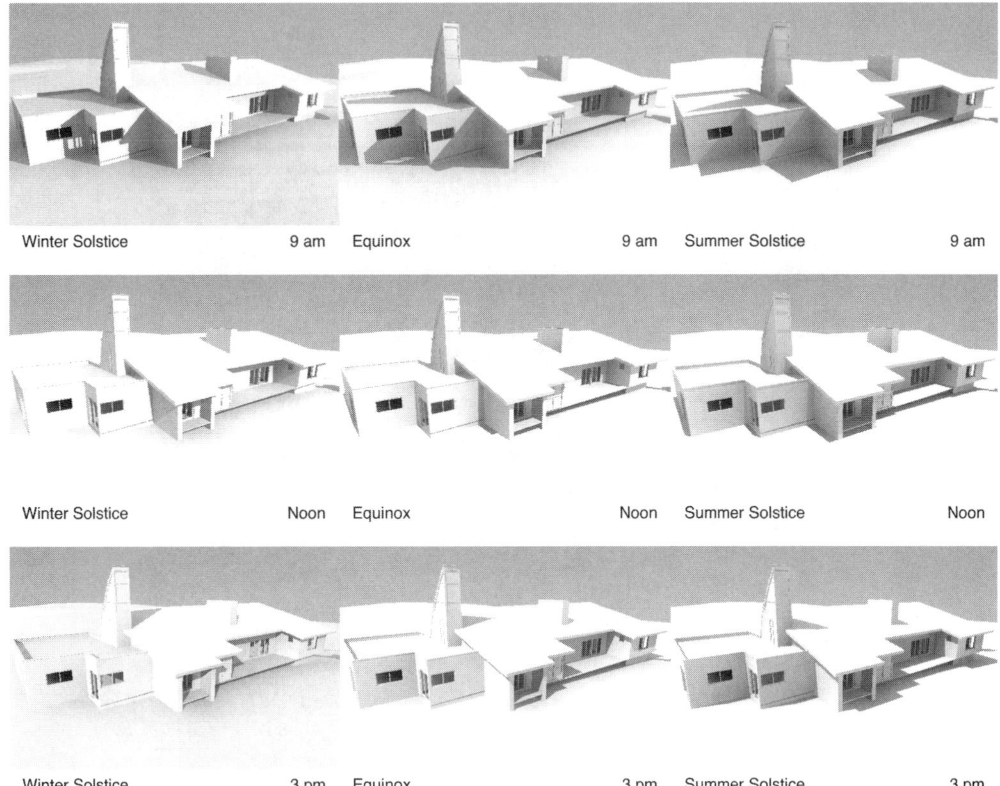

FIGURE 5.7 A matrix study of still images showing sun shading on the same model, from the same view, at selected times of selected dates. The user may increase the number of dates in the years and/or times of day to study.

- Prepare rendered views with shadows on for a few hours throughout the day; perhaps 9 a.m., noon, 3 p.m., and 6 p.m. (or slightly earlier if the sun has already set by then).
- Arrange the renderings in small or thumbnail views on a sheet, as a matrix of dates crossed with columns. As with solar animation movies, the model need not be highly detailed, colored, or textured to be effective (Fig. 5.7).

Most applications will automatically set a directional light source with the correct azimuth (bearing from south or north) and elevation (angle above the horizon). Otherwise, there are several online tools to calculate these. For example, NOAA's Web site[2] allows the user to drag a marker on a zoomable world map to locate the building site (Fig. 5.8).

Sun views (what the sun sees)

Early in architecture school, when some of us were just becoming consciously aware of the relationship between the sun and building form, we would tilt our models or crane our heads to simulate the perspective of the solar disk. What we as the "sun" could see would be directly illuminated; any part of the model concealed by an overhang or projection would be in shadow. Setting the viewing angle of the BIM model equal to the sun's position offers a similar insight; anything visible to the viewer is "seen" by the sun, and therefore illuminated (Fig. 5.9). Anything else is in shadow. In some cases, the BIM sun is a directional light object whose azimuth and elevation are calculated by the

[2] NOAA's Solar Calculator can be accessed at www.esrl.noaa.gov/gmd/grad/solcalc/.

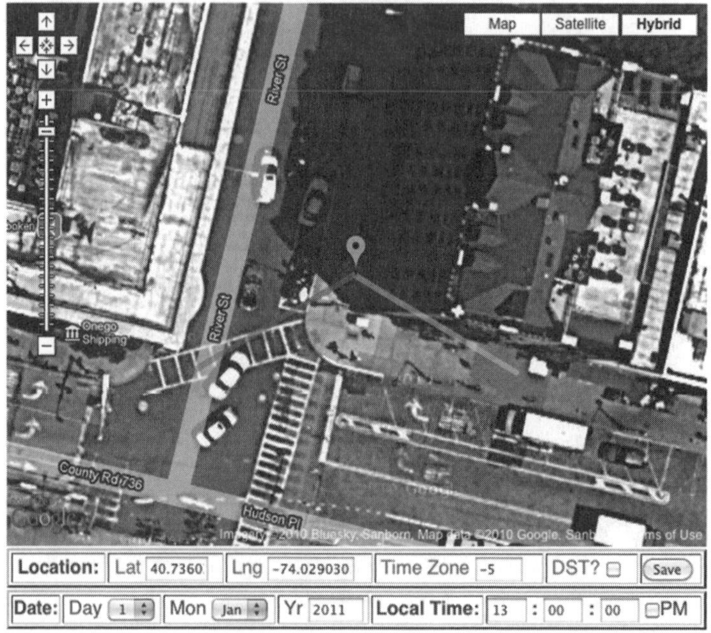
NOAA Solar Calculator
Find Sunrise, Sunset, Solar Noon and Solar Position for Any Place on Earth
Show: World Cities U.S. Cities GMD Observ.'s GMD Data Sites SurfRad
Click one of the small pins near (and in the same time zone as) your desired location. Use the control on the left side of the map to zoom in or out. Place the large pin in the exact desired location. You can use the Save button to have your computer remember the current location for next time. Check the DST check box if Daylight Saving Time is in effect for your site.
Map
Satellite
Hybrid
River St
River St
County Rd 736
Hudson Pl
Location: Lat 40.7360 Lng -74.029030 Time Zone -5 DST? Save
Date: Day 1 Mon Jan Yr 2011 Local Time: 13 : 00 : 00 PM

Equation of Time (minutes):	Solar Declination (degrees):	Apparent Sunrise:	Solar Noon:	Apparent Sunset:	Current Az/El (degrees):	
-3.55	-22.98	07:20	11:59:39	16:39	195.3	24.79
Show on map:		Sunrise		Sunset	Current	

FIGURE 5.8 Screen shot of a location on the NOAA Solar Calculator. The user may specify sunrise and sunset direction for a given date, as well as solar azimuth for a specific moment.

Imagery ©2010 Bluesky, Sanborn Map. Map data ©Google, Sanborn.

program; in Vectorworks, for example, clicking on "set view to light" aligns the view to be parallel to the directional light "rays." If the sun's view needs to be set manually, the user can set it manually by first calculating the sun's azimuth and elevation using the NOAA calculator.

Sun chart projections

Polar coordinate sun-path diagrams are fairly familiar (3D representations of sun-paths are shown in Figs. 5.10 and 5.11). 2D sun-paths can be quickly generated for any latitude thanks to the University of Oregon's free online tool.[3] A 3D hemisphere centered on the building model or point of interest and scribed with the sun's path can help quantify the total number of hours per year that the given point "sees" the sun.

[3] University of Oregon's free online tool can be accessed at http://solardat.uoregon.edu/PolarSunChartProgram.php.

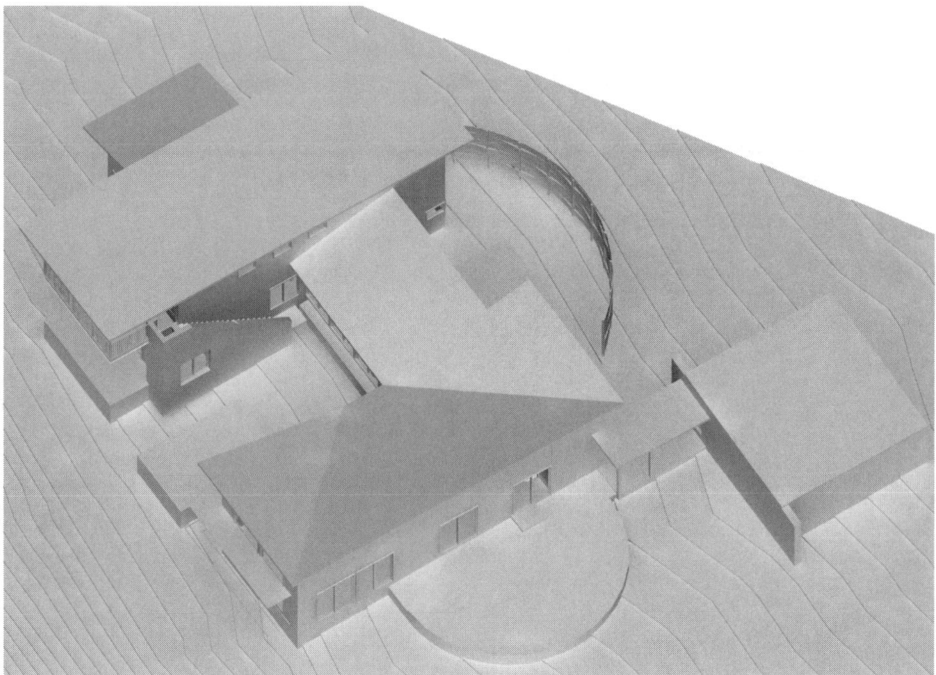

FIGURE 5.9 This is another view of the same model found in Figure 1.18, but in this case the view is set to model the sun on a September afternoon. This is a quick and effective view to evaluate adjustments to shading design. Note that the projection is orthogonal (the sun is so far away that a view from it would have hardly any perspective— its rays are nearly parallel). Also, there are no shadows (the sun never "sees" a shadow).

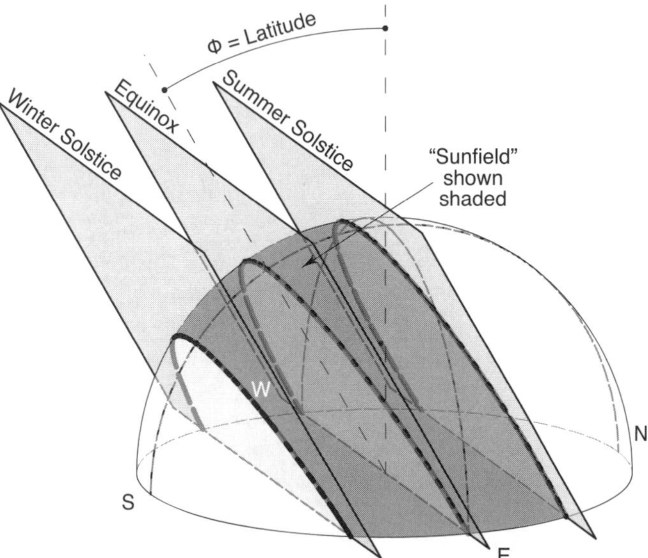

FIGURE 5.10 The shaded area bounded by the horizon and the solstice sun paths represents the area of the sky visited by the sun throughout the year. If this "sun field" is visible from a point in or about a building, then at some time during the year that point gets direct solar exposure.

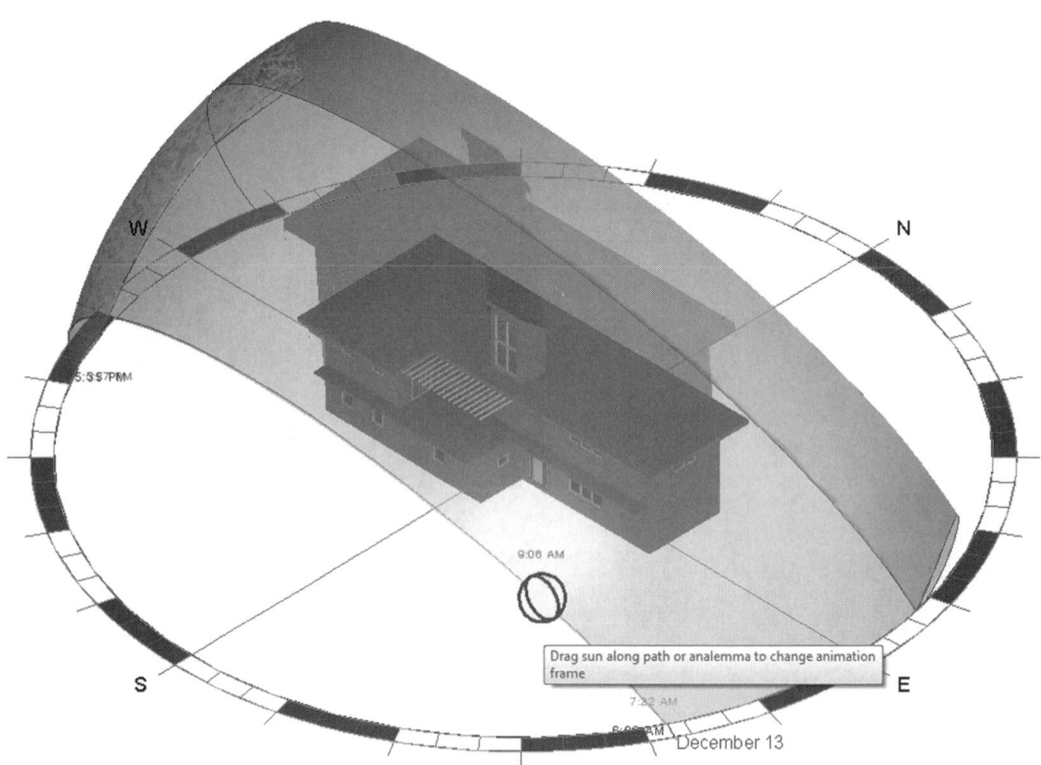

FIGURE 5.11 Like SketchUp, Autodesk's Project Vasari has an interactive interface that allows real-time variation in sun position.
Image courtesy of Justin Firuz Dowhower, LEED AP.

This annual analysis is impossible to determine from a single solar animation, and is prohibitively tedious to determine from a series of animations.

While some applications automate placing such a 3D sun-path, "virtual heliodon," model around the BIM model, it may be useful for the user to construct an annual sunfield. After generating the appropriate sun chart for the building's latitude from the University of Oregon site, the BIM user places a hemisphere over the building model. The dome should be of a sufficient size to completely enclose the model and allow for extra room. The exact size is secondary since the same sun paths on two or more concentric domes will appear collinear from the point of view of the center of the dome. However, a sufficiently large dome will serve multiple points in a building without having to be relocated.

Next, construct three parallel oblique planes inclined towards the equator (e.g., a plane for the northern hemisphere would be inclined toward the south). The angle of elevation above the horizon should be equal to 90° minus the site's latitude; put another way, the plane's angle from vertical is equal to the site's latitude. One plane should intersect the base of the hemisphere exactly on the east-west line; the intersection of this plane and the hemisphere represents the sun's path on both the spring and autumn equinoxes. For the sun's path on the winter solstice, the lowest path of the year, the second of the parallel planes should be placed north of the equinox plane. In plan, the line of this plane should intersect the base circle of the hemisphere at the sunrise and sunset points of the winter solstice. It may be useful to overlay the sun chart, resized so that its perimeter circle is the same size as the base of the hemisphere, as a guide to locate the base of the winter solstice plane. As with the equinox, the curved line on the surface of the hemisphere resulting from the intersection of the dome and the winter solstice plane represents the sun's path on the winter solstice. Repeat the procedure for the summer solstice, placing its corresponding plane south of the equinox such that both the summer and winter solstice planes are equidistant from the equinox plane. Once again, the intersection of this plane and the hemisphere represents the sun's path on the summer solstice. Figure 5.10 illustrates the three sun paths resulting by the intersection of these three planes and the hemisphere.

If desired, the surfaces of the hemisphere outside the boundary of the solstice planes may be clipped away, leaving a curved band representing all the possible sun positions throughout the year for the given latitude. From any vantage point in the BIM model (such as the middle of a room looking out a window) the *visible area* of the hemisphere bounded by the solstice paths represents the *total time* throughout the year that the sun is directly visible from the point of interest.

Solar animations and models

Since buildings are used year-round, a rendering of shading conditions at a single moment in time is of limited usefulness. Solar animations are intended to overcome that limitation, and broadly include representational tools that depict the sun's movement over time—or more accurately the movement of shadows cast by the sun—whether over the span of a day, a season, or a year.

Interactive animations

Models in which the viewer operates a slider or some other gestural metaphor to "move" the sun, thereby interactively adjusting sun shadows, are possibly the most satisfying but the least *quantitatively* useful form of sun study. An excellent (near-BIM) example of this is SketchUp's Shadow Settings floating palette, which allows the user to manipulate two sliders (one for time of day and the other for time of year; Fig. 5.11). While this type of tool is helpful in gaining an intuitive grasp of the sun's effect on a building, and is potentially useful in designing shading devices, a serious drawback is the lack of quantitative data. One cannot, for example, readily and quantifiably compare two different shading devices, except by inspection.

Seasonal animations

Of somewhat greater usefulness are true solar animations such as those saved as Apple QuickTime or Windows Media Player files. Typically these are for a single day of the year, taken from a fixed vantage point (the building is static; the only thing that is animated in the scene are shadows cast by the sun). These movies are particularly helpful if they include a time counter, so that the user can stop the animation at any given moment and note the time, or observe at which time of day a particular shading condition begins and ends (Fig. 5.12).

In preparing these, it is most useful to capture several vantages of the building. However, the particular building design will determine which views should be taken:

- Oblique views from a building corner are typically effective for capturing two elevations simultaneously, provided they do not over-foreshorten the visible elevations such that windows and shading devices are obscured.
- Do not neglect the north elevation on the false assumption that north elevations do not get direct sun. A quick glance at a sun-path chart will immediately reveal that in the summer, north façades get direct sun early in the morning and late in the afternoon. How much sun hits these areas is dependent on latitude (the closer to the equator, the more north sun in summer).

A few rendering pointers may help make the solar animation faster to generate while remaining effective:

- Solar animations need not be lengthy to be valuable. Movies as short as five to seven seconds can be quite effective; very long movies can be a bit tedious to sit through with little practical advantage.

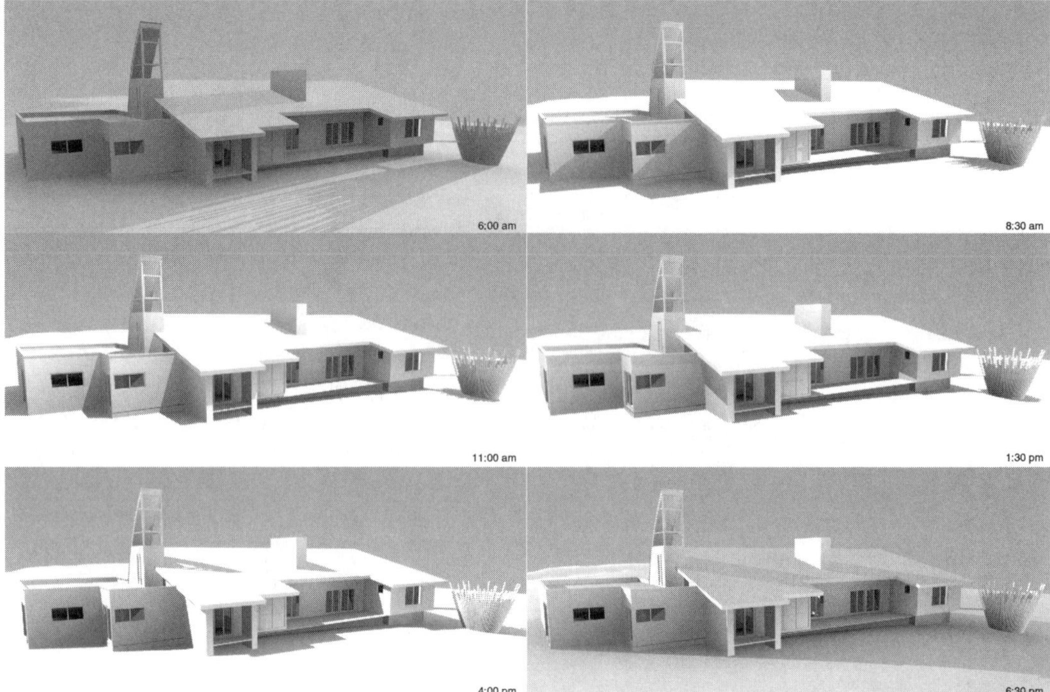

FIGURE 5.12 Solar animations are by nature problematic to represent on a page; here a series of six stills begin to suggest the tool's usefulness in evaluating building orientation, glazing sizing and location, and shading device design.

- Unless a high-quality presentation is desired, the model should be kept simple to minimize rendering times. Textures and even colors can usually be ignored; even the digital equivalent of a foam-core model can be a useful design tool (Fig. 5.13).
- Animations need not be high-resolution to be constructive. Remember that doubling a rendering's image area quadruples the number of pixels, commensurate with a lengthening of rendering times. An animation is simply a series of static renderings sequenced together, frame after frame. A 1000-pixel-wide animation is nice, but even movies half that width can be quite instructive.

A good rule of thumb is to make solar animations that are intended as *design studies* into small enough files such that they are suitable for Web viewing. Of course, presentation movies can be much higher quality, if the user is prepared to wait for the renderings.

Daylighting

According to recent US Department of Energy figures, about 15.4 percent of US electricity is consumed in lighting residential, commercial, and industrial buildings. When one considers that even a relatively efficient fluorescent lamp converts about only 22 percent of the energy it consumes into light and 78 percent of the energy becomes waste heat, it's evident that much of the electricity consumed by lighting is wasted inefficiently (Fig. 5.14). This in turn increases building cooling loads, with a corresponding increase in cooling, ventilation, and operating costs. Cooling equipment must be upsized in order to handle the lighting load, and this equipment costs more to run.

Moreover, diffuse natural light is the most efficient known source of lighting buildings, with a luminous efficacy of 130 to 160 lumens produced per Watt (lm/W) of heat. Compare those figures to fluorescent lamps with an efficacy of around 100 lm/W. Diffuse sky-light outperforms all other

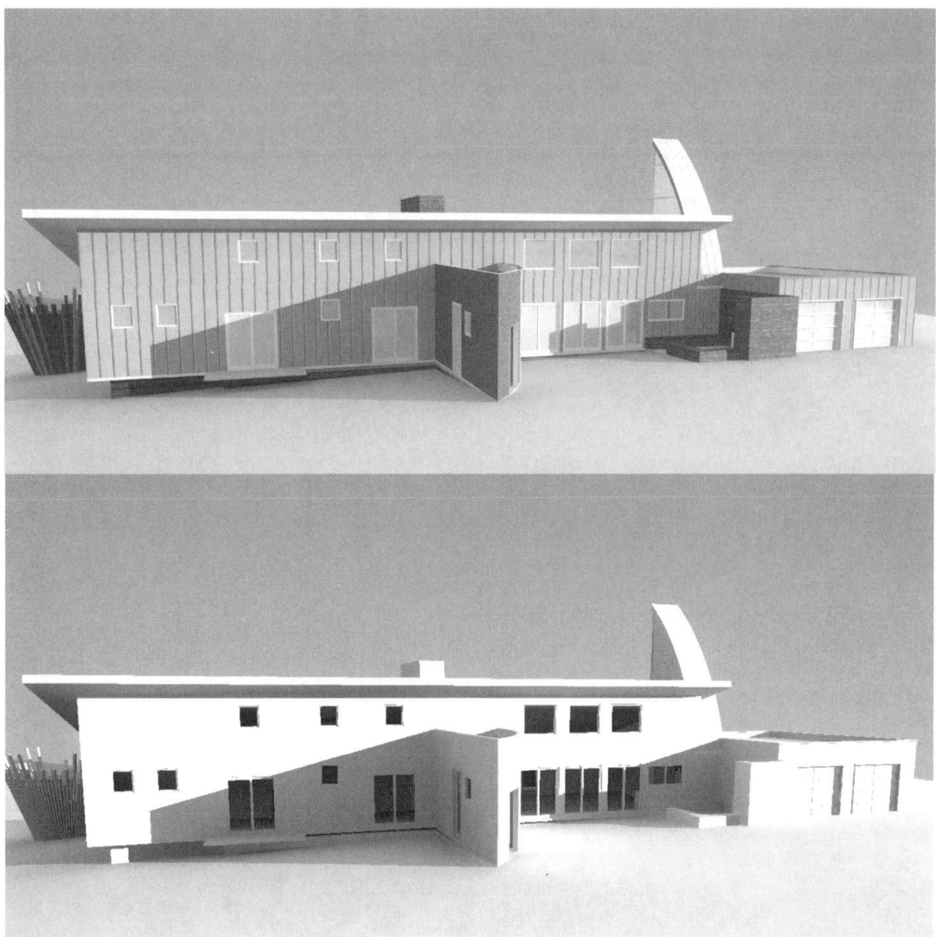

FIGURE 5.13 Models need not be colorful or highly rendered to serve as useful subjects of sun studies. These two views are of the exact same BIM model; the lower view has simply had all color and texture turned off (incidentally, with faster rendering times). This technique may even make the sun-study model more legible. Further, this image suggests that sun studies can be usefully applied to early models—perhaps even before materials have been selected.

light sources—even high pressure sodium lamps (Fig. 5.15). As a result, proper daylighting not only reduces or eliminates daytime operation of electrical lighting, but it reduces the need to cool those lights.

However, it is not sufficient to simply add a lot of glass to a building and declare it "daylit." Correct daylighting requires the right amount of light and the right kind (diffuse). Overlighting a space even with daylight can create unnecessary cooling loads, and an over-bright space creates glare problems for its occupants. My architectural lighting students spend a great deal of effort carefully analyzing their designs for correct daylighting, using light meters in physical models as well as analytical software. There are several analysis approaches that the BIM practitioner can undertake to ensure more successfully daylit projects, whether or not more detailed analysis is undertaken later with Ecotect, Daysim, or Green Building Studio.

Window-height to room-depth ratio

A common, and very simple, rule of thumb for determining the area of adequate daylighting for a

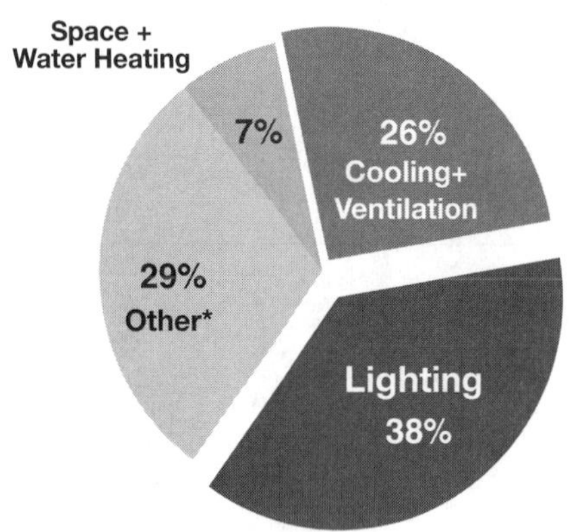

FIGURE 5.14 Commercial buildings' greatest electrical use is for lighting—38 percent of all electricity used is for illumination. In 2003, commercial buildings in the Unites States consumed 1,340 trillion Btu's of electricity. This does not account for the increased cooling load that lighting generates. Consider that fluorescent lamps (which have a far greater luminous efficacy than incandescent lamps) produce about 78 percent waste heat for 22 percent light.

Data source: US Department of Energy, Annual Energy Review 2009, Report No. DOE/EIA-0384 (2009).

window of a given geometry is the 2.5H rule. That is, a space will be adequately daylit for a depth equal to 2.5 times the window head height above the floor (Fig. 5.16). This rule of thumb presupposes a host of assumptions:

- glazing is clear, not translucent, and is relatively clean;
- sky conditions are overcast (this is actually an assumption made in a variety of daylighting design guides, for reasons discussed further on);
- there are no major obstructions outside the window(s) in question;
- the window sill is at or below *task* or *work plane*—the plane where the illuminated task is set to take place. In many cases, the task plane is 30" above finish floor (AFF), at desk height;
- windows are assumed to account for approximately half the length (not the area) of the fenestration wall.

Light Source	Lamp Life	Luminous Efficacy
Incandescent	750	15
Halogen	4,000	16
Mercury	24,000+	45
Fluorescent/Compact	10,000	70
Induction Lamp	100,000	76
Fluorescent/T8	20,000	89
Metal Halide	20,000	90
Fluorescent/T5	16,000	93
LED	50,000	100
Direct Sun	—	100
High Pressure Sodium	24,000	104
Global Sunlight (Sun + Sky)	—	119
Low Pressure Sodium	16,000	140
Sky	—	153

FIGURE 5.15 Luminous efficacy is the ratio of a light source's lumen output to the watts of power required. The higher the value, the less heat produced by the light source for the same illuminance. Even with the advent of LEDs and advances in fluorescent lamps, diffuse light from the sky is the most efficacious light source readily available.

Data courtesy of Charles K. Thompson, AIA, IALD, LC, IESNA, Archillume Lighting Design, Inc.

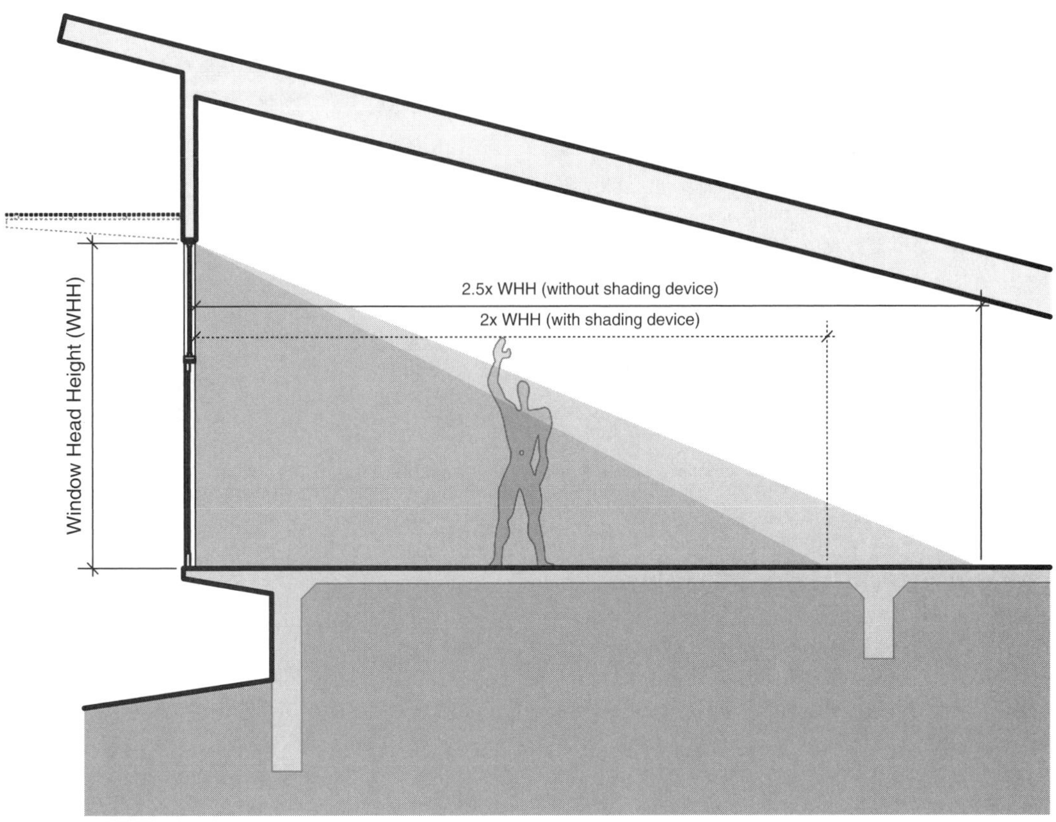

FIGURE 5.16 This diagram illustrates the well-known 2H and 2.5H guides for daylight penetration into spaces. Note that H refers to window head height—not glazing height—assuming the sill is at or below the task plane (usually 30" AFF).

Window head heights in the BIM model can be checked against room width to verify compliance with the 2.5H rule; a simple way to achieve this is to prepare a schedule or worksheet that returns an error statement (perhaps "*WINDOW TOO LOW*" or "*ROOM TOO DEEP*") with the window head height is less than 2.5 times the room width. A Space object, or even a simple polygon representing the floor area, can provide the room's characteristic width (obviously, the dimension perpendicular to the plane of the window wall). In cases where windows have shading devices, then it is commonly accepted that the 2.5H rule should be adjusted to 2H.

Estimating average Daylight Factor

Daylight factor (DF) is a simple measure in use for decades to predict or assess whether a point in a given architectural space will receive adequate daylighting for an occupant to comfortably perform tasks. It is the ratio of outdoor diffuse horizontal illuminance on a cloudy day to indoor illuminance at a given point:

$$DF = E_{point}/E_{outdoor\ horizontal}$$ [Equation 5.1; Grondzik et al. 2010, 598]

Where *DF* is usually expressed as a percentage, and *E* is illuminance (in lux or footcandles). The Illumination Engineering Society (IES; formerly the IESNA) recommends daylight factors from 0.5 percent to 6 percent, depending on the type of space; *Mechanical and Electrical Equipment for Buildings* (MEEB; Grondzik et al. 2010), on the other hand, reports Millet and Bedrick's values ranging from 1.5 percent to 8.0 percent, depending on task and general latitude (Fig. 5.17).

Task	DF, southern	DF, northern
Ordinary seeing tasks *Reading, filing, easy office work*	1.5%	2.5%
Moderately difficult tasks *Prolonged reading, stenographic work, normal machine tool work*	2.5%	4.0%
Difficult, prolonged tasks *Drafting, proofreading poor copy, fine machine work, fine inspection*	4.0%	8.0%

FIGURE 5.17 A synopsis of suggested Daylight Factor values reported in MEEB.

DF as a design guide has two major drawbacks. It assumes overcast skies, which tends to underestimate illuminance in predominately clear-sky climates. This is partially taken into account in Millet and Bedrick's recommendations, which distinguish southern latitudes with ample wintertime daylight. Secondly, daylight factor by itself does not directly indicate whether there is actually enough illuminance (in lux or footcandles) at a point to adequately perform a task, as it is entirely dependent on outdoor illuminance, which is obviously highly variable from hour to hour.

Nevertheless, DF is a very useful design tool, as it *generally* informs the architect whether a space has adequate daylight. For precise calculations of interior illuminance levels, far more sophisticated methods must be employed, and there is a role for BIM to play in those as well. In preliminary design, however, there are some relatively simple calculations that can be built into the BIM model to inform the design and help optimize daylighting.

In 1979, Lynes gave the average DF for a rectangular space illuminated by windows (that is, sidelit, as opposed to top- or skylit):

$$DF = \frac{A_{glazing}\tau_{vis}\theta}{2A_{total}(1-\rho_{mean})}$$

[Equation 5.2; Reinhart & LoVerso 2010]

Where $A_{glazing}$ is the net glass area; τ_{vis} is the visual glazing transmittance (sometimes expressed as VT); θ is the sky angle (the angle between the vertical and a line from the center of the window to the top of an outside obstruction; for an unobstructed view $\theta = 90°$); A_{total} is the total interior room surface area, including glazing; ρ_{mean} is the mean reflectance (from above 0 to 1.0) of all the surfaces in the space, area-weighted by material.

Of these variables, the BIM model can easily report the two area values. The value τ_{vis} is known from the BIM window properties, or can be assigned from manufacturer-provided data. The value ρ_{mean} would be a bit tedious to calculate manually, but here again BIM can help. The user should assign a reflectance value to all surfaces in the space, and from that, ρ_{mean} can be calculated in a BIM worksheet for each surface of area A, reflectance ρ, and the total area A_{total}:

$$\rho_{mean} = (A_1\rho_1 + A_2\rho_2 + A_3\rho_3 + \cdots + A_n\rho_n)/A_{total}$$

[Equation 5.3]

This leaves only the variable sky angle, θ, which is the value that is most problematic to automatically get from the BIM model. However, if obstructions are modeled as recommended in "Adjacent structures and vegetation," then a section can be easily derived from the BIM model to accurately, albeit manually, determine θ.

For an interesting yet somewhat technical discussion of Lynes's formula and the role of daylighting rules of thumb in design, the reader is directed to Reinhart and LoVerso (2010). As Reinhart and

LoVerso demonstrate, Lynes' formula and subsequent variations are remarkably accurate at predicting average daylight factor, as determined by comparisons to Radiance simulations.

A word of caution: some sources suggest that there is no upper limit to the amount of allowable winter daylight, provided that glare is controlled. This ignores the fact that it is possible to passively overheat a space in winter, as demonstrated in the following two scenarios:

- The building is internal-load dominated. In this case, internal cooling loads like occupants, artificial lighting, and equipment are significant enough to overwhelm envelope heat loss and the building requires winter *cooling*.
- Even in a small, normally external-load dominated building, the envelope is sufficiently well insulated that heat loss is minimal; significant additional solar heat gain can tip heat transfer balance to overheat the space.

It is therefore suggested that the designer observe the maximum and minimum south-facing glass ratios recommended in Chapter 7 and implement those in the BIM model.

Light shelves

Lynes' equation fairly accurately predicts average DF in a space; certainly the results are acceptable as a design guideline. But note that it calculates the *average* daylight factor; it does not, for example, indicate what the DF will be for a specific point of interest in the space. Furthermore, it is clear from experience that most spaces have an abundance of daylight at or very near the glazing wall, but that as distance increases the illuminance sharply drops off. This is illustrated by the 15/30 daylighting rule of thumb: a sidelit space whose wall *length* is roughly 50 percent window will have adequate daylighting in the first 15 feet from the glazing wall, it will require some supplemental electric lighting up to 30 feet from the windows, and it will be wholly dependent on artificial lighting thereafter. This phenomenon also explains the ideally narrow north-south massing of sustainable, envelope-dominated buildings.

One can easily imagine a Lynes' equation analysis of a space that would indicate a wholly satisfactory average DF, but this could be the result of very high DFs near the fenestration wall(s) and inadequate DFs deeper in the room. *Light shelves* are exterior and/or interior horizontal projections, placed just above eye level with glazing above and below, whose essential function is to redistribute the DF gradient. That is, they introduce more shade at the window wall, decreasing DF there, but thanks to their high diffuse reflectance, they project more light deeper into the room. Of course, because they never have perfect diffuse reflectance ($\rho < 1.0$), there is some net overall loss of average DF. Nevertheless, light shelves help redistribute overabundance of light at the window wall to deeper and darker recesses of room (Fig. 5.18).

Of little or no benefit on north-facing façades, light shelves are most effective at south-facing windows. Their usefulness is rather limited on east- and west-facing building sides unless they are significantly wider than the windows they shade.

Unfortunately, there are no light-shelf-sizing rules of thumb that can be quickly applied to a BIM model. On the other hand, properly placing and sizing them can best be achieved through modeling and lighting analysis, and as we've seen, BIM is an excellent starting point for modeling the geometry on which those analyses are based; the same techniques described above for iterating and refining sun shading devices are wholly applicable to light shelves. Indeed, for the lower glazing, an external light shelf is essentially just a shading device.

For a comprehensive discussion of light shelves and daylighting, the reader is directed to Lechner (2009) and the International Energy Agency's source book (2000),[4] respectively.

Ray-traced renderings

By the 1980s, researchers like Greg Ward (primary developer of Radiance, an industry-standard free

[4] The International Energy Agency's source book can be accessed at http://btech.lbl.gov/pub/iea21.

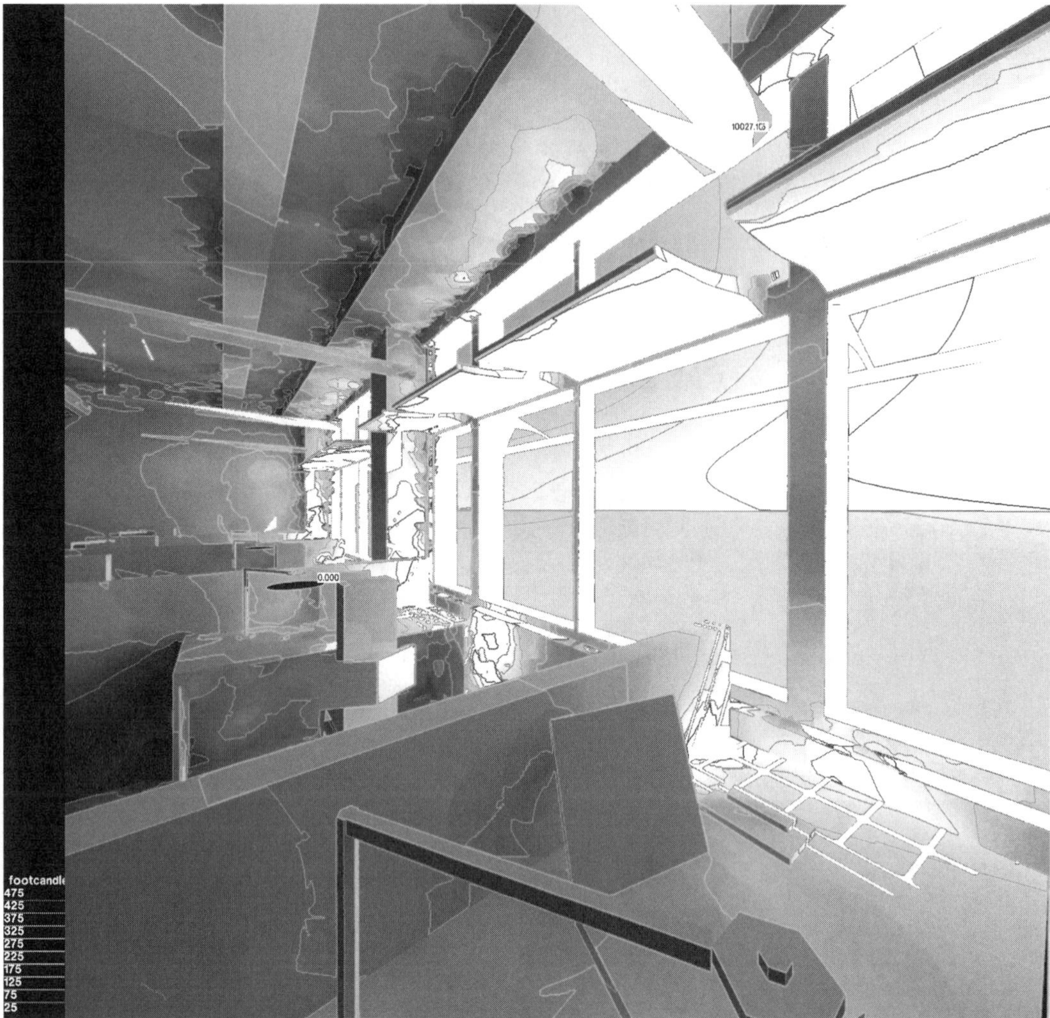

FIGURE 5.18 Performed in Radiance, this isolux contour analysis of a space with internal light shelves demonstrates the benefit of reflective shading devices. The areas below and near the light shelf are somewhat more shaded than they would be otherwise, while the reflective top of the shelf projects more natural daylight onto the ceiling and deeper into the room.

Simulation by Adam Pyrek.

application) were writing computer programs to accurately predict illumination levels within architectural spaces based on a modeling technique called backwards ray tracing. Their algorithms traced reflected, direct light paths *back* from their termination points to a virtual observer's eye, rather than tracing the rays *forward,* from the source. The significant advantage of the former method over the latter "naïve ray tracing" is that only the light rays that mattered (those observed from a given point in space) were calculated, which is computationally a much more tractable problem.

Since that time, specialized Unix software available only to researchers or lighting consultants has given way to powerful applications that can run on desktop and notebook computers (Fig. 5.19). Modern rendering applications (including those included as modules of BIM software) are now capable of

FIGURE 5.19 This diffuse (north light) daylighting study in BIM is an example of a useful qualitative daylighting study. The improved rendering engines incorporated in today's BIM authoring software with the goal of producing more compelling presentations can also be effective lighting analysis tools—to a point. Unlike dedicated lighting analysis software like Radiance, these renderings do not provide illuminance values. Also, the user is able to "fudge" the lighting by changing light characteristics away from physics-based values. This might make renderings seem more lifelike, but that verisimilitude is at the cost of accuracy.

Ashe Laughlin Studio by Agruppo.

rendering photo-realistic scenes that are uncanny in their verisimilitude. However, as any experienced renderer knows, in most applications it is very difficult to achieve realistic scenes by rigorously including every light source and correct material reflectance. Often, the user must employ tricks or "cheats" like fill lights, hidden light sources, or atmospheric effects to create a scene that *looks* realistic.

This is fine (and in many cases preferable, as it's simpler) if a rendering is desired. But this method is useless as a study, as it can only produce lighting results that meet the user's expectations. For an analysis that accurately predicts lighting conditions for the purpose of making informed design decisions, a rigorous method like that offered by Radiance or similar physics-based programs is required (Fig. 5.20). The latter may also produce an attractive rendering, depending on the visualization type selected. Some images produced may look photorealistic, others may have illuminance (lux) contours superimposed, or they may be false-color renderings with a yellow-to-blue color scale that indicate quantifiable lighting levels on surfaces. Since Radiance has become an open-source program, applications like Ecotect have included modules that optionally make use of the underlying Radiance code for analysis.

In recent years, rendering applications (as distinct from lighting analysis software) have incorporated rendering engines based on real physics; Maxwell Render is just such a program. These programs are bridging the gap between pure analytical lighting programs and purely visual renderers. Maxwell, the freeware Kerkythea, and other physics-based renderers may be used analytically, but the user must be disciplined and not "fudge" light source and atmospheric settings, nor elect to include hidden sources. If electric lighting is also to be analyzed, actual luminaire IES files must be assigned to artificial light sources to insure accurate results (Fig. 5.21). These files describe the exact photometric characteristics of a light fixture and its associated lamp and are usually available from manufacturers (Fig. 5.22).

Both Maxwell Studio and Kerkythia support 3DS and OBJ file formats; Maxwell Studio also supports DXF file imports. Maxwell Render (the rendering engine of the software) includes plug-ins that integrate the renderer directly with several 3D CAD or BIM applications, including ArchiCAD. Revit and Vectorworks users must export their models to 3DS or DXF formats to Maxwell Studio, and then render with Maxwell Render. Another renderer, Cinema4D, is the new rendering engine for Vectorworks Renderworks (Fig. 5.23), and Vectorworks also directly exports BIM models to Cinema4D as a result.

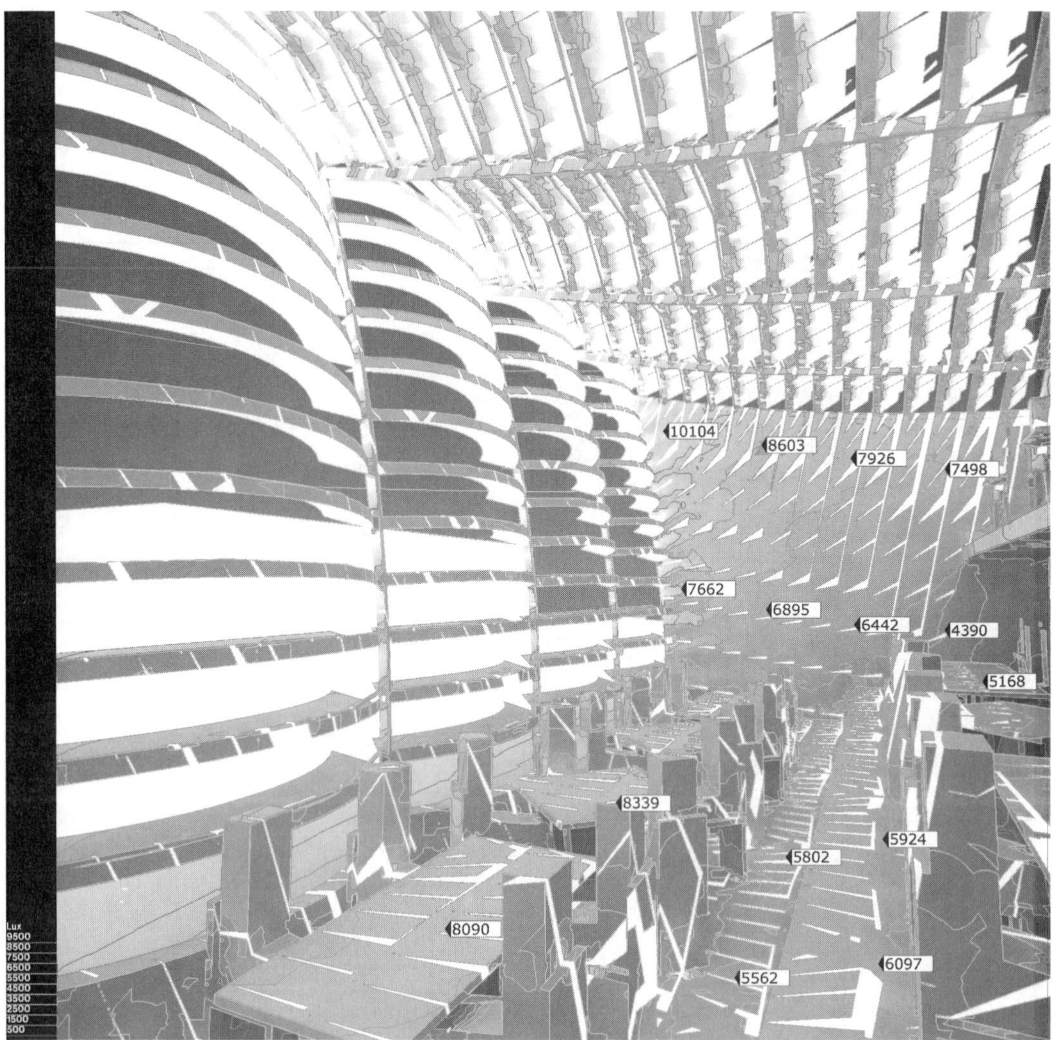

FIGURE 5.20 This is a forced-color illuminance analysis produced in Radiance. The forced colors are not obvious in this black-and-white reproduction, but note the illuminance (lux) values indicated throughout the space. Such an analysis in Radiance does far more than give an impression of the space—it accurately predicts illuminance to help the designer refine the project to meet required lighting goals while not overlighting the space.

Simulation by Adam Pyrek.

BIM daylighting workflow summary

For BIM, a productive workflow could be summarized as follows:

1. Apply the design guidelines and rules of thumb outlined above to develop and refine early proportion, massing, and glazing design decisions. Note that many of these guides do not deeply consider material reflectance; this is not a great problem as defining material reflectance is likely premature at this stage.
2. Iterate the design several times entirely within BIM using these design guides to best optimize daylighting.

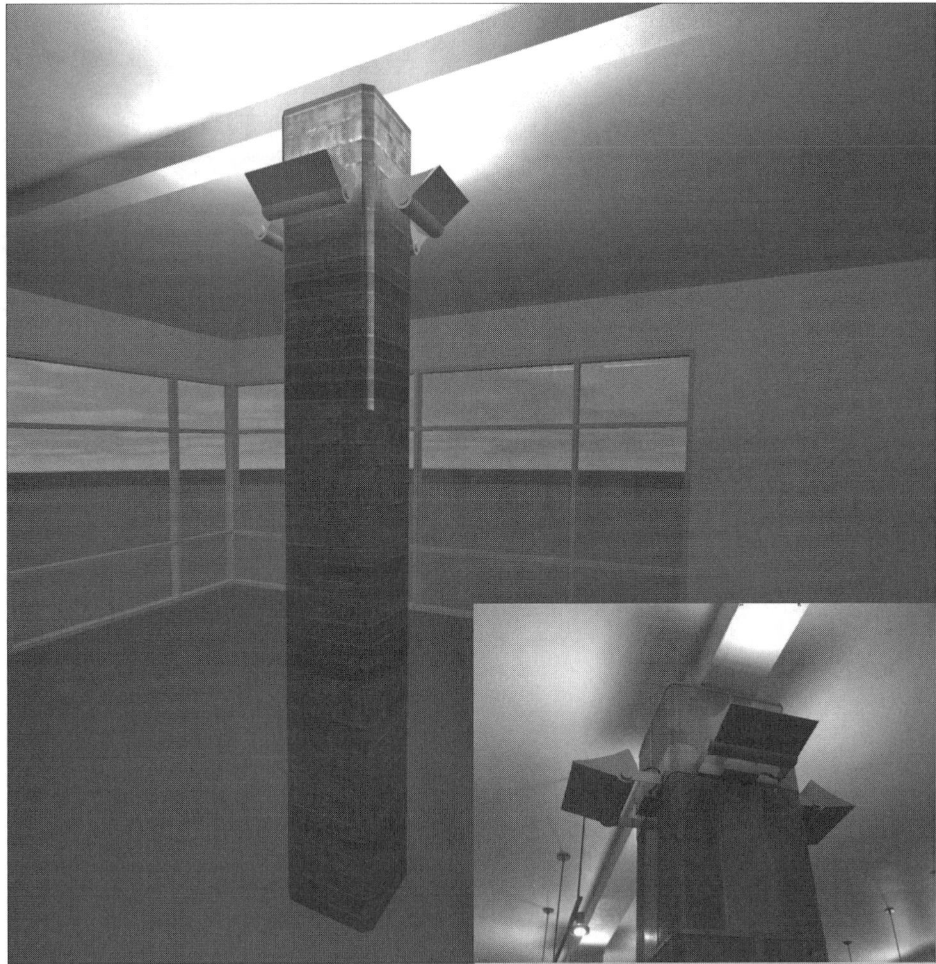

FIGURE 5.21 A BIM rendering (produced in Vectorworks with Renderworks) of a space using IES photometric data for the asymmetrical luminaires employed; the inset is a photograph of a similar real-world condition.

3. Once the design seems to best satisfy daylighting guidelines as well as other programmatic and architectural considerations, export the model and run a daylighting analysis, using Ecotect, Green Building Studio, or a similar program's default algorithms.
4. Refine the design accordingly, executing design changes within BIM. Iterate this step as required.
5. Optionally perform further analysis, still within Ecotect, but using the Radiance or Daysim engines, for more accurate but lengthier results.
6. Again, refine and iterate step 5 as required.
7. If desired, export and perform an accurate-physics rendering of the model.

A word of caution: even if the BIM model is rendered with accurate physics-based algorithms (Fig. 5.24), renderers will not provide the kind of illuminance analysis (such as isolux contours) that Radiance would afford.

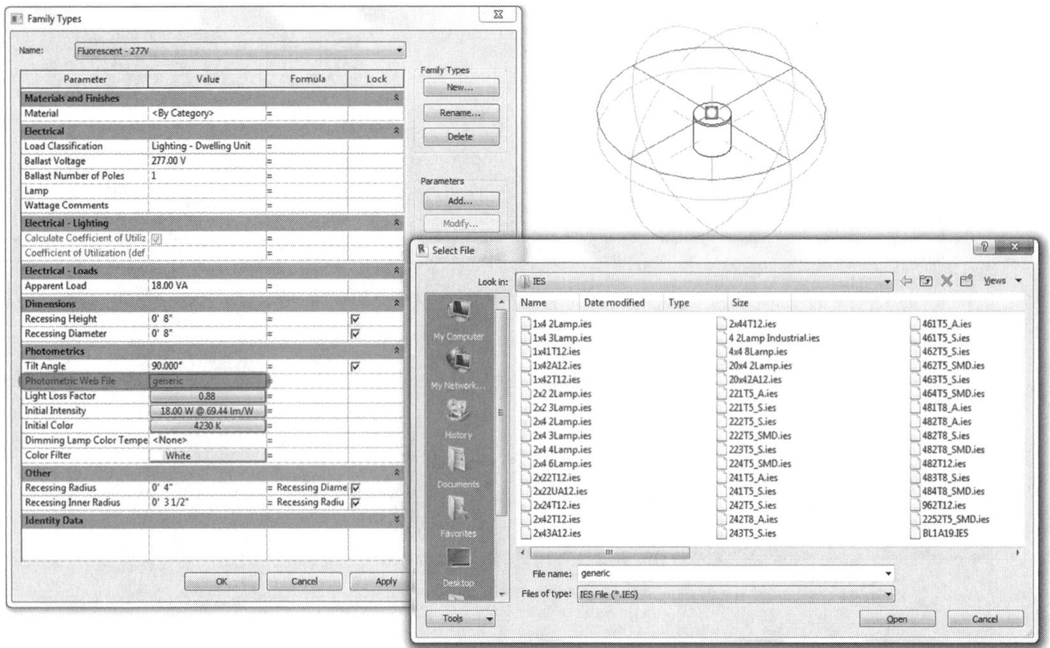

FIGURE 5.22 Photometric data for a Revit light; note the ability to import manufacturers' IES-formatted photometric data for greater lighting simulation accuracy.

Image courtesy of Justin Firuz Dowhower.

FIGURE 5.23 This photorealistic rendering of a residential interior space was done entirely within Vectorworks Architect (with the Renderworks module), without any post-processing by other rendering applications or Photoshop. As with any photorealistic rendering, results are largely dependent on user skill and patience.

Image courtesy of Daniel Jansenson, Architect.

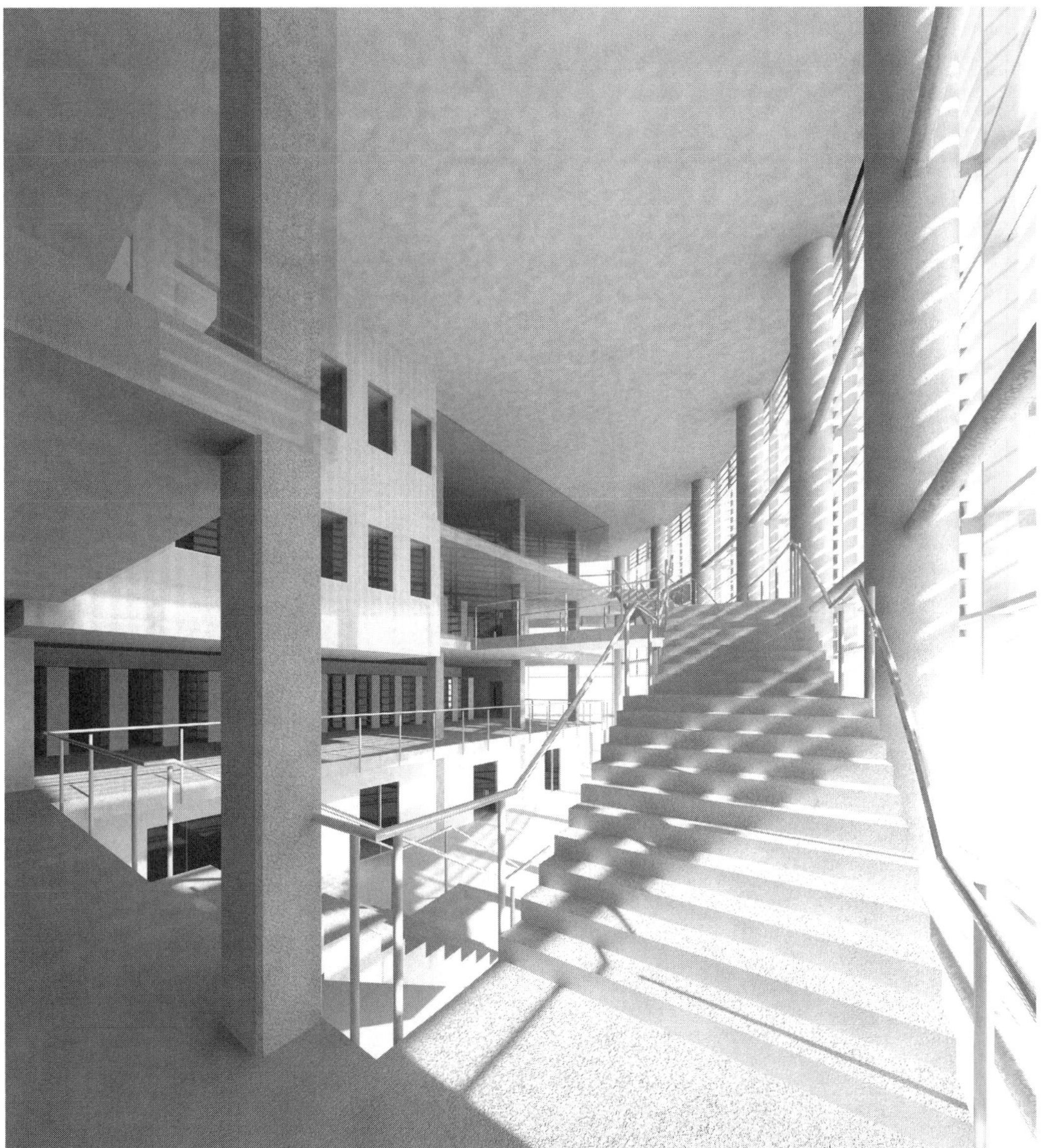

FIGURE 5.24 Another BIM photorealistic rendering, this one of a Revit model of the proposed Library Building at Durham University.

Image courtesy of _space architecture, UK.

■ Case Study: Ross Street House, Madison, Wisconsin

By Carol Richard
Design firm: Richard Wittschiebe Hand
Client: Carol Richard and Fred Berg

The goal of the owners was to design and build a modern, affordable, and sustainable single-family home that would last the couple throughout their retirement years (Fig. 5.25). The owners, an architect and her husband, an engineer, undertook an integrated design approach toward the project. This allowed them to work on the project together, which was another key project goal.

FIGURE 5.25 The Ross Street House is a LEED for Homes Platinum project designed from its inception with BIM, whose form is dominantly given by passive solar concerns.

Photo courtesy of Carol Richard, Richard Wittschiebe Hand.

The 50'-wide by 130'-deep city lot faces due south and falls off gradually to the rear. It is located on the near-west side of Madison in a modest neighborhood. The undeveloped, infill site was chosen because of its proximity to essential services, parks, and bike paths, and because it is only one mile from the University of Wisconsin.

The concept of the design is that of a carefully controlled light box, and BIM (ArchiCAD) was extensively used in developing the home from its inception. Several sun studies informed the development of the brise-soleil on the southern elevation of the home, and guided the form of the building (Fig. 5.26). The louvers are designed to allow the sun to penetrate deep into the space between October and February while shading the windows from May to August. In addition, ArchiCAD was useful in determining the location of the photovoltaic (PV) panels located on the detached garage; the home was modeled at various times throughout the year to minimize the amount of time the panels would be shaded.

FIGURE 5.26 ArchiCAD was used throughout the design process, from developing massing models of adjacent homes in evaluating the project's impact on nearby structures, to optimizing the spacing and dimensions of the southerly brise-soleil to maximize direct solar gain in winter (solstice, above) and deny heat gain in summer (below).

Renderings courtesy of Carol Richard, Richard Wittschiebe Hand.

(*Continued*)

A large bank of windows faces due south. Light is controlled through a fixed exterior brise-soleil, designed to be indexed to the site latitude (Fig. 5.27). At the summer solstice, no direct sunlight penetrates the space. At noon on the winter solstice, sunlight penetrates through to the rear of the open floor plan. There is limited exposure to the west and east; however, three round windows facing west are located in the open stairwell. These "portholes" activate the space. Carefully placed ribbon windows to the east provide the dining area and main bedroom with morning light.

The building form is simple—the two-story open plan "light box" volume contains the primary living spaces (Fig. 5.28), while support spaces are contained in an adjacent one-story volume. The entire house is about 1,700 square feet, excluding the basement (Wisconsin foundations must be deep in order to penetrate the frost line, so a basement is an economical additional space). Provisions for a future elevator in this retirement home allowed placement of the main bedroom on the upper level. The resulting building is scaled to be in harmony with the neighborhood. Materials, such as the 6" tongue-and-groove cedar siding and metal roof, were chosen carefully to be sustainable and durable, but also to blend with the neighboring houses. Adjacent homes along with the designed home were computer-modeled early in the design to ensure contextual compatibility.

FIGURE 5.27 A comprehensive BIM model was developed and maintained throughout the design process. The project team, which consisted of an architect, an engineer, a LEED-certified landscape architect, and, later, a contractor, made continuous use of the model as a tool.

Rendering courtesy of Carol Richard, Richard Wittschiebe Hand.

FIGURE 5.28 In addition to visually expanding the modestly scaled space, light-colored surfaces improve diffuse reflectance of daylight, reducing energy expenditures.

Photo courtesy of Zane Williams.

The project was registered as a LEED for Homes project. Numerous green strategies were employed. The landscape is entirely composed of native perennials and no turf grass. All rainwater falling on the site is either collected in cisterns or directed via bioswales to a rain garden. The photovoltaic panels located on the detached garage generate approximately 58 percent of annual demand, less than the PV Watts prediction of 3045 kWh, by about 16 percent. Collectors are fixed panels and it takes some time for the snow to melt clear of the PV array. The well-insulated, leak-tight house envelope (under 1 ACH) requires an energy-recovery forced ventilation system that works in harmony with a three stage high-efficiency furnace. The Ross Street project received a Home Energy Rating System (HERS) rating of 42, such that projected energy use was to be 42 percent of that of a similarly sized Wisconsin house built in accordance with the 2006 energy code. At the end of the first year, actual usage corresponded to a HERS rating of approximately 23.

The project met the goals of the program with a simple, well-considered and integrated design solution (Fig. 5.29). The result was a comfortable, livable home with the play of sunlight on interior surfaces providing passive heating as well as visual excitement throughout the year. The home achieved LEED for Homes platinum level certification—the first project to do so in the state of Wisconsin.

(*Continued*)

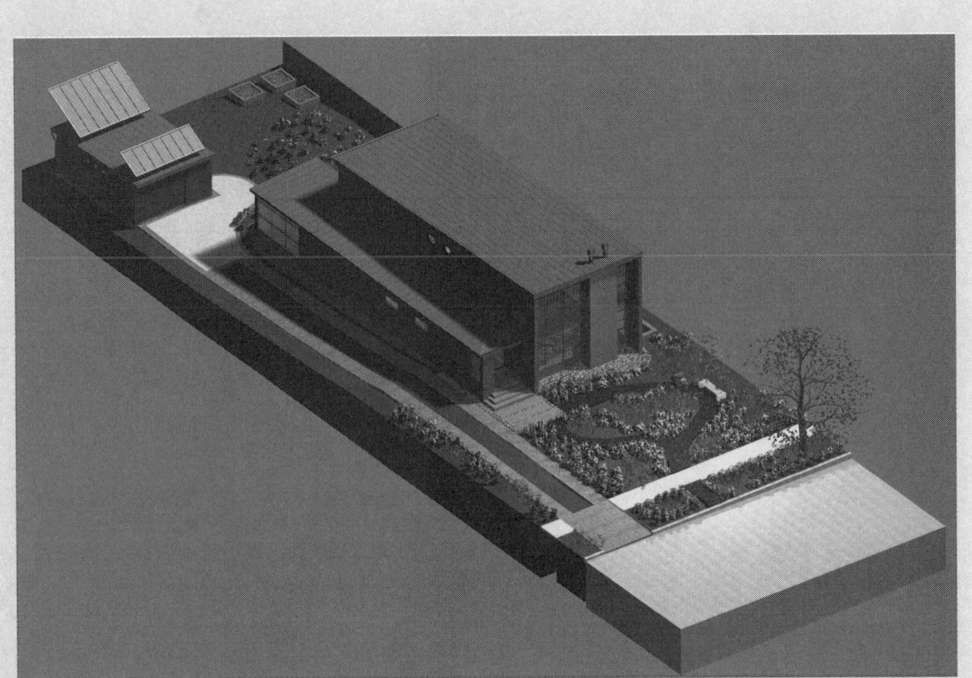

FIGURE 5.29 The solar collector array is located over the detached garage, away from any shading structures. Note the higher array tilt, appropriate to the project's northern latitude.

Rendering courtesy of Carol Richard, Richard Wittschiebe Hand.

Chapter 6

Passive Cooling

As has been suggested in this book—as well as elsewhere at great length—the designer's primary strategy for energy efficiency in sustainable design is a reduction in energy loads (Fig. 6.1). (This is why chapters on solar geometry, daylighting, passive cooling, and passive heating are presented before chapters on energy systems.) There is roughly an order of magnitude greater effectiveness in reducing energy consumption over increasing energy production (which can be done via lower carbon emitting, alternative energy sources). In crude terms, every dollar spent on insulation is worth ten spent on installing solar photovoltaics (PVs). PVs are more visible and therefore may make an

FIGURE 6.1 Jackson Clements Burroughs's Trojan House in Melbourne, Australia makes extensive use of natural ventilation for cooling: from a thermal chimney for interior spaces to a wooden rain screen that ventilates and cools the building envelope.

Photo by Emma Cross.

architectural statement, but there's little that is "green" about a building with an aggressive amount of glass located in a hot climate which offsets its cooling load with a solar array.

Passive thermal controls seek to minimize cooling and heating loads with a minimum of mechanical systems. Moreover, passive cooling and heating are potentially "free," in that much of the relevant strategies can be achieved by appropriate configuration of the building without recourse to expensive or exotic technologies (Fig. 6.2). As a point of departure, consider architectural forms developed before the advent of mechanical and electrical systems. Whether they were vernacular or "high" architecture, pre-mechanical cooling design responses were almost universally climate-appropriate, and may suggest appropriate responses for a given climate and region. For example, in the aftermath of Hurricane Katrina, Alex Wilson and architects Bill Odell and Mary Ann Lazarus of HOK delivered a lecture to the American Institute of Architects (AIA) on Sustainable Design in the Post-Katrina Era suggesting that "passive survivability"—that is, a building's ability to allow its occupants to survive a disaster for a short or long period of time—is a design objective lying on a continuum with sustainable design. Historic, pre-mechanical system buildings are valid and useful examples of passive survivability (Fig. 6.3).

It may also be said that passively achieving thermal comfort in hot climates or during hot seasons seems more challenging than passive heating. In part, this is because a high degree of insulation goes a long way in making cold buildings comfortable, due to efficient capitalization of modest internal or external loads. It is, moreover, quite possible to over-insulate in a hot climate, leading to moisture control problems if the envelope is not carefully designed and constructed. In addition, the simple measures that work for passive heating (for example, insulation, heat sinks) do not address humidity, a key component of thermal discomfort in certain

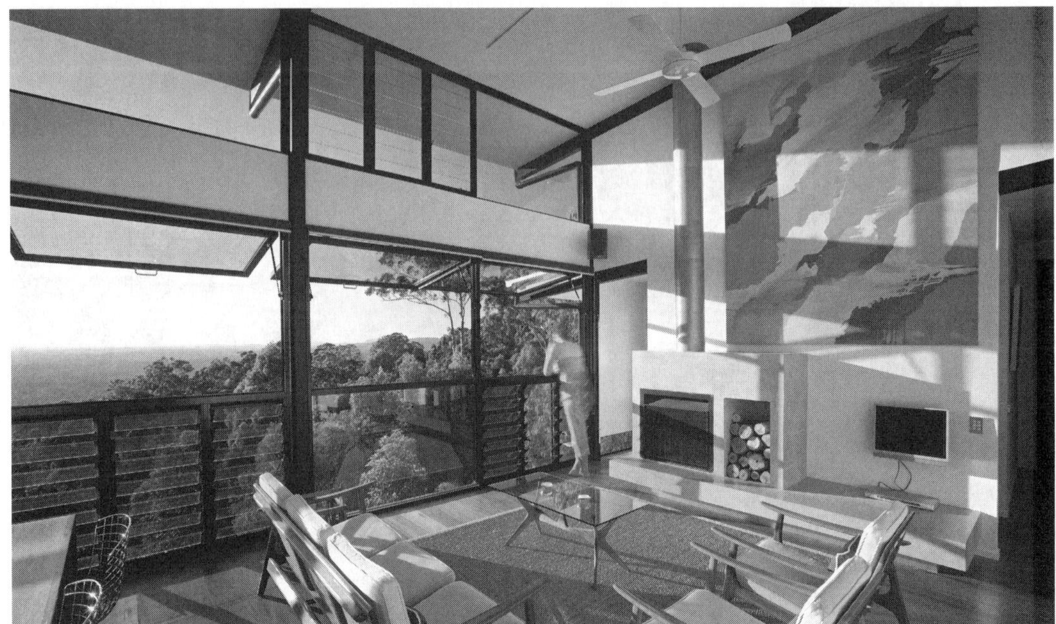

FIGURE 6.2 Not all glass architecture is unsustainable; this project by Bark Design Architects makes appropriate use of operable glass for natural ventilation.

Photo by Bark Design Architects/Christopher Frederick Jones.

FIGURE 6.3 This early twentieth-century train depot from Granger, Texas, is a clear example of the passive survivability of historic structures. Now relocated to the author's home in Austin, the building's tall ceilings, large, symmetrical operable windows, and eight-foot eaves provide passive cooling through stratification, ready access to wind-driven cooling, and excellent shading.

hot climates. And finally, passive cooling seems to lead to more obvious architectural expressions. Shading devices, wind-driven natural ventilation, and the stack effect are among the passive cooling strategies that suggest formal expressions.

Appropriate responses for local climates

Remarkably, too often architects select inappropriate or suboptimal passive cooling design approaches for a given climate or region. Designers may select natural ventilation systems for a hot, dry climate like the American Desert Southwest, or hope to rely upon the thermal mass of its structural system in helping to cool a building in the Gulf Coast region. An understanding of appropriate strategies is therefore critical. This following overview should be helpful, but for discussions with greater depth and detail the reader is referred to analyses by Lechner (2009) and Grondzik, Kwok, Stein, and Reynolds (2010). The former tends to provide a more conceptual presentation of the material, while the latter is generally more technical and serves as an excellent reference.

The psychrometric chart was developed by mechanical engineers to represent the relationship between the temperature, humidity, and density of air under various conditions. In the past, the American Society of Heating, Refrigerating, and Air-Conditioning Engineers (ASHRAE) identified a single comfort zone that detailed temperature and humidity ranges in which most human subjects would be comfortable. Recognizing that people's expectations of comfort and modes of dress vary

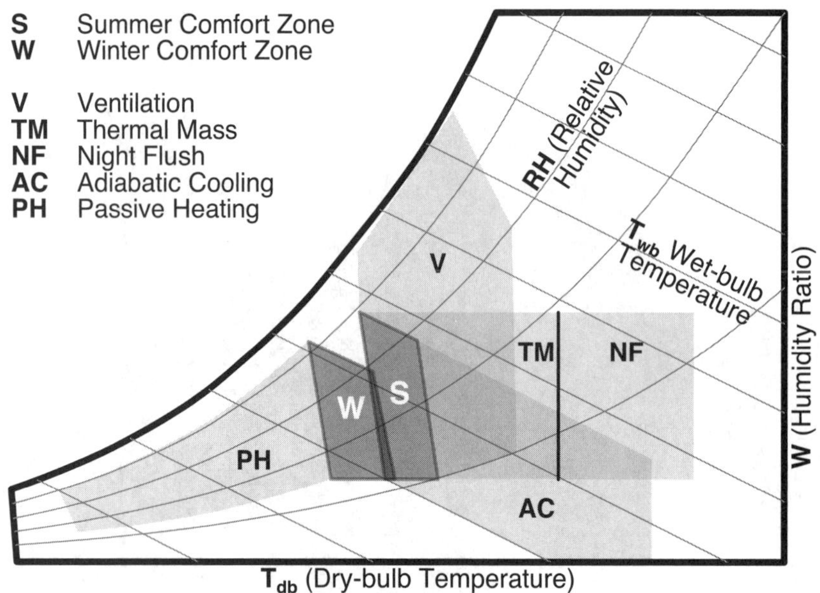

FIGURE 6.4 Here, passive cooling strategies and their abilities to affect the comfort zone under a variety of hot atmospheric conditions are mapped on the psychrometric chart. This is a useful visual tool to aid the designer in selecting appropriate passive cooling approaches for a particular climate.

with season, the single comfort zone has been more recently divided in two: a summer comfort zone and a winter comfort zone. In designing passive cooling systems, the key consideration is that comfort is determined by (dry-bulb) temperature and humidity. For cooling, it's also important to account for the biological mechanisms that our bodies employ: perspiration and evaporation.

The psychrometric-bioclimatic chart (Fig. 6.4) graphs the appropriate responses to various cooling needs based on climate. Of course, not all days in a hot-dry climate will be hot and dry, but passive architectural responses are generally static; dominant conditions drive design responses.

Hot-dry

Under hot-dry conditions, not only are temperatures above the comfort zone, but humidity is as well—whether measured as relative humidity (the percentage of water vapor saturation for a mass of air at a given temperature and pressure) or humidity ratio (the mass of water vapor to mass of dry air). Unlike dry-bulb temperature, wet-bulb temperature (of equal values along the diagonal lines on the chart) accounts for both the energy of an air mass due to its thermal properties and the energy embodied in the water vapor. The result is that wet-bulb temperature is a better measure of human comfort than dry-bulb temperature alone, as it closely approximates enthalpy—a measure of the *total* heat of air, including sensible (temperature) and latent (humidity) heat.

In the psychrometric chart in Figure 6.4, hot and dry air lies down and to the right of the summer comfort zone, roughly along lines of equal enthalpy. That is, the enthalpy in the hot-dry zone is the same as that in the comfort zone. All that is needed is to trade off humidity for sensible heat, and comfort can be achieved with no net addition or removal of energy. This is called an adiabatic process. For hot-dry climates, then, the primary cooling strategy for low-energy comfort is to add moisture to the air, which will absorb the energy of the air, lowering the dry-bulb temperature. The wet-bulb temperature

FIGURE 6.5 A traditional badgir, or wind tower, in the Iranian city of Yazd. These centuries-old structures are marvels of passive cooling architecture, and an outstanding example of passive thermal controls as architectural formgivers.

Image © Mary Loosemore.

will remain fairly constant, but comfort will improve. This is the principal behind lower energy mechanical systems like swamp coolers, and traditional vernacular cooling responses such as courtyards with water elements and the Persian badgir of the ninth century (Fig. 6.5). Natural ventilation alone, however, will not achieve comfort in this climate. Ventilation tends to lower perceived humidity first, and may also bring excessive dust from the hot-dry environment.

How much moisture should be provided? How can the building design help propagate moistened air into spaces? What rate of natural ventilation to circulate wetted air can be achieved? Effective implementation of proven approximations within BIM can help the designer quantify the responses to these questions and influence the design.

Hot-temperate

Buildings with hot summers where the humidity ratio is consistent with that of the summer comfort zone cannot effectively use an adiabatic cooling stratagem. Following lines of constant enthalpy on the chart from hot, moderately moist conditions miss the summer comfort zone. In these conditions, the appropriate, passive approach is to lower sensible heat (dry-bulb temperature), and to maintain humidity. This can be achieved by providing thermal mass (Fig. 6.6). With this strategy, dense materials like stone, concrete, or water serve as "heat batteries," charged by sensible heat during the cooling load cycle (during the day) and depleted during the heating cycle (at night).

Thermal mass is therefore most applicable when days are too warm and nights too cool, serving to even out temperature fluctuations in the 24-hour cycle. If there is so much absorbed heat that it cannot all be released overnight, or would overheat the nocturnal space, then additional ventilation via mechanical or passive "night flushing" may be necessary.

Here again, BIM can help answer quantitative questions early in design. How much thermal mass is appropriate? Can existing structural systems fulfill thermal mass requirements, or should they be augmented? Is night flushing needed, and if so, can it be adequately provided passively, without use of fans?

Hot-humid

If adiabatic cooling is problematic for hot-temperate conditions, it is completely inappropriate for hot-humid climates—a brief inspection of the psychrometric chart above reveals that adiabatic lines from the hot-humid region completely miss the summer comfort zone. Moreover, thermal mass may serve as a "heat battery" for sensible heat, but it does nothing to address the latent heat of these psychrometric conditions. Under the right conditions, thermal mass in this climate may contribute to condensation, or sweating, on the thermal mass surface.

When conditions are both hot and humid, look to the human body's response. In the process of

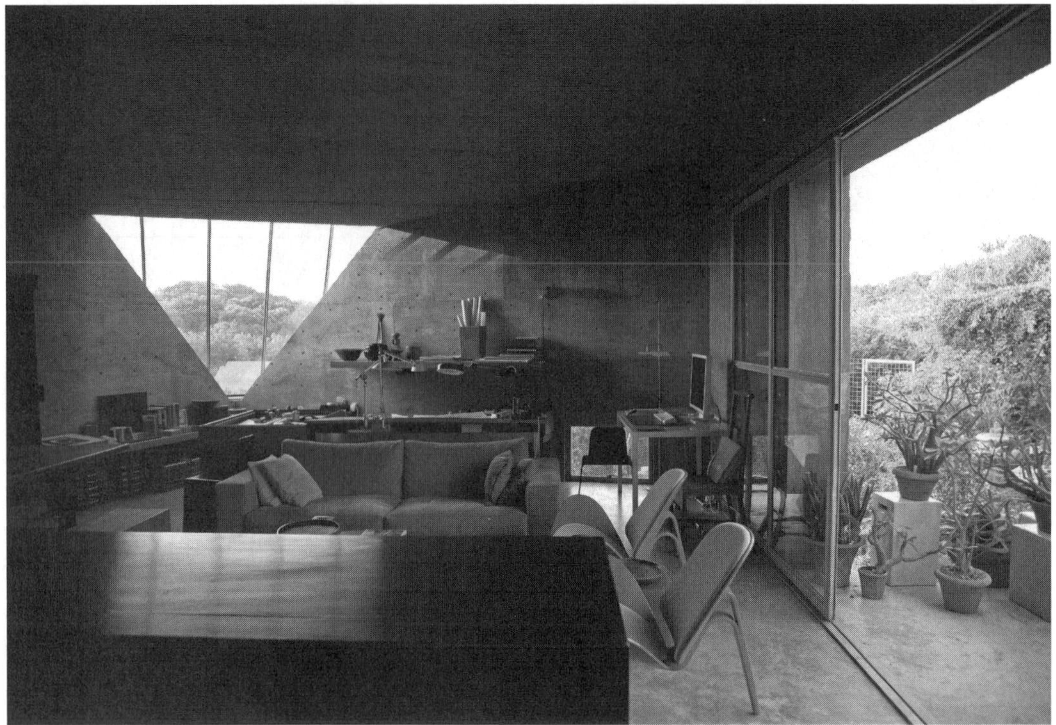

FIGURE 6.6 Architectural concrete is highly durable, offers innumerable plastic possibilities in its formal expression, readily takes imprints from formwork, and serves as ready thermal mass. While a far less effective heat sink—or "heat battery"—than water, it is structurally more useful.

Image courtesy of Mell Lawrence Architects.

evaporating from human skin, perspiration draws energy both from the air and skin, thus cooling our bodies. Benjamin Franklin, in his letter to John Lining dated June 17, 1758, astutely observed this phenomenon:

> May not this be a reason why our reapers in Pensylvania [sic], working in the open field, in the clear hot sunshine . . . find themselves well able to go through that labour, without being much incommoded by the heat, while they continue to sweat, and while . . . drinking frequently . . . but if the sweat stops, they drop, and sometimes die suddenly . . .

When the air is laden with moisture, it will not readily absorb perspiration; in that case the solution is to entrain air over the body to maximize absorption. There are two architectural responses to encourage natural ventilation. Wind-driven ventilation is typically most effective, but it requires, well, wind, which may not always be reliable. Indeed, wind is typically more prevalent at night, when cooling needs are usually lowest, with the exception of night flush cooling. Alternately, the architect may design for stack effect ventilation, relying on warm air's natural buoyancy to ventilate the building. This second option is generally less effective than wind-driven ventilation, but more predictable. Of course, the strategies may (and probably should) be employed together (Fig. 6.7).

Both wind-driven and stack ventilation are in part predicated on environmental conditions: wind speed and direction, and ambient temperature. However, the rate of air movement is also largely

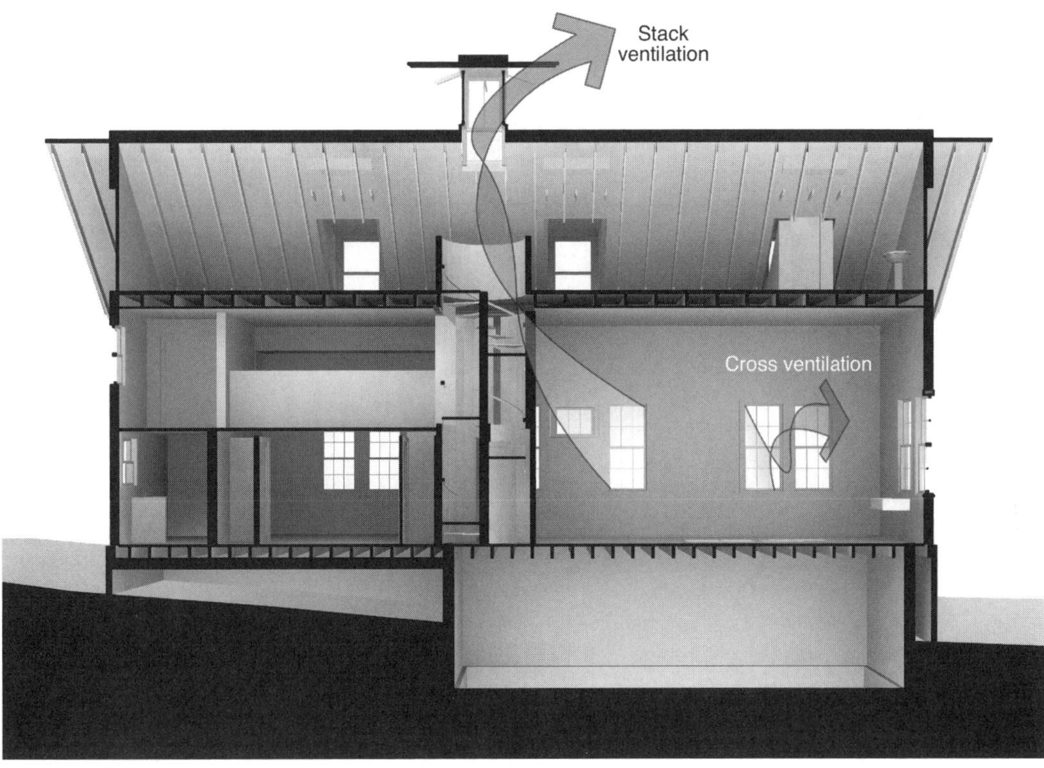

FIGURE 6.7 In this architectural example of wind-driven and stack ventilation, the lantern at top is both a thermal chimney vent and a daylighting device.

influenced by architectural elements, such as the size and placement of openings and the heights of thermal chimneys. In other words, natural ventilation is dependent on building geometry, which can readily be quantified in the BIM model. A BIM workflow can quantify the relative impact of design decisions on effective natural ventilation rates.

Rules of thumb and sizing guidelines for cooling strategies

With the preceeding in mind, we'll consider strategies and techniques in the use of BIM that contribute to energy efficient buildings. As in the general discussion of sustainability and design found in Chapter 1, early consideration of passive cooling at the conceptual and schematic design phase will have the greatest impact on building performance with the least computational overhead. Further, these strategies are considered singly for the sake of clarity; in reality a passive, high-performance building may—and probably must—successfully synergize two or more approaches to effectively control thermal comfort.

Much of the following discussion is an adaptation of rules of thumb and engineering approximations to BIM. These have been developed over the past decades when today's energy modeling was unavailable, and have the advantage of being readily adaptable by non-scientist architectural practitioners to interactive BIM reports and worksheets. The reader is cautioned that being approximations, these methods may not accurately predict actual building performance. (For that matter, detailed energy modeling does not necessarily accurately forecast performance either, due in large part to unpredictable patterns of energy consumption by building occupants.) Rather, these performance-modeling rules of thumb, dynamically linked as they are to the BIM model, are intended to help the designer evaluate competing designs. For in-depth discussion of the engineering literature that forms the basis of these rules of thumb, the reader is again referred to MEEB (Grondzik et al. 2010).

Approximate summer heat gain

A significant challenge in performance-based passive cooling design is the calculation of cooling loads. This may be simplified somewhat by accounting for worst-case conditions, but cooling load calculations are inherently complex. Contributing to this are the at-times interrelated mechanisms of heat transfer: conduction, convection, radiation, and evaporation. In addition, seasonal and daily movement of the sun, combined with the cumulative nature of climate-dominated cooling loads, makes accurate energy modeling an involved and computationally demanding effort well beyond the scope of current BIM applications. As a result, true energy modeling is performed using dedicated applications, with geometry and hopefully material data supplied by the BIM model (see Chapter 11).

It's possible, of course, to defer cooling load calculations until the design is sufficiently advanced to justify detailed energy modeling. In that case, the designer would evaluate competing designs based on their relative performance, but would not be able to confirm whether even the best-performing design being considered was able to meet comfort demands.

An alternative is the use of a simple modeler. One example for residential projects is Home Energy Efficient Design (HEED), a free program by UCLA (energy modelers used in collaboration with BIM are discussed more fully in Chapter 11). A distinct advantage of this approach is that even a user-friendly modeler is more likely to accurately predict building performance than hand calculations. Early design stage-load calculations, drawing on data such as wall assembly areas from the BIM model, gives the designer early feedback on design changes as they are made. The immediacy of design feedback may be the most compelling reason to take the trouble to perform early energy performance calculations with data from the BIM model, even if that data must be manually transferred and the building recreated in the basic energy modeler.

On the other hand, the degree of architectural control in energy modelers such as HEED tends to be cruder, so complex or unusual geometries may not be well represented. Further, design iterations must be recreated in the energy modeler, which may be time consuming and discourage iterative design.

In decades past, the ASHRAE *Handbook of Fundamentals* offered methods for cooling load calculations intended to be performed manually (before the advent of widespread and cheap computation). Methods like Total Equivalent Temperature Differential method with Time Averaging (TETD/TA) and Cooling Load Temperature Differential method with solar Cooling Load Factors (CLTD/CLF) are very useful, but are nevertheless approximations and fairly intensive to implement. A version of the latter is presented in MEEB (2010, Chapter 8 and Appendix F), for those readers interested in incorporating this method directly into a BIM model without reference to separate energy modeling. Keep in mind, however, that such load calculations are approximations, and require a degree of engineering experience and judgment to implement successfully.

Effective solar shading

The first rule of sustainable energy use is to reduce demand. For cooling envelope-driven buildings, solar gain is the chief load of interest. The designer must consider solar geometry and how best to shade the building in hot months, while allowing winter heat gain and minimizing the impact on desirable views and natural ventilation (Fig. 6.8). Summarizing from the previous chapter, consider these BIM approaches to achieving appropriate solar shading:

FIGURE 6.8 The golden rule of solar shading: keep the summer sun off. A broad-brimmed hat tilted to the south should do the trick!

Sun angles

In designing shading devices, it is typical to simulate sun angles for three significant dates: summer and winter solstices, and either the vernal or autumnal equinox (the solar geometry is identical for both of the latter). Optimize the BIM model geometry to exclude summer sun and ensure deep penetration of winter sun (Fig. 6.9). The time-tested shading configurations of shading devices are quite valid: horizontal overhangs for southern orientation, vertical for east and west—and even north (the north summer sun can penetrate a space at a low altitude early in the morning and late in the afternoon, as the sun rises and sets north of east and west in the summer).

Bear in mind, however, that while solar geometry about the imaginary time axis from one solstice to another is symmetrical, climate is not (Fig. 6.10). As discussed in the previous chapter, two opposite dates in the spring and fall may have identical solar geometries, but very different temperatures, wind, cloud cover, and so on.

In architecture school in Texas, a professor of mine's admonition was for us to "see what the sun sees." By that he meant that we should tilt our (at the time physical) models such that our vantage was that of the sun at a particular moment of interest: anything we could see would be bathed in sunlight; anything concealed would be shaded. This useful, low-tech method of verifying shading device effectiveness is applicable to BIM as well. Once a sun angle is established (typically automated based on project location and desired date and time), sight along a parallel line of one of the sun's rays in an orthogonal projection. (The building's astronomical distance from the sun is such that the sun's rays are nearly parallel, and an orthogonal projection simulates this). Whatever portion of the building that is perceptible from this view is sunlit; anything else is in shadow for that particular sun position (that is,

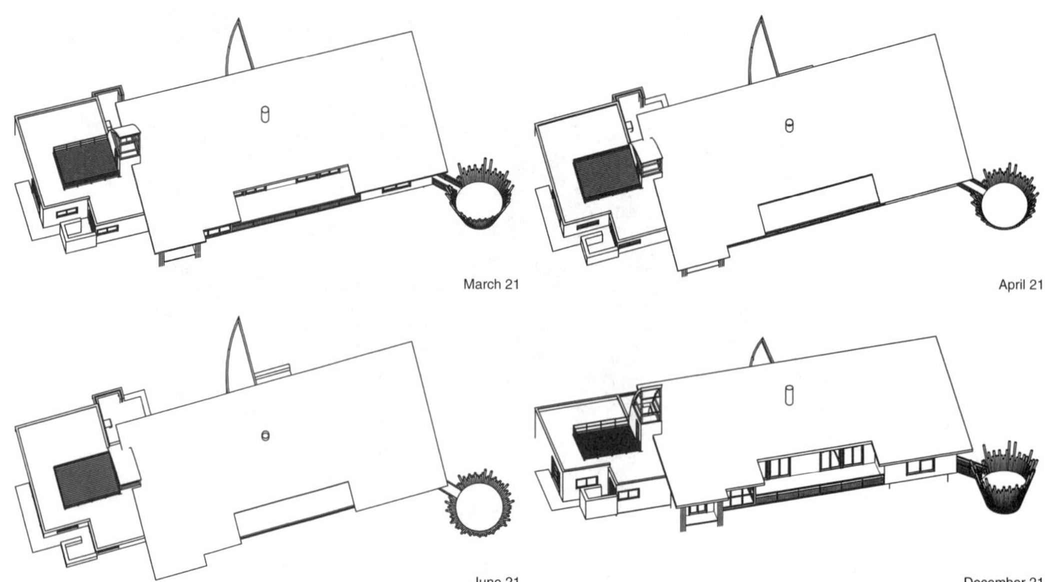

FIGURE 6.9 These four orthogonal building projections have been chosen at key times of year to assess the effectiveness of shading devices: at the solstices and an equinox, as well as the time when the ratio of Heating and Cooling Degree days suggests that the building should be shaded (see Fig. 5.3). These "sun views" do not require shadows (the sun never "sees" a shadow), nor should they be perspective projections (the sun is 93 million miles away, so rays are for all intents parallel).

at that moment). Vectorworks, for one, automates this with the little-known "set view to light" button in the light object's Object Information pane.

Solar animations

Daylighting analysis applications like Ecotect provide useful daylight factor and daylight autonomy analysis of buildings or individual spaces (see Chapter 11). These are particularly helpful in making detailed and quantified design decisions in selecting materials based on reflectivity, for example. However, there is also value early in the design process in making qualitatively informed design decisions. BIM applications, like ArchiCAD and Vectorworks Architect as well as 3D modelers like SketchUp, allow solar animations to be created even at the conceptual design stage. Animations are particularly useful if generated from the southwest and southeast for the solstices and equinox, and from the north for the summer solstice (Fig. 6.11).

Remember that to be effective, the solar animation need not be:

- detailed
- textured
- long
- or have a high frame rate

Remember that a short solar animation of an accurate but low-fidelity model (the BIM equivalent of a foam core model) can be quite instructional, and need not represent a significant modeling overhead (Fig. 6.12).

Ventilation

For both hot-dry and hot-moist conditions, natural ventilation is fundamental to passive cooling, albeit as we've seen for very different reasons. In the former case, natural ventilation is the direct means of

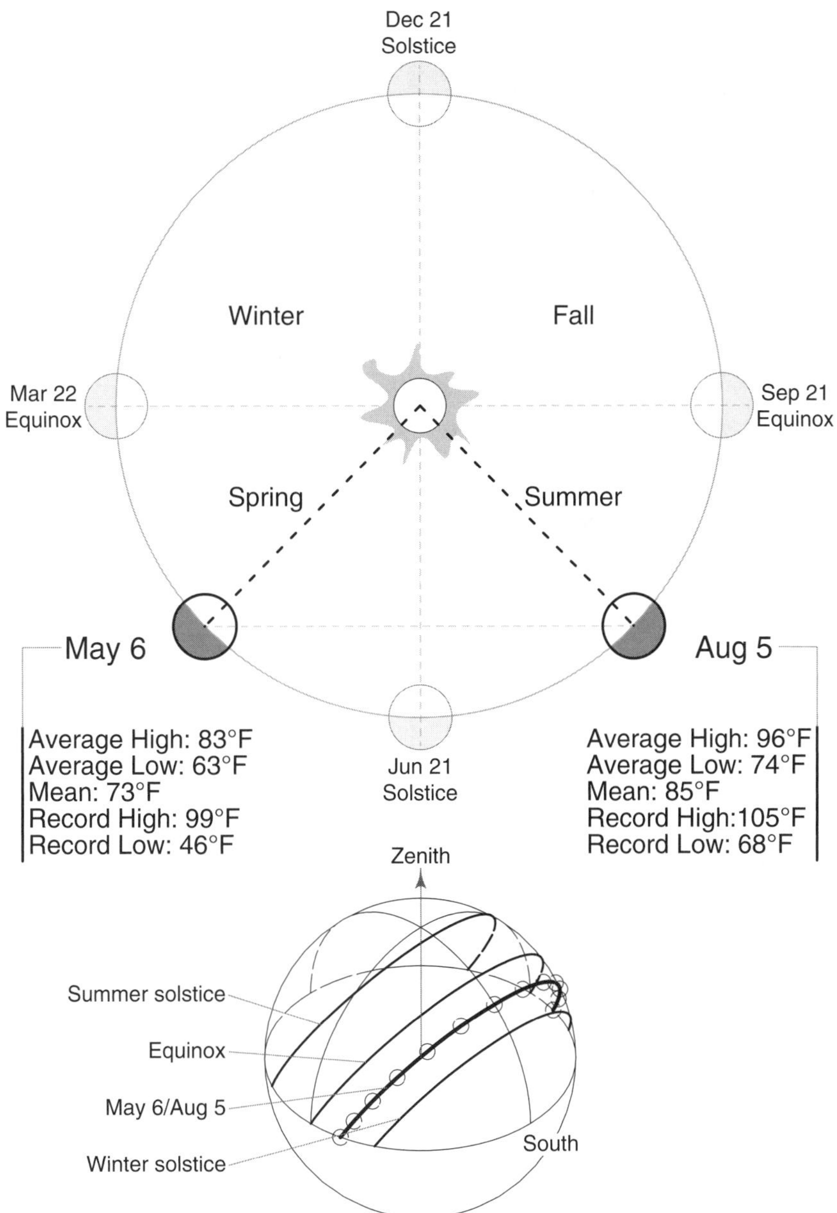

FIGURE 6.10 For any point on earth, solar geometry is symmetrical about an imaginary "time axis" between solstices—sun angles and times are the same for a pair of days a given number of days before and after a solstice. However, weather data can be radically different for these paired dates, depending on the locale. Designers must therefore be sensitive to climate and not just solar geometry when designing shading devices.

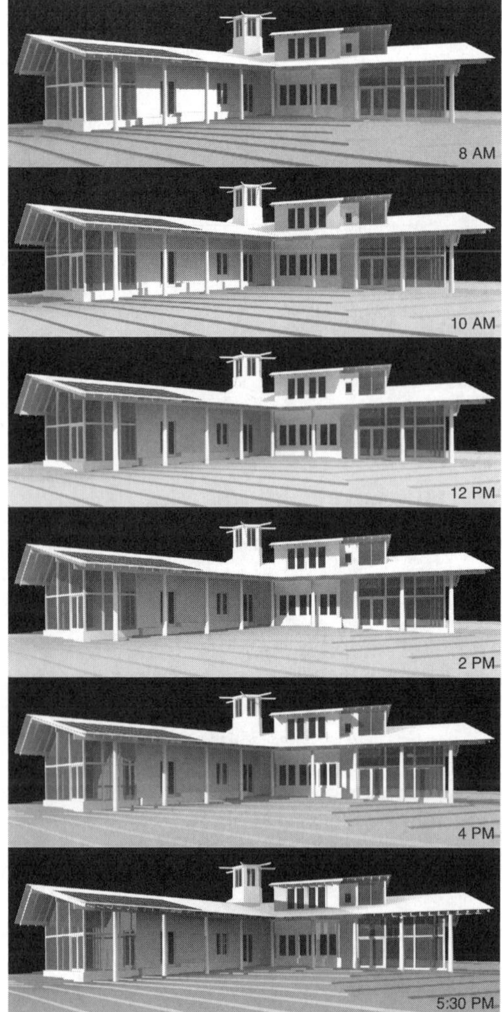

FIGURE 6.11 These stills from a solar animation of the Bee Ranch project (see the case study at the end of Chapter 9) are among several that were key in designing appropriate shading on south, west, and east elevations.

cooling the body and providing comfort. For the latter, ventilation is the mechanism by which humidity is added uniformly to a building's air mass and helps ensure well-mixed conditions. Other than mechanical means of providing ventilation (which is necessary at times), there are two-centuries-old passive ventilation strategies available: capitalizing on the wind, or taking advantage of warmer air's natural tendency to rise.

Cross ventilation

Wind-driven, or cross, ventilation is dependent on wind direction and intensity, as well as aperture sizes. Wind roses indicating annual wind direction and speed are commonly available for most cities in the United States, since meteorological data is collected at major and municipal airports. However, prevailing wind direction is highly affected by local geographical phenomena (nearby buildings, topography, bodies of water, and vegetation). For large unobstructed sites, a published wind rose may be reliable. There is no substitute, however, for onsite investigation. Wind roses are included in analytical software like Ecotect, and published online at a variety of sites. The EPA's web site, for example, has a collection of wind roses for 139 separate zip codes.[1] Wind data is also available on the Web for most airports.

The air displacement volume rate, *V,* in cubic feet per minute, can be approximated as:

$$V = C_v A_v \qquad \text{[Equation 6.1; ASHRAE 2005, 27.10]}$$

The building should when possible be oriented broadside to prevailing summer winds; orientation is reflected by C_v, the effectiveness coefficient, ranging from 0.5 to 0.6 for winds perpendicular to the window and 0.25 to 0.35 for wind blowing obliquely to the window. *A* is the area of inlets (in square feet), and *v* is the prevailing wind velocity in feet per minute (convert miles per hour to feet per minute by multiplying the former by 88). If wind data are not available, the value of 7.5 mph (660 fpm) is typically used.

All of these variables may be accounted for in a BIM model (Fig. 6.13). C_v may be assigned by the design according to orientation, and *v* is known from meteorological data and input by the user. The BIM model may report *A* on a dynamic basis, as the model is changed throughout the design process. By comparing the resulting *V* of competing designs, derived from BIM reports of their respective effectiveness coefficients and net operable opening

[1] Zip code data can be found at http://www.epa.gov/ttn/naaqs/ozone/areas/wind.htm.

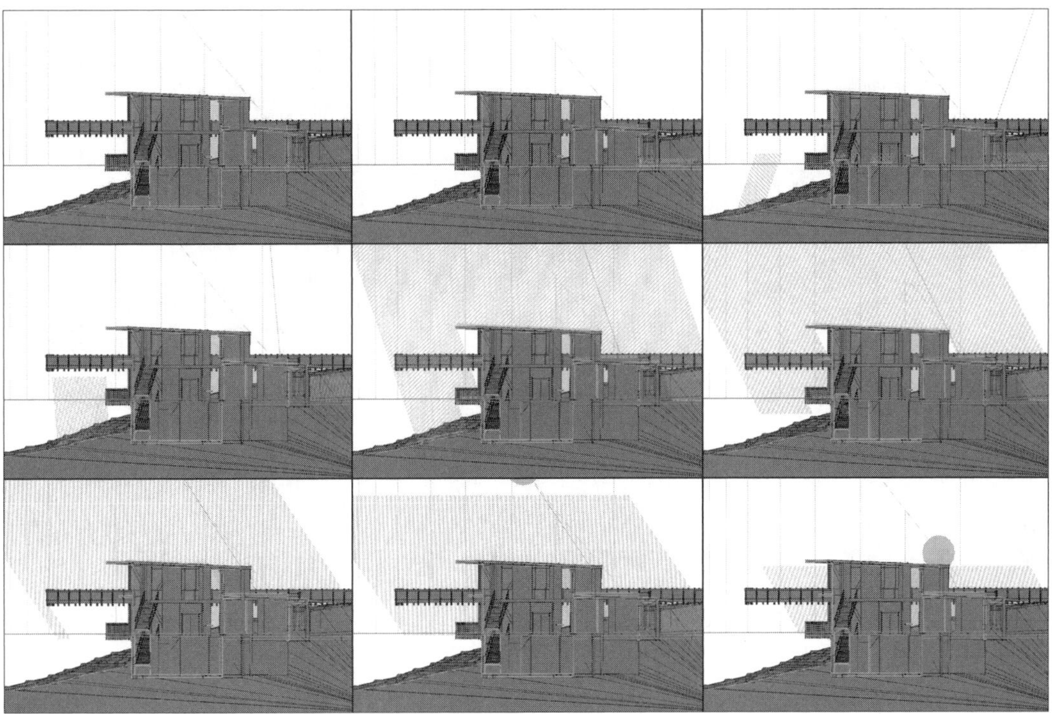

FIGURE 6.12 These series of still images from an Ecotect animation were based on a BIM model of the Battelle Darby Creek Environmental Center (see the case study at the end of Chapter 7). The BIM geometry need neither be highly rendered nor detailed to yield useful design information.

Photos courtesy of DesignGroup.

areas, the architect may quantify two or more designs' comparative total natural cross ventilation.

In many cases, simply being able to quantifiably compare ventilation rates among design options is sufficient. However, the designer may want to know how much ventilation is required to cool a building. Here we run the risk of straying away from design rules of thumb and into energy modeling; again, remember that these are design guidelines, not predictions of actual performance.

In estimating heat transfer, it is assumed that indoor temperatures can approach outdoor temperatures, within about 3°F. Even with perfect heat transfer, indoor temperatures obviously could not be below outdoor temperatures. From this perspective, natural ventilation is useful in offsetting internal heat loads only, such as those generated by occupants (people), equipment, and lighting. However, consider that:

- If the building is well shaded, outdoor air may be at or near comfortable temperatures;
- If adiabatic cooling is employed for hot-dry conditions, then as the inlet air enters the building and is humidified, its dry-bulb temperature will drop. The lower temperature may well be within the comfort zone;
- Most importantly, adequate natural ventilation potentially expands the summer comfort zone, as shown in Figure 6.3.

Sensible heat removal (q_v) is:

$$q_v = V\,(1.1)\,\Delta t$$

[Equation 6.2; Grondzik et al. 2010, 208]

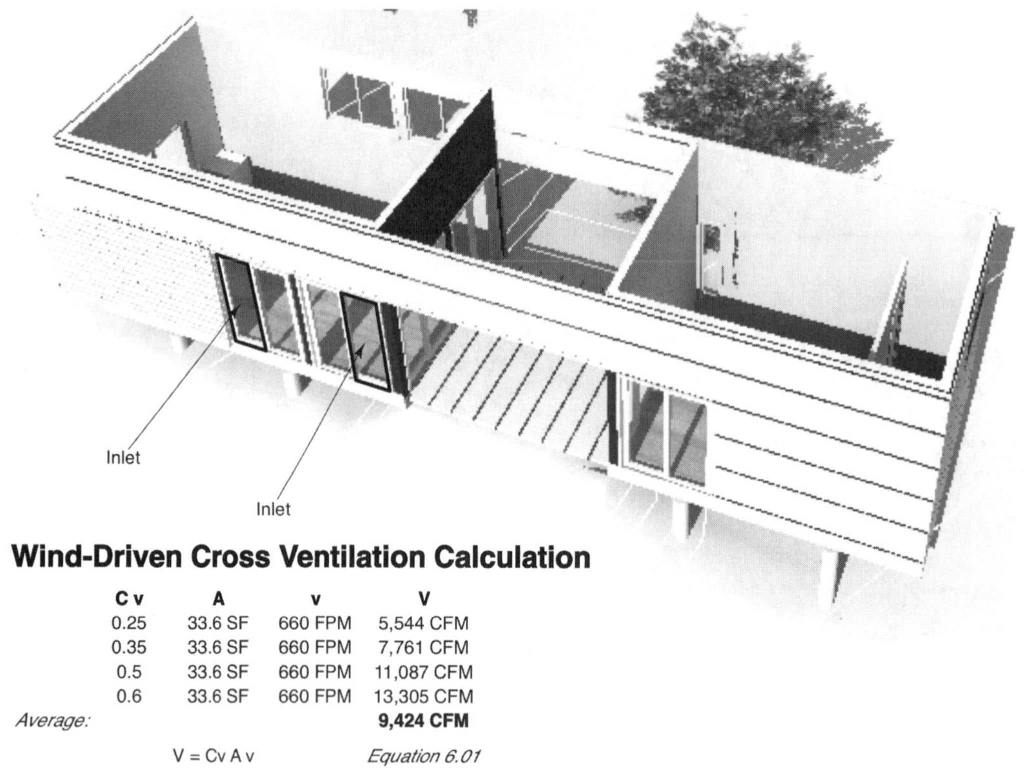

Wind-Driven Cross Ventilation Calculation

	Cv	A	v	V
	0.25	33.6 SF	660 FPM	5,544 CFM
	0.35	33.6 SF	660 FPM	7,761 CFM
	0.5	33.6 SF	660 FPM	11,087 CFM
	0.6	33.6 SF	660 FPM	13,305 CFM
Average:				**9,424 CFM**

$$V = C_v A v \qquad \textit{Equation 6.01}$$

Where:

Cv = effectiveness coefficient: 0.25, 0.35, 0.50. 0.60, depending on wind orientation to window
A = inlet area, square feet
v = prevailing wind velocity, feet per minute (miles per hour · 88)

FIGURE 6.13 Simple cross ventilation calculations may be approximated in a BIM schedule.

V is the air displacement volume rate in cubic feet per minute calculated in Equation 6.1. Assume that Δt (the difference between indoor air and outdoor air dry-bulb temperature) is 3°F, representing the least *sensible* heat that can be removed by natural ventilation alone. The product is read in Btu/h ft^2; compare to average cooling loads by building type and climate in Grondzik et al. (2010, Appendix F.3) or as determined by energy modeling software (see Chapter 2).

Again, without detailed energy modeling of a completed design, load calculations are very approximate only. Furthermore, even detailed load modeling may not accurately estimate actual occupant patterns of behavior, which may have a significant influence on cooling loads.

As an alternative to calculating *heat* loss by natural ventilation, one might consider the effective reduction in indoor air *temperature* by natural ventilation. Temperature can be thought of as a measure of the density of heat. The advantage of considering the former is that it is a far simpler value to measure, and is one that building occupants can readily appreciate as an indication of comfort. On the other hand, solely calculating temperature reduction due to ventilation does not consider cooling loads resulting from heat added by solar insolation, people, lights, and equipment.

The maximum recommended air speed for sedentary indoor occupancy is 160 feet per minute (1.8 mph); at or below that and loose paper is not disturbed. At 160 ft/min, indoor air temperature may be reduced by 4.7°F when the temperature of building interior surfaces is equal to the air temperature; when surface temperatures are 9°F higher than air temperatures, cooling is 5.4°F for a 160 ft/min ventilation speed. Since the volume of air is assumed to flow through the inlet and outlet, divide *V* (in cubic feet per minute) as calculated within the BIM model according to Equation 6.1, by the average area of inlet and outlet aperture area to get the speed of air in feet per minute. Of course, aperture area data are available from the BIM model; the cooling from air speed calculation can also thereby be included in the building model.

Stack effect

Warm air's natural tendency to rise has been exploited architecturally for centuries to provide natural ventilation when wind-driven ventilation was unavailable or unreliable. Accurately predicting rate of airflow due to the stack effect is problematic, as a rising warm air mass represents a complex system involving interrelated mass transfer (movement of air) and heat transfer (through convection). True modeling of the phenomenon involves computational fluid dynamics (CFD), well beyond the capabilities of any available BIM modeler.

On the other hand, ASHRAE has published a far simpler formula that approximates the air flow rate by volume. This formula can be built into a BIM model to calculate volume flow rate in cubic feet per minute, *Q*:

$$Q = 60 \cdot C_d \cdot A \cdot K \sqrt{(2g \cdot h(t_i - t_o)/t_i}$$ [Equation 6.3; ASHRAE 2005, 27.11]

The discharge coefficient (C_d), a correction factor for aperture openings of disparate sizes, can be expressed as:

$$C_d = 0.040 + 0.0025\ |(t_i - t_o)|$$ [Equation 6.4; ASHRAE 2005, 27.11]

For multiple inlets, C_d can be approximated as 0.65. The area of inlet(s), *A*, is reported by the BIM model. When the inlet area and the outlet area are not the same, use the lesser value for *A*, multiplying it by up to 1.39 according to the following formula:

$$K = 1.388 - (e^{-(A_1/A_2)})$$ [Equation 6.5]

Note that in the above equation, when the apertures are of equal size, $K = 1$; at an area ratio of 6 or more to 1, *K* approaches 1.39. The exponent ratio A_1/A_2 always considers the larger of the two apertures in the numerator, so that ratio is always 1 or greater. The other expressions in Equation 6.3 are *g*, the gravitational constant at 32 ft/s^2 (there can be no buoyancy without gravity); *h*, the stack height, in feet; and t_i and t_o—the indoor and outdoor dry-bulb temperatures, respectively, expressed in degrees Rankine (that is, degrees Fahrenheit plus 459.67). Since BIM modelers do not link to weather data, and one would have to mathematically model the upper temperature, assumed values for t_i and t_o are usually assigned.

In Equation 6.3, note that the air flow rate *Q* increases with aperture area, height of the stack, and the temperature difference between upper and lower openings. In order to encourage the greatest possible value for the temperature differential, place inlets under deep shade, preferably to the north. Outlets should be high and glassy, like small greenhouses, so as to maximize the outlet temperature (Fig. 6.14). Indeed, this is exactly the approach of Monticello and antebellum houses of the American South, with wraparound porches (cool inlets) and glass cupolas (hot outlets).

Once the above formulas are included in the BIM model and the appropriate aperture representations (likely window objects) are attached to the values *A* and *h*, changes to the model's stack height or window sizes will automatically result in recalculated results for the airflow rate volume (Fig. 6.15). This is extremely useful early in design when the designer is developing building massing, determining the height of thermal chimneys, and selecting and locating operable windows. For the cooling capacity of stack-effect ventilation, refer to one of the two methods suggested above for

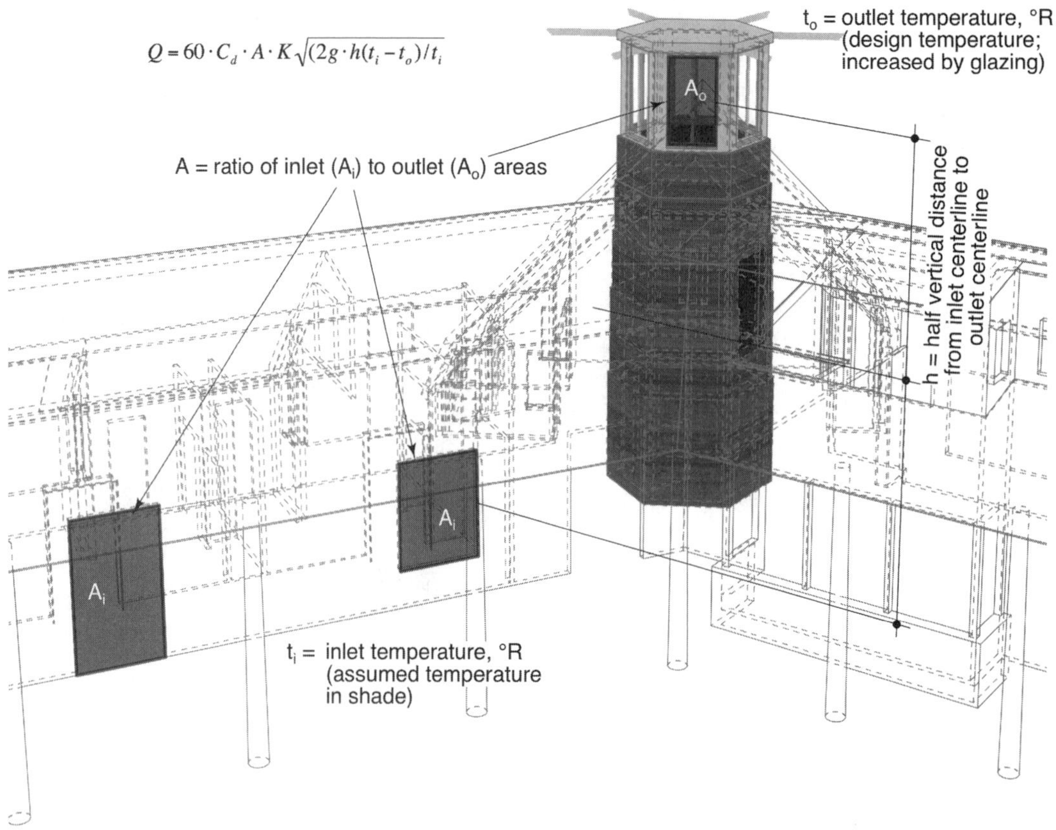

FIGURE 6.14 For a completely accurate simulation of the cooling capacity of the stack effect, one would need to employ computational fluid dynamics (CFD). ASHRAE's approximation (see Equation 6.03) has the virtue of being far more tractable. Here, the variables that the architect controls are highlighted.

cross-ventilation (see Equation 6.2; 4.7°F to 5.4°F for a 160 ft/min ventilation speed).

Evaporative (adiabatic) cooling

Swamp coolers, while using considerably less energy than vapor-compression cycle air conditioning, are nevertheless mechanical devices. For a fully passive system, one must look to combining natural ventilation with humidification of inlet air. One such approach and the subject of research in the 1990s is the cool tower, adapting principles used in Persian badgir to the American Desert Southwest. One or more tall wind towers with wetted absorbent pads serve as inlets for hot, dry air. The air is driven into the building by wind, passing over the pads where it is adiabatically cooled (see Fig. 6.4). The amount of cooling can be estimated by a series of short equations (see Equations 6.6 through 6.8), which can as usual be incorporated into BIM with a schedule or worksheet. First, the temperature of the cooled air is estimated by the following equation, where t_{cooled}, t_{DB}, and t_{WB} are cooled, dry-bulb, and wet-bulb temperatures, respectively:

$$t_{cooled} = t_{DB} - 0.87\,(t_{DB} - t_{WB})$$

[Equation 6.6; Grondzik et al. 2010, 305]

The first, of course, is the temperature of interest, and the latter two are derived from climate data

Thermal Chimney Calculations

Cd	T in	T out	A, lower	A, upper	A	K	g	Z, lower	Z, upper	ΔHnpl	Q	V	V
0.45	85 °F	105 °F	*55.0 SF*	*22.6 SF*	2.4	1.3	32.2 FT/S2	*3.5 FT*	*13.6 FT*	5.1 FT	**2,698 CFM**	**1.4 MPH**	**119.2 FPM**

Q = 60 Cd A K (2g ΔHnpl (To - Ti) / (To + 459.67))^(1/2)   *Source: ASHRAE Handbook of Fundamentals 2005, page 27.11*

Where:

Cd = 0.40 + 0.0025 ITi -ToI
A = Aperture area ratio, lower:upper
K = Aperture area ratio coefficient (empirical), where K is approximately 1.388 - e^-A (Source: François Lévy, M.Arch, MSE)
ΔHnpl = Distance to neutral point, assumed to be half of ΔZ
T out = Temperature at outlet (upper) aperture (user supplies value in °F, automatically converted to °R (Rankine; °R = °F + 459.67)
T in = Temperature at inlet (lower) aperture (user supplies value in °F, automatically converted to °R (Rankine; °R = °F + 459.67))
g = Gravitational constant

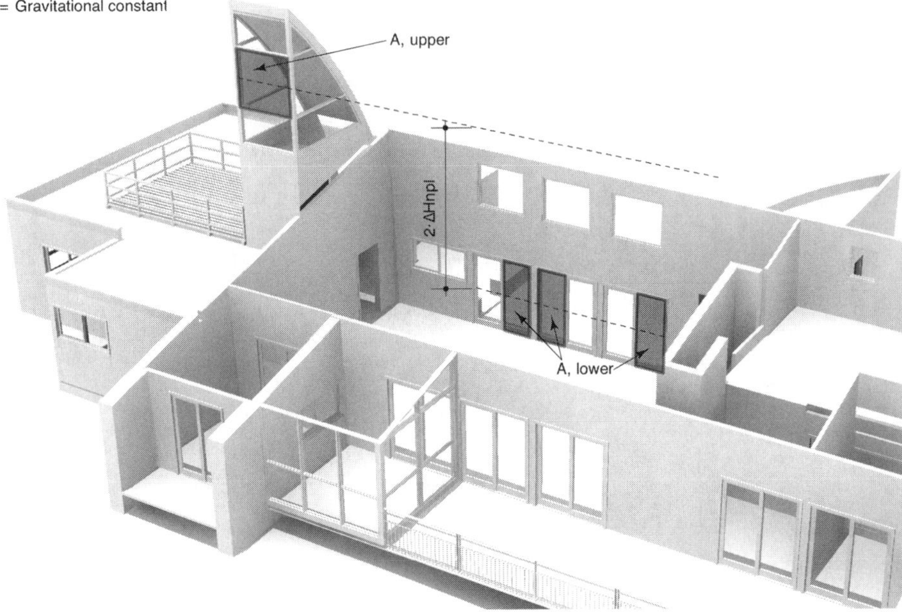

FIGURE 6.15 In this model, a stack-effect calculation has been integrated in BIM. The worksheet responds dynamically to changes in aperture sizes and relative heights and provides an updated airflow rate estimate.

or set to design temperatures. Note that knowing temperature is not enough; one needs to know the total cooling capacity in Btu/hr. Equation 6.06 is independent of building geometry; however, the airflow rate through a cool tower, *V*, is given by:

$$V = 2.7 \cdot A\sqrt{h\left(t_{DB} - t_{WB}\right)}$$ [Equation 6.7, Grondzik et al. 2010, 305]

In this equation, *A* is the area of the wetted pads and *h* is the height of the tower. Note that unlike Equation 6.3, the above expression does not consider relative aperture sizes; only the area of the outdoor air inlet (the wetted pads) is a factor. Moreover, *A* and *h* are architectural features, and their values are reported in the BIM model and used to calculate *V*.

The total cooling capacity of the cooling tower is calculated using the values determined in previous equations:

$$\text{Btu/hr} = 1.1\ V\ (t_{int} - t_{cooled})$$ [Equation 6.8; Grondizk et al. 2010, 305]

In this calculation, *V* is from Equation 6.7, Equation 6.06 gives t_{cooled}, and t_{int} is the maintained

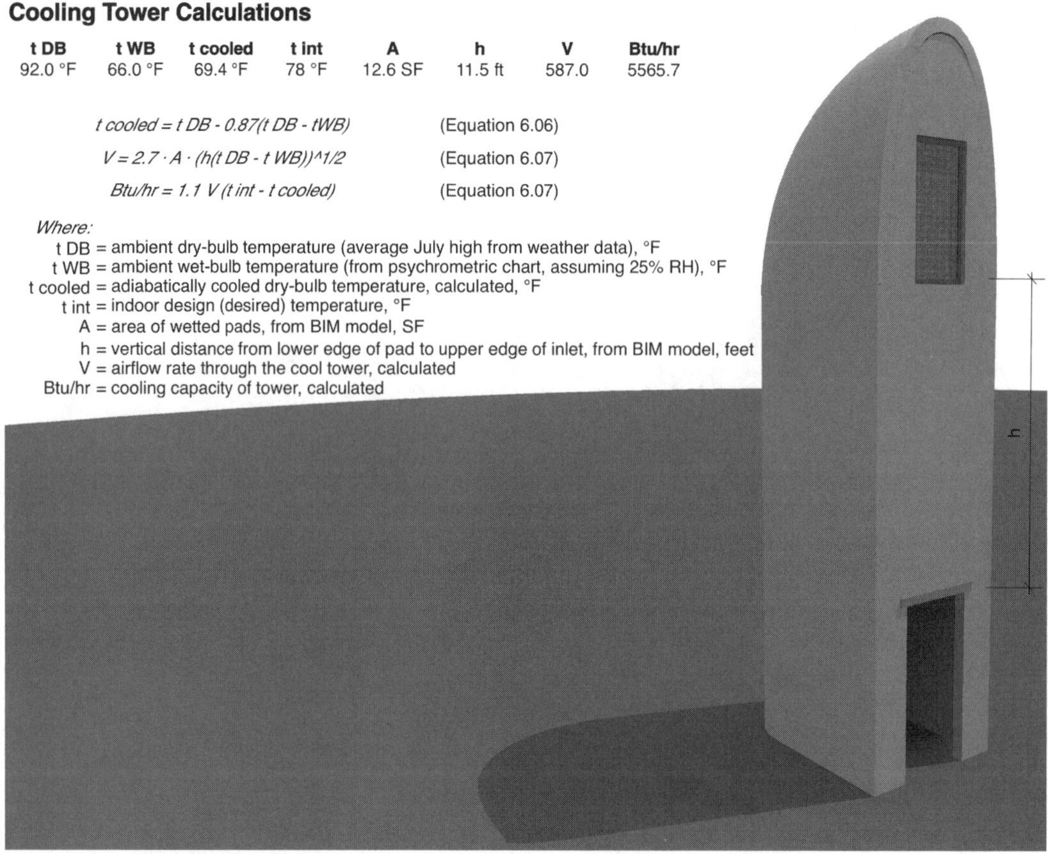

Cooling Tower Calculations
t DB | t WB | t cooled | t int | A | h | V | Btu/hr
92.0 °F | 66.0 °F | 69.4 °F | 78 °F | 12.6 SF | 11.5 ft | 587.0 | 5565.7
t cooled = t DB - 0.87(t DB - tWB) (Equation 6.06)
V = 2.7 · A · (h(t DB - t WB))^1/2 (Equation 6.07)
Btu/hr = 1.1 V (t int - t cooled) (Equation 6.07)
Where:
t DB = ambient dry-bulb temperature (average July high from weather data), °F
t WB = ambient wet-bulb temperature (from psychrometric chart, assuming 25% RH), °F
t cooled = adiabatically cooled dry-bulb temperature, calculated, °F
t int = indoor design (desired) temperature, °F
A = area of wetted pads, from BIM model, SF
h = vertical distance from lower edge of pad to upper edge of inlet, from BIM model, feet
V = airflow rate through the cool tower, calculated
Btu/hr = cooling capacity of tower, calculated
h

FIGURE 6.16 This simple BIM model of a cool tower uses readily available average weather data combined with values from the model geometry to calculate the tower's cooling capacity. One can vary the height of inlet to the building (in this example, the lower doorway and wetted pads, as well as the area of the latter to optimize the tower design).

dry-bulb temperature of indoor air. These three simple formulas can be incorporated into the BIM model and linked to tower height and wetted aperture size to optimize cooling tower height and wetted pad size (Fig. 6.16). For example, the *Z*-value (height above floor) of the inlet (wetted pad opening) may be used for *h*, and the area, *A*, of the inlet opening(s), whether modeled as a window object, custom family (Revit), or custom symbol (ArchiCAD or Vectorworks).

Thermal mass with night flushing

For the skin-load dominated buildings of interest in this book, most thermal loading occurs during the day (this also the case for internally loaded buildings without significant nighttime occupancy). The thermal mass's capacity to absorb heat by day is limited by its ability to shed absorbed heat overnight. So-called night flushing extends the thermal mass capacity to cool by day, with a commensurate extension of the psychrometric comfort zone (refer back to Fig. 6.3).

For moderate-mass buildings (for example, exposed slab on grade construction with lightweight wall and roof construction), nighttime ventilation cooling capacity (in Btu's per day foot squared, Btu/day·ft^2) may be approximated by the following equation:

$$\text{Btu/day(ft}^2) = 358 - (t_{out} - t_{MDR})^{1.366}$$

[Equation 6.9; after Grondzik et al. 2010, 245]

The summer outdoor design temperature (the dry-bulb temperature for which the architect is designing) is expressed as tout; t_{MDR} is the mean daily temperature range, a climate datum available from MEEB appendices and on the web. High-mass buildings (for example, at least two square feet of three-inch thick exposed concrete surface for every square foot of floor area) use the following formula to approximate cooling capacity in Btu/day:

$$\text{Btu/day(ft}^2) = 546 - (t_{out} - t_{MDR})^{1.456}$$

[Equation 6.10; after Grondzik et al. 2010, 245]

These two equations will yield values that are, in most cases, within 10 percent of those given by graphs in MEEB (Grondzik et al. 2010), with calculated results that average under a 1 percent error. Such inaccuracies should be tolerable for design purposes. These formulas may be incorporated into the BIM model to dynamically determine the area of thermal mass required to compensate for internal and external loads. By attaching the exposed area of available thermally massive materials to calculations, the additional thermal mass, if any, may be optimized to overcome preliminary design cooling loads (Fig. 6.17).

Detailed calculations that determine hour-by-hour cooling of the thermal mass is beyond the scope of this book, but the interested reader is referred to work done by Grondzik and colleagues (2010). Such calculations are probably best accomplished with detailed thermal modeling, rather than incorporated into a BIM model.

Roof ponds for cooling

The roof pond is another effective implementation of the thermal mass strategy, one that has been known since the 1940s. It relies on direct radiation to the sky to complete a heat transfer cycle. Roof

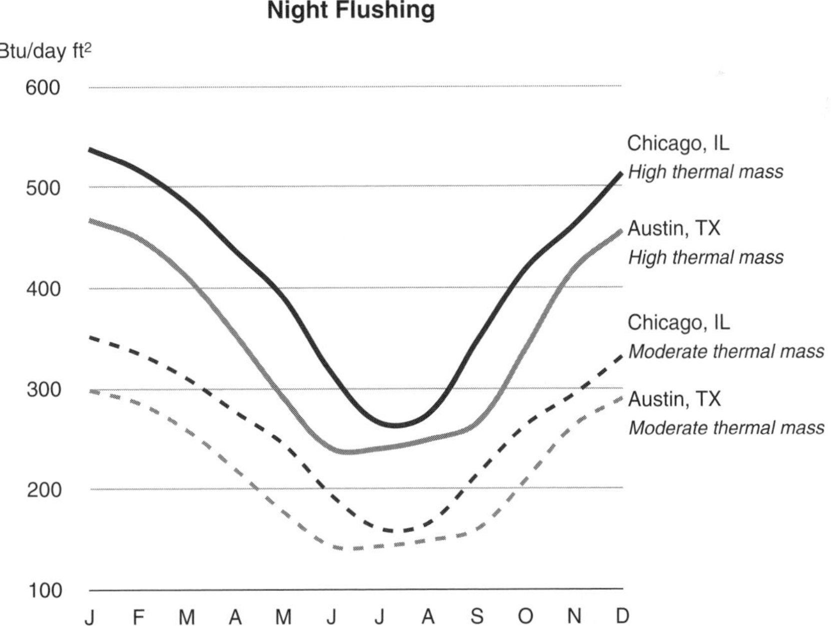

FIGURE 6.17 Using weather data for Austin, Texas, and Chicago, Illinois, the night-flushing potential in Btu/day ft² is plotted according to Equations 6.9 and 6.10. All twelve months of the year are shown, although night flushing would be realistically used only in warm months (that is, "shade" months in Figure 5.3, for the two respective locales).

ponds may be used to help cool buildings in the summer as well as heat them in the winter (we'll discuss winter applications in Chapter 7). The summer cooling principle is simple: a mass of water on the roof absorbs heat from the occupied space below by day, and then later radiates that heat to the black body of the night sky. Since heat flows from high to low temperatures, the water must be cooler than the space below. In order to avoid the roof pond's being heated by day, a retractable insulation layer may cover it until night. Roof ponds are only effective for the story directly below them, and they only address sensible heat gain or loss. Thus they are ideal for climates with manageable humidity.

In the United States, roof ponds are rare and considered somewhat exotic. When they are found, the water tends to be stored in large, sealed bladders as a precaution against leaks and to prevent evaporation. In Iran, where roof ponds are heavily researched, the water in the roof pond tends to be open to the air. In the latter case, leaks may be a greater concern and water must be replenished to offset evaporation losses. But in either configuration, the required area of the pond is dependent on how much energy it may absorb and release. According to MEEB, storage capacity in Btu's per day per square feet is:

$$\text{Btu/day ft}^2 = 0.7 \cdot d_{pond} \cdot (62.5\ \text{Btu/ft}^3\ °\text{F}) \cdot (t_{pond} - t_{min})$$

[Equation 6.11; Grondzik et al. 2010, 250]

The first value is a corrective constant. The depth of the pond, *d,* is in feet—generally 4 inches (0.33 feet); 62.5 Btu/ft³ °F is a constant due to the

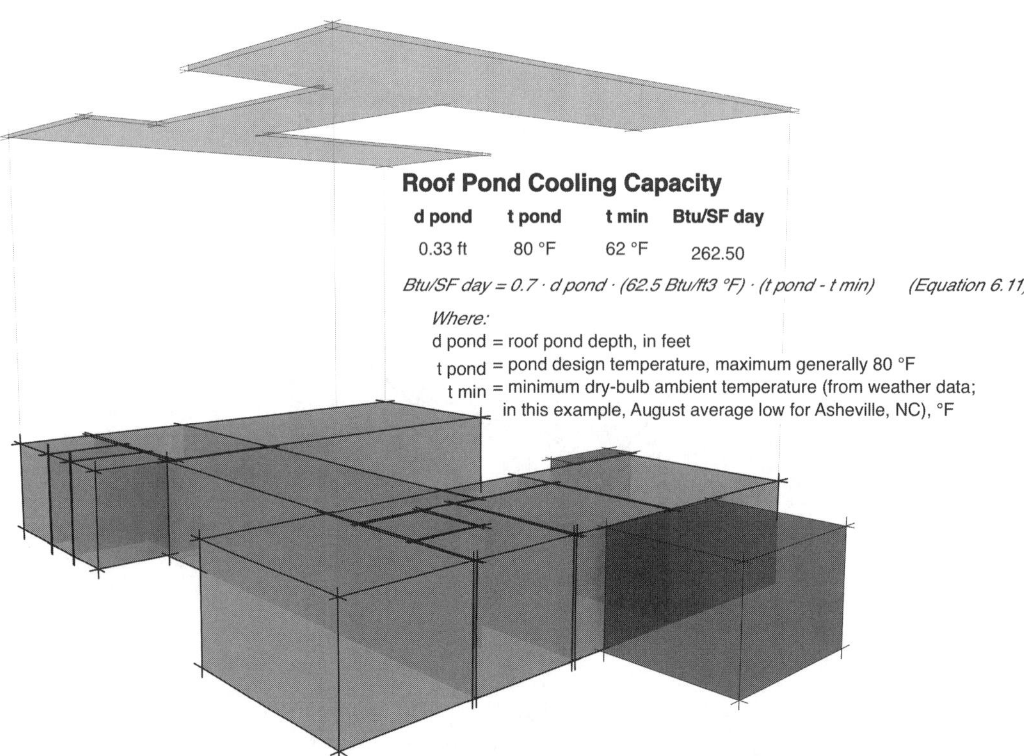

Roof Pond Cooling Capacity
d pond
t pond
t min
Btu/SF day
0.33 ft
80 °F
62 °F
262.50
Btu/SF day = 0.7 · d pond · (62.5 Btu/ft3 °F) · (t pond - t min)
(Equation 6.11)
Where:
d pond = roof pond depth, in feet
t pond = pond design temperature, maximum generally 80 °F
t min = minimum dry-bulb ambient temperature (from weather data; in this example, August average low for Asheville, NC), °F

FIGURE 6.18 The cooling storage capacity (in Btu/day ft²) is a function of maximum roof pond and minimum summer nighttime temperatures, and roof pond depth. Here, the latter is linked to the BIM schedule. Comparing the cooling capacity to building cooling loads would allow appropriate sizing of the roof pond for summer cooling.

density and specific heat capacity of water. The design temperature, $t_{pond,}$ is the desired pond temperature; 80°F is practical maximum. The summer minimum temperature, $t_{min,}$ for the site is from climate data, and represents the average daily low (nighttime temperature).

To size the roof pond, compare the building heat gain (or loss, as in the case of heating) in Btu/h ft^2 times the number of hours per day of occupancy or cooling (say, nine hours), divided by the pond-heat storage calculated in Equation 6.11. The result will be in square feet of pond per square feet of building area of the floor below the pond.

The salient characteristics to be parameterized in BIM are the pond depth and area, or its volume (Fig. 6.18). A solid prism such as an extrusion, or even a Space object may therefore be used to represent the pond, again reporting its values to a worksheet incorporating the relevant formula. As the building design evolves and the roof pond's extent and depth is adjusted, the designer can determine if it is adequately cooling the floor below.

▪ Case Study: Hadlow College Rural Regeneration Centre, Kent, United Kingdom

By James Anwyl

Design firm: Eurobuild

Client: Hadlow College

James Anwyl, founding partner at Eurobuild, a company specializing in PassivHaus architecture and construction, designed and built the Rural Regeneration Centre for Hadlow College, which is one of the top three agricultural colleges in the UK. The Rural Regeneration Centre is the first certified PassivHaus educational building in the UK (Fig. 6.19).

The 3,770 square foot (350 m^2) building includes two teaching spaces, a kitchen, offices, showers, and toilet rooms. Partially funded by the South East England Development Agency (SEEDA), a regional development agency, the building was intended as a new teaching facility for the agricultural students and for occasional local community use. Upon discussion with the Kent planning department, Eurobuild changed the location of the new building, which was originally destined for a virgin green field to the south of the current location. Instead, the planners approved Eurobuild's intention to use the footprint (and some existing walls!) from a number of redundant cow sheds on the college's fully operational dairy farm. Over 95 percent of the original shed structure was retained on site and used for non-structural backfill and a significant proportion was reclad to match the new lumber.

The building's main purpose is to enable seminar-based teaching—it houses a staff office and meeting space, alongside a significant exhibition area used to display the college's expansive land-based study program. One of the college's requirements was a "Wet Working Area," a semi-outdoor space for machinery and livestock demonstrations. A sliding window from the main seminar room allows students to watch these demonstrations as part of their studies. This space made use of the preserved brick and block work at the northeast corner

(*Continued*)

FIGURE 6.19 This photo of Hadlow College's Rural Regeneration Centre shows the building at its completion. Designed in accordance with the PassiveHaus Institut's principles and PassivHaus Institut's Planning Package (PHPP) calculation tool (in the United States, see *www.passivehouse.us*), the Centre successfully employs large amounts of north-facing glass for daylighting, and overcomes the thermal losses entailed by other means.

Image courtesy of James Anwyl.

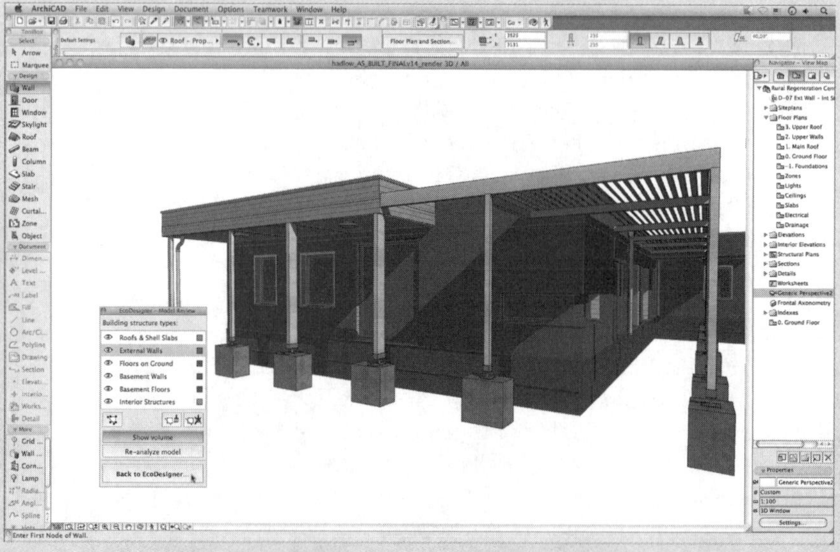

FIGURE 6.20 Design decisions may be analyzed for their energy implications directly within ArchiCAD using EcoDesigner. In this image, building components are assigned structure types and verified prior to analysis.

Image courtesy of James Anwyl.

of the former calf shed; the original walls are concealed behind a continuation of the larch cladding.

Constructed of super-insulated, closed panels, the structure was designed using BIM (ArchiCAD) and assembled in just three days (Figs. 6.20 and 6.21). In under ten days overall, the structure was airtight to a very high standard: 0.34 air changes per hour. Prefabrication led to a high quality finish with significant time savings.

A monitoring system has been installed to track the energy consumption of the building over the next two years and beyond for Eurobuild to learn from the "as built" building performance in relation to weather and usage patterns. The information communications technology (ICT) display, ventilation unit, and heat pump are monitored individually, in addition to a number of lighting and power circuits. The students and staff can see the results displayed on a very visible monitor in the exhibition area and via the online Building User Guide.

The building employs a number of sustainable technologies including a super-efficient Drexel & Weiss Aero Centro mechanical ventilation system with heat recovery, triple glazed windows, and a ground-source heat pump for both heating and cooling. Since carbon dioxide sensors (to measure occupancy and automatically control mechanical ventilation

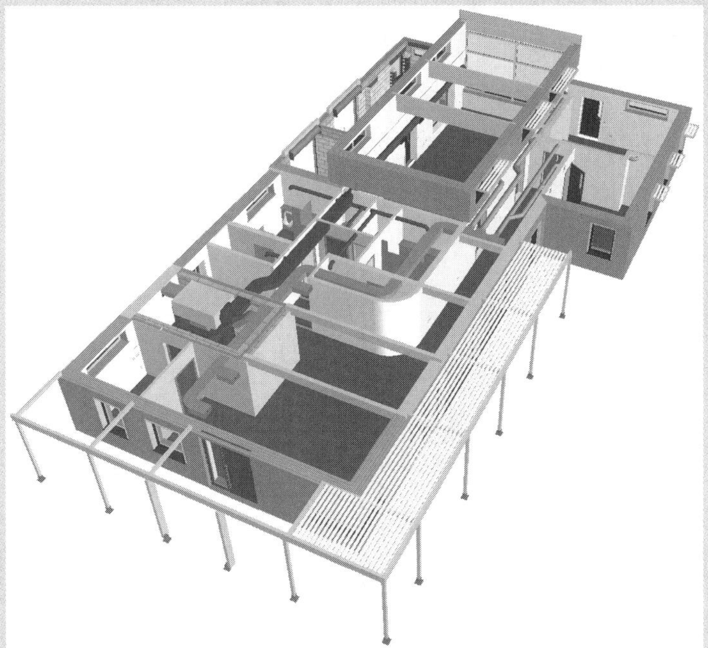

FIGURE 6.21 The ArchiCAD BIM model of the Rural Regeneration Centre includes mechanical and structural components, in addition to being an architectural virtual building.

Image courtesy of James Anwyl.

(*Continued*)

for appropriate fresh air) were not affordable, the seminar and demonstration spaces are ingeniously equipped with manual switches. When these spaces are occupied, the ventilation rate will increase above 16 CFM/person (8 l/s/person). The bathrooms all have waterless urinals, low flush toilets, timed water-saving taps, and moderated flow showers. Low-energy T5 fluorescent lamps are used throughout the building and the lighting was carefully planned using DiaLux software.

Natural slate laid on the screed gives a flooring depth of 2.75 inches (70 mm), while the medium density concrete block partition walls increase internal thermal mass and absorb the solar gain from the large south façade. Cooling is governed primarily by the ground source heat exchanger in the ventilation unit and backed by the heat pump and underfloor pipework. In addition, the seminar room windows are time- and temperature-controlled to enable night flushing for free cooling at night. Individual window pergolas and a colonnade across the south façade prevent overheating in summer. Solar geometry was modeled in 3D in ArchiCAD (Fig. 6.22), and then verified with EDSL's Tas energy simulation software and backed up by PHPP analysis.

All the lumber used in the project was derived from FSC sources or from sustainably managed forests in Austria, and apart from two 3-foot (1-meter) lengths of steel section (4" x 2" or 100 mm x 50 mm) there is no metal in the superstructure. This was a conscious decision to minimize life cycle costs and embodied energy. As a result of the careful planning, it seems likely from pre-assessment that the building might achieve the Building Research Establishment Environmental Assessment Method (BREEAM) "Excellent" rating; it has already achieved PassivHaus certification.

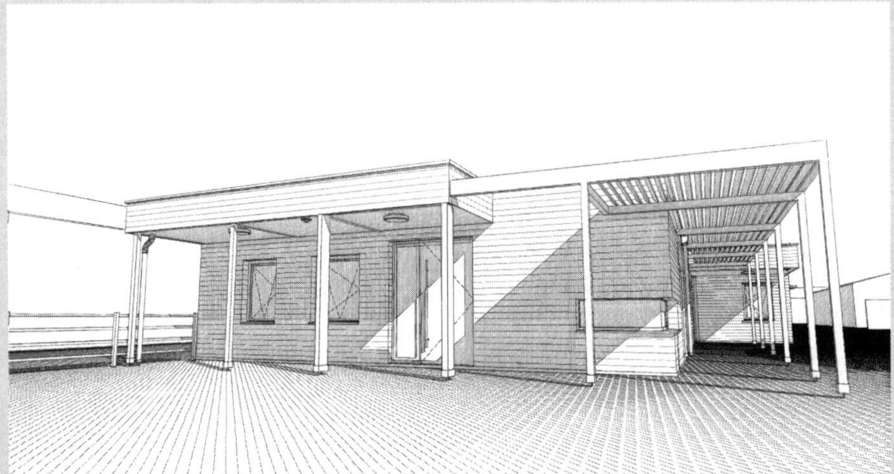

FIGURE 6.22 A sketch rendering of the BIM model for the Hadlow College project. Construction documents consist of annotated and dimensioned graphical views of this model, and the model provided the data for preliminary energy design and later energy simulation.

Image courtesy of James Anwyl.

With an insulation value of over R-56, the wall and roof panels use 15.75 inches (400 mm) of recycled "blown" cellulose insulation. These panels were made in Eurobuild's partner factory in Austria and transported directly to the site near Tonbridge, Kent. The factory is ultra-compact and one of the most advanced timber frame facilities in the world. Eurobuild is working to deliver more PassivHaus residential and education projects in the UK.

Chapter 7

Passive Heating

In its current manifestation, a key component of sustainable design is to incrementally lessen human impact on the biosphere by reducing building energy use. Barring breakthroughs in energy generation, materials resource management, and pollution control, all our buildings will have to evolve to the point where they have net-zero energy use—not unlikely within a generation. Eventually, we must go beyond that, to the point that the built environment—and all of human society—mimics natural systems' zero waste design, reusing all resources in a perpetuating cycle.

To minimize energy expenditures for heating our buildings, the appropriate approach is to maximize passive heat gains while controlling envelope losses. The former includes external gains from solar insolation, and internal gains from occupants, lighting, and equipment. Most passive heating design seeks to maximize external gains, while ignoring internal ones (for reasons outlined further on in this chapter). For colder climates, it is critical to design for *appropriate* maximum passive heating, all the while not overheating spaces. Moreover, even cold climates have warm seasons, and vice versa, so passive heating strategies must be seasonally indexed to avoid poor performance in summer. And as with passive cooling strategies, not all passive heating techniques are appropriate to every project, nor to every climate.

Determining and optimizing envelope heating losses can be achieved as with any exercise in envelope design, applying the principle of conductivity times area. However, in the case of heating losses, slabs on grade and basements are special cases that require variant approaches to estimating losses. As with other instances of designing for optimal performance, the application of a few straightforward rules of thumb to the BIM model can yield dynamic reports that better inform the architect (Fig. 7.1).

Implementing passive heating calculations in a BIM model is slightly more direct than for cooling. As we've seen in the previous chapter, performance-based passive cooling design is challenging in part due to the calculation of cooling loads. Heating load calculations are somewhat simplified by the adoption of worst-case climate assumptions. They also ignore the internal cooling loads—occupants, equipment, and lighting—that would otherwise contribute to heating the building.

As with passive cooling, the BIM user must enter climate data manually. To minimize data entry and more importantly to account for worst-case conditions (without overheating the building), use climate data for so-called 99 percent design temperatures. That is, outdoor temperatures will be below these values only 1 percent of the time, and this is the condition for which the building is designed. Climate data tables from *MEEB*, the ASHRAE *Handbook of Fundamentals*, and elsewhere report these 99 percent conditions.

Throughout this book, a performance-based design methodology is proposed that is more quantitatively accurate than "intuitive" design approaches, but it requires less computational overhead and technical knowledge than proper energy modeling. It is further expected that as appropriate, this sustainable BIM design

FIGURE 7.1 Passive House in the Woods, Wisconsin. TE Studio used the Passive House Planning Package (PHPP) as the primary optimization tool, supported by data gleaned from the BIM model. Exterior surface areas and interior floor areas were read from the ArchiCAD virtual building, while the mesh tool was used to model a challenging site with trees. 3D visualization was used to "walk" the property for ideal placement of the home.

Image courtesy of TE Studio.

methodology may be concluded with detailed energy modeling. (Fig. 7.2) The energy simulation preferably should use the BIM model as the basis of the building geometry, thus avoiding inefficiencies and potential errors from duplicate data entry.

Humidity responses for cold climates

As with passive cooling, architectural responses for heating needs must be designed appropriately for the climate. However, unlike with some passive cooling techniques, passive heating strategies as a rule only address sensible heat, not latent heat. This may be problematic, as winter air is far drier than warm air. Colder air with the same relative humidity (*RH*) has a far lower humidity ratio (*W*), the ratio of water vapor mass to dry air mass, than warmer air with the same *RH*. As a mass of colder air is sensibly heated, *W* remains constant, whereas *RH* decreases (Fig. 7.3).

Typically, internal loads (such as occupants breathing or activities like cooking) are relied upon to humidify winter spaces. Unfortunately, there is no ready way to predict this simply within a BIM model. Fortunately, increased passive heating (within acceptable limits to avoid overheating a space) will not decrease *W*. Humidification does need not therefore to overcome "drying" of the space by passive means, it just needs to increase humidity to compensate for the natural lowering of *RH* due to greater sensible heat.

Rules of thumb and sizing guidelines for heating strategies

The quantitative passive heating analysis and design guidelines below were developed, as many

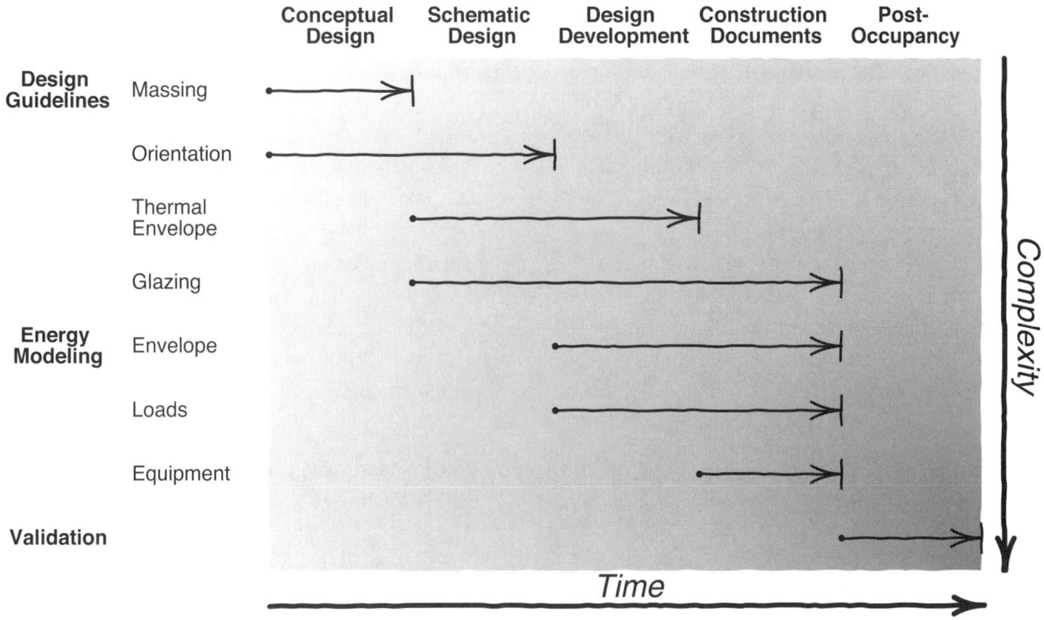

FIGURE 7.2 This matrix illustrates the role of design guidelines and detailed energy modeling in the design life of a project. Consider the MacLeamy curve (Figure 1.5) and its applicability to designing for energy.

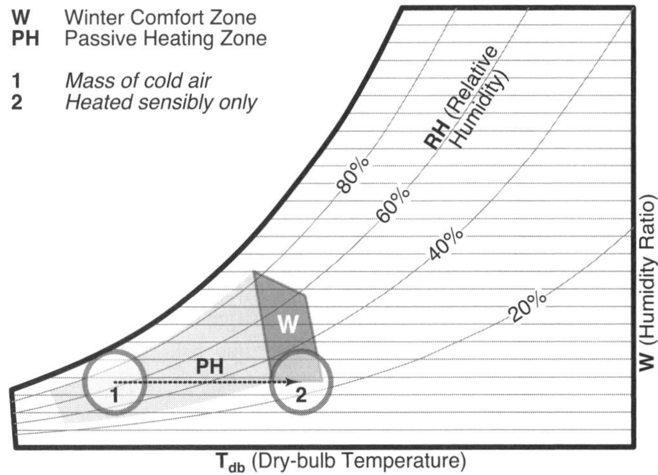

FIGURE 7.3 A mass of cold air may have a high relative humidity, but not because it actually contains a great deal of moisture (its humidity ratio, *W*, may be quite low). As the mass is heated sensibly (only), *W* remains constant since the mass of water vapor and dry air remain constant, but *RH* may drop dramatically.

of the rules of thumb suggested in this book, in the 1970s and 1980s as architectural responses to the perceived energy crisis of 1973 triggered by international oil cartel market manipulations. Predating as they do the age of ubiquitous, powerful desktop computing, these guidelines were designed to be tractable "hand" calculations. They are therefore suitable for inclusion in a BIM workflow.

Furthermore, in spite of buildings having existed for millennia, understanding their quantitative performance is not necessarily straightforward. New materials, for example, may interact in unexpected ways in given climates under certain conditions. Furthermore, the infinite variety of architectural responses to wall assembly design, building orientation, volume, and spatial organization contribute to the challenge of developing reliable, formulaic rules. (There are very good reasons why building scientists are still very much in business even to this day.) The formulas suggested here have been empirically tested and refined over decades.

The guides below are therefore selected for these reasons—simplicity and reliability. As always, these are intended for the BIM workflow as design guides only:

- to establish initial design parameters or for preliminary sizing;
- to evaluate the relative merits of competing designs; and
- to help refine an established design by quantitatively comparing design iterations.

These guides are not necessarily predictive of actual building performance, as has been disclaimed elsewhere.

Whole-building heat loss

In designing for passive heating in skin-load dominated buildings, it is typically assumed that internal cooling loads—sources of heat such as people, lighting, and equipment—do not contribute to the heating of the building. This has drawbacks and advantages. On the one hand, it does not accurately reflect reality, and is a missed opportunity to use internal heat gains to offset external losses. Moreover, it may lead to overheating in winter, especially if the building has no systems—even as simple as operable shading devices—to control winter insolation.

On the other hand, ignoring internal loads for early design phases has certain advantages. The design will thereby perform under worst-case conditions (low occupancy, lights off, lack of significant equipment heat sources). Design is simplified, since the designer need only consider solar heat gains and envelope losses. In energy modeling, internal loads are the most complex to calculate, as they are significantly impacted by usage patterns and schedules. By comparison, solar gains and envelope performance are far more tractable, computationally. Eliminating internal heat sources therefore simplifies the architect's early energy performance assessments, and makes modeling within BIM far more straightforward. Of course, as the design is assessed, refined, and carefully optimized for maximum performance, external energy modelers come into play (see Chapter 11).

Envelope assembly losses

There are four areas where buildings lose heat. Wall assemblies and their glazed subassemblies, windows, and roofs comprise three areas, and are commonly thought of as the "building envelope." These envelope assemblies are subject to conductive losses primarily, as well as radiation and convection losses, and losses due to infiltration of cold air (or exfiltration of warm air). For all but infiltration, the total assembly U-factor multiplied by the area of a given assembly determines heat loss. Floors and basements are subject to ground heat losses, and these are treated in the next section.

Opaque wall assembly heat losses

Total wall R-value (thermal resistance) or U-factor (thermal conductance) should be assigned at the time of creation of BIM wall types; it's generally easier to do so early in the project and helps to avoid possible errors due to missing walls when assigning data *ex post facto*. As mentioned in Chapter 4, total envelope heat loss is the conductivity of each envelope wall or roof type, *U*, multiplied by its area, *A*. Globally, this is expressed as:

$$q_{assembly} = U \cdot A(t_{in} - t_{out})$$ [Equation 7.1; Grondzik et al. 2010, 208]

It is immaterial whether walls are given R-values or U-factors, because one is the inverse of the other, so long as the same unit is applied consistently

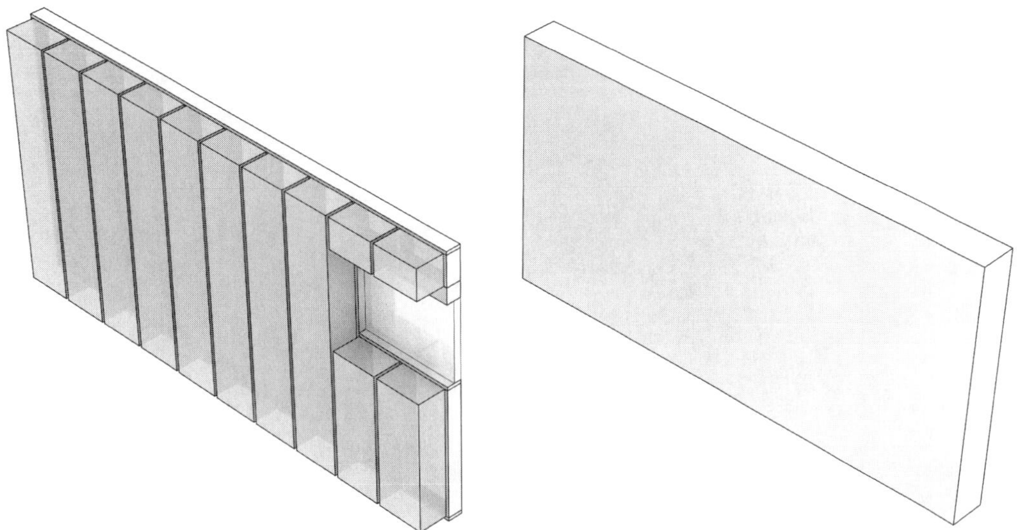

FIGURE 7.4 In these comparative "graphs," component R-value is represented by thickness. The U·A of frame wall components by relative volume is shown on the left. The slab on the right has the same total U·A as the wall assembly on the left; that is, it is represented as having the same total volume, only homogenously distributed.

throughout the project. If using R-values, the embedded expression of Equation 7.1 must be rewritten, substituting 1/R for U. One advantage of working with R-values is that these are additive for each component within a given wall assembly; U-factors are not additive. For example, in a wood stud frame wall, one sums the R-value of each wythe (exterior air film, siding, sheathing, stud or insulation, drywall, interior air film) to derive a total R-value. One cannot, however, sum the U-values of each of the above components and get a correct total assembly U-factor. There are innumerable print and online resources listing typical building material R-values (care should be taken, too, to consistently use Inch-Pound or Système International units).

Certain common wall types, the stud wall above for example, have different R-values at the insulation than at the stud (not to mention at headers, corners, edges of openings, and other conditions where structure fills the cavity). When assigning an R-value (or U-factor) to a wall type, calculate an *average* value, taking into account the percentage of the wall that is thermally bridged or under-insulated (Fig. 7.4). The Oak Ridge National Laboratory's web site[1] has online tools to help determine *average* R-values of common wall types. (For stud framing, *advanced framing* or *optimized value engineered* (OVE) framing is preferable to conventional wood framing for its economical use of materials and increased insulation—see Chapter 10.)

Glazed wall assembly (window) heat losses

As window thermal performance has radically improved in recent years, these have come to account for less of total heat losses for most buildings. Future advances will undoubtedly lead to even further performance improvements. Window performance is characterized by three factors generally: *solar heat gain coefficient* (SHGC, theoretically ranging from 0 to 1.0), *visible transmittance* (VT, also from 0 to 1.0), and U-factor (Fig. 7.5). *Emissivity* (ε) contributes to a window's SHGC, and coatings to control the emission of thermal radiation from the

[1] Available at www.ornl.gov.

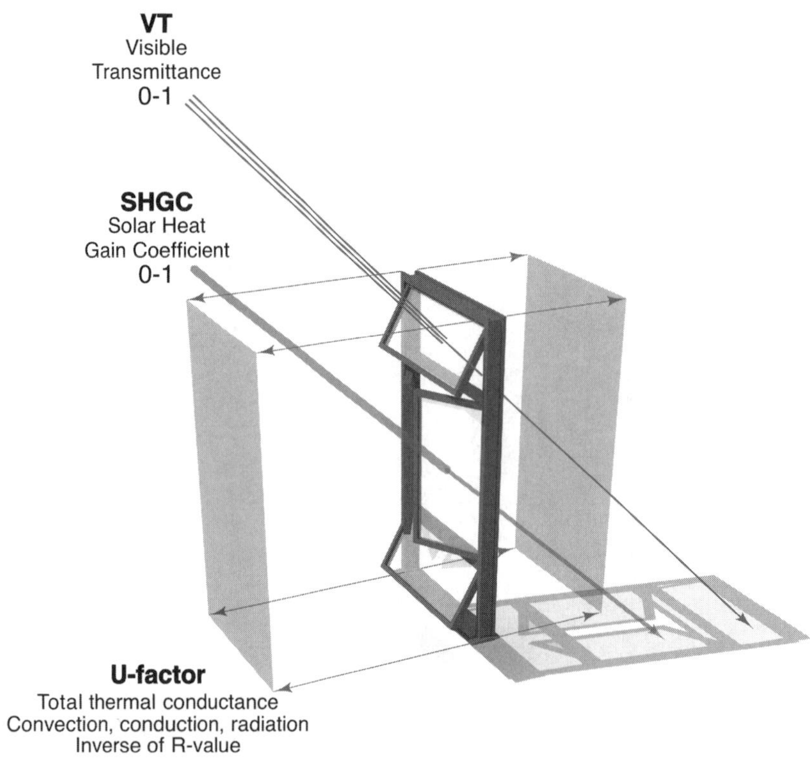

FIGURE 7.5 Visible Transmittance, Solar Heat Gain Coefficient, and U-factor of a window.

window glass are designed for particular climates. In the United States, "low-ε" coatings on glazing reflect infrared back into the space to encourage space heating, while so-called "Southern low-ε" coatings for warmer climates help block heat gain into the space in the first place. For warm climates, a high SHGC is desirable, as an important function of glazed assemblies is the admission of solar insolation to passively heat a space. In hot climates, a *maximum* SHGC will likely be code-mandated; for cold climates, a *high* SHGC is desirable.

The higher the U-factor, the greater the tendency the window as a whole will have to conduct heat. Thus for warm or cold climates, a low U-factor is ideal, although it is most critical in colder climates: total heat loss is dependent on the difference between indoor and outdoor temperatures. In colder climates, the outdoor winter temperatures are routinely 70°F or more below indoor set point temperatures; under hot conditions, temperature differences may be half that or less. As with opaque wall assemblies, glazed assemblies will use U·A for total conductance (Equation 7.1).

For the BIM user, it is generally not necessary (nor desirable) to differentiate subcomponents of windows. Manufactured windows have a U-factor provided by the manufacturer; this U-factor is not for the glazing alone, but the window assembly as a whole, including jambs and sashes, assuming correct installation. When querying the BIM model to report window area, do not therefore parse net glazed area (Fig. 7.6). Instead, use overall window unit size to determine the value of *A* for Equation 7.1.

In the context of this book, any sustainable project in a cold climate (or warm climate under cold conditions) is assumed to make use of passive solar heating. Since south-facing glass is a *source* of heat, it cannot simultaneously be a site for heat loss. Total

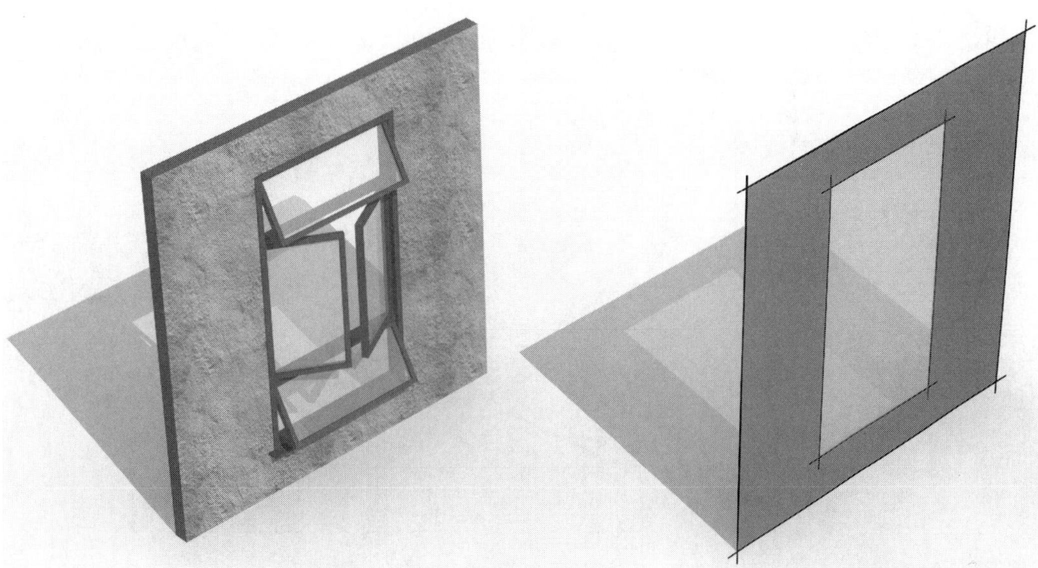

FIGURE 7.6 The BIM model may detail the window geometry for visualization and detailing purposes, but since window U-factor is global, for energy calculations the overall window characteristics applied to its total area are used.

glazed assembly heat losses therefore ignore any south-facing glass; multiply the area of non-south glass by window U-factors for the glazing U·A.

Roof assembly heat losses

As described in Chapter 4, *Massing Analysis,* roof assemblies functionally underperform for a given U-factor (or R-value; see Fig. 7.7). This diminishment in effective R-value is not linear, and can be approximately expressed as:

$$R_{effective} = (R_{cavity} - 9)^{-0.1}$$

[Equation 7.2; after Grondzik et al. 2010, 1621]

Hence, a metal roof with a calculated or cavity R-value of 50 would have an effective R-value of 34.5. The above formula slightly underestimates the effective roof R-value at lower values; for a more exact table of values, refer to Grondzik et al. (2010). Remember that when incorporating envelope thermal loss calculations in the BIM model, only count the area of the roof over conditioned spaces. This may require an additional step, depending on the nature of the building and level of detail of the model:

- For hipped or gabled roof forms, assuming the model is sufficiently detailed to incorporate separate soffit elements, subtract the eave area from the overall roof area. If the soffit is horizontal, divide the soffit area by the cosine of the roof angle, θ, to get the roof area over the soffit; this accounts for the roof area over the soffit's being greater than the horizontal soffit area:

$$A_{soffit\_roof} = A_{soffit}/\cos\theta$$ [Equation 7.3]

- For single-pitch (shed or skillion) roofs with vaulted ceilings, in lieu of reporting the roof object area, count uppermost floor ceilings over conditioned spaces. This method may miss areas over exterior walls (and possibly interior walls too, depending on how the model is constructed);
- For shed, gabled, or hipped roofs with horizontal ceilings, use the trigonometric function above, substituting ceiling area over conditioned space in lieu of soffit area, to determine the area of the roof above conditioned spaces;

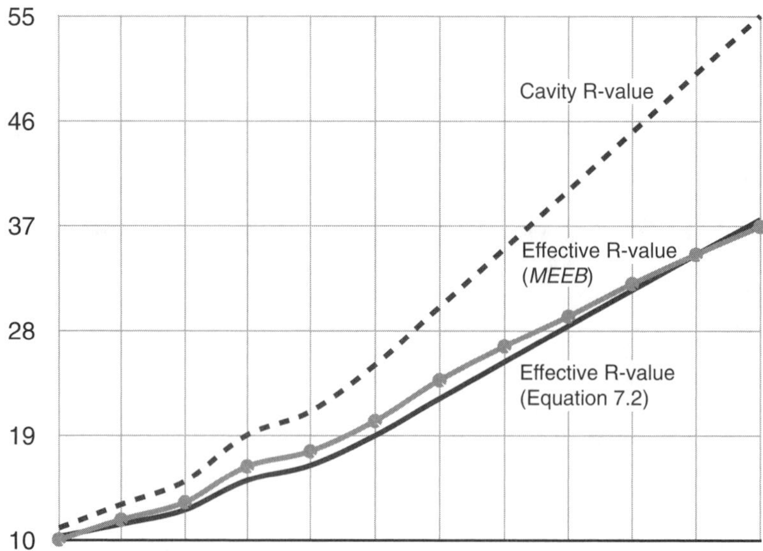

FIGURE 7.7 Actual metal roof R-value performance decreases nonlinearly as rated R-value increases. The dashed line represents rated R-value of a metal roof assembly, while the lower two curves represent effective roof R-values. The dark solid curve is from Equation 7.2, while data points on the light grey curve are from Grondzik et al. (2010).

- For atypical roof forms (curved or barrel) with overhangs over unconditioned areas, the modeler may want to include a separate invisible 3D surface that conforms to the roof, but only over conditioned spaces. As the roof is changed throughout design, the "shadow" roof must also be maintained, in order to return an accurate roof area value. Alternately, the roof insulation itself may be used to determine conditioned roof surface area, although care must be taken to use the entire roof assembly's R-value, not just the insulation R-value (Fig. 7.8).

In later design phases, exporting the BIM model to an energy modeler will yield superior thermal performance information compared to U·A calculations, for reasons outlined previously. An energy modeler will more accurately account for:

- roof surface performance based on material, color, and emissivity;
- roof orientation, and the effect of solar insolation; and
- effects of climate on annual performance, accounting for cloud cover, ambient air temperatures, relative humidity, rain, and wind velocity.

Infiltration heat losses

In winter conditions, when winds tend to be stronger than in summer, some heat loss will occur due to infiltration of cold air into the building. There are a wide variety of methods to estimate infiltration rates in existing buildings, but pressurization testing (the so-called blower door test) is common and more reliable. For buildings in design (which this book primarily addresses), the area of air leakage in *square inches* (A_L) can be estimated as the exposed building envelope area in *square feet* divided by 0.01 for tight buildings with an air-sealing specialist involved during construction, or by 0.02 for carefully sealed buildings constructed by a knowledgeable builder. (Looser buildings are unlikely to be designed by readers of this book.)

Heat loss due to infiltration is a function of (among other factors) the number of *air changes per hour* (distinct from *air replacements per hour*); the ACH calculation is embedded within the equation below, derived from earlier work and republished in the *Handbook of Fundamentals*. Infiltration heat loss

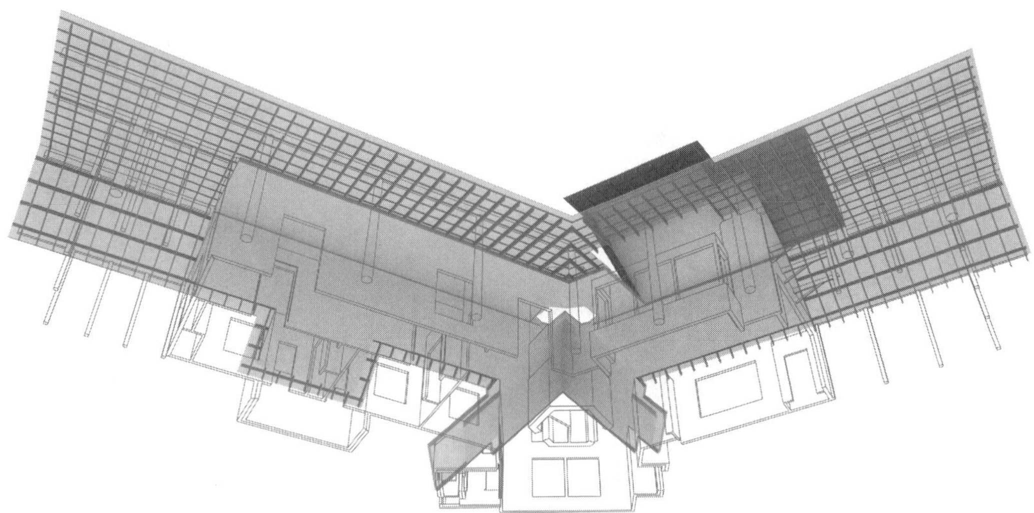

FIGURE 7.8 Some BIM roof models do not differentiate exposed eaves from roofs over conditioned space. A variety of modeling techniques can be used to compensate.

due can be expressed equivalently to U·A in units of Btu/h°F (which makes it easily additive with other envelope losses), and is best expressed as:

$$q_{vent} = V \cdot 0.018 . A_L \left[\frac{698 + H|\Delta t|\left(0.81 + 0.53(A_{L,flue} / A_L\right)}{1000} \right]$$

[Equation 7.4; ASHRAE 2005, 29.12]

Again, we have a formula that may look a bit daunting, but is, in fact, straightforward algebra. The constants in the brackets are assuming 15 mph winter winds. *V* is the conditioned volume of the building, and *H* is its height (to account for the stack effect and buoyant air movement)—both values can be readily given by the BIM model. As usual, Δt is the difference between the interior set-point temperature and the outdoor 99 percent design temperature. The areas of leakage, $A_{L,flue}$ and A_L, are values (in square inches) also determined from the BIM model (Fig. 7.9). The former can be mined from the model by including any fireplace flue's cross-sectional area in the calculation, and the latter as explained above is a function of the building area (also given by the model) and the aforementioned coefficients for building tightness.

Ground heat losses

The thermal conductivity of building materials, *U,* is a value that factors the material's conductive heat losses as well as those due to convection and radiation. Stated U-factors have been empirically derived by testing materials and assemblies in air; they are not reliable when considering earth contact, since only conductance is at play in this case, and soil is far more conductive than air. Further, the variance between soil and air temperature increases significantly with soil depth. For these reasons, the usual values for U do not accurately represent ground heat losses, and design guidelines for the virtual building must adjust the aboveground U-factors of walls to represent subsurface mechanisms of heat loss.

Slab losses

Empirical research shows that heat loss from a slab on grade occurs far more significantly at the slab's perimeter than under it. That is, the characteristic of interest in this case is the slab perimeter length, rather than its area. F_p is the perimeter (linear) heat loss coefficient, in Btu/h ft °F. According to ASHRAE *(2005)*, F_p varies from 0.49 for brick veneered CMU with R-5.4 insulation, to 2.12 for an

Variable	Description	Value
A_L	Area losses, building, ft²	166.6
A_L, flue	Area losses, flue, in²	238.5
V	Building volume, ft³	25,460.0
H	Building height, ft	29.0
Δt	Indoor/outdoor design temperature difference, °F	48.0

q vent 219,991.9 Btu/h °F

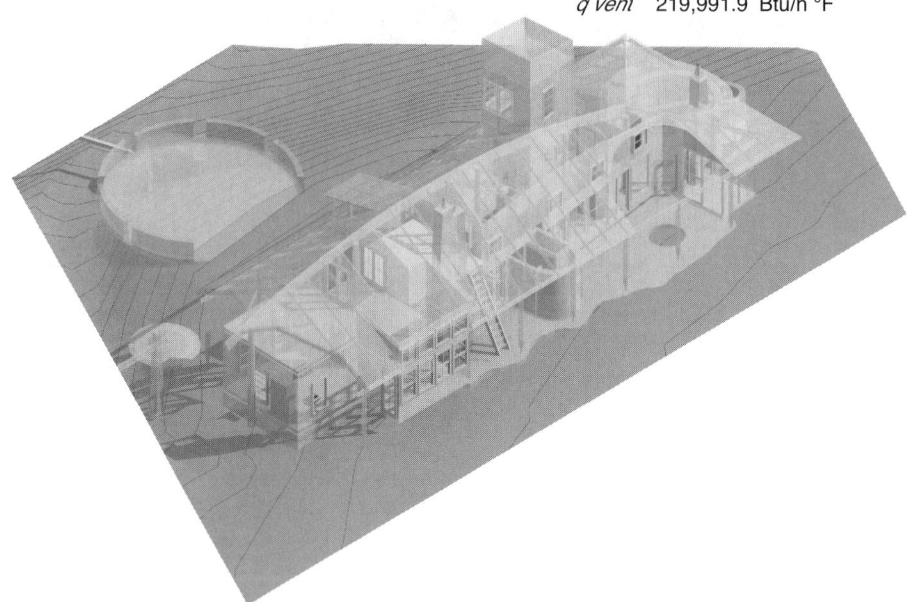

FIGURE 7.9 The BIM model may self-report infiltration losses by incorporating Equation 7.4 in a worksheet, provided the user supplies estimated values for estimated indoor and outdoor temperature differences.

uninsulated cast concrete wall with a perimeter heating duct nearby. Unfortunately, ASHRAE provides a very limited number of wall assemblies and their corresponding F_p values. Correlation of those values given to the wall type's R-values suggests that it may be possible to approximate a wall's F_p value as $R^{-1/3}$. The BIM model can readily report slab perimeter length, as well as assigned wall type R-values, incorporated into a worksheet or schedule calculating slab heat losses:

$$q_{slab} = P \cdot R^{-1/3} \cdot \Delta t \qquad \text{[Equation 7.5; after ASHRAE 2005, 29.12]}$$

Where Δt is the temperature difference between the inside set point temperature (reasonable at 68°F) and the outdoor 99 percent design temperature; P is the slab perimeter length, in feet; and R is the adjacent wall R-value, including *any insulation added at the slab perimeter* (commonly an inch of rigid insulation for cold climates; see Fig. 7.10).

For pier-and-beam foundations with crawlspaces, use U·A for the raised floor assembly, since there is no direct earth contact. More precise methods for estimating heat losses to vented and unvented crawlspaces or other unconditioned buffer spaces are provided by ASHRAE (2005).

Basement wall heat loss

Formerly, when buildings were less well insulated, about 10 percent of heat loss occurred through the ground. As building envelope assemblies elsewhere in the building have become thermally tighter,

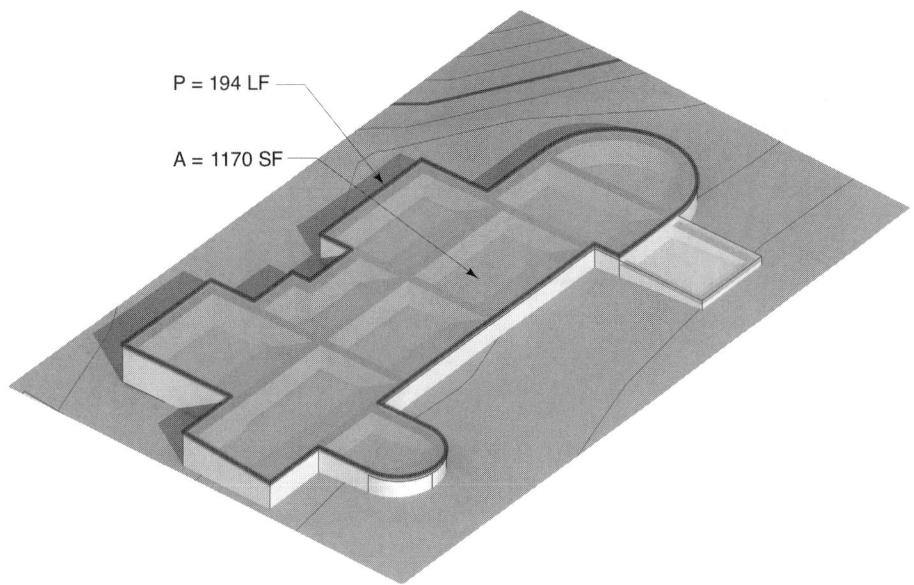

FIGURE 7.10 For heat losses at slabs, the characteristic of interest is the slab perimeter, not its area. Either value may be reported automatically by the BIM model with appropriate schedules.

ground losses have become responsible for a proportionately larger portion of total heat losses—30 to 50 percent by some estimates.

Heat loss through basement walls occurs differently than through aboveground envelope assemblies. Again, this is due to conductive differences between soils and air, the nature of below-grade of convection and radiation, and the fact that soil temperatures vary significantly with depth. In addition, variation in soil types and moisture content makes predicting heat loss through basement walls challenging. For over 30 years building science researchers have been devising simplified formulas to model heat loss through soil; a comparison of these simplified models reveals that they disagree with each other by as much as 50 percent.

For the BIM user, who will not use advanced finite element analysis (FEA) to numerically discretize the virtual building and perform detailed energy modeling, simplified approaches to approximate basement wall heat losses are useful, if imperfect, tools for evaluating designs. A formula for calculating the average U-factor of basement walls is given by ASHRAE (2005), with variables that can be applied to a BIM model. The slightly simplified equation below to calculate the U-factor of a basement wall may seem complex, but it is just a long algebraic expression with four variables:

$$U=\frac{2k_{soil}}{\pi\cdot h}\cdot \ln\left(h+\frac{2k_{soil}R}{\pi}\right)$$

[Equation 7.6; ASHRAE 2005, 29.12]

The average soil thermal conductivity is expressed as a constant, k_{soil}. Ideally, site soils would be tested, but in most cases an approximation may be necessary:

- sandy soil: 0.17 Btu ft/ft^{2}h°F
- clay soil: 0.14 Btu ft/ft^{2}h°F
- average soil: 1.0 Btu ft/ft^{2}h°F
- rock: 1.68 Btu ft/ft^{2}h°F

In these formulas, *h* is the height of the basement wall below grade (in feet), *ln* is the natural logarithm of the parenthetical value, and R is the R-value (total thermal resistance the wall assembly would have aboveground).

This formula can be included in a worksheet in the project file and the BIM model can query designated basement walls of given resistance, R, for their respective heights (h). Since all other values are constant, the worksheet can calculate the U-factor for basement walls of varying heights.

It's not uncommon to insulate the upper few feet of a basement wall, since winter temperatures near the surface are low in cold climes but tend to stabilize as depth increases. In cases where a basement wall is not homogenously insulated, the following more detailed expression for U may be used:

$$U=\frac{2k_{soil}}{\pi(h_2-h_1)}\cdot\left[\ln\left(h_2+\frac{2k_{soil}R}{\pi}\right)-\ln\left(h_1+\frac{2k_{soil}R}{\pi}\right)\right]$$

[Equation 7.7; ASHRAE 2005, 29.12]

Here, h_1 is the depth of the upper (presumably insulated) vertical segment of the wall and h_2 is the depth of the lower (presumably uninsulated) vertical segment of the basement wall. In this case, a preliminary massing model would need separate prisms to represent the basement, one for each segment (insulated and uninsulated). A more detailed BIM model of course would model differing wall types individually.

Summing heat losses

The total building heat loss is based on:

- Opaque wall assembly losses (U·A)
- Glazed assembly losses, excluding south-facing glass for passive solar buildings (U·A)
- Roof assembly losses (U·A, reducing roof R-value using Equation 7.2)
- Air infiltration losses (Equation 7.4)
- Slab ground losses (Equation 7.5), or
- Basement losses (Equation 7.6 for homogenously insulated walls, otherwise Equation 7.7)

All of the above are expressed in common units of Btu/h°F, and can be added to express the total building heat losses for a given design (Fig. 7.11). It may take some effort to set up a template file that incorporates the equations above, linking the architectural variables of BIM objects, families, layers, or classes. However, this initial setup is not much more work than creating standalone spreadsheets for these same calculations, with the advantage that the model, not manual data entry, provides variable values. Once calculations are in place of course, the model can give real time feedback as the design evolves, which is clearly a distinct benefit.

Whole-building heat gain

Passively heating buildings to minimize net energy expenditures requires balancing gains with losses. Once losses are at least generally known, then the architect must design passive gains (primarily from solar heating) to offset those losses, without overheating the space. There are several simplified methods for estimating gains; as might be expected, the designer must balance their simplicity and accessibility on the one hand with potential inaccuracies on the other.

Heat gain from glazing

Balcomb (1980) as reported in Gondzik et al. (2010) recommended south-facing glazing equaling in area between 7 and 13 percent of the building floor area for conventional wood-framed buildings with carpeted floors. An analysis of location-specific design guidelines suggested in his earlier *Passive Solar Design Handbook* reveals a general correlation in most cases between recommended maximum south-facing glazing area ($A_{SG\ max}$) as a percentage of building floor area and January *Heating Degree Days* (HDD65):

$$A_{SG\ max} = HDD_{Jan}/3883 \qquad \text{[Equation 7.8]}$$

Heating Degree Days (HDD) are a quantitative measure of the number of degree days in a period where ambient temperature is below a defined balance point temperature, generally 65°F (18°C). This

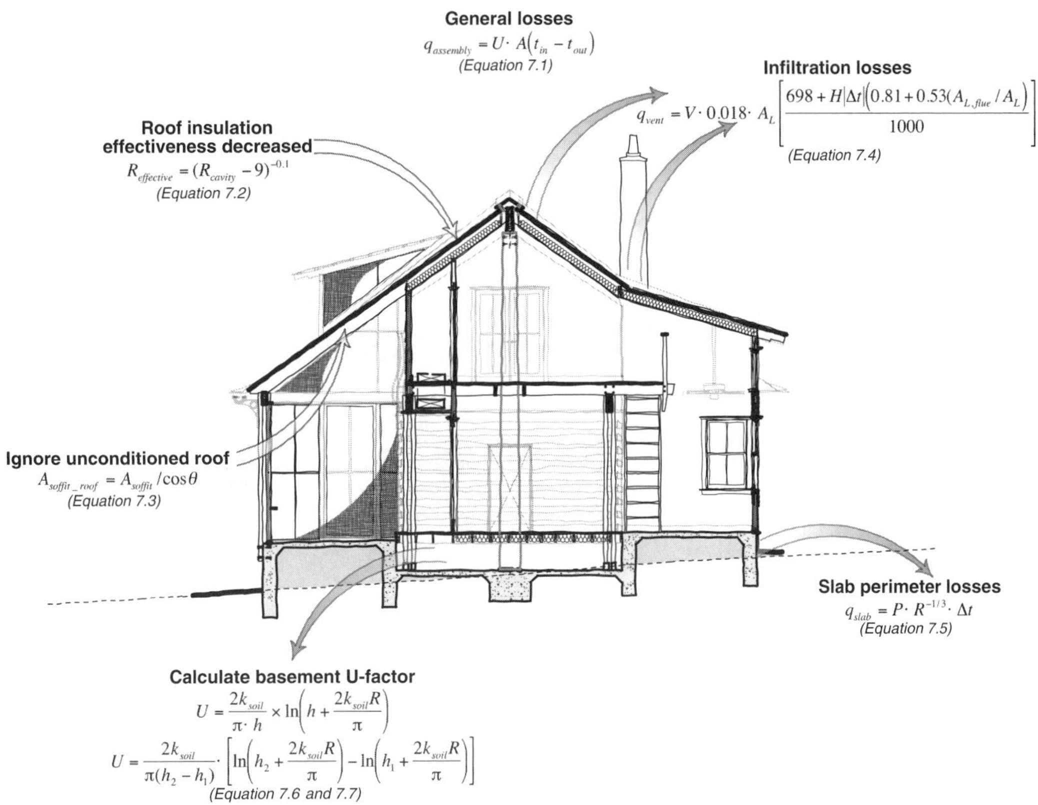

FIGURE 7.11 Heat losses from equations 7.2 and 7.4 through 7.7 are summarized in this building section. Nearly all variables can readily be determined from the BIM model. Total building heat loss is simply the sum of individually calculated losses: opaque wall assembly, glazing (excluding south-facing glass), roof, slab and basement, and infiltration. These losses are tedious to calculate by hand, but once the user has set up a BIM process to account for these, then updating estimated losses for numerous design iterations is trivial.

equation will yield values for maximum south-facing glazed area on average within under 10 percent of the values given in Grondzik et al. (2010, appendix F.1), which is itself adapted from Balcomb's (1980) data (Fig. 7.12). Values from the above equation tend to be least accurate and underestimate glazing area for hot, sunny climates with a very low January HDD value. For *minimum* recommended area, divide $A_{SG\,max}$ by 2 (south glazing minima equal to half the maxima is a common solar design guideline).

As an example, NOAA climate data for Chicago indicates a 30-year average of 1,333 HDD for January (in that month, one would expect an average daily temperature of 43°F below 65°F, or 22°F, since 1,333 divided by 31 is 43). Dividing 1,333 by 3,833 gives 0.348, or 34.8 percent. Thus, at least 17 percent and at most about 35 percent of the south façade should be glazed (compare with Grondzik and Balcomb, who also give that range as 17 to 35 percent).

In the BIM model, it is straightforward enough to report a schedule of south facing windows (Fig. 7.13), and compare the sum of their *net glazed area* (not the rough opening or unit area) to the maximum and minimum recommended values given by the Equation 7.8.

While solar geometry for passively heated buildings might seem to be correlated to latitude

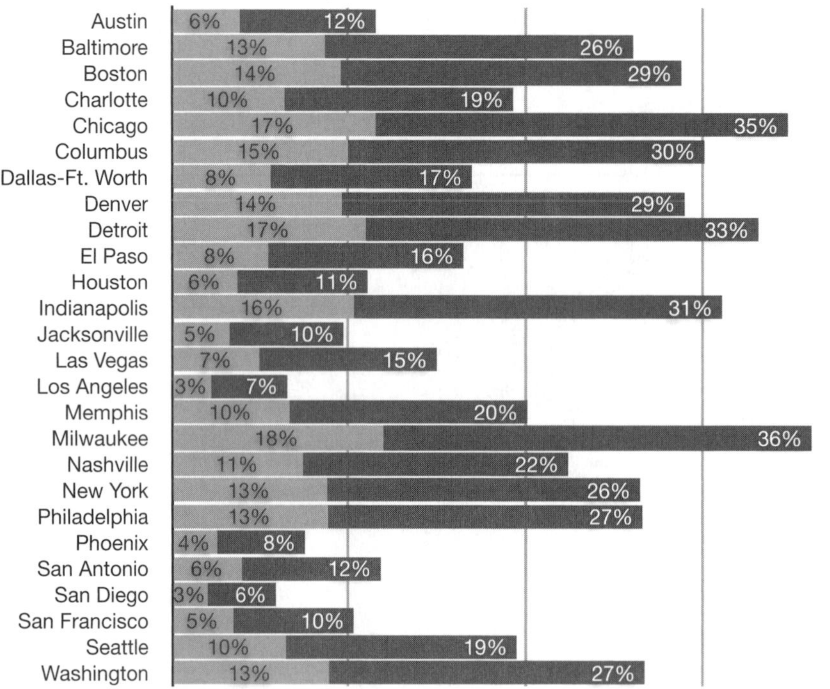

FIGURE 7.12 A sampling of average January Heating Degree Days for over 25 of the most populous cities in the United States was used to derive the minimum and maximum south-facing glass (as a percentage of building floor area) as an effective solar passive heating design guideline.

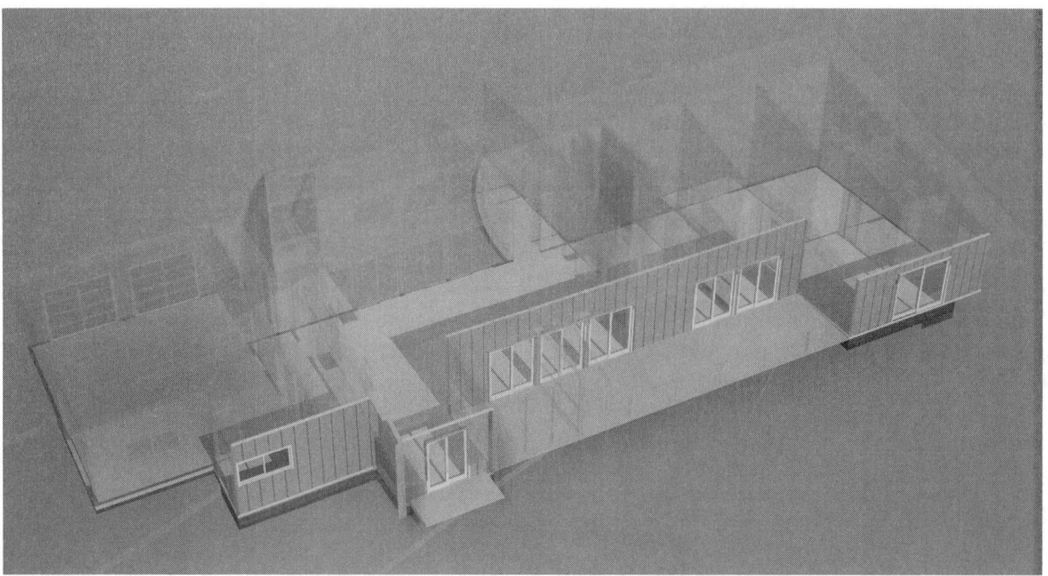

FIGURE 7.13 South-facing walls and their glazed components can be isolated in BIM and areas optimized as an appropriate percentage of total conditioned floor slab.

Degrees from due south			
East	**West**	γ_{opt}	η_{loss}
-6	**6**	**±0**	**0.0%**
-4	8	±2	-0.0%
-2	10	±4	-0.1%
0	12	±6	-0.3%
2	14	±8	-0.6%
4	16	±10	-0.9%
6	18	±12	-1.2%
8	20	±14	-1.7%
10	22	±16	-2.2%
12	24	±18	-2.8%
14	26	±20	-3.5%
16	28	±22	-4.2%
18	**30**	**±24**	**-5.0%**
20	32	±26	-5.8%
22	34	±28	-6.8%
24	36	±30	-7.8%
26	38	±32	-8.9%
28	**40**	**±34**	**-10.0%**
30	42	±36	-11.2%
32	44	±38	-12.5%
34	46	±40	-13.8%
36	48	±42	-15.3%
38	50	±44	-16.7%
40	52	±46	-18.3%
42	**54**	**±48**	**-19.9%**

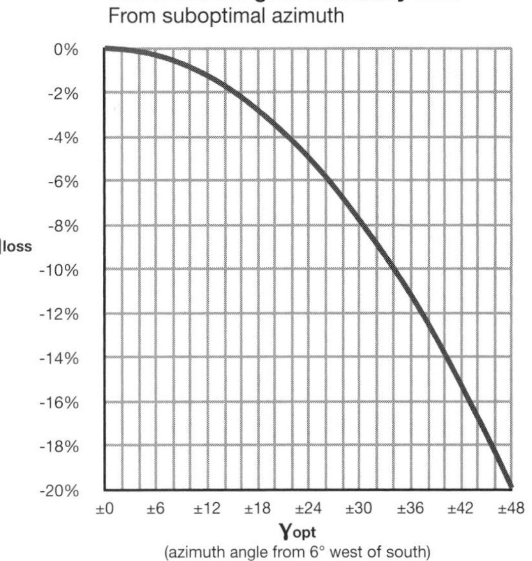

FIGURE 7.14 Data and graph showing the decreased efficiency for winter heat gain of windows, η_{loss}, resulting in window orientation away from the equator (south). Values are calculated from Equation 7.9.

(as photovoltaic and solar hot water systems are), latitude is only partially a predictor of winter conditions, outdoor design temperatures and overcast conditions. Consider that Seattle is slightly north of Fargo, yet obviously the two have strikingly different winter temperatures. There are numerous web resources with historically averaged or recent-year heating degree day data, both monthly and annually tabulated. NOAA has extensive data for hundreds of North American locations on their web site, but simple consumer-oriented calculators are also available.[2]

For solar photovoltaic and thermal collectors, it is commonly known that azimuth weakly affects collector efficiency, provided that the collector is within 15° of due south—as we saw in Chapter 5 and will revisit in Chapter 8. For vertical direct-gain glazed solar air collectors (that is, windows oriented generally towards the equator), *annual* performance is optimized if orientation is on average 6° west of south (or north in the southern hemisphere). In certain cases, the designer may orient the building slightly east of south, in order to increase morning insolation to offset overnight heat losses and take the edge off the morning chill. Within 18° east or 30° west of south performance is decreased by only 5 percent. While exact performance decrease for sub-optimal orientation is dependent on site conditions (obstructions) and climate (meteorological phenomena), in general it can be expressed as:

$$\eta_{loss} = -8.65 \cdot 10^{-5} \cdot \gamma_{opt}^2 \qquad \text{[Equation 7.9]}$$

Where η_{loss} is the decrease in efficiency of the solar collecting windows, as a percentage, and γ_{opt} is the number of degrees from optimum (6° west of south; Fig. 7.14). Applying the formula above to a few orientations reported in the *Passive Solar Design Handbook* yields similar results. Figure 7.14 lists a range of orientations and the corresponding loss in solar insolation collection efficiency that Equation 7.9 predicts; values in bold are

[2] For example, www.weatherdatadepot.com.

angles listed in the *Passive Solar Design Handbook* and agree with Balcomb's (1980) values.

By assigning γ_{opt} to BIM windows, the model can report in a worksheet or schedule the amount by which A_{SG} in Equation 7.8 should be increased to achieve an area equivalent to fully south-facing windows. Alternately, the designer can adjust Equation 7.8 as follows:

$$A_{SG} = \frac{HDD_{Jan}}{\left(3833 \cdot \left(1 - 8.65 \cdot 10^{-5} \cdot \gamma^2_{opt}\right)\right)} \quad \text{[Equation 7.10]}$$

Annual auxiliary heating estimates

An important question a designer may consider as the building design evolves is that of conventional heating equipment to compensate for any deficiencies in passive heating. Consider that sizing systems on the basis of design guidelines takes into account global, annual, or worst-case conditions. Further, these guides consider the building essentially in a steady state. That is, they do not take into account fluctuations in heat flow and temperature over time, nor do they account for the variability of weather. This is a distinct (and as stated previously) simplified approach taken by energy modeling, which simulates building performance on an hour-by-hour basis over the course of a climatically idealized year, based on three decades of weather data.

For example, a method for sizing the recommended area of south facing glazing in the BIM model has been suggested. Such a method does not directly take into account nighttime heat losses through the south glazing, and by itself does not address shifting daytime heat gain to overnight use by means of thermal mass—although there are separate guidelines for that, too. Because the south window sizing guideline is based on Heating Degree Days for the entire month of January, it may be inadequate for an unusually long period of overcast days, or lead to overheating in an unusually warm winter. Energy modeling, on the other hand, would potentially indicate which hours of the year saw too much solar gain, and which saw not enough. Generally, though, most sustainable architecture practices aim for optimal performance over the year, recognizing that a building is unlikely, however well designed, to never require additional energy. The goal is a *net* reduction in energy consumption.

To size mechanical heating equipment appropriately, the heating system must balance the total hourly heat loss, calculated as:

$$q_{total} = q_{wall} + q_{glazing} + q_{roof} + q_{ground} + q_{vent}$$

[Equation 7.11; after Grondzik et al. 2010, 258]

Each of the right-hand values is given by preceding equations; q_{wall} is from Equation 7.1, as are $q_{glazing}$ and q_{roof}. For solar heated buildings in most climates, it may be appropriate to omit the area of south-facing glass from $q_{glazing}$ based on the assumption that while the south glazing area is collecting net energy, it cannot simultaneously be losing it. Remember to reduce the U-factor of roof components per Equation 7.2, and q_{vent} is given by Equation 7.4. Finally, depending on whether the building is slab on grade or includes a basement will determine which value to use for q_{ground} (Equation 7.5 or 7.7), and buildings with both conditions will use each expression for a portion of their ground heat losses.

Estimating Solar Savings Fraction and optimizing thermal mass

Thermally massive passive heating relies on the heat storage capacity of dense materials like concrete, stone, or water to absorb excess heat by day and gradually release it at night. It is therefore ideal for climates with significant temperature difference between day and night (diurnal swing). If latent heat is an issue, other passive means must be paired with thermal mass to control humidity. Typically for winter conditions ambient humidity is insufficient for comfort, and moisture must be added.

As with cooling, when sizing the area of thermal mass materials for heating, count areas of 4-inch-thick exposed concrete, stone, or brick, or 12 inches of water—thicker thermal masses have little effect on daily building performance. *Solar Savings Fraction* (SSF; Fig. 7.15) is a value indicating the increased efficiency of a passive building over its conventional counterpart; for example, an SSF of 40 indicates 40 percent greater relative efficiency compared to a conventionally (non-solar) heated building. For a desired SSF, include 0.6 pound of water per square foot of building, or 3 pounds of masonry per square foot for every percentage point of desired SSF. To approximate the design area of exposed thermal mass recommended for a given building, multiply the thermal material constant (K_{mass}) by the exposed thermal mass area (A_{mass}) divided by the collector area (for example, a south-facing window; $A_{collector}$):

$$SSF = \frac{K_{mass} \cdot A_{mass}}{A_{collector}}$$ [Equation 7.12, after Grondzik et al. 2010, 1649]

The constant K_{mass} in the equation above is dependant on the thermal mass material. For water, K_{mass} is 1; for masonry, it is 0.137. (While less than half as dense as concrete, water has nearly five times concrete's specific heat capacity, per unit of mass.) Only count thermal mass surfaces exposed to direct solar gain for at least part of a clear winter day as "exposed thermal mass."

Roof pond sizing

The same roof pond that helps cool a building on a summer day can also help heat the floor below it on winter nights. Roof ponds for heating operate on the same principal as for cooling, albeit with an inverted schedule of insulated cover operation. By day, when insolation contributes to heat gains (as do to a certain degree internal loads), the pond's insulated cover is retracted to maximize solar heating. At night, the cover is deployed to prevent radiated heat loss to the black body of the night sky or convective losses to cold night air (Fig. 7.16).

Solar Savings Fraction estimate

K mass	A mass	A SG	SSF
0.137	1,254.3 SF	305.0 SF	**56.3 %**

SSF = K mass · A mass / A SG

Where:
SSF = Solar Savings Fraction
K mass = specific heat coefficient of material (masonry)
A mass = concrete and masonry surfaces exposed to winter sun, SF
A SG = South-facing glazing area, SF

FIGURE 7.15 Solar savings fraction, a measure of improved performance for a given passive solar building, may be estimated from the amount of south-facing glazing and exposed thermal mass. In this view of a BIM model, south glazing and internal thermally massive surfaces are isolated to illustrate the estimated SSF calculation.

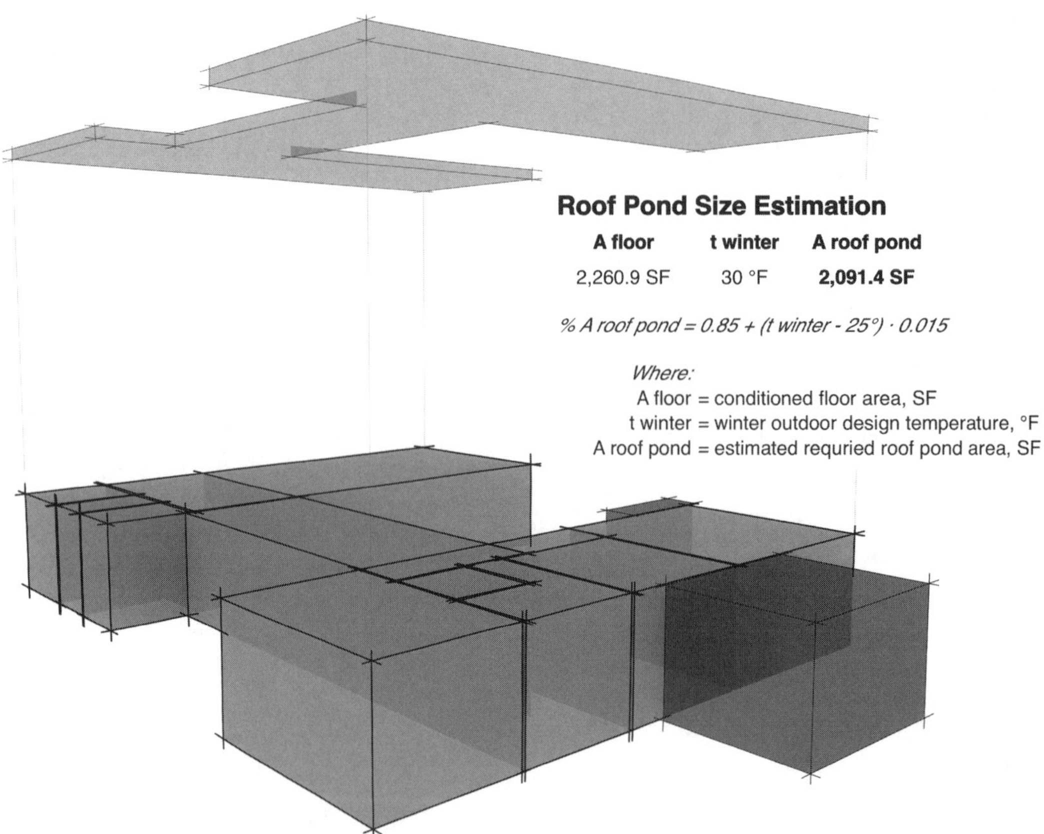

Roof Pond Size Estimation
A floor
t winter
A roof pond
2,260.9 SF
30 °F
2,091.4 SF
% A roof pond = 0.85 + (t winter - 25°) · 0.015
Where:
A floor = conditioned floor area, SF
t winter = winter outdoor design temperature, °F
A roof pond = estimated requried roof pond area, SF

FIGURE 7.16 A simple schedule can be created to estimate required roof pond size given the available roof area, floor area below to be thermally controlled, and winter design temperature.

Generally, the colder the winter, the larger the roof pond needs to be. For winters with temperature lows ranging from 25° F to 35°F (t_{winter}), the required roof pond area (as a percentage of the building floor area below it) is roughly:

$$A_{roof\ pond} = 0.85 + (t_{winter} - 25°) \cdot 0.015$$

[Equation 7.13; Grondzik et al. 2010, 238]

For climates with winter lows between 35°F and 45°F, the roof pond area percentage is:

$$A_{roof\ pond} = 0.6 + (t_{winter} - 35°) \cdot 0.03$$

[Equation 7.14; Grondzik et al. 2010, 238]

Roof ponds are not appropriate for cold climates with winter lows below 25°F. Under those conditions, the pond may freeze in winter, and/or snow accumulation may cover it and render it ineffectual. In addition, the northern latitudes of cold climates make for very low winter sun angles, reducing the effectiveness of daytime insolation. The noon sun on the winter solstice is 66.5° minus the site's latitude (Fig. 7.17). For a site in Chicago, for example, the winter solstice sun never gets higher than about 24.5° above the horizon, reducing the density of solar energy on a horizontal surface by nearly 60 percent.

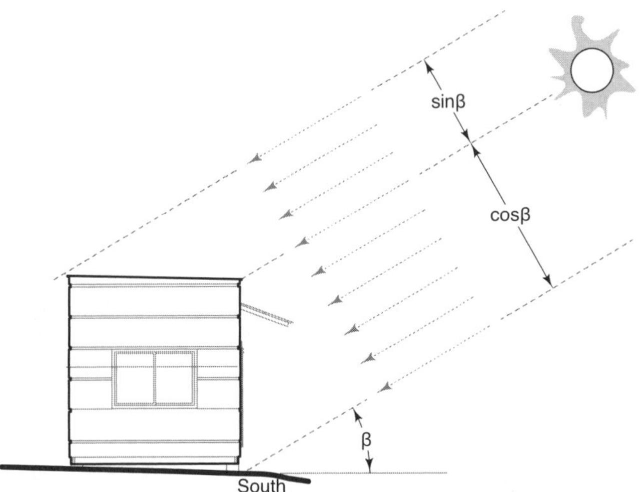

FIGURE 7.17 Solar insolation on a roof is reduced as a function of sun angle; this condition is particularly exacerbated under winter conditions with low sun angles.

▪ Case Study: Battelle Darby Creek Environmental Center, Columbus, Ohio

By Author: Brian Skripac
Design firm: DesignGroup
Client: Columbus and Franklin County Metropolitan Park District

DesignGroup, a 56-person architectural design firm based in Columbus, Ohio, has in its 38-year history considered sustainable design to be an integral part of the design process, as well as a key factor in defining building form. More recently, DesignGroup's working methods have undergone a valuable evolution through the adoption of Building Information Modeling (BIM). Over the past five years the firm's BIM expertise has grown to the point that all project work is designed in a BIM environment, spanning more than 50 projects that encompass more than 5 million square feet. This transformation has also allowed new technologies to become integrated into our design processes, ultimately representing a unique opportunity to synchronize the firm's sustainable design and BIM initiatives.

Because energy conservation is a key formgiver in all of our design projects, we've found the use of Autodesk's Revit Architecture to be a powerful tool in developing building information models at the earliest stages of a project's conception (Fig. 7.18). This modeling effort provides a more holistic approach to addressing the design challenges at hand. With model geometry in place we are able to better consider how to position the building on site, optimize its orientation, and capitalize on prevailing winds. These issues need to be studied early in the design process when these decisions can have the most positive impact on the building's performance over its lifecycle.

(Continued)

FIGURE 7.18 A rendered perspective view of southwest façade of the Battelle Darby Creek Environmental Center in design, seen from bottom of the site's promontory. The image was produced in Revit and postprocessed with Photoshop.

Image courtesy of DesignGroup, Columbus, Ohio.

The most recent example of this early sustainable analysis can be seen in a project that has just completed schematic design, the Battelle Darby Creek Environmental Center, a 10,000-square-foot educational building for the Columbus and Franklin County Metropolitan Park District. The Center will embody the client's vision of an environmental center that encourages visitors to learn about the diverse ecosystems found within the surrounding area: native prairies, creeks, wetlands, and forests. To complement these sustainable design ambitions, the project is pursuing LEED Gold Certification and will be one of the hosts of the 2012 World EcoSummit.

Leveraging Revit to quickly create multiple design iterations enabled the team to study a diverse range of solutions that looked to optimize the building's envelope and orientation for its unique climate and location. This early prototyping effort helped the designers to further develop two very distinct building layouts and orientations (Fig. 7.19).

Utilizing Revit's scheduling capabilities to easily quantify and understand the overall amounts of glazing (as compared to solid wall surfaces) in each design, the design team examined how these window-to-wall ratios would work in conjunction with each option's energy performance. Exploiting Revit's interoperability, the team exported models via the (WWRs) gbXML format to perform whole-building analysis in Green Building Studio. The results of this early analysis allowed the team to realize better than a 5 percent annual energy reduction simply due to a more favorable solar orientation (Fig. 7.20). Understanding how the optimized long north/south façade with a 46 percent WWR would outperform the less desirable east/west façade, which had a much smaller WWR at 28 percent, provided an immediate value to the project with no added cost to the design.

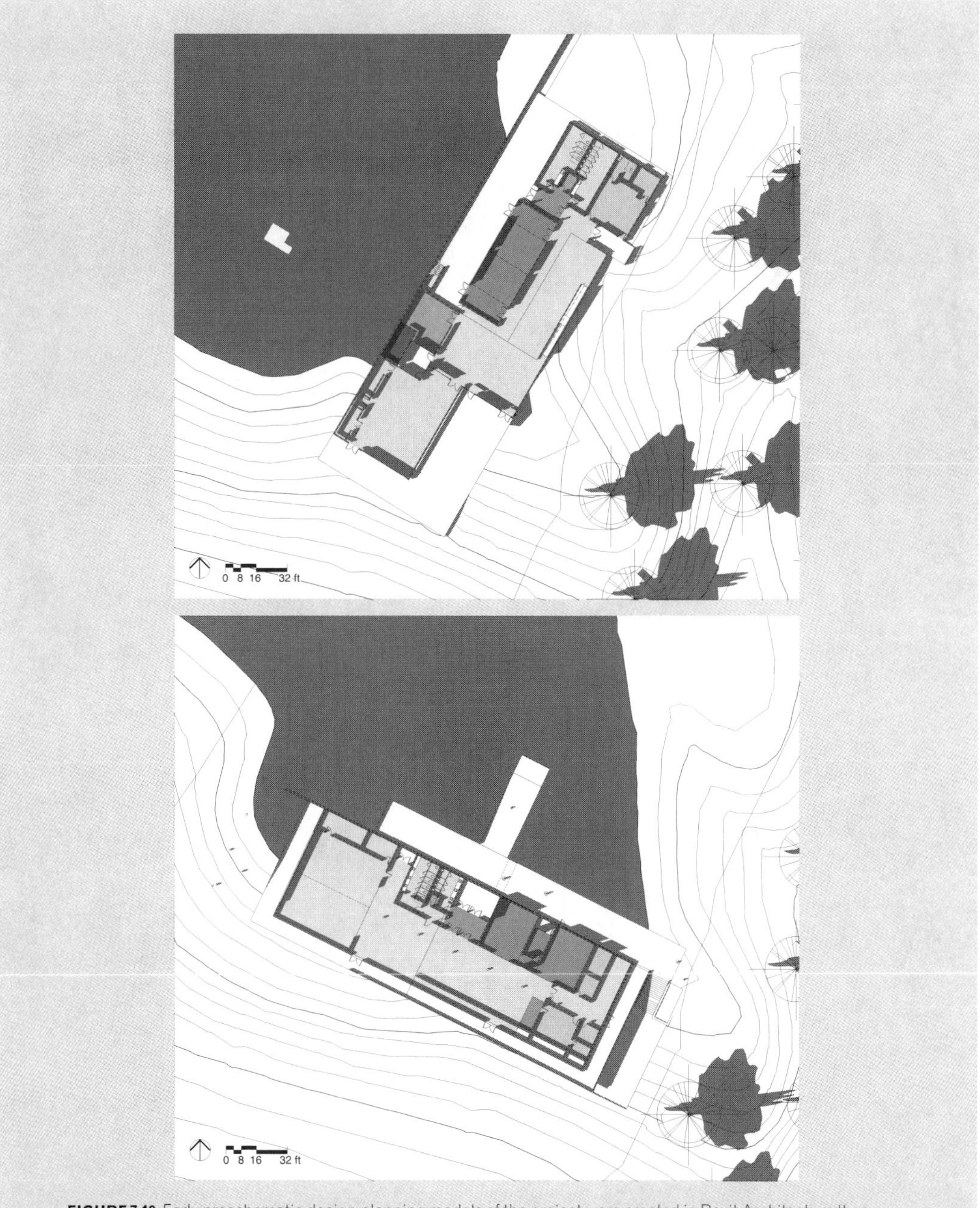

FIGURE 7.19 Early preschematic design planning models of the project were created in Revit Architecture then shared with Green Building Studio via a gbXML file to perform a whole building energy analysis to understand each option's energy performance. At top is the long east/west design with 28 percent Window-Wall Ratio (WWR); at the bottom the long north/south design has 46 percent WWR. The wall and glazing areas were calculated with Revit.

Images courtesy of DesignGroup, Columbus, Ohio.

(Continued)

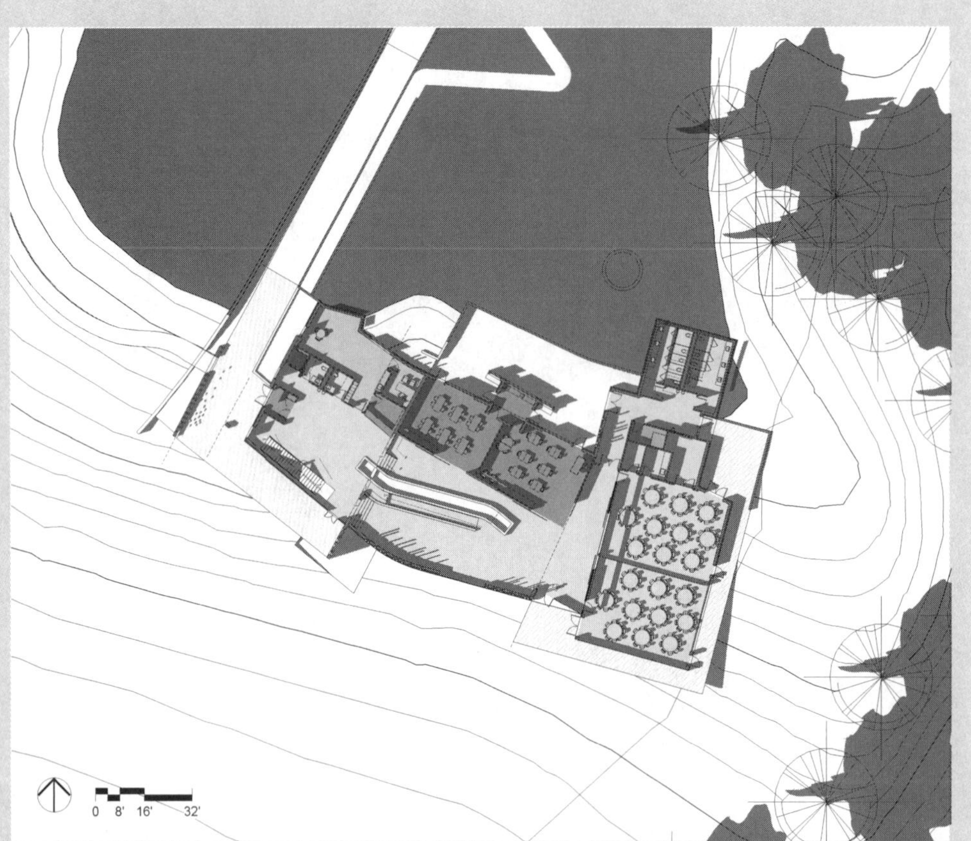

FIGURE 7.20 Schematic design floor plan of the Battelle Darby Creek Environmental Center as the design has evolved from the two competing schemes shown in the previous figure. As the project team developed the schematic design model they gained greater insight into the building's envelope performance and the amount and distribution of glazing throughout the design. The architects were thus able to leverage the early analytical feedback to optimize the design for a more favorable solar orientation and performance.

Image courtesy of DesignGroup, Columbus, Ohio.

Additionally, we found the daylighting analysis tools in Ecotect to be valuable in understanding the impacts of different daylight harvesting options in the project. With Ecotect we were able to study where to locate and how to size shading devices and roof overhangs, while maintaining a high level of daylight in the building spaces. At the same time, we were able to utilize this information in Green Building Studio to validate how these design decisions maximize and minimize solar gains to have the most positive impact on the building's overall energy consumption. The combination of all of these tools within a BIM workflow gave us the opportunity to balance both the qualitative and quantitative aspects of the building's design and performance (Fig. 7.21).

FIGURE 7.21 Rendered perspective view above drop-off area towards building entrance. The image was produced in Revit and postprocessed with Photoshop.

Image courtesy of DesignGroup, Columbus, Ohio.

FIGURE 7.22 As the design has continued to develop, BIM has proven invaluable for coordinating structural and consultant design work, as well as in continuing to visualize and analyze the evolving project.

Image courtesy of DesignGroup, Columbus, Ohio.

(Continued)

This type of feedback has proven to be extremely valuable at the early stages of the design process, enabling us to work with project elements that are typically under our scope of work, such as the building's orientation, envelope, performance, and glazing amounts and location (Fig. 7.22). If as architects we can make these decisions validated by actual analytical feedback, we will have a much better design, optimized from the outset and exceeding performance expectations.

Chapter 8

Onsite Energy Systems

It seems that energy is on everyone's mind nowadays, whether in the context of climate change or manmade disasters in the quest for more fossil fuels, or during political, social, and at times violent upheaval in oil-producing nations. Perhaps in part because of our fossil fuel dependence, and the ubiquity of cars, few members of the general public realize the significant impact our built environment has on energy consumption and carbon emissions. In the United States as in Europe, building operation and construction accounts for over 48 percent of our energy use, which is far more than that used for transportation (Fig. 8.1). Since the United States consumes about a fifth of the world's energy (albeit with increasing competition in this regard from rising economic powers like Brazil, China, and India), the building sector of the American economy consumes about one tenth of the world's energy.

The path we must take is to increase the use of alternative sources of energy while weaning our society from carbon-emitting and non-renewable resources. And this is a path we have begun to embark upon (Fig. 8.2). Texas alone in the last decade has seen nearly a fifty-fold increase in wind energy production, having surpassed the former leader, California, and providing almost 30 percent

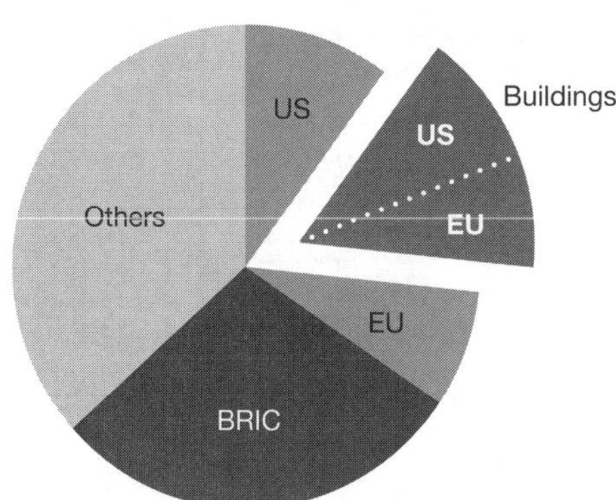

FIGURE 8.1 US buildings consume about 10 percent of world energy. Together, US and European Union (EU) buildings account for a sizable portion of world energy consumption—over half of the total energy consumption by BRIC (Brazil, Russia, India, and China).

Energy data by country: European Union, "EU Energy and Transport in Figures," 2010.

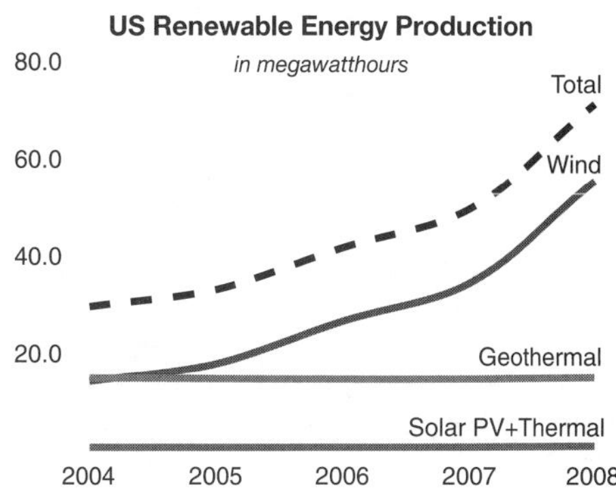

FIGURE 8.2 The installed base of photovoltaic and wind energy production in the United States has increased dramatically in the last 10 years for which data are available; nevertheless, renewable energy accounts for less than 7 percent of US energy production.

Data: US Energy Information Administration, Department of Energy.

of US wind energy. Solar photovoltaic energy production in the United States has increased tenfold over a similar period.

Yet in spite of these considerable advances, alternative energy sources only account for less than 7 percent of US energy production—about 15 percent if nuclear energy is included. At the current accelerated rate of alternative energy production increase, we will not curtail our carbon emissions fast enough to avert climatological disaster by relying on alternative energy sources alone. This is why the conservation measures that are at the heart of the design strategies discussed elsewhere in this book are essential. Every dollar spent on energy conservation—decreasing building energy consumption—is about as effective as ten dollars spent on alternative energy production.

Nevertheless, there is real value in increasing alternative energy production, particularly at or near the building site (Fig. 8.3). On-site, or distributed, energy generation has distinct advantages:

- *It eliminates transmission losses.* Depending on the grid, up to a quarter of generated electricity is lost to transmission; national average losses in 2007 in the United States were 6.5 percent of electricity produced according to the Department of Energy. However, there are also losses associated with converting direct-current generated electricity to alternating current for conventional (North American) appliances.
- *It represents a scalable energy source.* Provided that appropriate electrical systems are installed during construction, onsite building

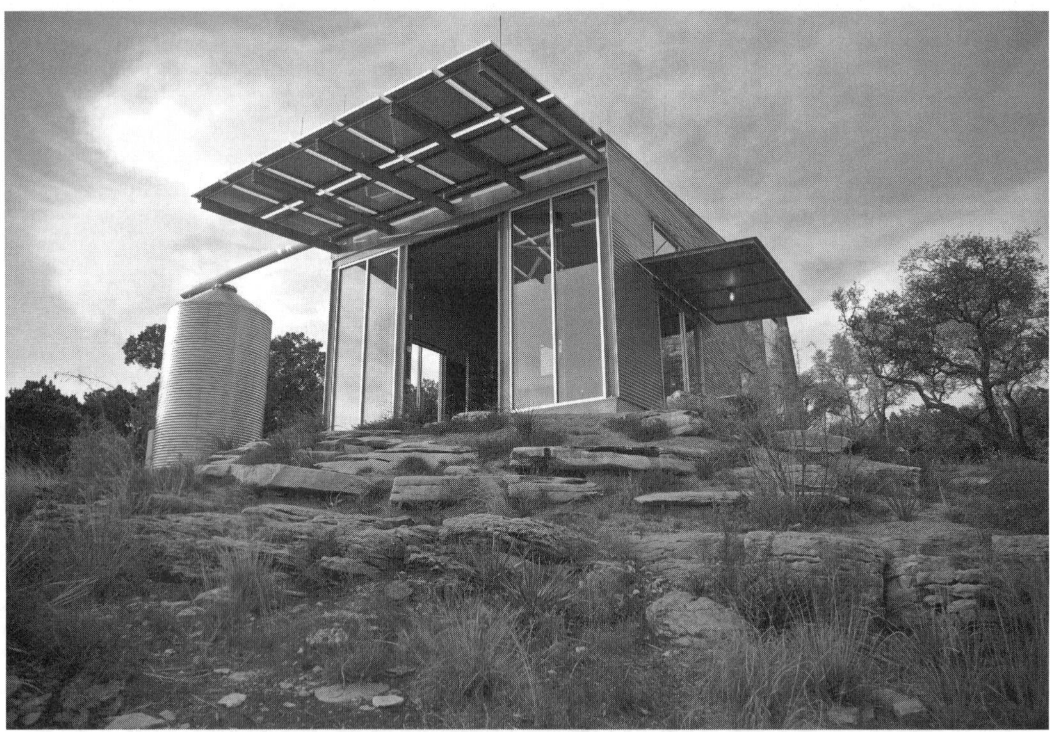

FIGURE 8.3 Onsite energy production can be an architectural formgiver, as well as serving other architectural functions, such as displacing cladding materials, as in the case of integrated photovoltaics, or serving as solar-indexed shading structure, as in this project. The awning surface is a 2.9-kilowatt photovoltaic module array sufficient to power this vacation cottage.

Image courtesy of Mell Lawrence Architects.

energy production (which tends to be direct current) can also be phased in, or increased incrementally.

- *It supports passive survivability.* One compelling approach to sustainable design is the "tight and right" method advocated by some, such as the PassivHaus Institut. Unlike purely passive buildings, this approach creates a super-insulated, tight envelope with (mechanically) controlled air intake and exhaust. Such a system is reliant on sophisticated albeit low-energy mechanical equipment; onsite energy production complements this approach well by helping ensuring continued mechanical operations. It also reduces demand as a first priority (creating "negawatts"), then providing sustainable energy sources to make up any deficits.
- *It is an opportunity for architectural expression.* While gratuitously adding photovoltaic arrays to a structure as a means of greenwashing is hardly good design, distributed energy production systems (particularly those that rely on geometry and location to be effective, such as solar and wind) can serve as legitimate architectural formgivers.
- *Building-integrated photovoltaics displace other envelope cladding materials.* There are, of course, several other onsite energy generation options than solar photovoltaics. But when PV is integrated in building materials, such as building-integrated photovoltaics (BIPV) roofing or wall cladding, it replaces conventional envelope materials. The increased cost of BIPV is therefore somewhat offset by the reduction in other cladding materials.
- *It capitalizes on subsidies.* There may be federal, state, and in some cases local subsidies available for distributed energy generation, in the form of cost rebates or tax incentives. Thanks to the 2005 Energy Policy Act, all public electric utilities in the United States are required to make net metering available upon request to their customers. With this arrangement, the utility is required to buy energy from the customer when a surplus is generated, albeit at wholesale rates. Newer electric utility meters can read and record both energy generated and used (they can be run forward and backward). Many utilities net-meter on a monthly billing basis.
- *It sustains technological innovation.* Of least direct benefit to a particular project, implementing onsite energy generation contributes slightly to demand and therefore altruistically supports and fosters advances in alternative energy technologies.

Solar photovoltaics

Perhaps the most visible if not iconic types of onsite energy generation are solar photovoltaic systems, by which sunlight is converted to useable (direct current) electrical power. While large-scale alternative energy production growth has in recent years been dominated by wind (see Fig. 8.2), for onsite energy production photovoltaics have certain advantages. In hot climates with an abundance of clear skies and direct solar gain, peak demand is indexed to peak production. That is, times of greatest power demand (due to cooling and ventilation loads) coincide with times of greatest production (summer). Contrast PVs with wind energy, which tends to produce most at night, when demands are lowest. In addition, wind speed and direction are highly variable and localized. Barring overcast weather, sun angles and obstructions are highly predictable.

BIM can be a useful tool in supporting the design and optimization of photovoltaics. The benefits are ordered here by increasing importance:

- **Maximizing exposure.** Sun studies of the BIM model with accurate latitude and building orientation can inform the designer on the optimal elevation and azimuth (angular distance from due south) for solar arrays. To approximate optimal elevation of the PV array, refer to the site's latitude and Figure 8.11; refer to the discussion in Chapter 7 for optimum azimuth.

- **Avoiding shading and self-shading**. While simple rules of thumb may inform the designer on the best PV array approximate elevation and azimuth, site-specific obstructions and the specific geometry of particular arrays make BIM shading studies critical to good PV performance. This is particularly true of arrays composed of crystalline-celled modules (mono or poly); cells are generally arranged in an electrical series within a single module in order to provide appropriate voltage. (For cells in series, each cell's voltage is added to the others; in parallel, amperage is cumulative). As a result, if a single cell within a module is shaded, the entire module is effectively offline.
- **PV synergy**. Integrating solar PV with other building performance concerns dependent on solar geometry: shading devices and daylighting geometry. In this regard, an integrated BIM approach to passive and active design is particularly effective. Building envelopes developed within a BIM workflow can be designed to simultaneously maximize annual solar collection and summer shading, while allowing appropriate daylighting and optimizing insolation on southerly glazing in winter.

Type

There are two general types of photovoltaic collectors available: those composed of arrays of individual cells with silicon crystal wafer layers and thin-film varieties (Fig. 8.4). The surface of the former type has the familiar blue-black appearance associated with PVs; thin-film PVs have no discrete "cells," and in some cases are integrated nearly invisibly with building cladding material.

Silicon: monocrystalline and polycrystalline PV cells

The technology behind silicon-based PV cells has benefitted from vast research and development investments made in the semiconductor industry over the past decades, and as a result silicon-based PV cells are the most efficient cells commercially available for general use. Currently, commercial cell efficiency is in the range of 15 to 18 percent under laboratory (optimum) conditions; actual *system* operational efficiency is less due to orientation for fixed arrays, climate, operating temperatures, dirt, shading, and system losses (from wiring and the transformer).

When considering cell efficiency, bear in mind that *system* efficiency—which considers losses at the module, array, power conditioning, and transformer level—is ultimately the most significant consideration. Nevertheless, cell efficiency is a good indicator of relative efficiency when selecting an appropriate PV technology. There is no difference at the module level between monocrystalline and polycrystalline cells, except that the former are more efficient—and more expensive. The latter have the characteristic mottled appearance associated with solar collectors due to their being composed of multiple silicon crystals (hence the name).

Thin film and integrated building materials

Different manufacturing processes and materials are used for thin-film PV than its silicon-based (Si) counterpart. While generally less efficient than Si PV (around 5 to 8 percent less efficient), thin-films are potentially less expensive because of lower material costs and larger substrate size, and they are growing in popularity in some markets (notably Germany). In addition, thin-film lends itself to true building-integrated photovoltaics.

Building-integrated photovoltaics (BIPV) represent one of the more exciting developments in building-generated energy sources. As the name implies, photovoltaic collectors are incorporated in building materials, typically in the envelope. Commonly BIPVs are found in roofing and wall cladding (Fig. 8.5); more novel products include fritted glass, which collects energy while displaying a visible pattern (Fig. 8.6). Applications for the latter range from logo-festooned building cladding to energy-collecting atria guardrails.

BIPVs offer a discreet alternative for architects hoping to avoid the cliché of photovoltaic modules arrayed on their buildings in a sort of technophilial pastiche. This discretion, however, comes at a price,

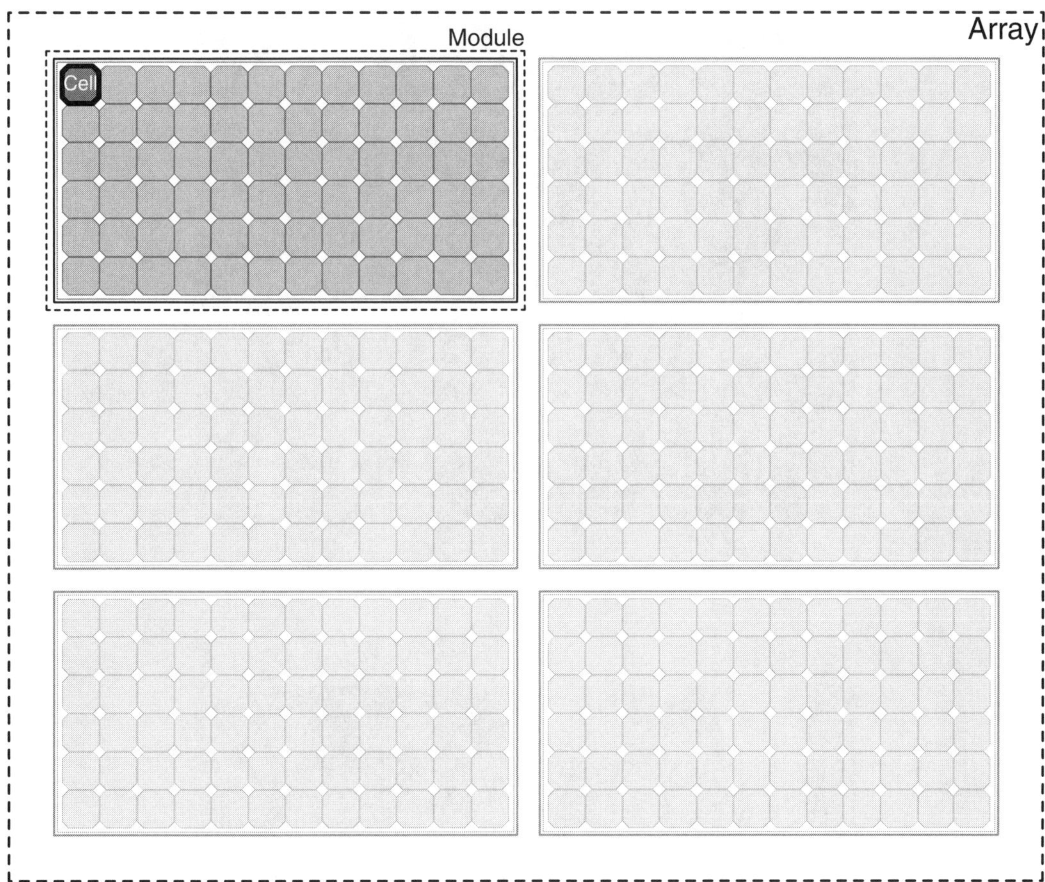

FIGURE 8.4 In crystalline silicon PV collectors, a series of cells constitute a module, which is typically, but not always, a panel (some panels are composed of multiple modules). Modules are typically arranged in parallel in an array, but depending on desired voltage, modules may be paired or tripled in series, and the series is then connected in parallel in the array. When a portion of a series is shaded, the entire series is affected.

albeit one that promises to decrease over time as the technology becomes more pervasive. BIPVs are less efficient than conventional PVs and there are some tradeoffs:

- Since BIPVs are not rack- or armature-mounted, those slight costs are avoided;
- As noted above, the cost of BIPVs is offset somewhat by a corresponding reduction in conventional cladding—whether in roofing, wall siding, or skylights.

In addition to increased material costs over non-energy producing cladding, there are energy penalties for BIPVs over PVs, associated both with technology and placement. BIPVs produce less power per unit area than conventional PVs (Fig. 8.7)—consequently more must be installed to generate the same power and meet building energy requirements. Furthermore, unless the building geometry is ideal for PV orientation (including both elevation and azimuth), system inefficiency may be further exacerbated by suboptimal BIPV placement

FIGURE 8.5 Building-integrated photovoltaics are commonly incorporated in roofing materials. In this case the modular nature of standing seam metal roofing makes it an ideal candidate for BIPV. This 5.1-kilowatt array of UniSolar BIPVs in San Antonio, Texas is part of a system that includes a Fronius IG 5100 Inverter that runs alternating current (AC) appliances.

Image courtesy of Meridian Solar, Inc.

FIGURE 8.6 A 3.5-kilowatt array of BIPVs constitute the glazing of this entry canopy at the Carlsbad Caverns National Park Visitor Center in Carlsbad, NM, capitalizing on the translucent nature of thin-film photovoltaics to provide shade and diffuse light.

Image courtesy of Meridian Solar, Inc.

for those portions of the envelope not ideally oriented for solar collection.

In addition to providing a modeling basis for performance due to orientation and shading as for other PV array types, BIM can also play an important role in analyzing the economic feasibility of BIPV. Accurate takeoffs of cladding material to be displaced by BIPV with associated labor and materials cost can be weighed against the solar PV subcontractor's bid or estimate. While the latter is best

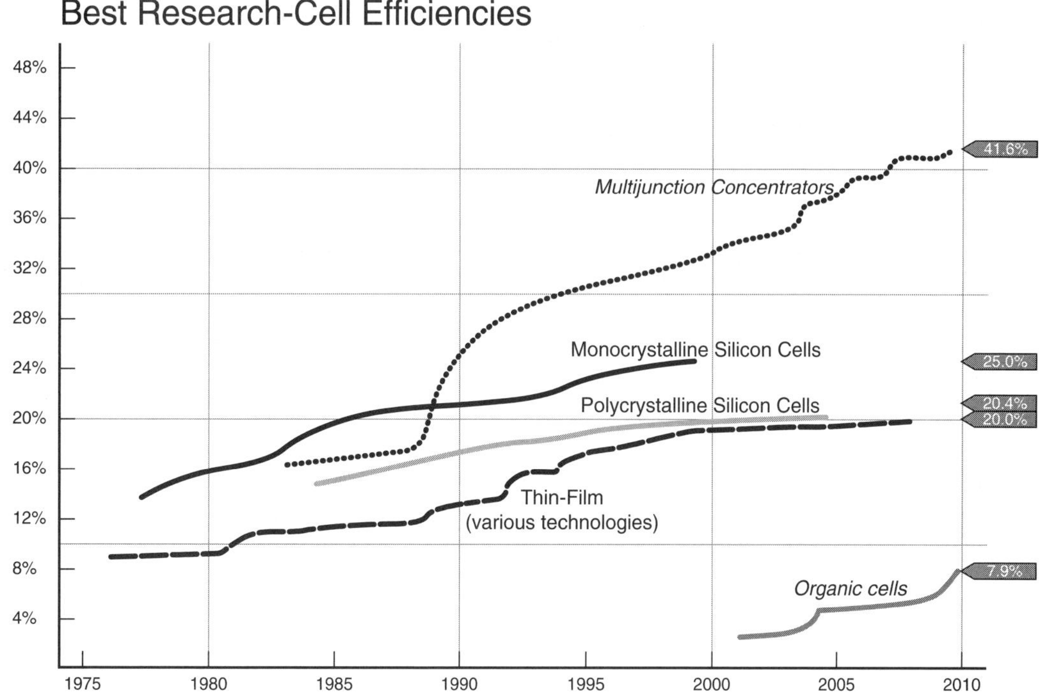

FIGURE 8.7 Photovoltaic cells have increased dramatically in efficiency over the past few decades, as can be seen in this graph based on data by the National Renewable Energy Research Lab (NREL; 2010). Italicized cell types (multijunction, organics) are types not typically used for general commercial PV arrays. Note that these values represent the best performance of experimental cells under laboratory conditions, not system performance under normal conditions. Commercially available cells perform more poorly due to the exigencies of mass production; nevertheless the graph serves to illustrate relative efficiency of competing technologies.

able to provide photovoltaic system cost estimates, the architect (working with a general contractor or a building cost database) is best able to provide appropriate data harvested from the BIM model.

Energy storage

As mentioned previously, a significant advantage of PV as an onsite energy candidate is that peak production tends to index closely with peak loads, especially in sunny climates. Even so, there may be times when a PV system's production exceeds loads (demand), and there will certainly be times when loads exceed production (whenever solar access is limited, such as at night, on cloudy days, or very early or late in the day). There is almost always therefore a need for energy storage (Fig. 8.8), whose capacity will vary depending on duration of denied solar access (number of consecutive cloudy days).

Indeed, solving the energy storage problem is a large part of alternative energy solutions; an attractive aspect of fossil fuels is their ready storage and transport. Due to the variable nature of energy requirements, PV systems for buildings other than the rare rustic shelter or pump house will incorporate some form of energy storage. Grid-tied systems store energy, too, by putting surplus energy back into the grid. In essence, in such systems the grid serves as the battery.

Sizing

The first step in determining the required size of a solar PV array is an estimate of loads. Typically a solar design professional will perform load calculations to determine the electrical demand required by lighting, appliances, and other equipment. For very simple estimations, the National Renewable Energy

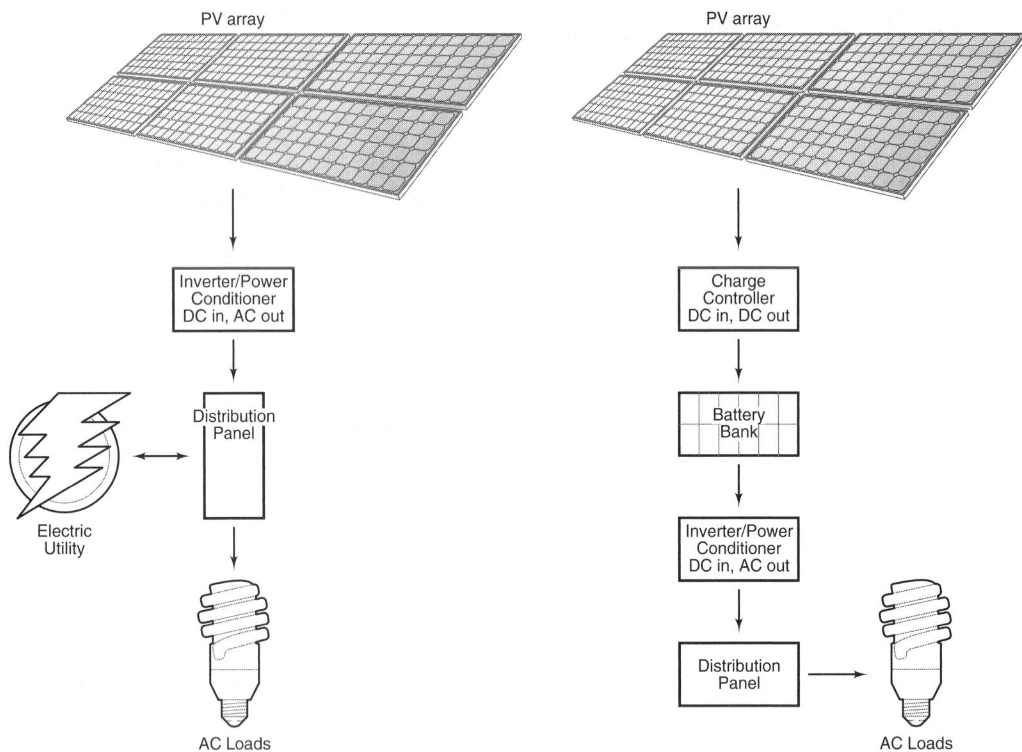

FIGURE 8.8 As even this simplified diagram comparing a grid-tied to battery-based PV system shows, the former is simpler and avoids the significant cost associated with batteries. Note the two-way arrow at left between the electric utility and the grid-tied system.

Laboratory's (NREL) online In My Back Yard (IMBY) tool has profiles for a hypothetical 1,800 SF, three-bedroom house in one of 20 US cities.[1] Assuming a grid-tied system with conventional (for North America) direct current (DC) equipment, PV load calculations may be performed by taking the sum of all appliances' wattage requirement, multiplied by the number of hours of use per day. The total Watt-hours per day (Wh/d) is multiplied by 1.2 for inverter losses (since PV arrays produce DC current which must be converted to AC for grid-tied systems) to obtain daily wattage per hour system requirement. In standalone systems, some appliances and equipment may be DC to avoid inverter losses, but many common consumer appliances may only be readily available for AC. For standalone systems, daily AC loads, if any, are added to any DC loads. Total loads are thus:

$$\Sigma(W_{AC} \cdot h/day \cdot 1.2) + \Sigma(W_{DC} \cdot h/day)$$

[Equation 8.1; after Howell, Bannerot, & Vliet 1982]

Preliminary estimates can be assembled with the BIM models by scheduling or tabulating AC or DC loads for individual pieces of electrical equipment and devices. The model can be set up to automate the tabulation and calculation of loads as the design evolves and devices are placed.

Location

When taking an integrated building approach to solar energy system design, the characteristics of the collector array will have an important influence

[1]The IMBY tool is accessible at www.nrel.gov/eis/imby.

AC ENERGY & COST SAVINGS

Estimated annual energy production for a 4.5-kilowatt array for Elgin, Texas.
Tilt is 15° to maximize summer collection (at a total energy collection penalty).

Station Identification	
City:	Austin
State:	Texas
Latitude:	30.30° N
Longitude:	97.70° W
Elevation:	189 m
PV System Specifications	
DC Rating:	4.5 kW
DC to AC Derate Factor:	0.770
AC Rating:	3.5 kW
Array Type:	Fixed Tilt
Array Tilt:	15.0°
Array Azimuth:	180.0°
Energy Specifications	
Cost of Electricity:	9.5 ¢/kWh

Results			
Month	Solar Radiation ($kWh/m^2/day$)	AC Energy (kWh)	Energy Value ($)
1	3.79	390	37.05
2	4.55	416	39.52
3	5.29	532	50.54
4	5.62	532	50.54
5	5.89	564	53.58
6	6.45	589	55.95
7	6.67	621	59.00
8	6.42	600	57.00
9	5.65	526	49.97
10	5.21	504	47.88
11	4.06	389	36.95
12	3.43	350	33.25
Year	5.26	6012	571.14

FIGURE 8.9 The PVWatts online calculator is a free tool for preliminary sizing of PV systems. Data that may be harvested from the BIM model (such as available collector array area, tilt, and azimuth) are useful for accurately using the Web tool.

on building morphology, even if not the single greatest determinant of form. Those characteristics are themselves interrelated, and include:

- Size
- Orientation (azimuth and tilt)
- Module efficiency
- Shading

Size is of course dependent on the loads to be met, and the ability of the array to meet them. That ability is in turn determined by module efficiency and array orientation and shading. BIM is best suited to study and optimize the placement of the array. Electrical loads, budget, and the collector module selected are factors contributing to array size that may be weakly influenced by the designer. However, array performance may significantly affect array size; an array optimized for azimuth, tilt, and shading will produce the same or more electricity than a poorly placed but larger array consisting of more modules.

Another useful free NREL online tool for non-solar experts is PVWatts (Fig. 8.9).[2] By means of this Web tool, energy production for a given solar

[2] The PVWatts tool is accessible at www.rredc.nrel.gov/solar/calculators/PVWATTS/version2.

PV array can be estimated, given the total wattage of the array, azimuth, tilt, whether the array is fixed or tracking (usually arrays are fixed), and location. The latter is crucial of course: drawing on weather data in a granular 40 km x 40 km grid of cells in the United States, and from a variety of discrete sites worldwide, PVWatts estimates solar insolation for a given site. The Web site reports monthly and annually energy production both in energy (kWh) and dollar amount saved (given local electricity rates).

Rapid design iterations may be developed to optimize the array using a combination of 3D modeling and sun studies in BIM, coupled with PVWatts calculations (which take mere moments). For example, changes in roof pitch may be evaluated architecturally in BIM, studied for shading (even self-shading for arrays whose modules are tilted up from the roof surface), and then the provisional array can be checked in PVWatts. One could easily imagine a scenario where an array might achieve unshaded operation by compromising on azimuth and/or tilt; BIM would be invaluable in determining the best tradeoff.

Azimuth and elevation

Tilt, or elevation, is the angle of the array up from the horizontal plane. Common rules of thumb for PV (and solar thermal array) tilt are depicted in Figure 8.14, and these are good starting values. For an architecturally integrated array (as distinct from building-integrated PV), roof pitch will likely be heavily informed, if not dictated, by ideal collector array tilt. In roof design, however, several agendas may compete with PV array optimization to determine final roof pitch (Fig. 8.10), some of which may be:

- preferred attic or lofted volume under roof
- height limitations due to zoning or solar access
- lines of sight obstructed by the roof
- sight lines to the roof
- aesthetic considerations or preferences
- surrounding architectural context
- relative costs

As a result, the designer may need to iterate several candidate roof designs to satisfy these and others (Figs. 8.11 and 8.12). Here BIM is invaluable as a visualization tool, obviously, but may be also quantitatively analyzed to determine:

- available roof surface area
- heights and volumes under roofs of various pitches
- comparative costs (see Chapter 10)

Solar thermal systems

While photovoltaic arrays generate electrical energy from sunlight through what is essentially an electronic process, solar thermal systems passively heat a fluid (often water) by solar radiation (insolation). Systems have a variety of applications; heated fluid is used either directly for heating or domestic hot water, or indirectly by means of a heat exchanger for closed-loop systems. Some (relatively) low-temperature systems are used for heating swimming pools, and innovative systems exist that even use solar thermal to heat air for heating. Interestingly, the design of residential solar thermal systems tends to be more involved than systems in commercial building applications due to the erratic scheduling of hot water needs, as well as increased demands during off-peak production hours—people tend to take hot showers and cook at home early in the morning or late in the day.

System types

Common systems are either open-loop, in which heated water leaves the collector for storage and eventual use, or they are closed-loop, in which the fluid in the collector (often an antifreeze mixture) heats end-use water through a heat exchanger (Fig. 8.13). The latter system is more complex and has higher first costs with minimal efficiency losses due to heat exchange, and can be more reliable and longer-lived as the collector is less subject to corrosion or clogging from mineral deposits. For all but swimming pool heating systems (where the collector

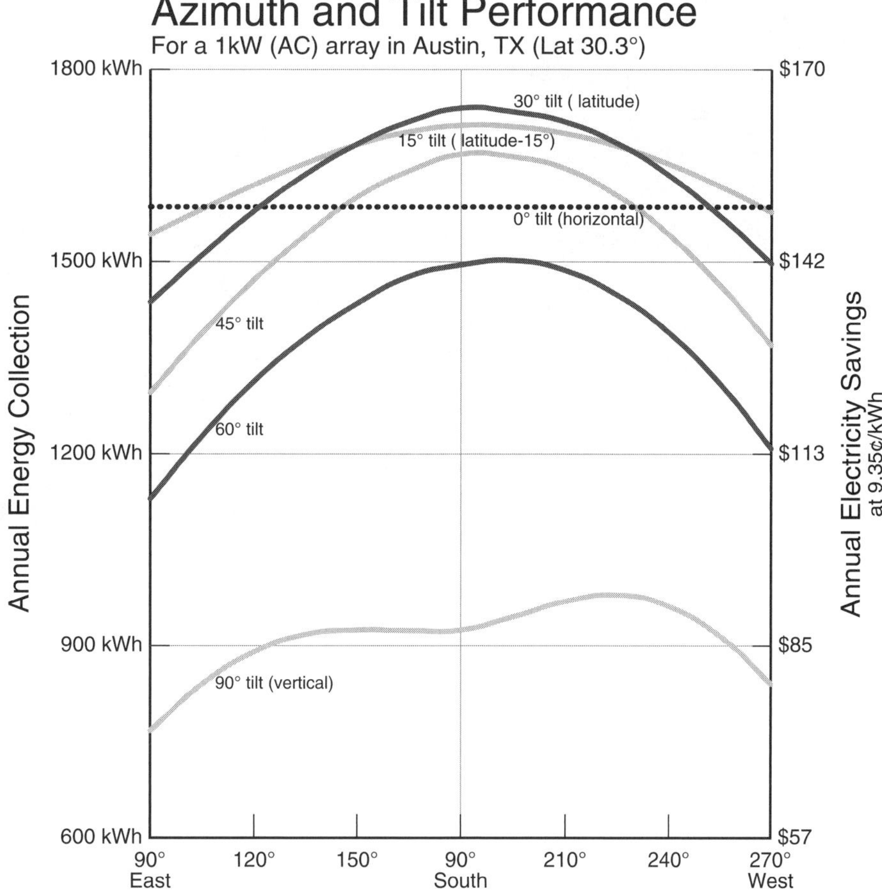

FIGURE 8.10 PV performance is strongly linked to elevation angle, and less strongly to azimuth (orientation), within limits. This analysis of PVWatts data for a hypothetical 1kW array in Austin, Texas (approximate latitude of 30°), shows that array performance for most tilts is fairly flat near an azimuth of 90° (due south), meaning that a slight deviation from south has little impact on array performance. Note also that performance is strongly linked to tilt. Furthermore, southerly arrays with a tilt equal to the site's latitude produce the highest annual energy, but arrays with a tilt of 15° less than latitude do best with easterly or westerly azimuths, with the greatest annual output (compare the 30° and 15° curves, respectively).

is little more than a large, black tube-filled mat that also serves as storage), the hot water storage is typically located indoors (some systems integrate the storage tank with the collector, but this exposes the tank to cold temperatures if the tank is not well-insulated). Methods are employed to allow for fluid drain-back to a collection tank at night or during overcast conditions; otherwise the system would lose heat to the near black body of the night sky.

Collectors

As with PV, collectors for solar thermal energy are the most prominent architectural feature of these distributed energy systems. Collectors are found in a variety of designs, from the coiled-tube, unglazed mats of pool heaters, to glazed, flat-plate collectors of varying sophistication, to one- and two-axis tracking collectors more commonly found in power plants and commercial applications. Overwhelmingly, the

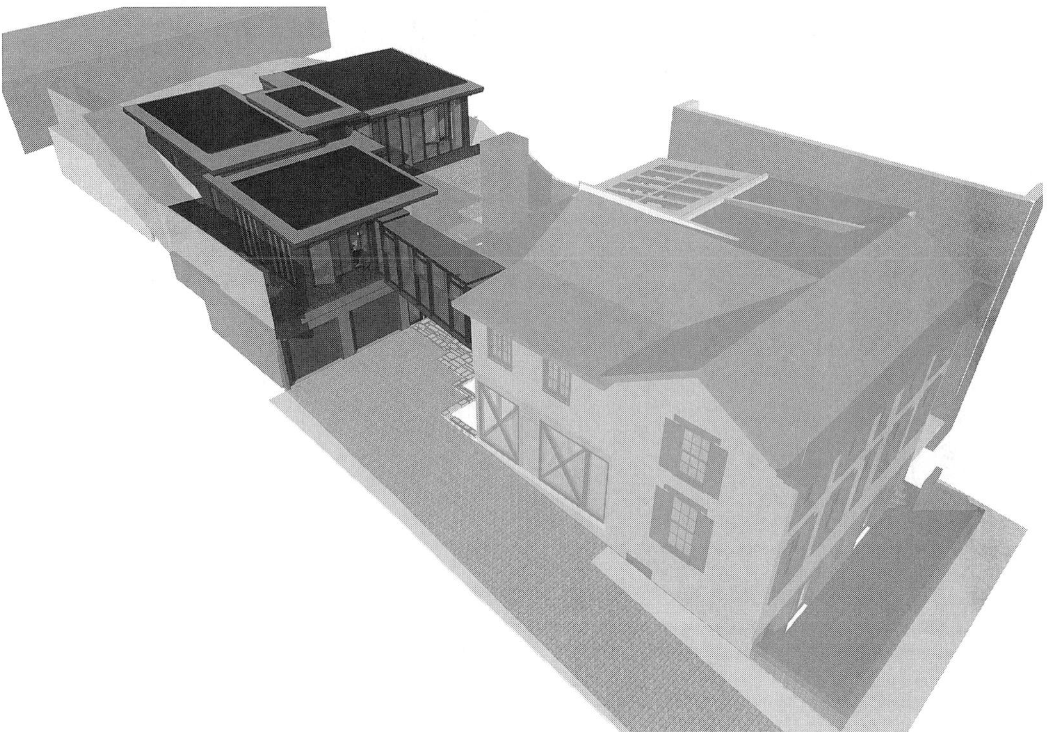

FIGURE 8.11 This BIM solar shading study of a residential addition in the Georgetown neighborhood of Washington, DC, was critical given the proximity of adjacent structures in this dense area. For historic preservation reasons, it was also a requirement that the addition and its solar collectors not be seen from the street, which was also confirmed by the model.

Image courtesy of Stephen DuPont AIA.

fixed, glazed flat-plate collector is prevalent in buildings. Collectors are available with single, double, or triple glazing, with or without low-emissivity coatings (as with windows), and the fluid coils may be painted with matte black paint or more exotic coatings that are even more absorptive.

Evacuated tubes, also called heat pipes, rely on convection to circulate the fluid in tubes set concentrically under vacuum, one to a pipe, within an array of larger black collector pipes. The curved surfaces of the array of tubes are insolated throughout the day to a greater degree than a fixed flat-plate collector, and the lack of convective losses through the vacuum leads to higher efficiencies over conventional flat-plate collectors. They have, however, higher first costs. Depending on the availability of roof or other collector supporting surfaces, increased efficiency (and therefore decreased collector array size) may not be the primary concern. If there's enough roof area to support a more expansive, less expensive system, then the lower first cost (and correspondingly shorter payback period) may be attractive.

All of these systems have a higher profile and tend to be visually more prominent than solar PV systems, and while solar thermal systems may certainly be architecturally integrated in the building design, there are not building-material integrated solar thermal counterparts to BIPV.

As with PV arrays, the solar thermal array size and placement are of significant concern to the architect (Fig. 8.14). Once the array size has been determined, its placement, orientation, and tilt can be verified in BIM using the same sun angle and

FIGURE 8.12 By incorporating neighboring trees and obstructions in the BIM model, positioning of collector arrays can be optimized to avoid shading. The farther roof in this image supports a PV array; the nearer (and steeper) roof is home to solar thermal collectors.

Image courtesy of Nathan Kipnis, AIA, LEED AP.

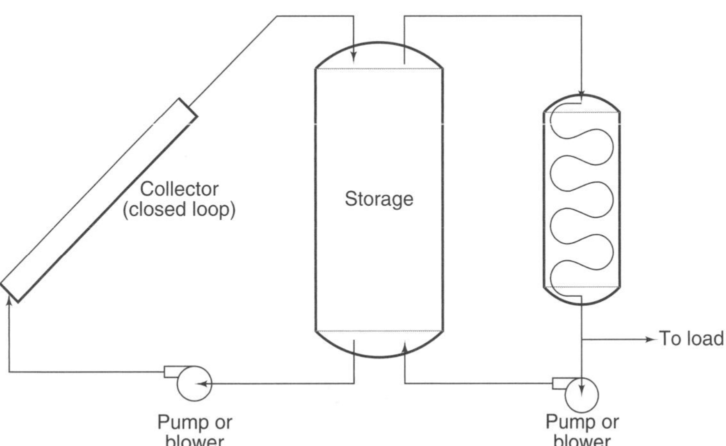

FIGURE 8.13 Diagram of a typical solar thermal system used for both heating and domestic hot water. To avoid heat losses, collector fluid is kept in an insulated drain-back tank at night. For system longevity and to avoid corrosion, the collector is often a closed-loop system, which provides heat exchange to water.

Optimal Tilt

For solar thermal and photovoltaic arrays

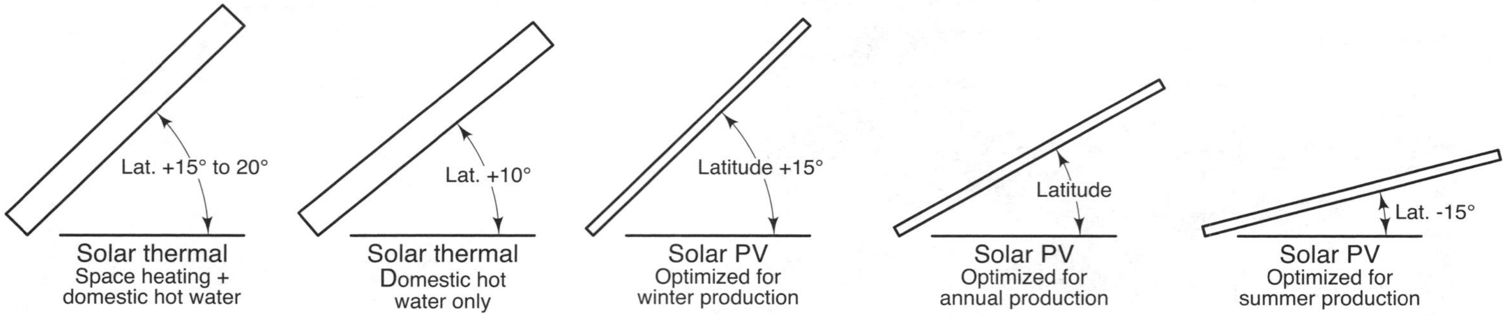

Lat. +15° to 20°
Solar thermal
Space heating +
domestic hot water

Lat. +10°
Solar thermal
Domestic hot
water only

Latitude +15°
Solar PV
Optimized for
winter production

Latitude
Solar PV
Optimized for
annual production

Lat. -15°
Solar PV
Optimized for
summer production

FIGURE 8.14 Simple rules of thumb may be used to determine collector elevation (tilt) for solar thermal and photovoltaic systems, as a function of site latitude.

shading analytical tools used for PV and passive cooling, heating, and daylighting strategies: solar animations, still renderings, and sun views.

A potential design issue that confronts the simultaneous architectural integration of solar thermal and solar PV is the differing optimal tilt for these two solar energy collection systems. Both systems perform best with an equatorial (south-facing) azimuth. However, optimal tilt for PV tends to be somewhat flatter than for solar thermal, especially in warmer climates. This is due to seasonal differences in peak demand. Electrical loads tend to be highest in summer when air conditioning demands peak; at this time of year the sun is higher and therefore the PV array should be closer to horizontal. For space heating, hot water demand is highest in winter when the sun is lower; hence the solar thermal array should be closer to upright.

For the architect, then, this is a design opportunity, and one that BIM's combined visualization capability and quantitative analytical tools are well suited to address (Fig. 8.15). Should south-facing roofs be set at varying pitches to optimize solar thermal and PV, respectively? Should a compromise be reached, whereby roof pitches are uniform, but suboptimal for both systems? If the latter, what should that roof pitch be? Regardless of which approach is taken, what are the volumetric ramifications for the solutions being studied?

There is, fortunately for the designer, no rule of thumb that will answer these questions. But BIM does offer a useful, expedient, and effective work methodology to better address these design issues.

Storage

Whether the solar thermal system is closed- or open-loop, some means of storing the energy collected must be employed. Typically, an insulated hot-water heater tank is used, particularly if a conventional backup system is to be used. For closed-loop systems, a second tank is required for drain-back (fluid is not left in the collector overnight), ideally close to the collector array. While hot water storage is not excessive, sufficient space must be allocated.

Wind turbines

Wind and solar tend to have somewhat opposite diurnal peak production cycles: winds tend to be greater at night, when of course solar production is nil. That said, nighttime is also when electrical demand is at its lowest, and so in that sense wind energy production is not well indexed to loads. On a large scale, this is an issue but of less concern as wind farms contribute to the grid. For onsite production, however, this poor load indexing may be a problem as effectiveness is thereby reduced.

Wind production has other problems that may make it less suitable for architecturally integrated energy production:

- *Startup speeds.* Turbines have a minimum startup speed; they are not designed to operate below certain wind speeds. For smaller turbines, the lowest startup speeds are around 7 to 9 miles per hour, in some cases 13 miles per hour. When winds are not sustained at these speeds, the turbine is not operable. Furthermore, turbine power output is dependent on wind speed; at startup speeds output will be minimal and strong, sustained winds are required for maximum output.
- *Wind is highly localized, both in direction and speed.* This has two important implications. First, wind roses recording wind speed and direction for a locale may not accurately represent wind at a particular project site even a few miles from the wind data site (typically an airport). At an even more localized scale, wind direction and speed are highly variable around buildings. Turbines operate best under *laminar* (streamline) flow conditions; *turbulence* (variation in wind speed and direction) decreases turbine effectiveness. Buildings encourage turbulent wind flow.
- *Height.* In addition to being placed as far from turbulent-producing obstructions as possible,

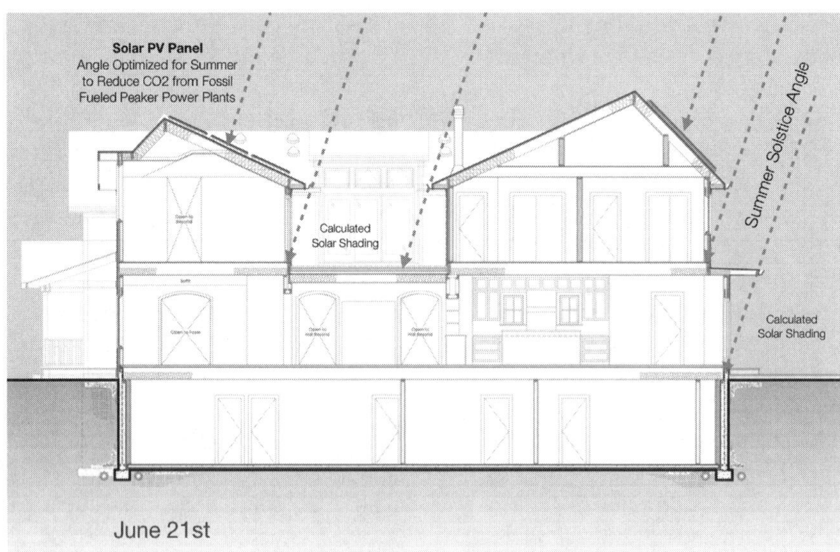

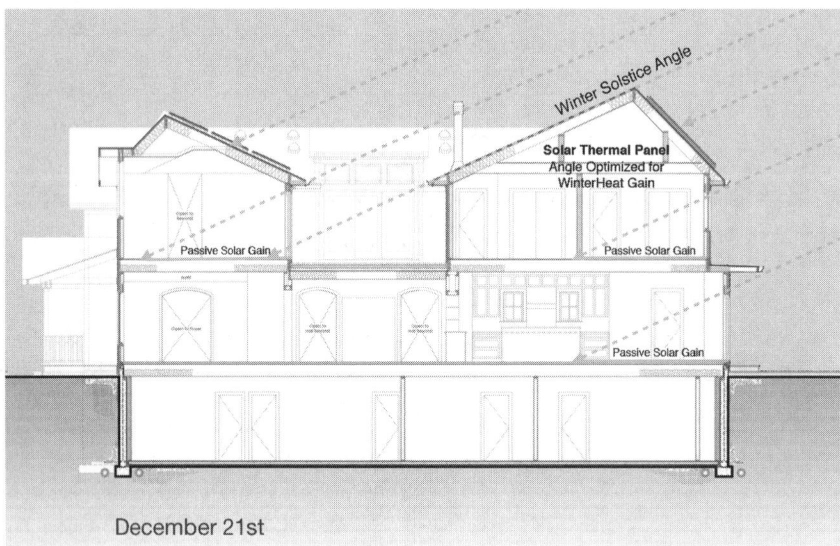

FIGURE 8.15 Given differing optimal tilts for solar thermal and PV collectors, the architect is faced with several potential design solutions. Here, roofs were dedicated to the respective collectors and their pitches selected for optimum collector tilt.

Image courtesy of Nathan Kipnis, AIA, LEED AP.

FIGURE 8.16 Examples of small turbines suitable for onsite wind energy generation; these were used in the Texas A&M University's 2007 Solar Decathlon competition entry.

Image courtesy of Center for Maximum Potential Building Systems; photo by Mimi Kwan.

turbines benefit from height. As Figure 8.17 illustrates, turbine power output increases non-linearly with height, due to the reduction of turbulence caused by the friction of air on the ground and other low obstructions (like buildings).

- *Noise and vibration.* Depending on the design (vertical or horizontal axis) and model, turbines are more or less noisy. Moreover, small sites may not afford a remote location for turbine placement. If integrated in the building design, care may be needed to isolate turbine vibrations from the structure.
- *Maintenance.* As they obviously have moving parts, turbines are more susceptible to needing maintenance than solid-state distributed energy systems.

This is not to say that wind turbines have no place near buildings. However, their application tends to be more specialized and must be carefully considered. Obviously, they are ideally deployed where there is plentiful and constant wind, and predominantly overcast locales may favor wind over solar.

BIM may be of qualitative use in visualizing an integrated turbine design:

- Turbine placement may be evaluated for architectural impact on the building itself.
- Given turbine height requirements, a 3D site and massing model may be necessary to establish views to the project from adjacent sites, depending on local ordinances and proximity to concerned neighbors.

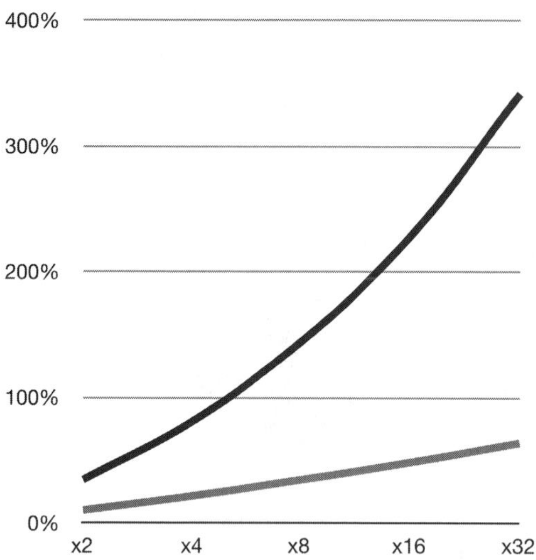

FIGURE 8.17 This graph charts the relationship between turbine height, wind speed, and wind power. As height doubles, wind speed approximately increases by a power of 1/7; wind power has a cube power relationship to speed, so power tends to increase to the 3/7 power with doubling of turbine height. Even under ideal conditions, however, wind flow is turbulent, while turbines operate at peak efficiency in laminar flow. Ideal airflow is especially problematic near buildings, which tend to contribute significantly to turbulence.

- If series photovoltaic modules are installed in the project, turbines may potentially shade some cells and affect PV performance.
- As a crude approximation of sound, a point light with appropriate drop-off settings could be placed at each turbine location; rendered illuminance at remote points could then be used to evaluate approximate noise impact.

Case Study: Cascadia Center for Sustainable Design and Construction, Seattle, Washington

By Brian Court

Design firm: The Miller Hull Partnership

Client: Bullitt Foundation

The Bullitt Foundation, the client for this 52,000-gross square foot office building, laid out specific project goals for the project's architect, The Miller Hull Partnership. The building was to meet the requirements of the Living Building Challenge, including net-zero energy and water expenditure, use of local and non-toxic materials and products, and the provision of natural light and ventilation for all occupied areas. The project would serve as a new prototype for sustainable mid-rise urban buildings, provide a replicable financial model for other developers, and help define a regional architecture for performance-based design. The program additionally called for the first and second floor to be occupied by institutional tenants, and floors three through six reserved for office spaces. In addition, the project was to include a 50,000-gallon rainwater cistern, a compost room, loading dock, and a greywater treatment green roof (Fig. 8.18).

FIGURE 8.18 Street view rendering of the Cascadia Center for Sustainable Design and Construction.
Image courtesy of The Miller Hull Partnership LLP.

Concept Phase

One of the primary design challenges Miller Hull faced was to maximize solar power collection without compromising daylighting. We used the parametric modeling software Grasshopper as a plug-in to the Rhino 3D modeling program, to better help us quickly study and manipulate the complex geometries of the solar array. The results were then exported to Ecotect, an environmental analysis program, and tested for daylight levels within the interior spaces. An iterative, back and forth process led to a solution that both maximized daylight levels and solar harvesting (Fig. 8.19). Miller Hull used SketchUp, another 3D modeling program, to study the impact of building height on neighboring structures and their solar access.

The City of Seattle passed the Living Building Ordinance, which created a pilot program whereby a dozen projects would be allowed certain zoning and code exceptions, if they could demonstrate that variances helped a project better meet the challenge of onsite energy production. The design team used Ecotect analysis grids to justify and achieve an additional 10 feet of building height.

Schematic Design/Design Development

Once the design of the photovoltaic array was established, we continued to work within Ecotect to refine floor plans, window fenestration design, solar heat gain, and glare control. The mechanical engineer, PAE Engineering, created an energy model using eQuest (energy

(Continued)

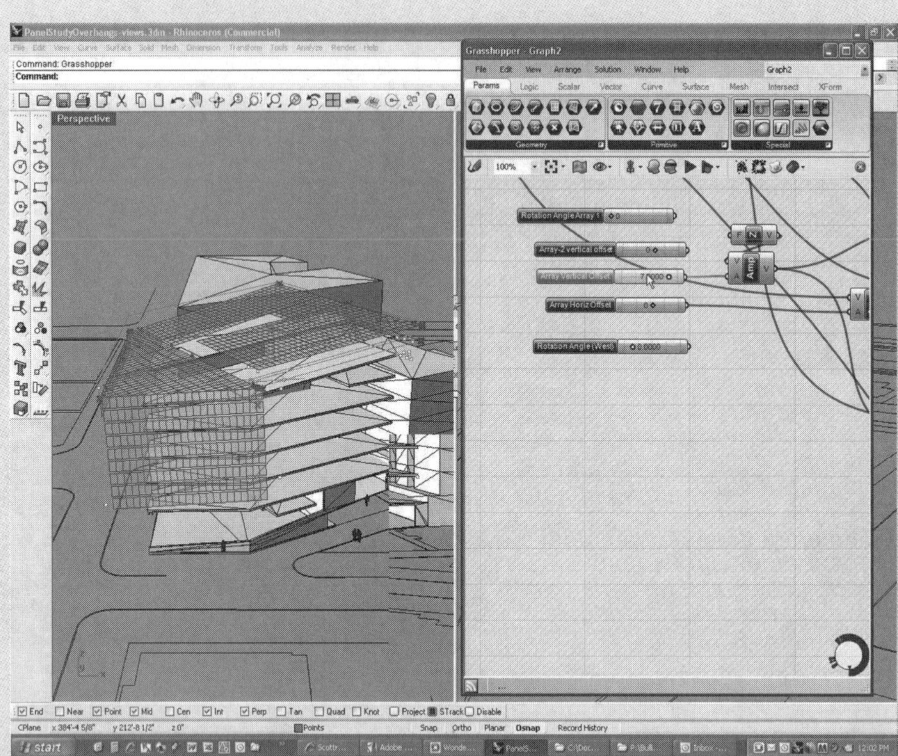

FIGURE 8.19 This view from the Rhino Grasshopper parametric model illustrates the iterative nature of BIM modeling. The design team used a series of models to quantitatively balance and optimize the daylighting needs of the building occupants with the photovoltaic collection potential of the solar array.

Image courtesy of The Miller Hull Partnership LLP.

modeling software based on DOE-2, a validated set of building energy simulation algorithms). They also created an energy simulation model using Environmental Design Solutions Limited (EDSL) Tas software that provides radiant and natural ventilation performance information. Mechanical engineers linked the two models, and Ecotect was used to further calibrate the DOE-2 model for daylighting analysis. The timber frame fabricator, Spearhead Timberworks, was brought into the design process. A coordinated Revit building information model was used for the architectural design process (Fig. 8.20).

Construction Documents

All consultants (mechanical, electrical, plumbing, and lighting) used Revit modeling to enable clash-detection early on and through construction documents. The timber fabricator maintained ownership of the structural components in the Revit model through the construction documents phase, thus eliminating time-intensive shop drawing review during construction. The mechanical engineers continued to maintain eQuest and Tas models. We integrated sub-contractor manufacture models for concrete and steel. As a result, construction-ready, a fully coordinated building model helped avoid delays in construction, streamline shop drawing reviews, and reduce change orders.

FIGURE 8.20 The detailed BIM modeling of the Cascadia Center for Sustainable Design and Construction facilitated the design, optimization, and detailing of the highly visible PV array.

Image courtesy of The Miller Hull Partnership LLP.

FIGURE 8.21 This rendering based on the BIM model shows the extent and design of the integrated photovoltaic array for the Cascadia Center for Sustainable Design and Construction.

Image courtesy of The Miller Hull Partnership LLP.

Chapter 9

Building Hydrology

The world's population has more than doubled since 1900, yet within that same span of time human consumption of water has increased over six-fold. In large part this is attributable to advances in hygiene and especially farming (worldwide, two-thirds of our water use is for agriculture). However, it is also due to the urbanization of the planet and the increased standards of access to fresh water such urbanization entails. Today, by UN estimates, 2.3 billion people live in water-stressed areas—defined as those places with under 1000 m^3 of total available water per capita per year. By 2025, 1.8 billion people will live in absolute water scarcity—under 500 m^3 of water per capita per year—and two-thirds of the world population may be under water stress (Fig. 9.1). Approximately 3.4 million people, mostly children, die each year due to water-related diseases. If 500 m^3 of water per person annually (362 gal/c/d, or gallons per capita per day) seems like a great deal, consider that this figure includes agricultural and industrial uses as well, allocated to each individual. As a point of reference, a hamburger patty requires almost 600 gallons of water to make (Mekonnen and Hoekstra 2010).

If you are reading this, chances are good that these figures do not apply to you, as poor and underdeveloped parts of the world are disproportionately susceptible to water shortage. A notable exception is the American Southwest at times the fastest growing part of the United States—regions of which are now considered to be either at or approaching water scarcity. Furthermore, we all have a responsibility as global citizens to do our part to support access to clean water worldwide. There is some consensus that in this century water will become the leading subject of wars of resource—and it has already been the flashpoint of armed conflict in the Middle East, central and south Asia, and south-central Africa (Fig. 9.2). Ten years ago, the UN estimated 300 ongoing water conflicts.

Any broad discussion of sustainability therefore must include water resources. Humans can survive without fossil fuels, but not without water. Global climate change combined with increasing populations will only exacerbate water problems, and at increasing rates. As professional architects and

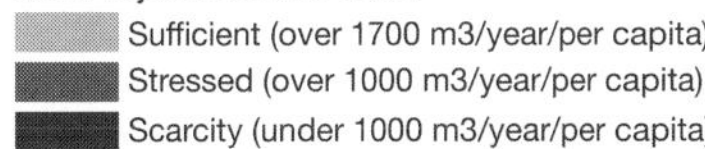

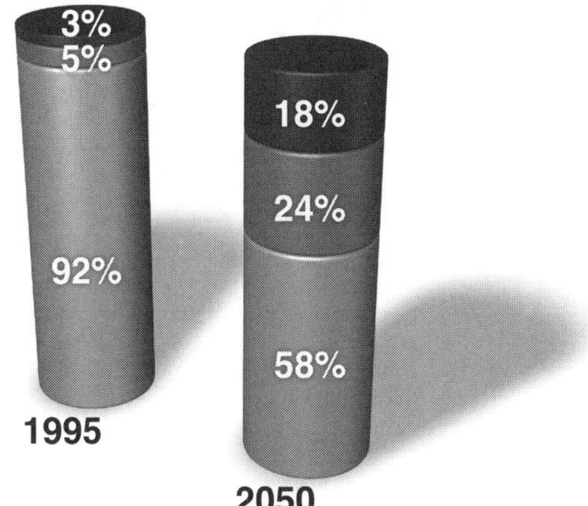

FIGURE 9.1 Water scarcity worldwide is a growing problem. Fifteen years ago 8 percent of the world population was living with water scarcity or stress; UN projections are that in less than 40 years almost half the world will experience water scarcity or stress.

designers, we have little direct influence on our agricultural system and public health policies, but an estimated 12 percent of fresh water use is dedicated to buildings. We do, therefore, have some impact on this issue given our influence over how buildings are supplied by, capture, and dispose of water. As that cycle is inherently quantifiable, there are opportunities to use BIM to improve architectural design for better water management.

Site design for water

A fundamental "systems principle" of all sustainable practices is to avoid expending energy (whether naturally occurring or artificially generated) to import a resource when it can be locally produced. Sustainable design should strive to maximize the resources at hand, establishing a closed loop as much as possible. This holds true for water as well, and to a greater degree the more arid the site. Potentially useful water should not run off, particularly if it may have to be imported later.

Moreover, as any structural engineer will attest, it is essential for the long-term performance of building foundations for the site to have positive drainage away from the building (Fig. 9.3). Positive drainage is also important for reasons of indoor air quality to discourage excessive moisture in the building envelope. Liquid water accumulation near building edges not only directly increases the localized ambient water vapor, but also encourages plant growth, which in turn fosters liquid water and vapor accumulation. This only increases opportunity for water in the building envelope, potentially leading to mold and/or long-term structural damage.

Establishing positive drainage can be accomplished without resorting to BIM or modeling. After all, longstanding drawing (that is, 2D) conventions, like topography lines and building sections, are still useful site-design tools. However, like any drawing, these require active coordination by the designer. Any conditions that are not drawn are potential errors. As with the building proper, modeling the

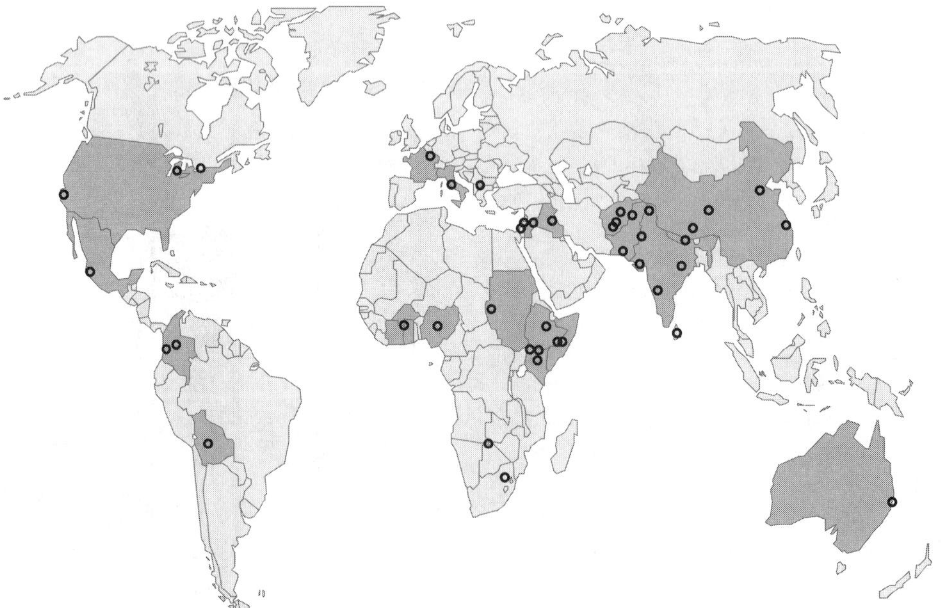

FIGURE 9.2 A world map showing twenty-first century violent water conflicts through 2008, ranging from a single violent death to organized, government-sanctioned armed conflicts. Circles represent incidents, and the nations in which they occur are shaded.

From data compiled in "Water Conflict Chronology" by Dr. Peter H. Gleick of the Pacific Institute for Studies in Development, Environment, and Security.

FIGURE 9.3 BIM site models need not be static representations of the existing site, but can be edited to facilitate the design of positive drainage at building edges.

site in BIM with consideration given to controlling drainage therefore offers coordination advantages. Add to that the visualization benefits—both for design and presentation—and a considered, detailed site model becomes all the more attractive. Finally, with some BIM authoring software the site model can be quantitatively analyzed for slope conditions, as we've seen in Chapter 3.

For small sites especially, catchment and drainage may be competing agendas that, depending upon conditions, may be challenging to resolve. On the one hand, building health suggests aggressive drainage, which may be rendered more difficult if redirecting water away from the building footprint entails redirecting more water to an adjacent property. Moreover, if catchment is desired, then that water must be stored someplace, also potentially difficult on a small site.

As has been discussed in Chapter 3, some architectural BIM site models are static meshes. In these cases, design investigations of alternative site iterations require alternate site models. Other BIM applications, like Vectorworks Architect, include dynamic site models as one of their available parametric tools. Much of this discussion is aimed at the latter, but with additional effort the same results can be achieved with "static" site models—it may simply require the extra steps of drawing a revised set of contours at each iteration, and then re-meshing a new site over them.

Runoff and impervious cover

Runoff has environmental impact in urban and suburban areas. As development increases and more areas are paved, rainfall quickly accumulates as runoff rather than slowly percolating through pervious soil.

Here careful modeling and area analysis can make or break a project. If impervious cover limitations are enforced by the local jurisdiction, a few square feet of ground cover more or less may make all the difference, and absolutely accurate takeoffs are critical. As with other material takeoffs (see Chapter 10), BIM schedules allow the dynamic reporting of quantities in real time as the design evolves. If partial pervious cover is allowed within a project's jurisdiction, then the impervious cover schedule can credit hard ground cover by the appropriate accepted percentages. Such partial cover would vary depending on the nature of the cover in question, pervious concrete, open-cell pavers, and so on. Generally, automobile traffic tends to render most open-cell cover fully impervious over time, due to compression and the accumulation of oils.

Flow and slope analysis

Two-dimensional contours can be read in a conventional site plan, but Vectorworks allows two significant other site model graphic presentation modes that facilitate design. Flow arrows are automatically arrayed on the site within a chosen grid interval and indicate direction of water flow on the site. This is a quick visualization method to analyze whether a particular site design is meeting the desired drainage objectives (Fig. 9.4). Unfortunately, these arrows indicate direction but are not true scalars; they are all of uniform length, regardless of local slope at each arrow.

Another Vectorworks site model graphic representation has been mentioned earlier: color-coded slope polygons. These indicate degree of slope, within user-defined ranges: one color for slopes in the 0 to *x*-percent range, another for *x* to *y*-percent, another for *y* to *z*-percent, and so on. They do not indicate direction. However, both flow arrows and colored slopes may be displayed simultaneously, effectively simulating true vectors by representing direction (arrows) and degree (color of underlying site polygons).

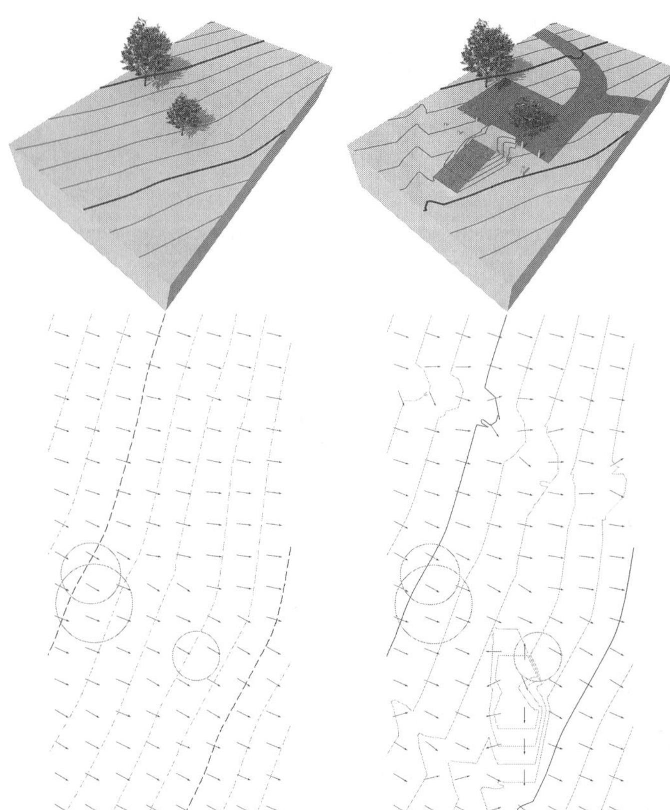

FIGURE 9.4 Two views (rendering at top and site plan below) of an existing (left) and proposed site detail (right) illustrate the graphical analysis possibilities of site models. Arrows indicate direction (although not rate) of water flow.

Rainwater harvesting

Weather patterns have been increasingly variable due to global climate change. Periods of draught are longer, while rainfall is more intense when it does occur. At the same time, in the United States, some of the greatest development growth rates occur in areas like the West, where water is scarcest. Small wonder then that there has been a renewed and growing interest in some regions in the age-old practice of rainwater harvesting. For architects, rainwater harvesting is not only an opportunity to design more sustainably, but also celebrating water capture with expressive roofs and cisterns can be an exciting and satisfying formal design exercise.

In most municipal utility-served portions of the United States, it is not permissible to use harvested rainwater for drinking water, although it may be used to supply toilets and urinals, provided appropriate system design measures are taken. If this seems insignificant, consider that in the United States, personal water consumption can be broken down as follows (see also Fig. 9.5):

- Drinking and cooking: 3 gal/c/d
- Bathing and personal hygiene: 21 gal/c/d
- Clothes and dish washing: 14 gal/c/d
- Waste transport: 32 gal/c/d

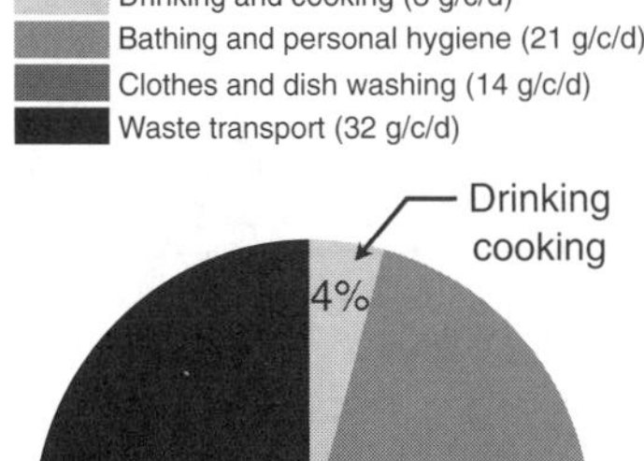

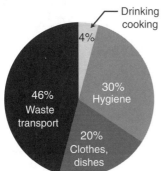

FIGURE 9.5 Personal water consumption by use. Nearly half is for waste transport—flushing the toilet. Note that these figures and percentages are for personal use only, and do not count landscape use.

Hence, almost half (46 percent) of the average individual water consumption is for waste transport. Even in an urban environment where rainwater harvesting may not be used for potable purposes, there is an opportunity to use it for waste transport, with a substantial reduction in municipal water use. Rainwater-fed water supply lines may only be tied into a utility-served supply system with appropriate back-flow prevention valves and rigorous inspection (understandably, utilities are reluctant to chance contamination of the public water supply). In rural areas without a water utility, however, the entire water supply may be provided by an appropriately designed rainwater harvest system.

It's also quite common (but underappreciated) for a municipal water utility to be one of the municipal electric utility's biggest customer: it takes a lot of energy to pump water around a sprawling American city. Hence reducing water usage also reduces overall community energy consumption.

Austin Energy (the city-owned public utility in Texas's capital city) has one of the most pioneering, progressive and well-respected Green Building programs in the nation. Their rainwater system-sizing worksheets are of particular merit. Originally intended for manual estimating of appropriate roof harvesting area and cistern sizing, the calculations are straightforward and suitable for inclusion in user-defined BIM worksheets or schedules. They may also be applied to any locale, and are not limited to central Texas. A useful manual on rainwater harvesting (written for Texas but applicable anywhere with appropriate rainfall data) is also available at the Texas Water Development Board web site.[1]

There are a variety of considerations in cistern and rainwater system design that are beyond this book's scope, including roof washing, guttering, tank maintenance and cleaning, and pumping and

[1] Manual is accessible at http://www.twdb.state.tx.us/publications/reports/RainwaterHarvestingManual_3rdedition.pdf.

disinfection. Numerous excellent and authoritative resources discuss rainwater systems; rather than repeat such material here, the present discussion will concentrate on calculating system sizing in BIM.

Climate data

For rainwater harvesting system sizing, there are two climate figures of merit: annual rainfall and monthly rainfall (particularly for summer months), both measured in inches of rain. Frozen precipitation is converted to equivalent rainfall (typically 10 inches of snow to 1 inch of rain). A couple of easy-to-use sources are worldclimate.com and weatherbase.com, both of whose data originate from a variety of weather station sources. Potentially more reliable but far more troublesome to use is the TMY (typical meteorological year, 1991–2005) data, available by city. TMY data are downloadable in comma-separated value (CSV) format (readable by spreadsheet applications), but list precipitation hour-by-hour over the period in the data set. The user may need to do a bit of post-processing to derive monthly rainfall averages. On the other hand, many energy modeling applications from eQuest to Ecotect use TMY data, and, as such, may be a more convenient way to process weather data.[2]

Load calculations

The average American personal water usage is 70 gallons per day. For purposes of sizing cisterns and systems, however, a smaller figure is typically used—40 or 50 gallons. The smaller figure is justified for a couple of reasons:

- The cistern is the single most expensive component of the rainwater system (in my region of the country, I estimate about a dollar per gallon of capacity). Lowering construction costs is a compelling motivator to decrease consumption below the national per capita average.
- It may be assumed that building owners who value a rainwater harvesting system (Fig. 9.6) are inherently prone to less water use than the average consumer.

These figures exclude yard irrigation, which can be quite a substantial additional load. We will assume in this discussion that landscaping is responsibly designed using drought-tolerant native plants.

If in doubt, the architect should determine as best as possible the water use habits of the building occupants through an interview process, and adjust daily average consumption figures accordingly. In sizing the system, assuming water is to be used for potable and non-potable functions, multiply the longest expected drought (in days) by the expected occupant per capita daily consumption, V_{daily} in gal/c/d, and the number of occupants, N_{occ}:

$$V_{occ} = D_{drought} \cdot V_{daily} \cdot N_{occ}$$ [Equation 9.1; Austin Energy 2000]

Drought duration ($D_{drought}$) will vary by region (for example, the rule of thumb for central Texas is 100 days). For some project types, this equation may be incorporated in the BIM model, as N_{occ} may be a function of building area.

A swimming pool in the project will represent both a potential for water loss due to evaporation, as well as a storage opportunity. For outdoor pools, evaporation rate is a function of psychrometric characteristics—temperature and humidity ratio—and activity (that is, splashing). In the United States, rates range for 30 inches a year (Maine) to 140 inches a year (for example, Death Valley; Fig. 9.7). Losses can be nearly eliminated with a pool cover, which also helps secure the pool from accidents and may help meet life safety codes by replacing the fence requirement. If the pool is uncovered, the simplest method to calculate evaporation loss is to locate annual losses for the site in feet (D_{evap}), multiply by the pool area given by the BIM model (A_{pool}), and convert to gallons:

$$V_{pool} = 7.48\ \text{gal/ft}^3 \cdot A_{pool} \cdot D_{evap}$$ [Equation 9.2]

The product (V_{pool}) is then part of the total required rainwater harvest capacity for the system.

[2] TMY3 files for US cities may be downloaded from http://rredc.nrel.gov/solar/old_data/nsrdb/1991-2005/tmy3/.

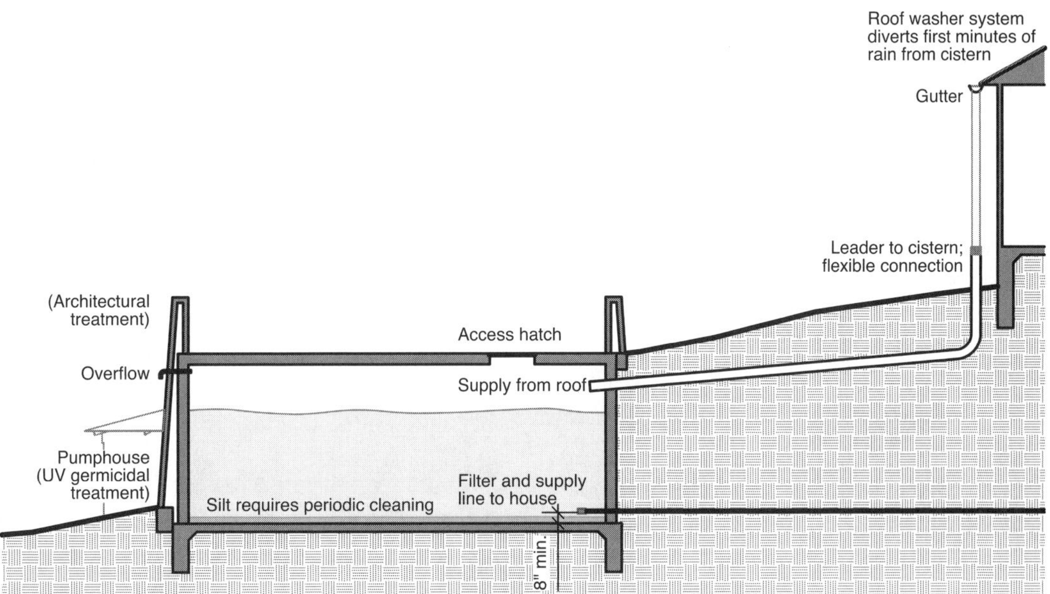

FIGURE 9.6 A sectional diagram of the basic components of a rainwater harvesting system intended for potable use. Roof washing is essential, as roofs accumulate dust, bird droppings, and decaying plant material that create sediment and contaminant problems. Designs vary, but the simplest systems divert the first few minutes of rainfall away from the cistern with a counterbalanced vessel that flips the diverter toward the cistern once it has filled. Leaders should have flexible connections to account for building movement. The supply line from the cistern should be maintained above the bottom of the tank by a few inches (a concrete masonry unit [CMU] spacer is commonly used), as sediment accumulates in the cistern. The cistern must be covered to avoid bacterial growth encouraged by sunlight, and an access hatch (for maintenance and cleaning of the tank) should be provided. Ideally, the cistern is tall enough to allow someone to move about the empty tank freely. There are a variety of systems for disinfecting water before supplying the building; one uses germicidal UV lamps to kill harmful microbes.

For irrigation, plants and soil themselves have storage capacity, so the rainwater system can be decreased accordingly (Fig. 9.8). In this case, annual rainfall values are insufficient; the designer must account for monthly summer rainfall, as well as whatever summer rain will be directly diverted from the roof to irrigation. The procedure is as follows:

- Assuming plantings require an inch of rainfall per week, the summer rainfall requirement is 17.5 inches (there are seventeen and a half weeks in June through September). If the local summer season is longer or shorter, adjust this figure accordingly.
- Using climate data, find the average summer rainfall (June through September), and then divide by 3 for a dry year; this is the summer design rainfall, or R_{summer}. Subtract the summer design rainfall by the summer requirement to find the summer rainfall deficit.
- Multiply the dry summer deficit by the irrigated area (A_{irr}, which may be calculated by the BIM model) and 0.623 in/ft² to find the irrigated deficit rainwater volume in gallons.
- The roof is also catching water in the summer; multiply the BIM-generated roof catchment area (A_{roof}) by the summer design rainfall (R_{summer}) multiplied by a conversion factor of 0.52 gallons per inch of rainfall per square foot of roof.

The procedure above is summarized in the following equation:

$$V_{irr} = A_{irr}\,(17.5 - R_{summer})0.623\ \text{in/gal ft}^2 - A_{roof} \cdot R_{summer} \cdot 0.52\ \text{gal/in ft}^2$$

[Equation 9.3; Austin Energy 2000]

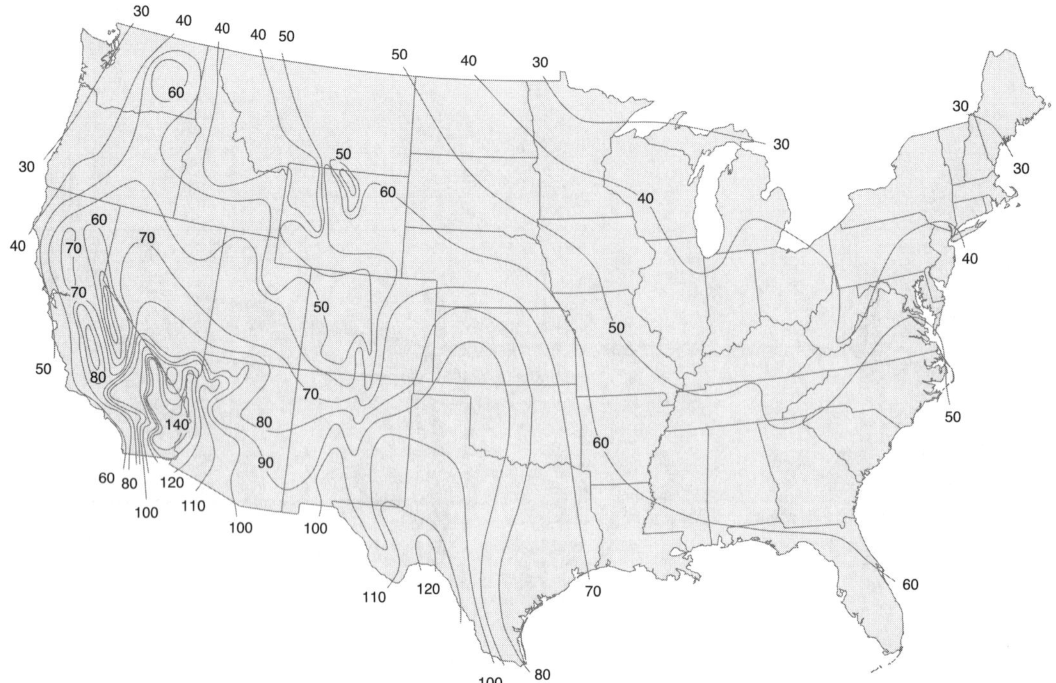

FIGURE 9.7 Map of the continental United States with contours indicating annual evaporation rate in inches. Redrawn by the author, from research by Dr. Muniram Budhu of the Department of Civil Engineering and Engineering Mechanics, University of Arizona.

Permission courtesy of Geotechnical, Rock and Water Resources, the University of Arizona.

The total load volume (V_{load}) to meet occupant water needs over a hundred-day drought (V_{occ}), swimming pool replenishment (V_{pool}), and irrigation requirements (V_{irr}) is simply:

$$V_{load} = V_{occ} + V_{pool} + V_{irr}$$ [Equation 9.4; Austin Energy 2000]

Roof area optimization and cistern sizing

The first component in a rainwater system is, of course, the catchment area, which is typically the roof. For some designs, a dedicated rain-barn's roof (which may also shelter the cistern) may serve this role, or rainwater may be harvested from the primary building roof (Fig. 9.9). If used for potable water, then the roof material is of concern and should be selected appropriately. The ubiquitous composition shingle roofing is not a suitable material for potable water catchment. Other materials, like galvanized metal roofing, are controversial due to concerns of zinc being leached into the water supply. However, it appears that zinc levels are safe in most cases. Smooth roofs like aluminum allow rapid runoff, self-clean more quickly, and accumulate fewer contaminants.

For sizing roofs, the characteristic of interest is the area *in plan* (*not* the roofing area, measured normal to the slope). The area of roof face(s) to be used for harvesting (A_{roof}), is linked in the BIM model to a worksheet or schedule, and the corresponding annual rainwater collection potential (V_{rain}) in gallons is:

$$V_{rain} = 0.52 \cdot A_{roof} \cdot R_{annual}$$ [Equation 9.5; Brown, Gerston and Colley 2005]

Where R_{annual} is the annual rainfall, in inches, for the site. By dynamically linking this calculation to the BIM roof, as the design evolves, the catchment

Design Data				
Available roof footprint	**2,200**	ft²		
Harvest capability	**37,100**	gallons for average year		

Occupancy		
Occupants	**4**	persons
Daily consumption	40	gallons per day
Drought	100	days
Occupant consumption	**16,000**	gallons
Pool	**288**	area, ft²
Evaporation loss	16,157	gallons
Irrigation		
Garden	**1,500**	ft²
Requirements	1	inch per week
Rainfall area coefficient	0.623	inches of rainfall per gallon
Length of summer	17.5	weeks June-Sept
Required water	16,363	gallons required in summer for garden
Summer rainfall (June-Sept)	4	inches June-Sept, 1/3 average rainfall
Natural rainfall received	3,534	gallons, June-Sept
Deficit	12,828	gallons
Summer roof harvest	4,324	gallons for above roof June-Sept
Irrigation requirement	**8,504**	gallons
Storage Required	**40,661**	gallons
	7.48	gallons/ft³
	5,436	required volume, ft³
Circular:	**24**	ft. desired diameter = 12.0 depth, ft
Prism:	**400**	ft² available area = 13.6 depth, ft

	Rainfall
J	1.61
F	2.16
M	2.33
A	2.48
M	4.58
J	4.09
J	2.04
A	2.06
S	3.15
O	3.46
N	2.32
D	2.15
Annual	**32.43**
Evaporation (inch/year)	**90**
Evaporation (feet/year)	7.5
Gallon/inch rain/roof ft²	0.52

User input data

FIGURE 9.8 A rainwater harvesting sizing calculation worksheet. Such a worksheet or schedule in the BIM model is populated by model geometry to automatically account for harvesting roof, occupancy, landscaping, and pool area to dynamically size the cistern as the design evolves.

area may change. Conversely, the design may be adjusted to optimize the harvested water. Bear in mind that the entire roof need not be dedicated to catchment.

For adequate rainwater harvesting, the catchment volume (V_{rain}) should equal or exceed the load volume (V_{load}) as should the cistern if it is to sustain the project's water needs. There are of course a wide variety of cisterns or tanks available, from polypropylene plastic tanks to bladder-lined wood tanks to above- or in-ground ferro-cement cisterns. All should be covered to keep the stored water as clean and bacteria-free as possible (Fig. 9.10). If multiple tanks are desired, then it's a simple matter to determine the number required. For determining the dimensions of a cylindrical or prism-shaped cistern, calculate its volume in cubic feet by dividing capacity in gallons by 7.48. Basic geometry can find a required diameter for a cylinder of a given height, or vice versa:

$$H_{cyl} = \frac{V_{load}}{\pi(d_{cyl}/2)^2} \qquad \text{[Equation 9.6]}$$

For complex cistern geometries, it may be worthwhile to create a small worksheet or schedule that tracks volume as the design evolves, perhaps dynamically checking it against both water design load and roof catchment area.

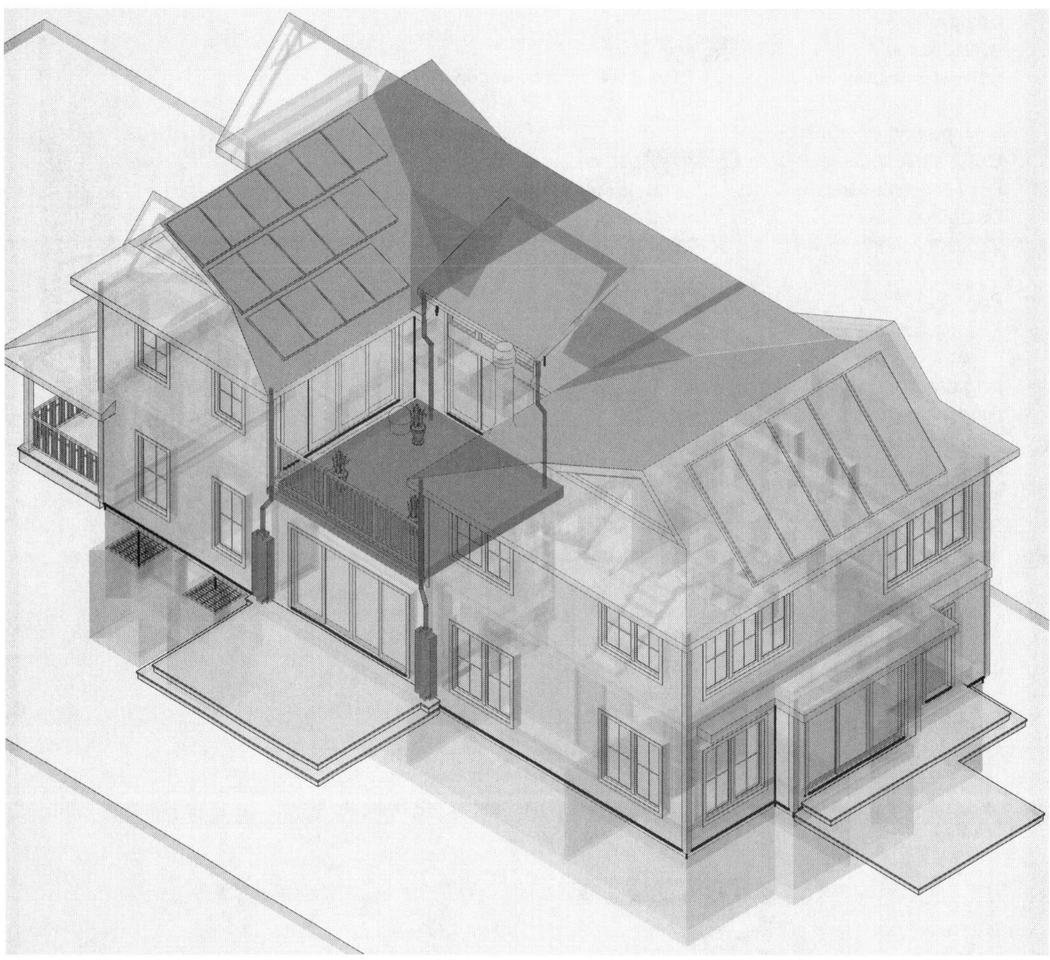

FIGURE 9.9 This LEED-platinum-targeted project incorporates a metal roof that is asymmetrically arranged to maximize water collection that can be funneled onto the green roof terrace below it. Metal was selected as best for water collection, plus it was made from local, recycled content material. The green roof itself is accessible and positioned adjacent to the second floor hallway and master bedroom, such that it can be seen and enjoyed every day. The three rain barrels are "Rainhogs"; unlike typical round barrels, they are rectangular in section such that they may be set flat against the walls. Excess water will flow to thirsty gardens nearby, an economical alternative to the 5000-gallon cistern originally planned.

Image courtesy of Nathan Kipnis, AIA, LEED AP.

Plumbing fixture efficiency

To comply with performance requirements of codes or to earn points in green rating schemas, it may be necessary to quantitatively demonstrate reduced water consumption relative to a stipulated baseline performance. Usually the code or rating system will indicate the calculation method. A sample case for a given plumbing fixture might be:

$$V_{waste} = N_{use} \cdot Q_{gpf} \cdot D_{flush} \cdot N_{occ}$$ [Equation 9.7; Austin Energy 2011]

Where V_{waste} is the daily wastewater volume, in gallons; N_{use} is the number of typical uses per day for a given fixture; Q_{gpf} is the flow rate in gallons per flush; D_{flush} is the typical duration of a flush; and N_{occ} is the number of full-time occupants (or equivalent). All of these variables are usually given or are a

FIGURE 9.10 The Lower Colorado River Authority (LCRA) Redbud Center, designed by Barnes Gromatzky Kosarek Architects, celebrates rainwater harvesting and water usage as architectural elements. [Figure 9.10]

Image ©Thomas McConnell Photography.

function of the specific fixture, except for number of occupants. The above calculation or similar ones are performed for both the design case and a conventional baseline, and can readily be included as part of a BIM fixture schedule, populated by the instanced fixtures themselves (Fig. 9.11). Occupancy values may be manually assigned or a function of floor area; if the latter, the virtual building can provide that value, too.

To determine eligibility for green building rating credits, the design is compared to the baseline, and the (presumed) percentage of improvement is compared to the baseline to determine the number of credit points, if any:

$$\text{Reduction percent} = (V_{design} - V_{baseline}) / V_{baseline}$$

[Equation 9.8]

Both the design (V_{design}) and baseline ($V_{baseline}$) volumes in the equation above are expressed as annual values (daily volume in gallons multiplied by number of days per year that the building is occupied).

Sizing constructed wetlands

Referring back to the average annual per capita consumption above, half of direct water consumption is for waste transport. An effective and accepted stratagem to address this problem is to reduce plumbing fixture water usage. For buildings relying on low-pressure dose septic systems, however, some of the wastewater may be used for surface irrigation. For projects that are not tightly integrated in the urban infrastructure, *constructed wetlands* are an alternative to septic systems. These systems mimic natural ones, harnessing natural physical and biological processes to filter, clean, and purify wastewater within the context of a whole cycle. Constructed wetlands reduce

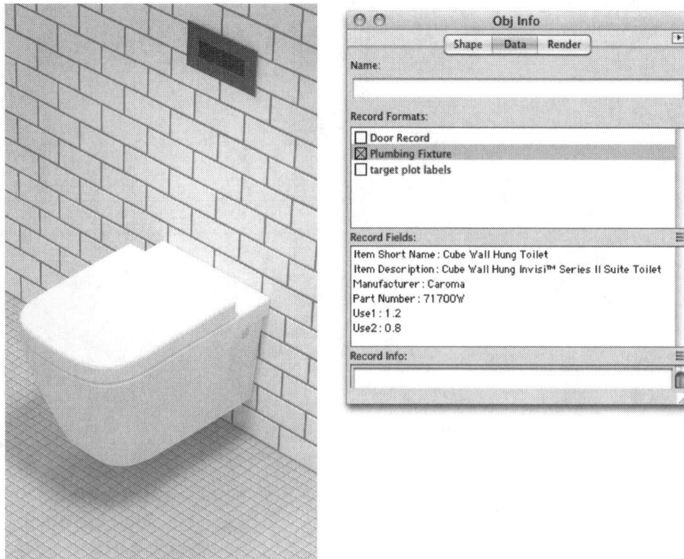

FIGURE 9.11 Extremely low-flow fixtures, like this Cube Wall Hung Invisi Series II Suite Toilet, modeled and rendered in BIM, use even less water than older low-flow fixtures. This particular toilet uses 0.8 gallons per flush (1.2 for dual flush). These values and other product data can be attached to the custom component and used for dynamic calculations and automated schedules.

Image courtesy of Caroma USA.

biochemical oxygen demand (BOD) loads, as well as reducing *total suspended solids* (TSS).

Natural wetlands are nature's filters, and are likened to the kidneys of the biosphere. They occur wherever water covers the soil, or is present at or near the soil surface for some or all of the year. Wetlands are found in every biome on earth, in fresh and saltwater environments, from tundra to temperate and tropical areas. They are the interface between terrestrial and aquatic or marine ecosystems. Once considered unhealthy wastelands to be drained (by Vitruvius among many others), one has only to look at the aftermath of Hurricane Katrina and the BP gulf oil spill to understand the beneficial—and fragile—role that wetlands play.

Ecologically, wetlands (whether natural or constructed) are nutrient sinks, and therefore resources for life. They store water, and then slowly release it, thus controlling flooding. They are among the most productive ecosystems, comparable to rainforests and coral reefs. When healthy and not compromised by human over-development, wetlands protect coastlands from extreme events. Wetlands support specialized flora that have adapted to hydric soils and saline conditions—some of those plants are well suited to phytoremediation, a process of redressing certain forms of water and soil pollution with carefully selected and managed plantings. For fauna, these habitats are vital to avian and other wildlife, as well as fisheries. And finally, they have a role in the human world, serving as recreation areas and sources of renewable natural resources.

The US Environmental Protection Agency (EPA) has a list of principles for wetland restoration available on their Web site.[3] While intended for larger-scale application, many of these principles would serve an architect well when designing any sustainable project:

- Preserve and protect aquatic resources
- Restore ecological integrity
- Restore natural structure

[3] List of principles is available at http://www.epa.gov/owow/wetlands/restore/principles.html.

- Restore natural function
- Design for self-sustainability
- Work within the watershed/landscape context
- Use passive restoration when appropriate
- Understand the potential of the watershed
- Restore native species, avoid non-native species
- Address ongoing causes of degradation
- Use natural fixes and bioengineering
- Involve a multidisciplinary team
- Develop clear, achievable, and measurable goals
- Monitor and adapt where changes are necessary
- Use reference sites
- Focus on feasibility

As an example of dynamically sizing a constructed wetland from data in the BIM model, we'll consider one such system domesticated for general use, the Wastewater Garden (WWG). Its predecessor was the sewage treatment and recycling systems that were designed and implemented in Biosphere 2. From 1991 to 1993 this constructed wetland safely treated and recycled human-generated wastewater back into the virtually sealed environment of the experimental, eight-person habitat (Fig. 9.12). The following WWG sizing information is provided courtesy of Dr. Mark Nelson, a member of the first Biosphere 2 crew and Wastewater Garden expert.

Superficially similar to a traditional septic system, the WWG treats water in three major steps (Fig. 9.13). The first treatment step occurs in a

FIGURE 9.12 The intensive agricultural biome in Biosphere 2 in early 1994.

Photo by Gill Kenny. Reprinted with permission from Synergetic Press.

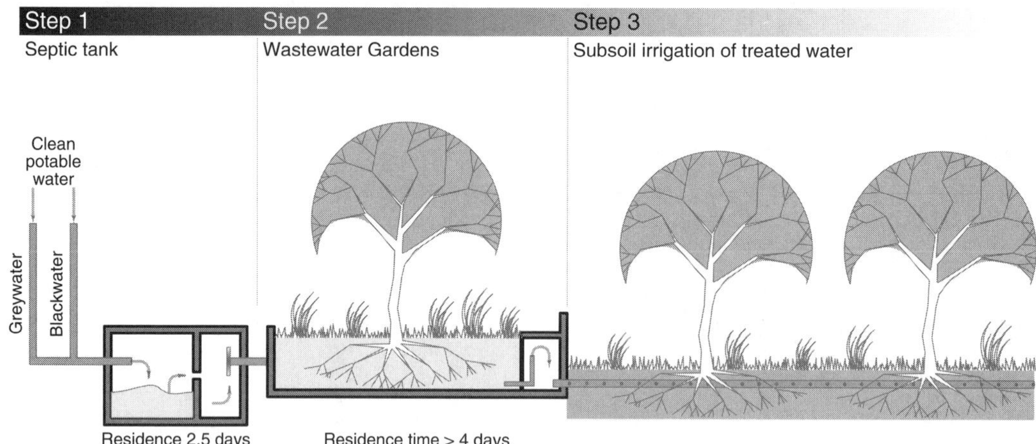

FIGURE 9.13 Diagram of the Wastewater Garden system, redrawn by the author from a figure by Dr. Mark Nelson. Plants in the Wastewater Garden itself must be carefully selected for their characteristics and suitability to the local climate; there is far more flexibility in the selection of drain field flora.

sedimentation tank, similar to a septic tank, to settle and digest biosolids. Greywater and blackwater reside in this tank for three days; the tank's capacity is therefore sized as three times the daily flow. Sedimentation storage itself is either comprised of two tanks or a single tank with two-thirds of its volume in first compartment and one-third volume in the second compartment behind an internal baffle wall. A conventional septic tank filter, sized to accommodate daily flow, is placed at the outlet pipes of the sedimentation tank. This filter is hardened plastic and is simply removed and washed if it begins to clog, ensuring that solids won't pass the septic tank and enter the constructed wetland, where they would fill gaps in the gravel.

The slope of piping from the building to the sedimentation tank should be at least 2 percent. Pipes from both the sedimentation tank (Fig. 9.14) to the WWG and from the Garden to the final subsoil leach drain area may be 1 percent. Here inspection of the 3D geometry of the BIM building and site model may help to confirm tank depth and relative locations of the garden and field.

The second step in the treatment process is the Wastewater Garden itself. For each full-time resident, provide approximately 0.7 square feet of WWG area; this will allow at least four days of residence time in the Garden. Areas with high rates of evapotranspiration (see Fig. 9.7; evapotranspiration rates will be similar) will likely result in longer residence times and more effective treatment. For treatment of toilet and kitchen wastewater only (blackwater), the WWG should be 0.4 square feet per gallon per inhabitant, prorated for occupancy for part of the day. The constructed wetland should be 0.65 meter deep (25 inches), with a water level of 0.6 meter and a 0.05-meter (5-inch) dry gravel layer above to ensure no odors and prevent accidental direct contact. A perimeter berm of 0.20 meters (8 inches) prevents rain runoff into the constructed wetland.

The third and final step in the treatment and reuse of wastewater is subsoil irrigation of a "leachdrain" area. This may be planted with any valuable shrub and/or tree species depending on soil type and water table depth, with the exception of root crops and trees with invasive root systems (such as fig trees). The leachdrain area may be home to productive species such as fruit trees, timber trees, or cut flower shrubs (Fig. 9.15). All plant species must be fully water-tolerant.

An indirect dependency may be established between the BIM-model's floor area and the required size of the leachdrain field. Occupancy

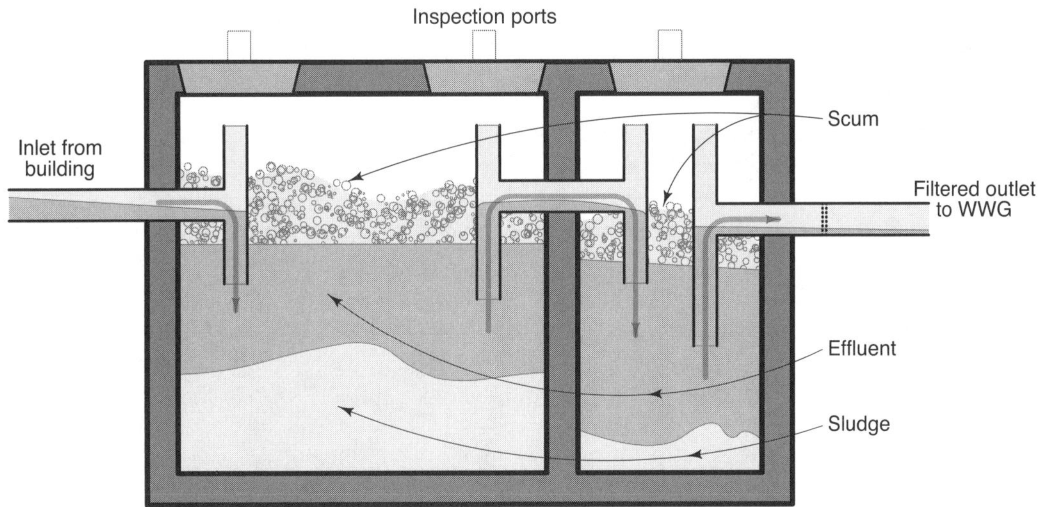

FIGURE 9.14 A standard two-compartment septic tank, sized appropriately, serves as waste material residence for almost three days.

FIGURE 9.15 Wastewater Garden in a courtyard between family house and guest rooms at Coco Eco Bed and Breakfast, Coconut Well, Broome, West Australia.

Image courtesy of Mark Nelson, Wastewater Gardens.

(if not programmatically known) is dependent on floor area; total lengths of subsoil irrigation trenches for greywater and blackwater WWG leachfields are calculated from the number of occupants, depending on soil type:

- Sandy soil: 2 m (6′-6″) per full-time occupant
- Loamy soil: 4.4 m (14′-5″) per occupant
- Light clay soil: 8 m (26′-3″) per occupant
- Heavy clay soil: determined by testing

These guideline values assume 0.3 meters wide by 0.5 meters deep gravel trenches (1 foot wide by 1.5-feet deep gravel at the bottom of a 3-foot deep trench).

For greywater recycling systems, the lengths of subsoil trenches needed per full-time occupant (or equivalent) are as follows, assuming 100 liters (about 26 gallons) per day per capita of greywater load:

- Sandy soil: 1.4 m (4′-6″) per full-time occupant
- Loamy soil: 3 m (9′-10″) per occupant
- Light clay soil: 8 m (16′-5″) per occupant
- Heavy clay soil: determined by testing

These are preliminary sizing guidelines only, of course; a knowledgeable consultant must be retained for properly designed and subsequently constructed wetlands. However, these values, when linked to the model, can guide the designer in the sizing and placement of the sedimentation tank, WWG, and leachdrain field. This in turn may influence site design considerations, potentially including the siting and even the orientation of the building itself.

Gutter sizing

Any structural engineer working in regions with expansive soils will vouch that gutters are a foundation's best friend. Architectural engineers moreover will advise against vegetation (which retains moisture) against the edge of the building due to the potential to encourage mold growth. In both these cases appropriately sized gutters are key to keeping undesirable water (whether in liquid or vapor form) away from the building perimeter. In many cases gutters are treated as an afterthought, a minor roofing accessory that is mentioned in the project specifications manual and appears in building sections or eave details.

In some cases, however, gutters may play an architectural role, particularly as a component of a rainwater harvesting system, or if expected to carry an extraordinary amount of water (a celebrated example of this is Overland Partner's Ladybird Johnson Wildlife Research Center near Austin). There are several gutter manufacturer Web sites that offer online calculators for sizing gutters approximately based on rainfall data and contributing roof area. For half-round gutters (a personal favorite), the gutter diameter (G_{ϕ}) is approximately given by the following equation,

Gutter Sizing

A	R	G ø
1,799.3 SF	3.0"	5.0"

$$G_{ø} = 2\cdot\sqrt{(A_{roof} \cdot R_{i})/280*\pi} \qquad \textit{Equation 9.09}$$

Where:

A = Contributing roof area, square feet
R = Rain intensity (1-hour, ten-year), inches
G ø = Half-round gutter diameter (rounded up to nearest inch)

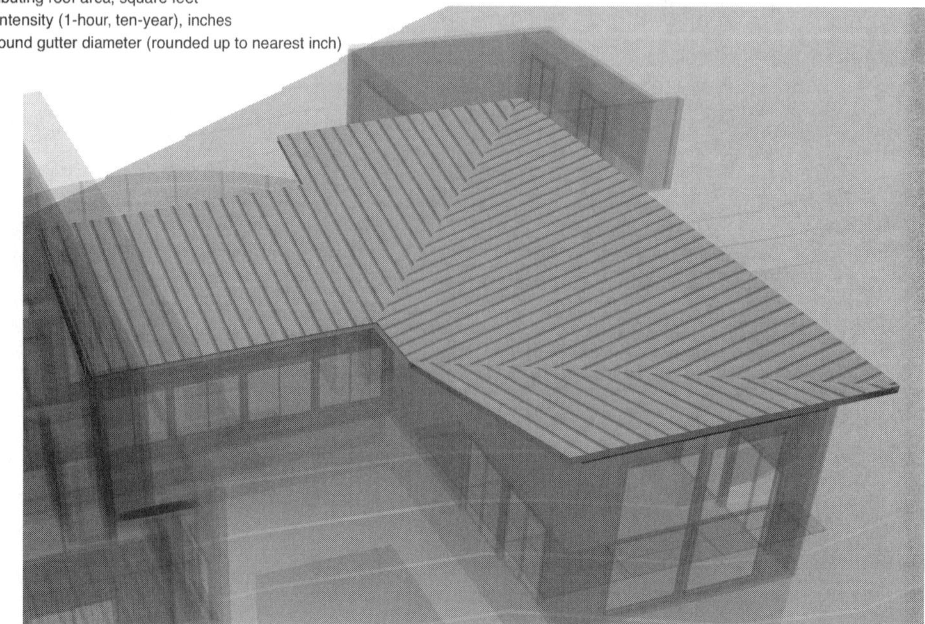

FIGURE 9.16 In this BIM model, a worksheet tabulates projected (plan) roof area to calculate half-round gutter sizing according to Equation 9.09, rounding up gutter diameter to the nearest inch. For BIM applications that only measure actual (normal) roof area, (plan) projected roof area is roof area multiplied by the cosine of the pitch.

where A_{roof} is the roof projected plan area in square feet and R_i is the rainfall intensity in inches per hour:

$$G_{\phi} = 2\cdot\sqrt{\frac{A_{roof}\cdot R_i}{280\pi}} \quad \text{[Equation 9.9; after SMACNA 1993]}$$

Rainfall intensity can be found on maps provided on the National Oceanic and Atmospheric Administration (NOAA) web site.[4] Other architectural sources (such as Ramsey and Sleeper 2007) provide charts for sizing rectangular gutters based on rainfall intensity, roof distance between leaders, and pitches of roofs. Equation 9.09, however, has the advantage that it can be incorporated into a BIM schedule to dynamically inform the user of appropriate gutter sizing based on the contributing roof area (Fig. 9.16). It is therefore most useful as a preliminary design and sizing relationship, rather than a determinate of final gutter sizing.

[4] Rainfall intensity data can be accessed at http://hdsc.nws.noaa.gov/hdsc/pdfs.

▪ Case Study: Bee Ranch, Navasota, Texas

By François Lévy
Design firm: François Lévy Architect

Any off-grid building occupied year-round poses significant design challenges. With no reliance on community electrical or hydrological infrastructure, it is critical that all systems be sized and designed correctly, and emergency backup systems be provided. This particular project, located in rural Central Texas east of Austin and northwest of Houston, is sited on property held by the owner's family since the nineteenth century. As in many places in America, neighboring farmland has been gradually converted to housing subdivisions. Not wanting to encourage further development and sprawl by bringing utilities to the site, the owners opted for an off-grid approach to their future family home (Fig. 9.17).

FIGURE 9.17 Rendered view of Bee Ranch looking north. South-facing roof pitch is designed for optimal summer PV collection, given anticipated cooling loads. At the same time, the roof is elevated to create a tall, shaded southerly colonnade, also providing tall indoor spaces for air stratification and loft space opportunities. See also Figure 6.11 for sun shading studies. BIM model and rendering by the author.

(Continued)

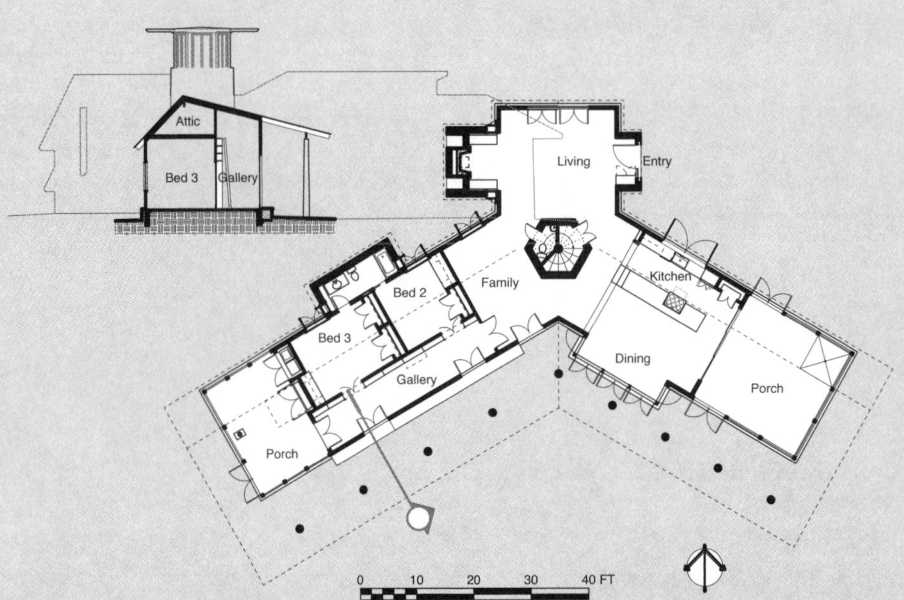

FIGURE 9.18 Ground floor plan and section of Bee Ranch. The north-facing living room has substantial glazing for daylighting with minimal heat gain. The large screened porches to the east and west provide substantial shade to the narrow elevations of the house. Drawing views of BIM model by the author.

This single-family home is thus intended to be entirely off-grid, both in its use of energy and water. The resource design strategy has been to "first reduce, then regenerate." The building's siting and orientation emphasizes southern exposure (Fig. 9.18), with the most south-facing roofs pitched for optimal annual solar collection. At the same time, the winter north wind at the open farmstead can be fierce, a fact the owners knew from generations of experience. North roofs, therefore, are steeper to proportionately account for more of the envelope, as they have roughly double the R-value of their supporting walls.

The short living wing of the tripartite plan is oriented due north, while the public and private wings fan out at equal angles to the east-southeast and west-southwest, respectively. Large screened porches at the ends of the long wings expand the livable area cost-effectively, provide transition zones between the working agricultural area and the home, shade the narrow east and west building elevations in the hottest part of the summer, and support rainwater collecting roofs.

The roof is the central design element of the house. Sheltering the long southerly façades from the high summer sun, the roof is set high on the south to create tall cool rooms in summer and let in the low winter sun. It maximizes attic storage, is pitched to provide shelter from the cold north wind, and it serves to harvest the region's plentiful rainfall. The exposed roof structure is architecturally emphasized and creates another transition space above the tall south colonnade.

Preliminary calculations showed that the building program area alone would yield enough water to meet the storage needs for the family of five. In a rainwater harvesting system, however, the most expensive component is the cistern; roof and cistern must be sized

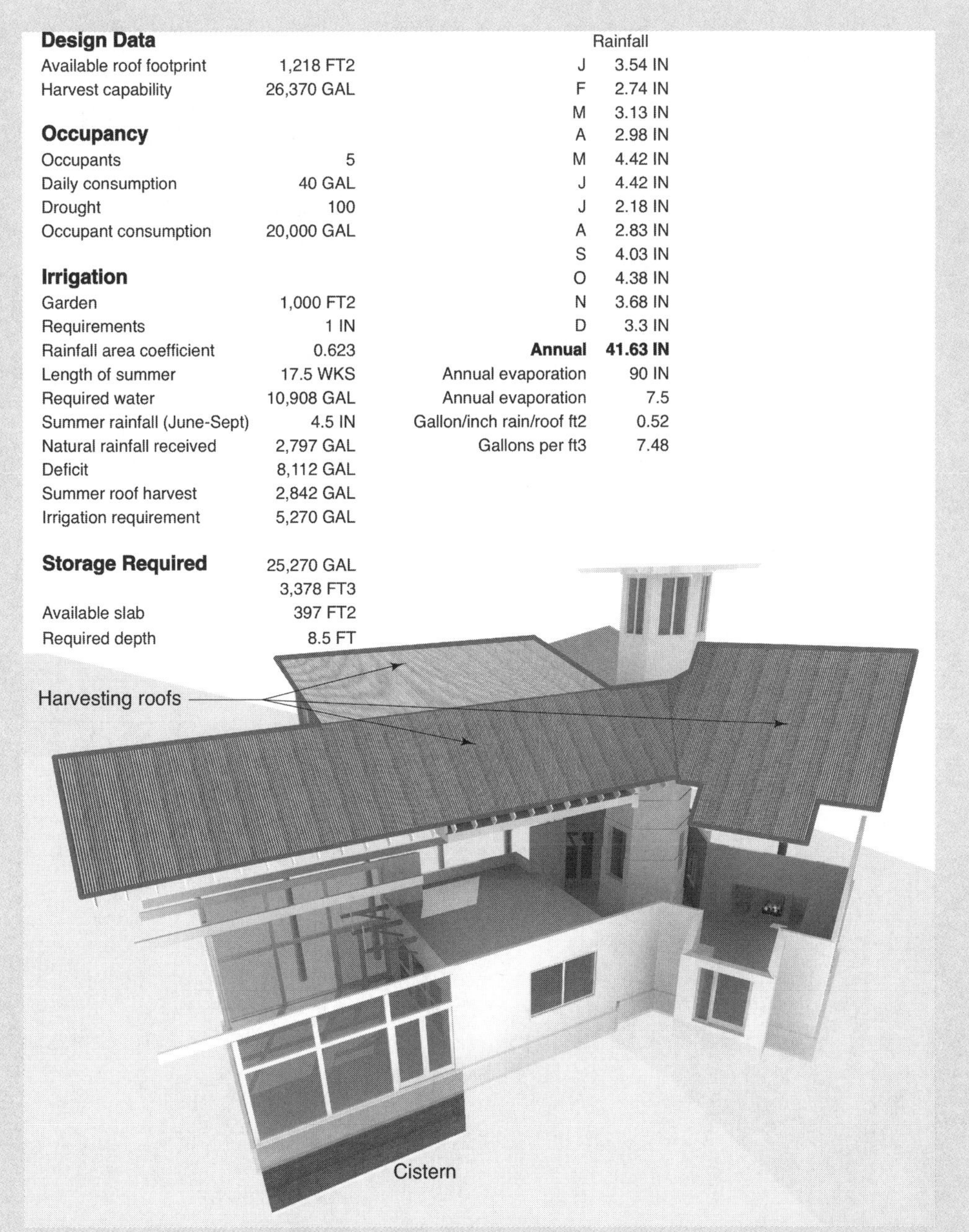

Design Data
Available roof footprint 1,218 FT2
Harvest capability 26,370 GAL
Occupancy
Occupants 5
Daily consumption 40 GAL
Drought 100
Occupant consumption 20,000 GAL
Irrigation
Garden 1,000 FT2
Requirements 1 IN
Rainfall area coefficient 0.623
Length of summer 17.5 WKS
Required water 10,908 GAL
Summer rainfall (June-Sept) 4.5 IN
Natural rainfall received 2,797 GAL
Deficit 8,112 GAL
Summer roof harvest 2,842 GAL
Irrigation requirement 5,270 GAL
Storage Required 25,270 GAL
3,378 FT3
Available slab 397 FT2
Required depth 8.5 FT
Rainfall
J 3.54 IN
F 2.74 IN
M 3.13 IN
A 2.98 IN
M 4.42 IN
J 4.42 IN
J 2.18 IN
A 2.83 IN
S 4.03 IN
O 4.38 IN
N 3.68 IN
D 3.3 IN
Annual 41.63 IN
Annual evaporation 90 IN
Annual evaporation 7.5
Gallon/inch rain/roof ft2 0.52
Gallons per ft3 7.48
Harvesting roofs
Cistern

FIGURE 9.19 This exploded perspective rendering of the Bee Ranch harvesting roofs and cisterns shows sizing data and calculations. Annual rainfall data determine the roof's capacity, and therefore suggests appropriate roof areas for collection. The roof is designed to concentrate harvesting surfaces (outlined) to minimize leaders and downspouts; the cistern is similarly located. The west screen porch and the cistern are sized together, as latter is situated below the former. The building is most out of grade here, which minimizes excavation. BIM model and rendering by the author.

(*Continued*)

FIGURE 9.20 View from the northwest. North roofs are at a steep pitch to help shelter conditioned spaces from the cold winter north winds. BIM model and rendering by the author.

together to insure that the roof can fill the tank. Several contributing roofs were candidates as harvesting surfaces, and two locations were considered for the cistern. A worksheet in the Vectorworks BIM file calculated annual harvested rainwater volume as a function of roof face areas; based on that information and considerations of leader and downpipe locations, three roof surfaces were selected as harvesting surfaces.

At the same time, it was decided that the cistern should be located under the slab (the local soils are not rocky nor difficult to excavate); in this way cistern costs would in part be shared by the foundation (Fig. 9.19). In the interests of indoor air quality and controlling humidity, only the porch areas were considered as water storage candidates. The porch floor areas (minus the plan area of the cistern walls) were therefore linked to the BIM worksheet to determine the necessary cistern depth to store enough water to weather a 100-day drought.

Other sustainable systems have been designed integrally with the catchment roof. Obviously the southern roof's pitch supports efficient solar collection while being optimal for summer shading and daylighting. The building is sited to capitalize on prevailing summer breezes to augment the passive cooling of the central thermal chimney. Walls and roofs are appropriately insulated and designed to use advanced framing techniques to maximize thermal resistance and minimize thermal bridging (Fig. 9.20). These systematic passive measures reduce the home's energy requirements; appliances and lighting are carefully selected to minimize energy loads. These reduced energy requirements are met through a photovoltaic array and solar thermal collectors for domestic hot water and radiant floor heating.

Chapter 10

Materials and Waste

For much of this book we have considered BIM in the service of sustainability in the context of energy usage, with the exception of the previous chapter on building hydrology and some of our discussion of site design and analysis in Chapter 3. Given the contemporary concern with the environmental ramifications of our society's fossil fuel addiction, those energy concerns have been quite appropriate. In Chapter 9, however, we broadened the discussion to include water resources, and now consider material use and its optimization with BIM.

An estimated 40 percent of raw materials in our economy are dedicated to the construction of buildings. In the United States, the construction industry accounts for roughly 30 percent of the waste output, generating 136 million tons per year. Fisk, Levin, and Bierman-Lytle (1992) offer one approach that begins to address this issue. Their suggestion is to build options in architecture by mimicking four of nature's "rules":

- Natural systems are highly redundant: one system seems always to be duplicated at a scale larger and smaller than the system being addressed;
- Conservation of resources (energy and materials) seems to occur through the integration of highly connected components that often serve multiple functions;
- Nature limits, whenever possible, the number of conversion steps, and the distance between these steps tends to accomplish all needs at the smallest possible scale;
- All the actors in every living system function in a way to ensure a continuous life cycle of materials (Fig. 10.2).

Optimizing building materials and reducing waste does not alone transform our artificial systems into natural ones; in a natural system, there is no waste. But waste reduction is a step in the right direction and is achievable by

- reducing consumption (optimizing materials use);
- sourcing renewed (salvaged) and renewable resources;
- selecting materials with the least processing and greatest benefit; and
- employing materials produced as close to the project site as possible, to reduce transportation environmental impact (and costs).

As BIM is widely used, there is a tendency to emphasize software use for productivity gains, and interoperability for process efficiencies (see the discussion in Chapter 11). And these are worthwhile aspects of the process. But given that the BIM model inherently inventories all modeled components of the virtual building, there are several opportunities to query the model to better control material waste. Along the way, the designer can help reduce construction cost, or at least more accurately predict it.

Material takeoffs and cost calculations

Accurately predicting construction costs has been a significant motivator for adoption of BIM in larger projects. Indeed, large-scale construction

FIGURE 10.1 A testament to the accuracy possible with BIM. The framing model, middle, was extracted from the comprehensive BIM model at top. A few months later, the architect took the construction photo at bottom from the same vantage.

Bley Sleeping House Addition by Agruppo. Photo by Andrew Nance.

FIGURE 10.2 The Advanced Green Builder Demonstration (AGBD) is a structure featuring numerous sustainable building techniques including a 13,200 gallon rainwater harvesting system and two methods of straw-earth construction. The AGBD is the first modern building in the United States to use 100 percent Portland Cement-free concrete. The concrete used in the building is a fly-ash, caliche mix developed by the Center for Maximum Building Potential Systems (CMBPS). The AGBD is designed with the lifecycles of water, energy, and materials in mind; it incorporates local and recycled materials and is designed for easy disassembly. It currently serves as the main office site for CMBPS.

Photo by Paul Bardagjy.

companies were early adopters of BIM precisely for the ability to precisely quantify materials (accurate takeoffs, of course, require accurate models; Fig. 10.1, above). Anecdotally, construction companies have placed such a high premium on model accuracy that they have rebuilt BIM models in-house (and thereby lose the interoperable efficiencies touted by BIM advocates). The benefits of material takeoffs are hardly limited to large projects; quantity surveys of small projects are particularly beneficial. These buildings tend to have smaller budget margins, and even a small error may lead to project-damaging cost overruns. But among residential contractors it seems at times that cost estimates are as much an art as a science.

In a traditional design-bid-build (DBB) project, there is a gap between design and estimating. There is imperfect communication between the architect, who has access to digital project documentation and therefore can prepare detailed takeoffs, and the contractor with access to detailed historic cost information, current bids, and proprietary trade cost information. Without open communication, each party's detailed information is of limited usefulness. Of course, even with traditional project delivery, accurate takeoffs, whether coarse or detailed, can be put to good use. For integrated project delivery (IPD), or design-build (DB) firms with both design control and access to cost information, BIM coupled with cost data offers the compelling possibility of

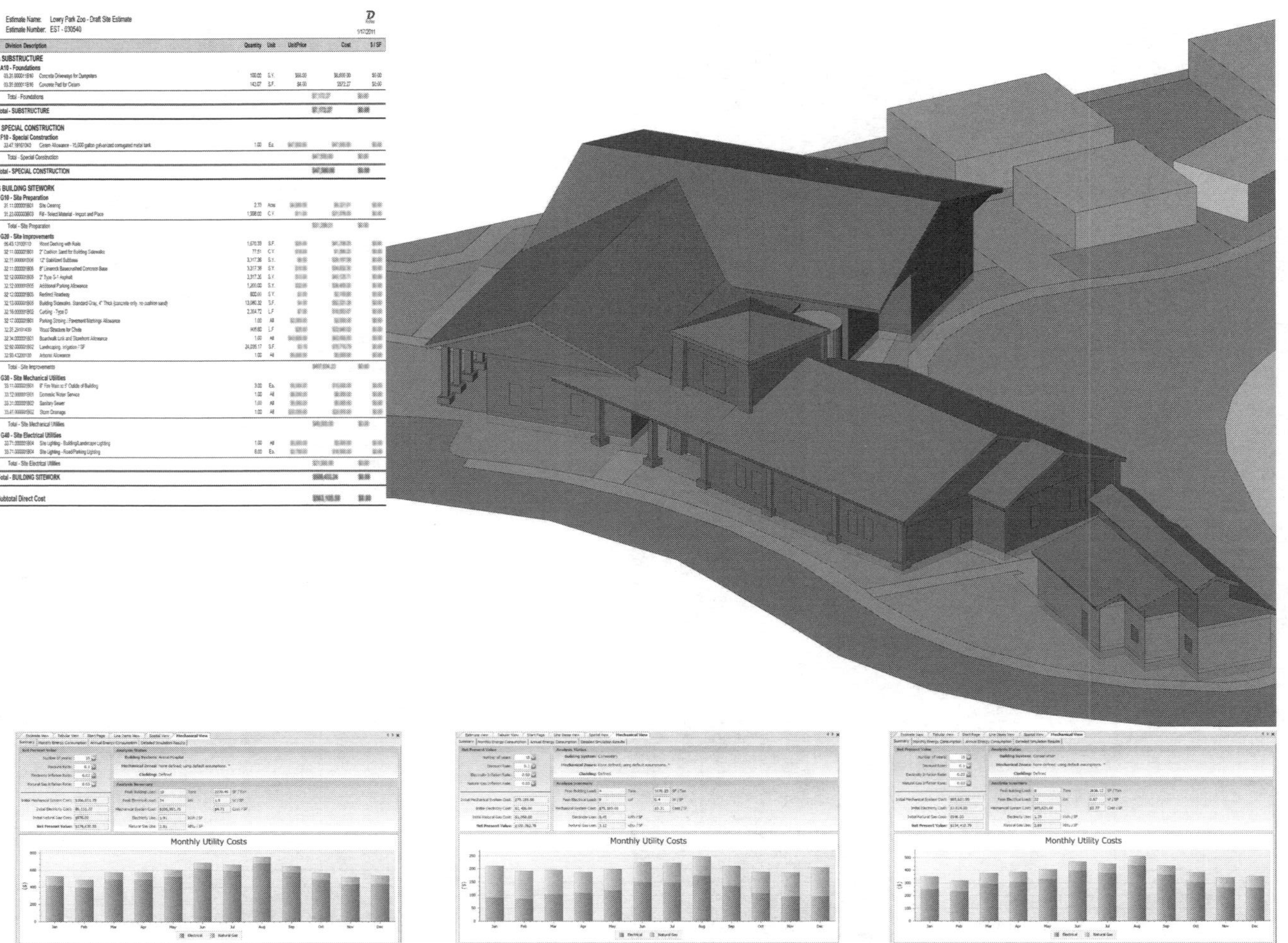

FIGURE 10.3 A schematic design cost analysis of the Lowry Park Zoo Animal Hospital Project consists of three main buildings and additional holding and quarantine areas: an Animal Hospital, a Conservation office and a research building, and the Commissary to facilitate food preparation and storage for the zoo animals. Each building will also serve as observation attractions for zoo guests. Cost reports, images, and energy analysis were done in DProfiler, the Beck Group's proprietary building information modeling software.

Image courtesy of Beck Architecture LLC.

using this data to design appropriately: information in the service of design.

Coarse calculations (area calculations)

As a contractor once said to me: "Give me a schematic design, and I'll give you a schematic cost estimate." That admonition notwithstanding, cost analysis based on early design information is useful in confirming preliminary budgets, holding to them, and checking project scope creep. The designer may not have access to up-to-the-minute material and labor costs, but a general historical cost analysis can still be useful. One approach is to review past projects to find a total project cost (C_{proj}) and break down gross square footages by type as multiplied by a ratio of base unit area cost:

- Conditioned space (A_{cond}) equal to 100 percent of base square footage cost;
- Enclosed unconditioned space (A_{uncond}) multiplied by a cost ratio (R_{uncond}) of, for example, 75 percent of base square footage cost;
- Covered outdoor areas (A_{cover}) such as porches, with a cost ratio (R_{cover}) of, say, 50 percent of base square footage;
- Hardscaped areas (A_{terr}) including terraces and decks, with a cost ratio (R_{terr}) of, for example, 25 percent of base square footage.

The values of the cost ratios *R* above are somewhat subjective, and those provided are obviously examples. To derive a past project's base unit area (C_{sf}) multiply each area *A* by its respective cost ratio *R* according to the following formula:

$$C_{sf} = C_{proj}/(A_{cond} + AR_{uncond} + AR_{cover} + AR_{terr})$$

[Equation 10.1]

This equation can be modified to account for areas with cost ratios *R* greater than 100 percent to represent particularly expensive building areas (Fig. 10.4). The equation may also be expanded to include additional categories of construction, such as differentiating elevated decks from terraces.

The square footage cost for past projects can then be applied to a proposed project, simply by multiplying the base unit area cost by the construction area and cost ratio—that is, by rearranging the previous equation into the following:

$$C_{proj} = C_{sf}(A_{cond} + AR_{uncond} + AR_{cover} + AR_{terr})$$

[Equation 10.2]

The cost ratio values (*R*) may be applied to BIM space objects, floor slabs, or polygons; once a probable unit cost of construction (C_{sf}) has been established and a schedule or worksheet has been created with the above formula, the BIM model can dynamically report estimated construction costs as the model changes.

Detailed takeoffs

As BIM applications have grown in sophistication, the degree to which generic 3D objects have been replaced with parametric models of real-world building components has only increased. This has had several effects:

- Virtual buildings have become easier to model, requiring less custom modeling on the part of the user;
- Building models have become more complex, both in their organization and in their design;
- Greater differentiation by object type has facilitated more detailed material takeoffs (Fig. 10.5).

In addition to this last point, the reporting tools available in BIM have improved. Whereas constructing schedules of materials was once a tedious process, it has become a far more automated one (Fig. 10.6). With minimal setup the BIM user can report linear, area, volumetric, and even mass values (if density is known) of object types or components—optionally within a given layer (or of a given class). Provided the model is accurately constructed, such takeoffs may include:

- Concrete volume for slabs on grade, including perimeter and internal grade beams;
- Wall areas of a given type (useful in estimating siding or masonry veneer quantities);

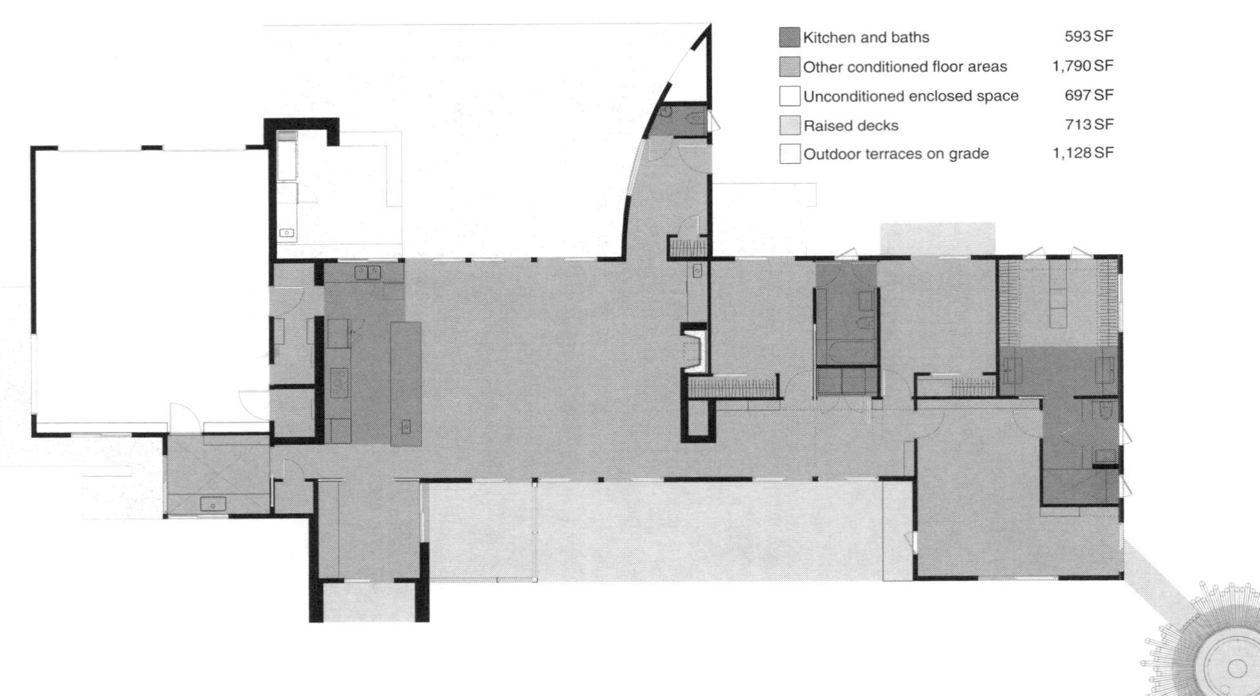

FIGURE 10.4 A simple method of estimating cost—hence material use—is to assign general cost per square foot for various area categories, from least intense (outdoor spaces) to most (finish-, plumbing-, and electrical-intensive areas like kitchens and baths). Such estimates are most accurate, of course, when there is reliable historic data. They also account for the inherent variations in building costs by area. In this color-coded plan, different "cost densities" are applied to different areas of the plan.

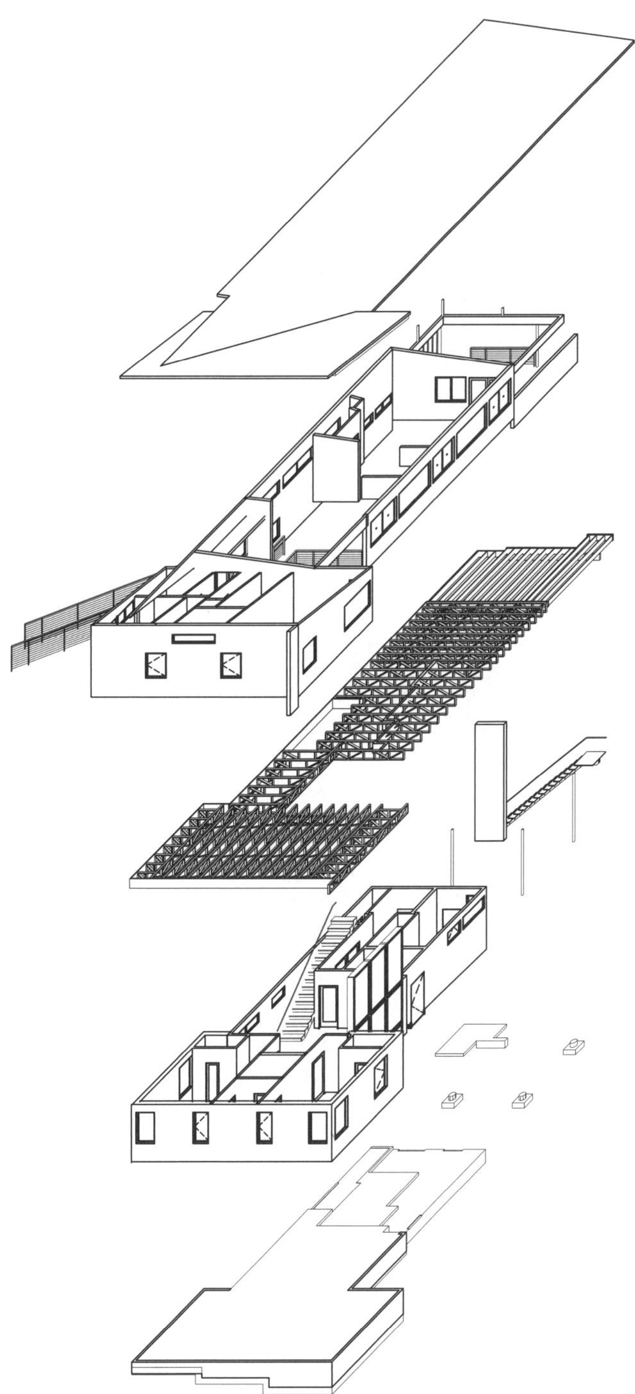

FIGURE 10.5 A detailed BIM model with every component delineated lends itself to detailed material takeoffs.

Rancho Encino Residence by Agruppo.

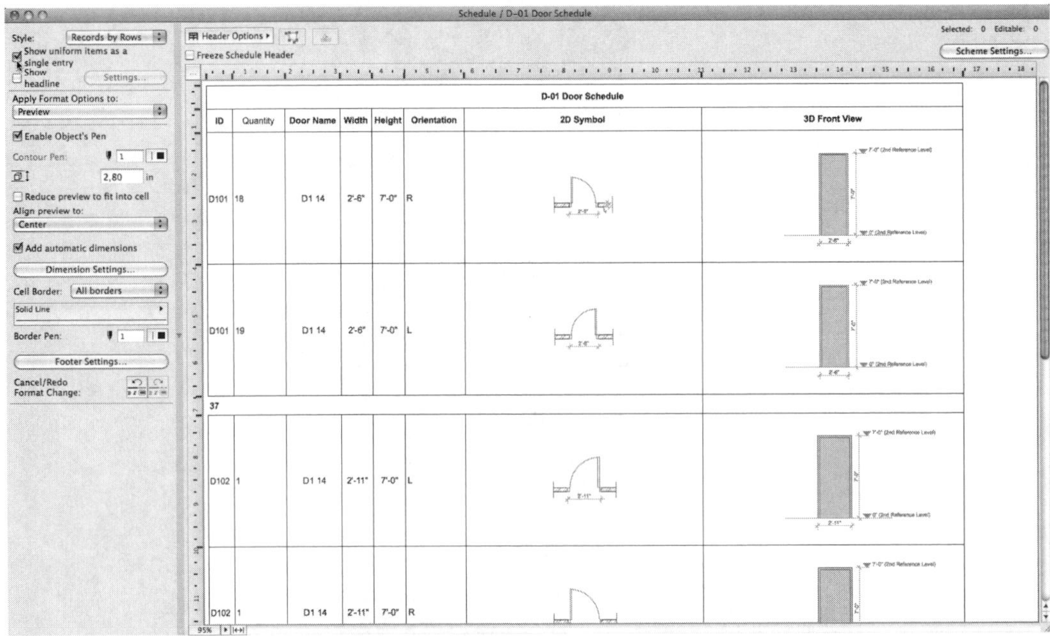

FIGURE 10.6 This detail of an automated BIM door schedule shows unit data, plan, and elevation views. The schedule can be updated to reflect model changes; in many cases the schedule is bi-directional, such that changes made therein update the model.

Image courtesy of Graphisoft.

- Roof areas;
- Framing member dimensions and quantities in some cases;
- Door and window schedules;
- Fixture counts for plumbing, lighting, power, and so forth.

Assuming correct material, labor, and equipment cost data, the BIM model can form the basis of a highly detailed and precise cost estimate, if gross approximations are no longer appropriate. Of even greater interest to the architect, takeoff data can better inform the designer of the first and environmental ramifications of alternative design decisions.

Advanced framing

There are a wide variety of wall system products as alternatives to dimensional lumber framing for smaller buildings, each with its own unique advantages and drawbacks. Two general wall system types are structural insulated panels (SIPs; Fig. 10.7) and insulated concrete forms (ICFs). SIPs or stress-skin panels are typically composed of rigid foam insulation laminated to and inserted between engineered wood shear membranes (formerly plywood, now usually oriented strand board, or OSB). The insulation and skin do most of the structural work, but SIPs additionally have dimensional lumber splines at their edges to serve as a fastening site for the adjacent panel. Some SIPs products omit the sheathing or employ a thin metal skin for shear, relying on cold-formed galvanized steel studs.

ICFs are available in a wide variety of proprietary systems. They commonly include an insulating aggregate such as expanded polystyrene or recycled and treated wood product as an insulating aggregate. ICF cavities are reinforced with steel (rebar or welded wire fabric) and filled with concrete (Fig. 10.8).

FIGURE 10.7 Construction photos of a SIPs project. Note the stacked stress-skin panels in the background at left, to the left of the small crane required for their placement. The image at right clearly shows the panelized construction, shop-fabricated openings, and wood stud spline edges characteristic of SIPs.

FIGURE 10.8 The LEED Gold-targeted 5,800 square foot Texas Parks and Wildlife Department Headquarters Building uses insulated concrete forms for the R-40 building shell. The design-build team was led by Jamail Smith Construction Co., and Stephen Oliver, AIA, LEED AP, of OPA Design Studio, both from Austin, Texas. Gordon Bohmfalk was the TPWD architect. Note the integrated reinforcing within each panel, the use of wood framing as formwork at openings, and the need for bracing against the pressure of the upcoming concrete pour.

Photo courtesy of Gordon Bohmfalk, Architect.

Both SIPs and ICFs offer generally better thermal performance than traditional stick framing for three important reasons:

- *Greater R-value.* The rigid insulation used in both products offers better thermal resistance than the loose fill commonly used in stick framing.
- *Less thermal bridging.* The absence or wider spacing of low R-value studs and plates (in traditional stick-framing up to 20 percent of the wall) results in a more uniform resistance to thermal conductance.
- *Tighter construction.* The nature of these wall systems makes them inherently less susceptible to air infiltration, with its attendant energy losses.

Nevertheless, stick framing is still highly popular in the United States. As is often the case, the prevalence of a technology has more to do with social dimensions than technical superiority. Stick framing's distinct advantages:

- *A huge labor pool.* Skilled carpenters are available in every community in the country, large or small.
- *Forgiving.* Framing errors are easy to correct.
- *Minimal specialized equipment.* Most SIPs are quite heavy and require small cranes for installation. ICFs are concrete-filled of course, and hoses are needed to fill them. In addition, care must be taken to brace the forms to avoid blowouts for tall lifts. Stick framing equipment easily fits in a small contractor's job box on the back of a pick-up truck.
- *Rapid erection.* In spite of the fact that panels are factory cut to very tight tolerances, SIPs are not, as a rule, erected faster than stick framing. Most ICF installation is similar to concrete block construction.

These and other factors conspire to make traditional dimensional lumber construction inexpensive and attractive to owners concerned with first costs. In an effort to capitalize on those benefits while making stick framing more sustainable, *advanced framing* (sometimes referred to as optimum value engineered, *or* OVE framing) was developed in the 1970s. It has become accepted in all major building codes, even though many building officials (and architects and builders) are unfamiliar with it. The goal of advanced framing is to use less structural material while providing for greater insulation. This is achieved with the following key measures:

- *Wider studs, wider spacing.* Exterior walls are framed with 2x6 studs at 24″ on center rather than 2x4s at 16″ o.c.; as a result, there is greater wall depth for more insulation, and studs occur less frequently to reduce thermal bridging.
- *Single plates.* Top (and sole) plates are single 2x6s and are not doubled. This requires coordination and care in roof framing layout, as rafters or trusses must align with a stud below them. Again, this measure reduces framing material use and reduces thermal bridging.
- *Two-stud corners.* Most corners are terribly over-built, and can be adequately framed with two studs in an L-configuration. Such corners can then be insulated, which helps reduce heat transfer and discourages mold growth in the wall cavity, which may occur due to condensation.
- *Insulated headers.* Rather than spacing header members with 1/2″ plywood to add up to the 5 1/2″ wall stud depth, provide rigid insulation spacers. Again, thermal bridging is reduced.

Coupled with modern foam insulations, advanced framing walls are more airtight and have better thermal performance than conventional stick framing (Fig. 10.9). Advanced framing in general is discussed in greater depth on the Department of Energy's Web site.[1]

BIM offers opportunities to evaluate and optimize advanced framing. On a very basic level, it

[1] Details are available in the Department of Energy's fact sheet, www.nrel.gov/docs/fy01osti/26449.pdf.

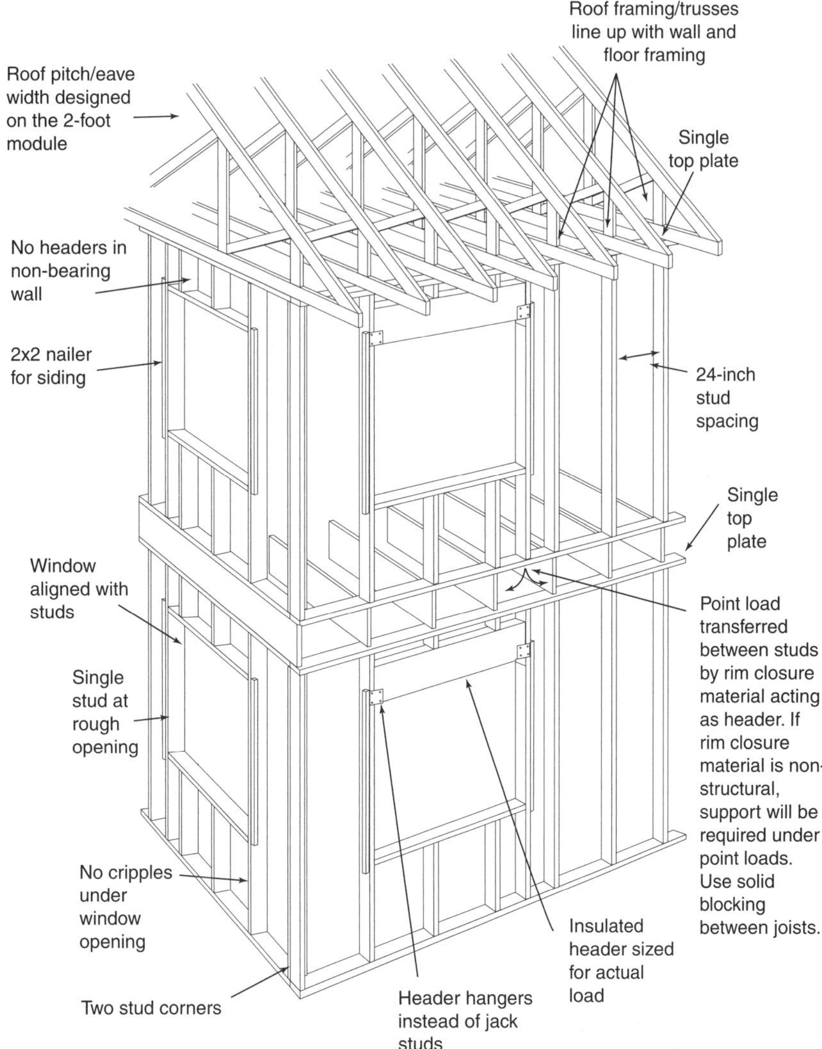

FIGURE 10.9 A graphical synopsis of advanced framing details from Lstiburek (2006). This optimized use of lumber allows for less material waste and greater wall insulation for superior envelope thermal and moisture performance.

Image reprinted by permission, Building Science Corporation.[2]

may be useful to substitute wall types for projects already under design with corresponding improvements in R-value and U·A calculations. In calculating total assembly U-factor, the designer must not neglect the different relative areas of thermal bridging. For a 20-foot length of wall ten feet high with no penetrations, the advanced framing wall is only 9 percent thermally bridged, versus over 13 percent for a conventional 2x4 wall (Fig. 10.10). (A 2x6 stud is also 1.6 times less conductive than a 2x4 stud, by virtue of its greater depth).

[2] Professional Web site available at www.buildingscience.com.

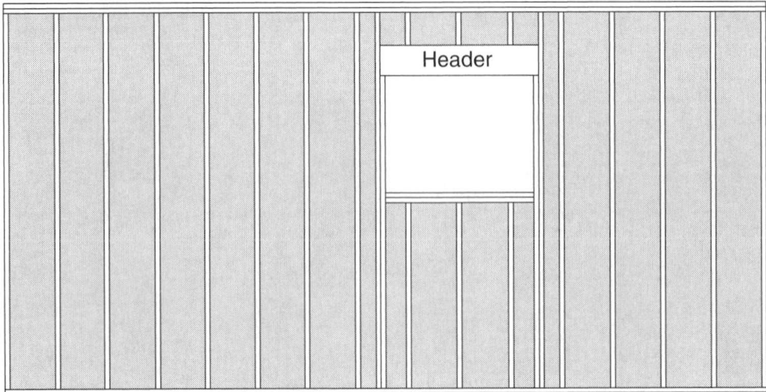

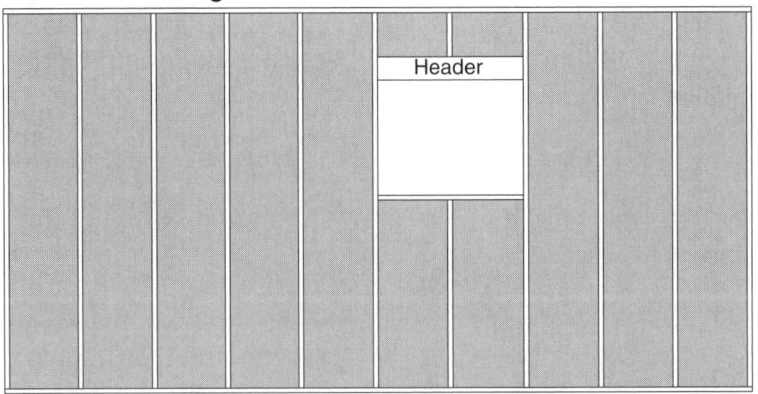

	Conventional	Advanced
	(2x4 studs at 16" o.c.)	*(2x6 studs at 24" o.c.)*
Studs	33.8 s.f.	20.8 s.f.
Insulation	155.8 s.f.	168.8 s.f.
Wood:Insulation Ratio	17.8%	11.0%
Increased R-value		1.7 times

FIGURE 10.10 Elevations of two 20-ft length and 10-ft tall framed walls, each with a single 2 ft x 2 ft opening in the same position. The conventional wall consists of 2x4 studs at 16" on center, with a double top plate, double sill plate at the window, cripples at the header, and uniform header size for all openings. The advanced framing wall has fewer studs that are 2" deeper and spaced 8" farther apart for more insulation. Additionally, it has a single top plate, an individually sized header with hangers, and no window cripples. As a result, there is a 70 percent net increase in thermal resistance.

On a more detailed level, BIM can facilitate a comparative analysis of advanced versus conventional framing. Walls of both types may be assigned an average stud count per length or area; this requires preparatory analysis to estimate framing density and material lengths. For those BIM applications that can automate wall framing, such as Vectorworks Architect or ArchiCAD with the Encina FrameWright add-on, then a project can be analyzed as both a traditionally framed structure and an advanced framing structure (Fig. 10.11). While BIM applications do not specifically have advanced framing built in, the wall framing options are flexible enough that advanced framing can be approximated in the model by stipulating appropriate framing member sizes, spacing, and top plate configuration. Two-stud (or "California") corners are trickier, and may need to be manually adjusted in the model.

In my practice, I have successfully employed this technique to demonstrate and document the economic feasibility of advanced framing. Automatic scheduling of framing materials for both scenarios combined with current lumber costs permitted the development of an accurate materials cost estimate demonstrating the increased per-stud cost for 2x6s being offset by reduced materials use. Of course, insulation costs are higher, but that is precisely the point—to allow more insulation.

Sheet materials

Modern building materials often come in sheet form: cement fiberboard, gypsum wallboard, oriented strand board (OSB), plywood (now more rarely used), metal roofing panels, SIPs, and so forth. To a certain extent, BIM can help optimize panelized construction, either grossly, by estimating quantities, or more precisely, by generating least-waste layouts (Fig. 10.12). This is a classic "knapsack problem" as it is known in mathematics.

Surface area takeoffs are the quickest and most direct route to estimating quantities of sheet materials; divide the total area by the per-sheet area. For irregular geometry, this method will almost always underestimate the number of sheets, as it assumes that off-cuts will be large enough to be reused; in fact they will often be wasted.

Solving the knapsack problem exactly and automatically requires a well-understood but complex mathematical solution. Digital fabrication machines like computer numerically controlled (CNC) routers or laser cutters have such algorithms incorporated into their operation to maximize the number of pieces that can be fit to a sheet. Without custom programming, BIM cannot accommodate these

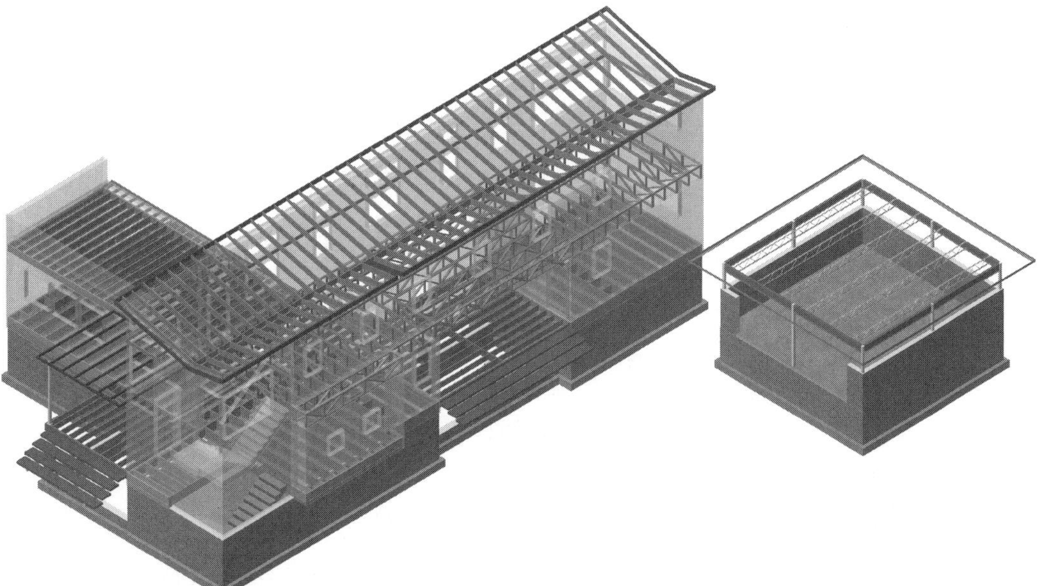

FIGURE 10.11 Most BIM applications automate the production of framing and structural models (articulating individual members) from the "slabs" of wall, floor, and roof objects.

Image ©2011 Nemetschek Vectorworks, Inc.

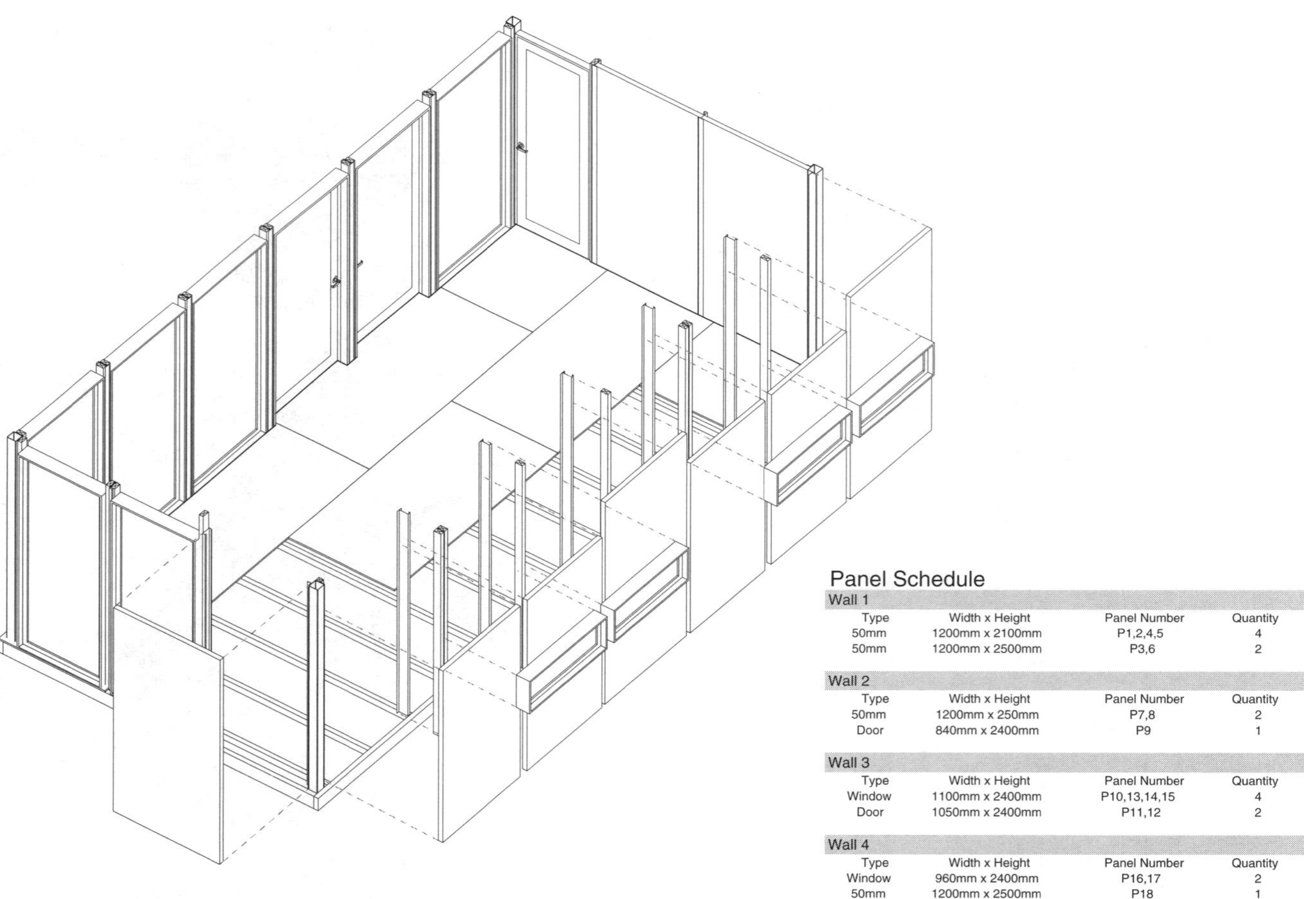

Panel Schedule

Wall 1			
Type	Width x Height	Panel Number	Quantity
50mm	1200mm x 2100mm	P1,2,4,5	4
50mm	1200mm x 2500mm	P3,6	2

Wall 2			
Type	Width x Height	Panel Number	Quantity
50mm	1200mm x 250mm	P7,8	2
Door	840mm x 2400mm	P9	1

Wall 3			
Type	Width x Height	Panel Number	Quantity
Window	1100mm x 2400mm	P10,13,14,15	4
Door	1050mm x 2400mm	P11,12	2

Wall 4			
Type	Width x Height	Panel Number	Quantity
Window	960mm x 2400mm	P16,17	2
50mm	1200mm x 2500mm	P18	1

FIGURE 10.12 An isometric view of an affordable prefabricated building module and an excerpt of the automatic schedule of components. The module is on a structural grid to work with plywood and wall panel dimensions. This module is part of a larger plan for modular courtyard housing and was an entry for the Free Green House Plan Competition.

Courtyard House Bedroom Module courtesy of Ben Allee.

so-called cutting-stock problems. On the other hand, rudimentary solutions can be approximated using simple rendering techniques. By applying an appropriately sized surface pattern to a BIM wall or floor component, for example, sheathing, drywall, or tiling can be simulated in the model. Resizing the pattern (when multiple sheet sizes are available) or changing its orientation can allow the user to approximate the best fit of a repeated regular dimensional sheet for a given surface. For a more precise graphical analysis, an orthogonal view of the model may be overlaid with a hatch or individual polygons to determine the best fit and to quantify off-cuts.

Preliminary life cycle analysis

Natural living systems evolve over such a long period of time that they are, as a result, inherently sustainable—or they would have collapsed long ago. By contrast, human systems are quite new. We've only had cities for 5,000 years or so, for example, which is a blink of an eye evolutionarily. Our human systems are almost universally designed as if we had unlimited natural resources, and just as importantly, as if we had unlimited waste sinks. Indeed, the concept of "waste" is entirely a human one, as there is no such thing in natural living systems. As we are discovering, not only is our environment not an unlimited sink for by-products and waste materials, it is not indefinitely capable of absorbing waste energy.

Awareness of these limitations has given rise to the discipline of life cycle analysis, whereby the true costs of human artifacts (usually manufactured products but buildings as well) are assessed. Life Cycle Assessment or Analysis (LCA) considers all the costs associated with a product, from raw material extraction, to processing and manufacturing, to transportation, operation, and eventual disposal. Some LCA considers costs to human and environmental well-being in addition to monetary costs. The process is highly detailed and the methodology by which different domains of cost assessment are weighted can be controversial. A complete LCA precisely identifies all environmental effects at every stage in the life cycle of a product or a process.

More appropriate to the expertise of architects is a kind of life cycle awareness, considering potential human and environmental impacts during design. There are several accessible tools to aid life cycle awareness, which architects can use, and even integrate into a BIM workflow. These are not traditional BIM tools, but like much of the discussion in this book they are quantifiable systems that rely on BIM data to inform the design process.

Malcolm Wells and the architectural value scale

Architect Malcolm Wells proposed in 1971 a simple scale, his "Wilderness-Based Checklist for Design and Construction," by which buildings could be numerically scored based on evaluations in 15 categories from *destroys/creates pure air* and *destroys/creates pure water* to *intensifies/moderates local weather* to is *ugly/is beautiful* (!). In each category a building is assigned a score from negative 100 (*destroys*) to positive 100 (*creates*) in 25-point increments, for a net rating that ranges from negative 1,500 to positive 1,500 (the latter only achievable by a natural system). Nearly 30 years later, the Society of Building Science Educators (SBSE), developed a Wells-inspired "Regeneration-Based Checklist for Design and Construction." Expanding on Wells' original categories to introduce seven more (for example, *serves as an icon for the apocalypse/for regeneration*), the SBSE checklist differentiates site design from the building and also allows ratings of 0, in contrast to Wells's original measure[3] (Fig. 10.13). This last detail is in keeping with John Tillman Lyle, in the notion that sustainability is just breaking even, while a truly regenerative approach to design goes far beyond that to regeneration—as do natural systems.

One might imagine a seemingly innocuous worksheet or schedule in the BIM file that compiles a score either from data gathered from the model, manual input, or both. For example, each BIM object can be classified as constituted of recycled or virgin materials, as a function of an object's layer

---

[3] The SBSE checklist is available at http://www.sbse.org/resources/docs/wells_checklist_explanation.pdf.

Regeneration-Based Checklist for Design and Construction

Project:

		degeneration				sustainability				regeneration	
		-100 always	-75 usually	-50 sometimes	-25 a bit	0 balances	25 a bit	50 sometimes	75 usually	100 always	
the site	pollutes air										cleans air
	pollutes water										cleans water
	wastes rainwater										stores rainwater
	consumes food										produces food
	destroys rich soil										creates rich soil
	dumps wastes unused										consumes wastes
	destroys wildlife habitat										provides wildlife habitat
	imports energy										exports energy
	requires fuel-powered transportation										requires human-powered transportation
	intensifies local weather										moderates local weather
the building	excludes daylight										uses daylight
	uses mechanical heating										uses passive heating
	uses mechanical cooling										uses passive cooling
	needs cleaning and repair										maintains itself
	produces human discomfort										provides human comfort
	uses fuel-powered circulation										uses human-powered circulation
	pollutes indoor air										creates pure indoor air
	is built of virgin materials										is built of recycled materials
	cannot be recycled										can be recycled
	serves as an icon for the apocalypse										serves as an icon for regeneration
	is a bad neighbor										is a good neighbor
	is ugly										is beautiful

negative score 2200 possible	positive score 2200 possible

final score:

FIGURE 10.13 SBSE's "Regeneration-Based Checklist for Design and Construction" is an update to architect Malcolm Wells's seminal "Wilderness-Based Checklist for Design and Construction." Human development (buildings) are rated on an equally weighted scale in categories that use natural systems as the model and standard, going beyond mere sustainability to regeneration.

Used by permission of SBSE.

(or class depending on software nomenclature), or as a custom object data tag. To score *Is built of virgin materials/recycled materials,* the regeneration checklist might compare the ratio of the number of virgin to recycled objects. For a more detailed analysis, the worksheet could report the ratio by volume, or even by mass if material densities were known. This ratio would then be translated to a scale of negative 100 to positive 100 points corresponding to 0 to 100 percent recycled material. A more subjective, but perhaps just as effective method, consists of alternating BIM views between virgin and recycled components and manually scoring the visual result by inspection.

Target plots

Another, more graphical method for ascertaining the sustainability of an artifact was developed by Graedel, Allenby, and Comrie (1995). These AT&T engineers proposed a matrix for assessing the sustainability of a product, scoring one to four points in five life cycle stages, from *premanufacture* through *refurbishment-recycling-disposal,* cross-referenced with five environmental concerns:

- Materials choice
- Energy use
- Solid residues
- Liquid residues
- Gaseous residues

Thus the matrix generated can be charted on a radial target plot (Fig. 10.14). The higher the score in any category, the closer to the center of the plot, and this gives the user an immediate graphical representation of a product's degree of sustainability.

This method is obviously a great simplification of LCA, as the title of their paper promises. A scale of 1 to 4 is a very coarse measure of performance, and these assessment values are subjective, albeit scored by an expert. The 25 categories are also quite general, and all are equally weighted. The authors of the paper were considering product design, and used a comparison of 1950s to 1990s automobiles as an example. Nevertheless, the methodology is one that professionals, who, although they may not be LCA experts, can usefully employ as methods of examination within their expertise. By extension,

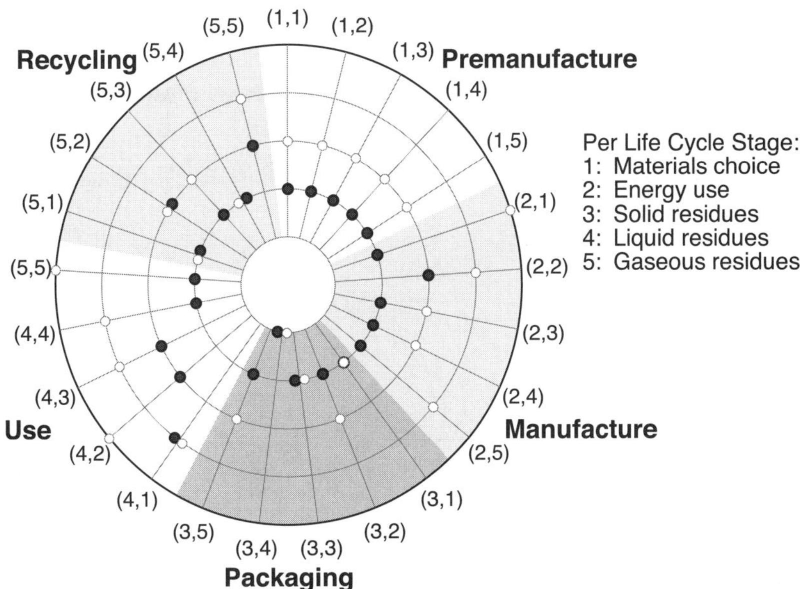

FIGURE 10.14 Original target plots put forth by Graedel, Allenby, and Comrie (1995) comparing automobiles of the 1950s with those of the 1990s. Of particular interest to architects and designers are the subjective yet expert assessment methodology and the graphical nature of the assessment matrix. Image by the author redrawn from the original.

Adapted with permission from Graedel et al. (1995).

the process may be applied to any human artifact, including infrastructure.

There is no "abridged life cycle assessment target plot tool" in any BIM application, although developing one might result in interesting design assessments. BIM can, however, support a target plot project assessment through material takeoffs of relevant building components. Examples of the five categories of the original paper are reframed in terms of buildings below:

- *Premanufacture.* What percentage of building raw material is sustainably sourced (by volume, mass, or cost)?
- *Building product manufacture.* Is the amount of energy used in building material manufacturing high? Do building material manufacturing processes produce excessive gaseous pollution? Is the construction of the building itself labor-, energy-, or material-intensive? Is there a significant solid waste stream during construction?
- *Building material packaging and transport.* Are building materials locally or regionally sourced?
- *Building occupation.* What is the offsite energy usage of the building? Does it consume a great deal of electricity, natural gas, or heating oil? How much water does it use?
- *Refurbishment-recycling-disposal.* Is the building designed for a long life? Does the design easily lend itself to adaptive reuse? Is it designed to be deconstructed and its materials salvaged, or is it likely to be torn down and sent to the landfill?

An experienced designer can subjectively (and accurately) score many of the above questions (Fig. 10.15). Portions of the rubric, however, will be more easily scored by the professional after

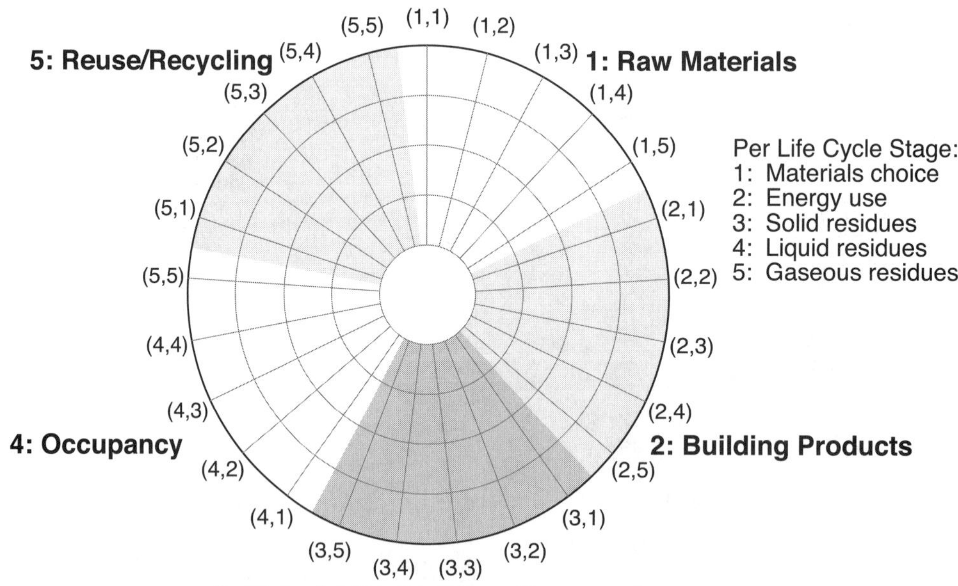

FIGURE 10.15 An example of a target plot repurposed (after Graedel et al. 1995) for the assessment of architectural sustainability. Expert evaluation of a project is carried out in five life cycle stages and in five categories. Scoring in each category can be aided by quantitative reports evaluated by the architect or designer.

consideration of the reports and schedules producible with BIM:

- Materials takeoffs
- Daylighting reports (Chapter 5)
- Passive heating and cooling calculations (Chapters 6 and 7)
- On-site energy production (Chapter 8)
- Water capture and use (Chapter 9)

Customizing the matrix

Neither the wilderness-based checklist nor target plots are widely recognized green-rating schemas; they are presented here to suggest innovative ways in which BIM may support assessments of a project's sustainability. As informal, internal design tools, therefore, they may be freely modified to better represent to the designer's professional experience. The goal is always to encourage sustainable design, and the tool should reflect that objective.

As case in point, for a design practice operating in a heavily urbanized environment, the architect may have little or no influence on site issues. Hence, those elements of the wilderness checklist may have a reduced weighting or be set aside altogether. For another practitioner, concerns of construction waste and building operations may far outweigh material premanufacturing, and the target plot may be adjusted to appropriately reflect the respective weighting of these environmental issues.

LEED material calculations

For some, green or sustainable design and the United States Green Building Council's Leadership in Energy Efficient Design (LEED) rating system are interchangeable. As of this writing, LEED has been adapted to meet a variety of project types:

- New Construction
- Existing Buildings: Operations & Maintenance
- Commercial Interiors
- Core & Shell
- Schools
- Retail
- Homes (Fig. 10.16)
- Neighborhood Development

There is mounting evidence, however, that LEED and similar green-rating systems are not without problems. Specifically, emphasis on energy efficiency has led to cases of poor indoor air quality (IAQ), in spite of LEED specifically addressing IAQ. Furthermore, LEED's initial emphasis (as the name implies) was on design. Now that many LEED buildings have been constructed and occupied, it has become clear that post-occupancy performance does not always match design intent. Building occupant behavior can trump system design, severely undermining actual building performance. And even energy modeling is not always a reliable predictor of actual performance. Finally, some LEED critics raise the issue of "point chasing," whereby designers game the system by seeking easier points in order to achieve a desired rating level, regardless of the appropriateness of the design measures taken for the particular project. These shortcomings notwithstanding, LEED has gone a long way to educate building stakeholders on the importance of energy efficiency and wise use of material resources.

BIM, with its ability to rapidly and accurately quantify materials, is an effective support for point-based green-rating systems. For example, in *LEED for New Construction and Major Renovations* (2010),[4] the following Materials and Resource (MR) credit categories can be quantified in BIM:

1.1 Building reuse: maintain existing walls, floors, and roof (various points are gained for 55, 75, or 95 percent existing construction maintained)

1.2 Building reuse: maintain existing interior non-structural elements

2 Construction waste management (LEED points earned for 50 or 75 percent recycled or salvaged)

---

[4] This publication is available at http://www.usgbc.org/DisplayPage.aspx?CMSPageID=2200.

FIGURE 10.16 The LEED Homes Platinum Margarido House was designed by Plumbob LLC and built by McDonald Construction & Development LLC. Among its many sustainable features are substantial use of locally sourced materials and sustainable building products, including thermally broken doors and windows; recycled concrete and glass counters; extensive use of concrete thermal mass floors and walls; a planted roof garden; permeable paving; and solar PV and thermal collection systems.

Photography by Mariko Reed.[5]

3 Materials reuse (points gained for 5 or 10 percent reused materials in project)

4 Recycled content (points earned for 10 or 20 percent of recycled building content)

5 Regional materials (LEED points gained for 10 or 20 percent of materials sourced regionally)

In *LEED for Homes* (2008), several MR credits are also directly applicable to BIM (many others are more applicable to the project specifications):

1.2 Detailed framing documents

1.3 Detailed cut list and lumber order

1.4 Framing efficiencies (including open web floor trusses, SIPs, framing member spacing greater than 16 inches, headers sized for loads, two-stud corners)

2.2 Environmentally preferable products (LEED points earned at 45 percent hard flooring, with more for 90 percent)

3.2 Construction waste reduction (using either pounds of waste per square foot or cubic yards of waste per 1,000 square feet)

The default (and detrimental) pattern in designing for building performance is that design decisions that affect performance (or, in this case, LEED points) are left until late in the design process. As a result, the LEED process may become more of an exercise in documenting decisions than in design. With BIM and facilitated material takeoffs, however, there are greater opportunities to evaluate the feasibility and impact of material choices earlier in the design. At that stage, decisions have a more meaningful influence on the sustainability of the project.

[5] Professional Web site available at www.marikoreed.com.

Case Study: Loblolly House, Taylor's Island, Maryland

By KieranTimberlake
Design firm: KieranTimberlake
Client: Withheld

Located on a barrier island off the coast of Maryland in the United States, Loblolly House was designed by architecture firm KieranTimberlake and was completed in 2006. The firm sought to fuse the natural elements of the site to the building's architectural form. As such, timber foundations minimize the house's footprint and provide savannah-like views of the trees and the bay, and the staggered boards of the east façade evoke the solids and voids of the forest.

This project introduced a new, more efficient method of building through the use of BIM and its integrated component assemblies, which reduced on-site construction time to less than six weeks. The building information model made simultaneous off-site fabrication of this project possible (Fig. 10.18). The geometric and dimensional certainty afforded by the model allowed parts of the building to be pre-assembled to the required tolerances. In addition, BIM enabled more efficient structural and mechanical coordination, greater management of

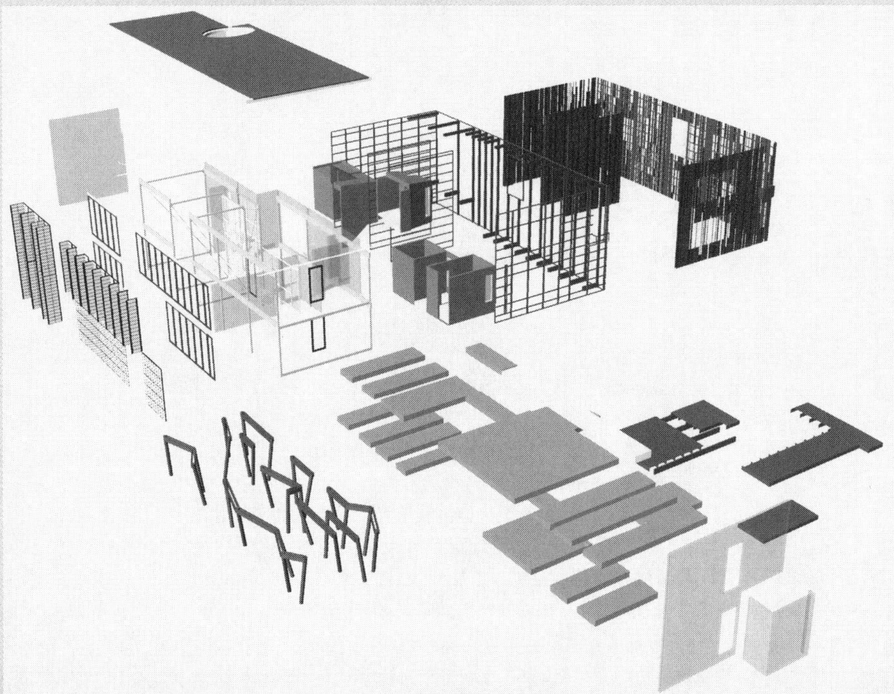

FIGURE 10.17 An exploded axonometric view of Loblolly House's major components.

Image courtesy of KieranTimberlake.

(Continued)

FIGURE 10.18 A component of Loblolly House was fabricated off-site and under controlled conditions. Thanks to the coordinated database of virtual building components, all details, schedules, part lists, and drawings were solely derived from the BIM model.

Image courtesy of KieranTimberlake.

materials and schedules for procurement, a clearer approach to assembly sequencing, and a way to control fabrication. BIM was the sole source of information from which all details, schedules, part lists, and fabrication drawings were derived.

The construction methodology confronted not only the question of how architecture should be assembled, but also the obligation to take responsibility for its disassembly. The essential elements—a scaffold, blocks, cartridges, and service spines—were detailed for rapid assembly, disassembly, and redeployment. The scaffold, comprised of Bosch Rexroth aluminum framing, was bolted together as opposed to being welded, which created a structural system for the house that could be disassembled without affecting the capacity of beam and column components to be reconnected. The bolted scaffold served as a frame into which the off-site fabricated kitchen, bathroom and mechanical blocks, and floor and wall cartridges were inserted without the use of permanent fasteners or wet connections (Fig. 10.19). Upon disassembly, cartridges and blocks were removed as whole units and column/beam scaffold sections were unbolted. Three service spines, integrated exclusively in floor cartridges, supplied energy, water, and data, with built-in connectors that could be readily accessed and unplugged (Fig. 10.20). The lack of adhesives and wet connections greatly improved the ease of redeployment while reducing the time required for extraction.

FIGURE 10.19 A component of Loblolly House being craned into place.
Image courtesy of KieranTimberlake.

Loblolly House preserves embodied energy with the easy disassembly and reassembly of its essential elements. The disassembly and redeployment potential is evident in the detailing and quality craftsmanship of the energy intensive aluminum scaffold, kitchen, bath and mechanical blocks, ceiling/wall cartridges, and service spines. This ensures a design-for-disassembly strategy where the components with the highest embodied energy can be disassembled and redeployed with a minimal loss of energy. The design also allows for alternative end-of-life material streams, including design-for-reuse, and as a last resort design-for-recycling. If recycled, there are ready and efficient markets for all materials used. The site's ecology is also addressed with the pile foundation which leaves little evidence that the house ever existed after it is disassembled and the piles are removed.

(Continued)

FIGURE 10.20 All energy, water, and data are supplied by three floor-cartridge integrated service spines with built-in connectors that can be readily accessed and unplugged.

Image courtesy of KieranTimberlake.

Chapter 11

Collaboration

In previous chapters, we've looked at sustainably designed projects realized through largely technological internal BIM operations. In this chapter, we will expand the sphere of BIM, enlarging it outside the space of a particular building model operating within a given application platform (Fig. 11.1). That is, we'll look at the potential impact BIM has on the design process as a whole, rather than simply at what happens while the user is at the computer. In some ways, this represents some of the most exciting aspects of BIM: the evolution of collaborative design (Fig. 11.2).

In drafted design documents, all drawing coordination is manual. The designer must interpret drawn elements and what they represent. Objects—whether they are traces of plastic lead on Mylar, or CAD arcs and lines—have no inherent meaning other than that inferred by the user. In BIM, objects carry meaning, or at least information. Coupled with a pervasive 3D model, this opens the possibility of this information being shared with members of the project team (Fig. 11.3):

- Owner
- Joint venture partners if any
- Engineers, consultants, and subconsultants
- General Contractor, subcontractors, and suppliers

This chapter discusses the role of collaboration in the context of BIM for envelope-dominated projects. We will look at mechanisms for effectively sharing BIM models, derived views, and general project information while allowing various stakeholders to exercise their respective expertise and design freedom. These mechanisms overlap and there are scores of common and obscure file formats; we'll touch on those that are most relevant to architectural practice in designing skin-load dominated buildings. File formats considered are organized according to their primary use: as *imported* background information, *exported* for consultant use, or serving as the medium of a closer back-and-forth *collaboration*. Of course, these are somewhat artificial distinctions, and some file formats (for example, DWG/DXF) may serve all three functions.

Some of the file formats that underpin collaboration inherently have sustainability ramifications, while others are important to any practice that incorporates BIM, whether it has a sustainable design emphasis or not. Since cooperation between and outside design disciplines is critical to designing wiser, more sustainable buildings, the discussion won't be limited to "green" formats like gbXML alone (Fig. 11.4).

Imported backgrounds

In a project team, other professionals will produce preliminary work to which the architect must refer, and over the life of the design process consultants and collaborators will contribute drawings and data. If the architect is fortunate enough to work with others who use the same BIM platform, then importing (and exporting) files for collaboration is straightforward and requires little discussion here—most

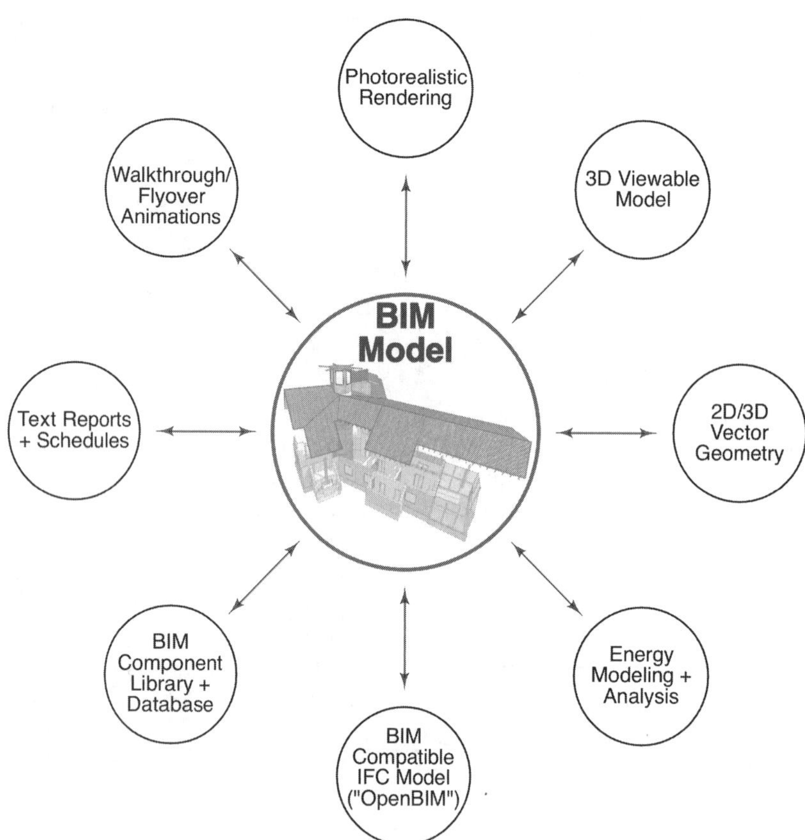

FIGURE 11.1 BIM is the lynch pin connecting a variety of various file formats and their users. Interoperability is a significant consideration, even in small practices and smaller-scaled projects.

Drawing by the author from a diagram by Justin Firuz Dowhower, LEED AP.

software manuals adequately address this topic (Fig. 11.5). However, in most instances that is not the case, and the BIM practitioner, like the CAD user, must learn to navigate and deal with an alphabet soup of software file extensions.

Survey data

2D topographic survey files (commonly in DWG or more archaically in DXF formats) may be imported into BIM to create terrain mesh models. An alternative is to construct a terrain mesh directly from individual points contained in a survey file containing tabular data that represents individual points in space (text files with tab- or comma-delimited coordinates) using ArchiCAD or Vectorworks (Revit Civil3D has this capability as well). For further discussion, see Chapter 3.

Importing 3D model components

3D file formats may be similar whether the architect is exporting from the BIM model or importing to it, but the purposes are often quite different. A common reason for importing 3D models is incorporating building or entourage components that may not be available among the BIM application's built-in object libraries, and when the user is either not inclined or too busy to model one "from scratch." This is particularly true of entourage objects (trees, posed people, vehicles), hardscape elements,

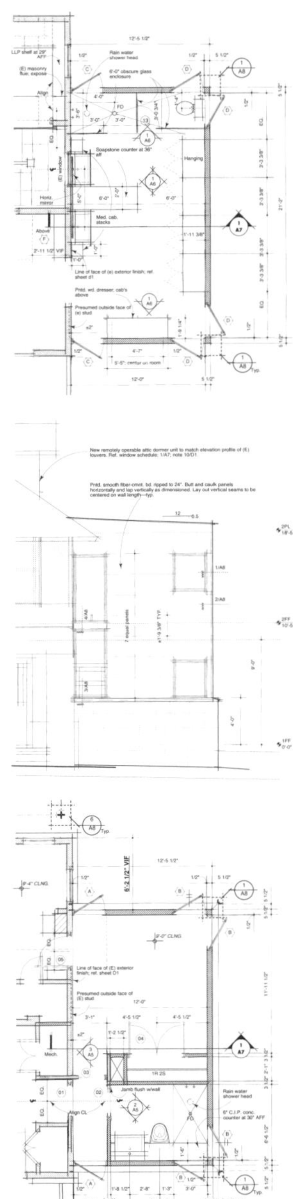

FIGURE 11.2 In manual and CAD drafting coordination between drawings of the same discipline has is been a manual process. Plans, sections, and elevations are visually inspected from agreement, and require interpretation by the draftsperson. BIM not only automates that internal coordination (that is, coordination within a single model), but also facilitates coordination across disciplines. To do so, however, requires technological tools: interoperable file formats. Just as critical are social structures, such as agreements and protocols to share data.

appliances, fixtures, and devices. Fortunately, Google's acquisition of SketchUp and distribution of the consumer version as a free application has created a groundswell of free SketchUp objects in their 3D Warehouse (Fig. 11.6). Unfortunately, the quality of these models is very uneven, and the potential user might spend a good deal of time sifting through dross to find a good model.

SketchUp Pro can export models as 3DS files, a popular format native to Autodesk 3ds Max, a high-end 3D modeler. Most BIM applications can import 3DS and even SketchUp files directly. In both cases, there may be some loss of applied textures or colors, so materiality may not be perfect. Importing at the right scale may also be problematic (although proportions should be preserved), so the user should verify the dimensions of model elements once they are imported and rescale appropriately.

Exporting files

Imported background files serve to provide the designer with accurate graphical and numeric data influencing design parameters. Exported files, on the other hand, tend to fall into one of two types:

- for presentation, whether to clients, community stakeholders, or regulatory approval
- to support design team collaborators with the architectural information they require for their work, which is often analytical in nature

The latter is of obviously greater significance to sustainable design practices, but renderings are critical to a practice too.

Engineering files

Most civil, structural, and MEP engineers even now still use conventionally drafted CAD files, almost universally prepared with AutoCAD. As with some of their architect colleagues, small engineering firms tend to work almost exclusively in 2D, and have not yet adopted BIM to the extent that larger firms have. Indeed, anecdotally it seems that among small firms engineers may lag behind architects in BIM adoption.

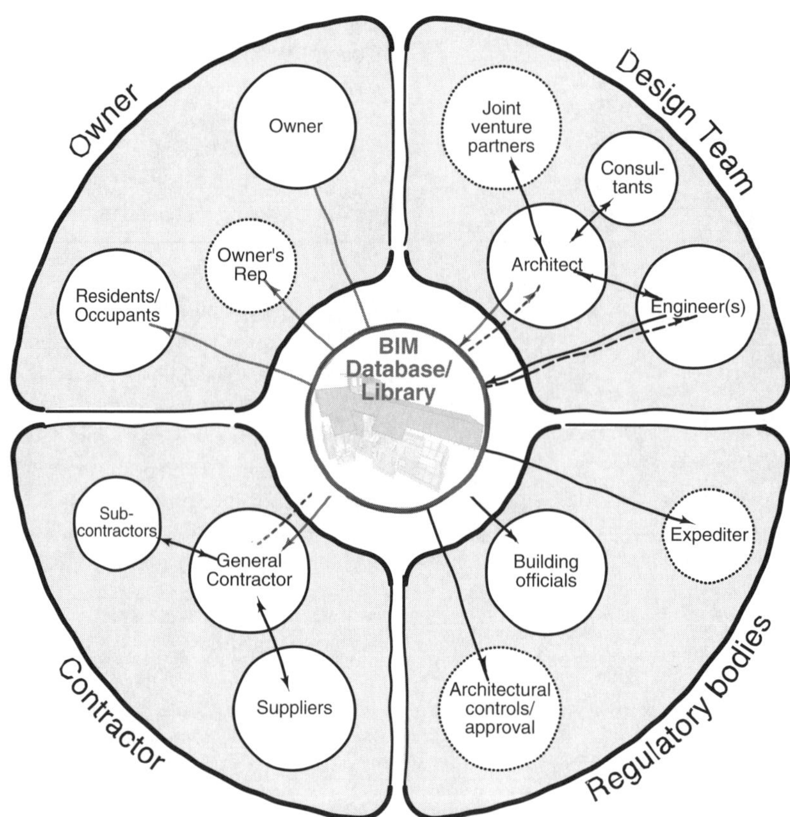

FIGURE 11.3 BIM has been described as being as much about the social structures enabling collaborative design and the sharing of information as the technology. This diagram of stakeholders includes some that may not be present in every project, but even in small projects there are opportunities for greater collaboration and communication. Arrows represent direction of model information flow, with dashed arrows representing weaker or less frequent flows.

All architectural BIM applications can import DWGs, but they remain 2D drawings only (Fig. 11.7). In reconciling the BIM and 2D worlds, the coordinating architect has a few options:

- Extract 2D views of the BIM model, "flattening" it, and compare these to provided 2D engineering drawings. This is essentially the conventional coordination workflow; the one, not inconsiderable, advantage over a pure 2D workflow is that the architectural portion of the BIM model is internally coordinated.
- In some cases, it may be possible to quickly model the engineering design in the BIM on the basis of provided 2D geometry, in essence "tracing" it then extruding it. "Push-pull" tools in applications like SketchUp and Vectorworks may make this graphically simpler and faster. Nevertheless, this is more work for the architect (who may not receive compensation accordingly). But with foresight and clear arguments demonstrating the value of 3D modeling over 2D coordination, the designer may be able to negotiate

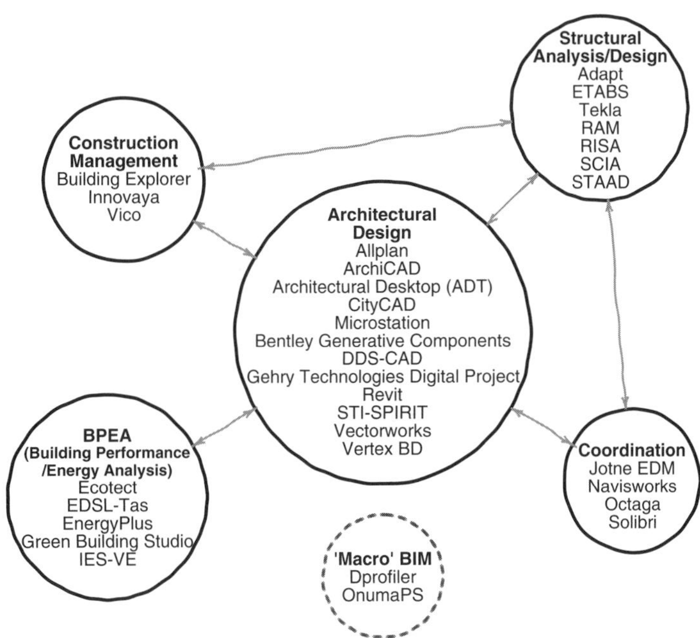

FIGURE 11.4 To bridge across disciplines, BIM must have a lingua franca, a file format by which different disciplines may share project geometry and data. A proprietary format would require that all disciplines use the same BIM software, which is problematic to say the least. An open, non-proprietary format like IFC allows everyone on the design team to exchange data.

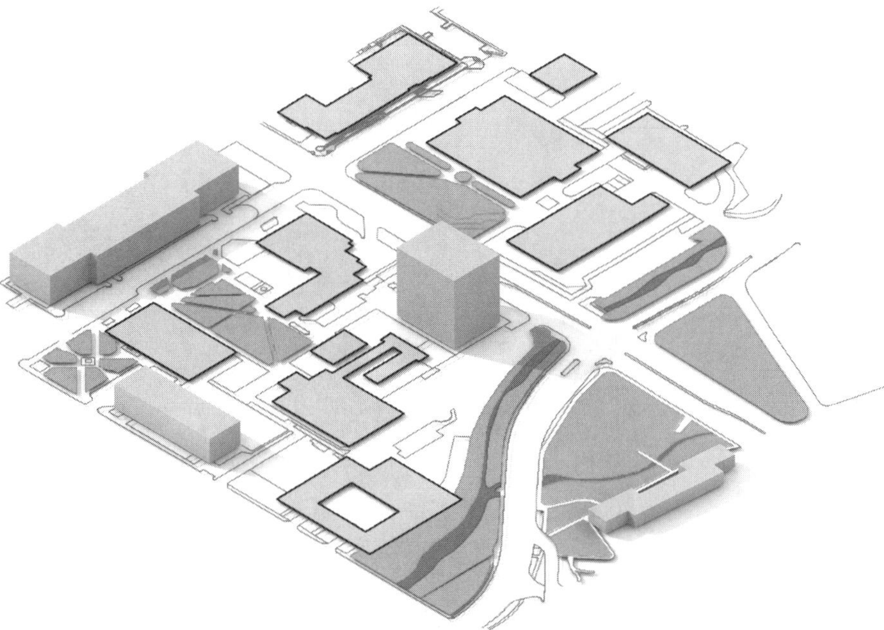

FIGURE 11.5 This campus site model in progress is based on a DWG file imported into a BIM application (in this image, on the ground plane). Building footprint polygons are pulled upward to form masses. Outlined ones have yet to be extruded.

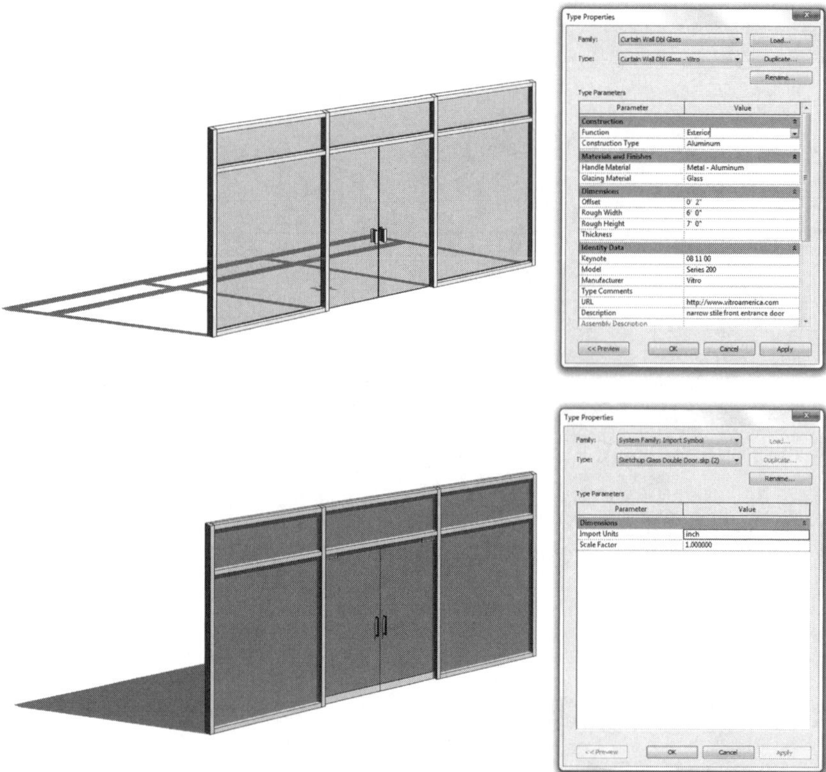

FIGURE 11.6 A native Revit door (above) has 3D geometry and data. A SketchUp model imported into Revit (below) may have the requisite geometry, but it lacks the data associated with doors. It cannot, for example, be automatically listed in a door schedule.

Image courtesy of Justin Firuz Dowhower, LEED AP.

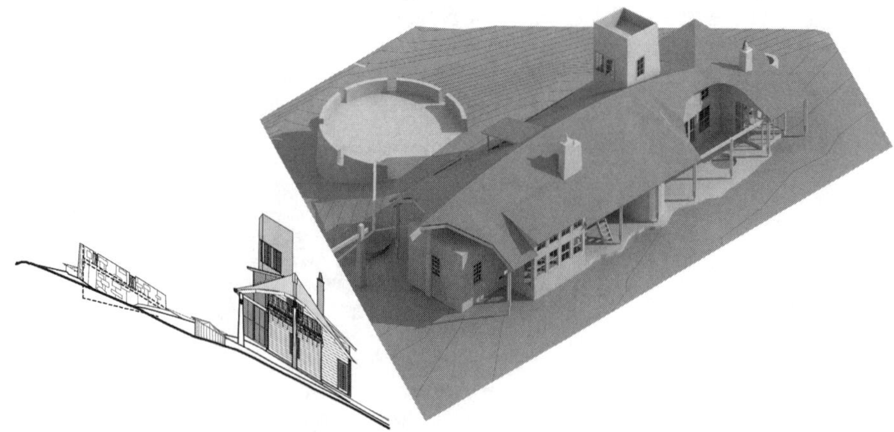

FIGURE 11.7 The BIM model seen here in a rendered isometric may be exported as DWG elevation, for example, but the result is either a 3D DWG mesh, or a "flattened" 2D DWG (depending on the export procedure), such as the view lower left.

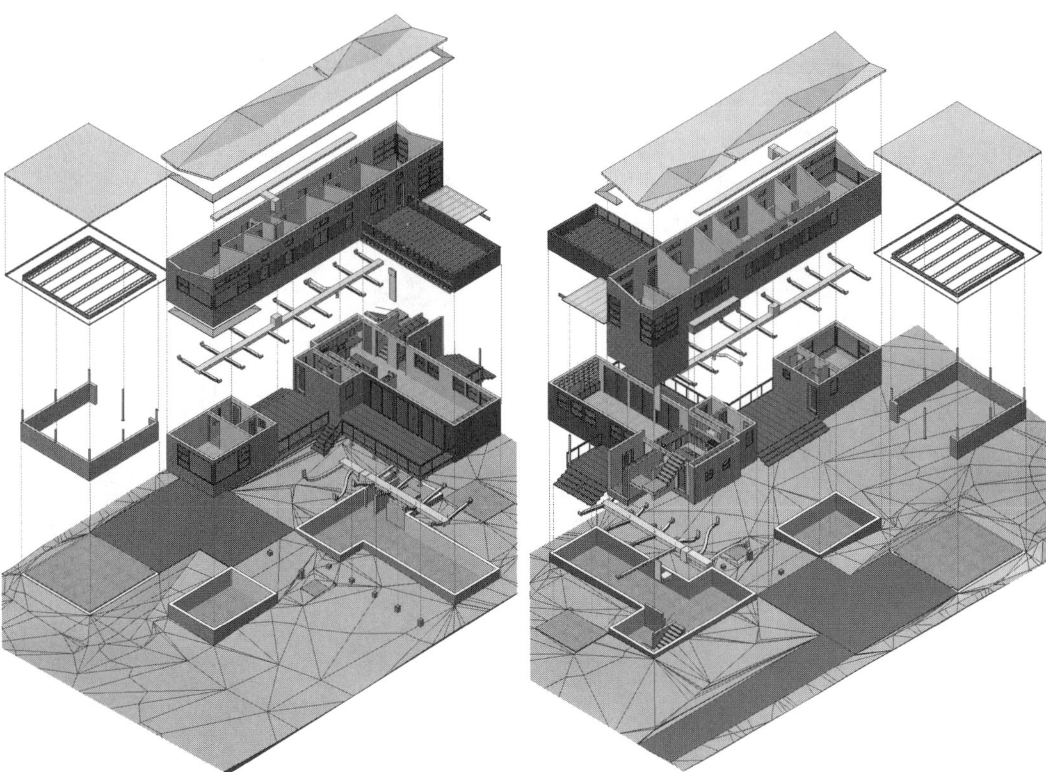

FIGURE 11.8 Two exploded views of a BIM model include structural as well as mechanical components. In some cases a single BIM model may contain all project modeling, or there may be multiple BIM models coordinated across disciplines. In both cases, BIM is an excellent coordination environment.

Image ©2011 Nemetschek Vectorworks, Inc.

additional services to cover such 3D conversion costs. Educating the client on the value of 3D coordination and clash detection is key. For example, in a well-known BIM pilot project, the GSA compared conventional coordination of construction documents (CDs) with BIM clash detection for the Jackson, Mississippi Federal Courthouse. The two independent teams reviewing the Jackson project got very different results: the BIM team found over a thousand times more constructability issues and conflicts than the 2D team. It is unclear, however, whether the study's methodology accounted for over-inflation of automated clash counts due to false-positive repetitions.

- Educate or encourage the engineer to model the components relevant to the latter's discipline in a 3D format, even if it is not editable once imported into the architect's BIM model. By far the best solution in theory, this may be the most difficult to implement in practice. It is very difficult to influence another firm to adopt a particular software platform, never mind an entirely new way of working.

Among engineering firms in the construction industry, mechanical engineers and contractors on large-scale projects are the likeliest to adopt BIM, primarily for collision detection. Structural engineers, too, find obvious and tangible benefit to BIM, thanks to the 3D structural analysis tools available through this workflow.

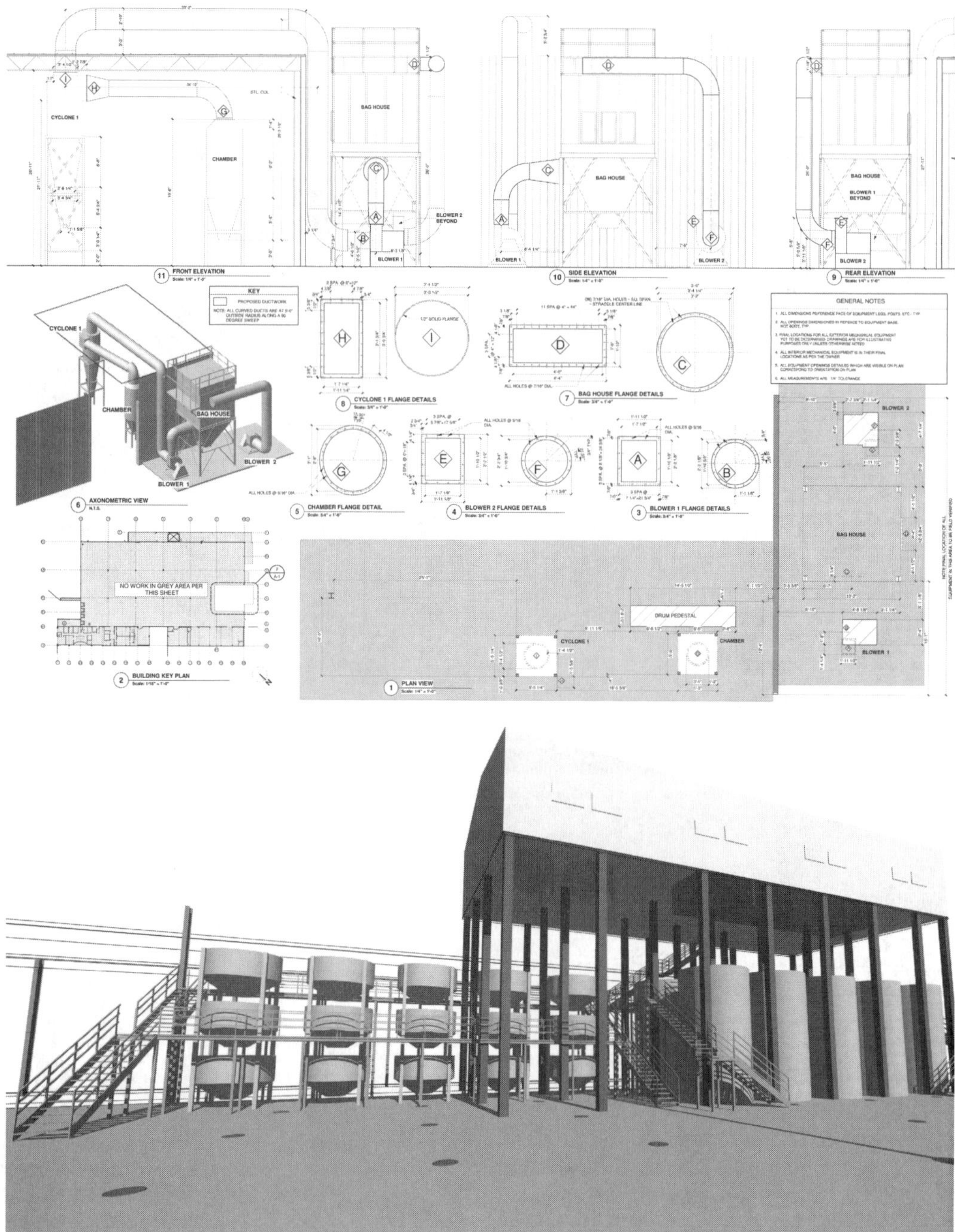

FIGURE 11.9 The Parkview El Milagro project expresses mechanical engineering didactically and tectonically. For this project, a coordinated architectural and engineering model was key to visualizing and avoiding clashes, as well as ensuring that components were dimensionally compatible.

Image courtesy of Frank Gomillion, GKZ, Inc.

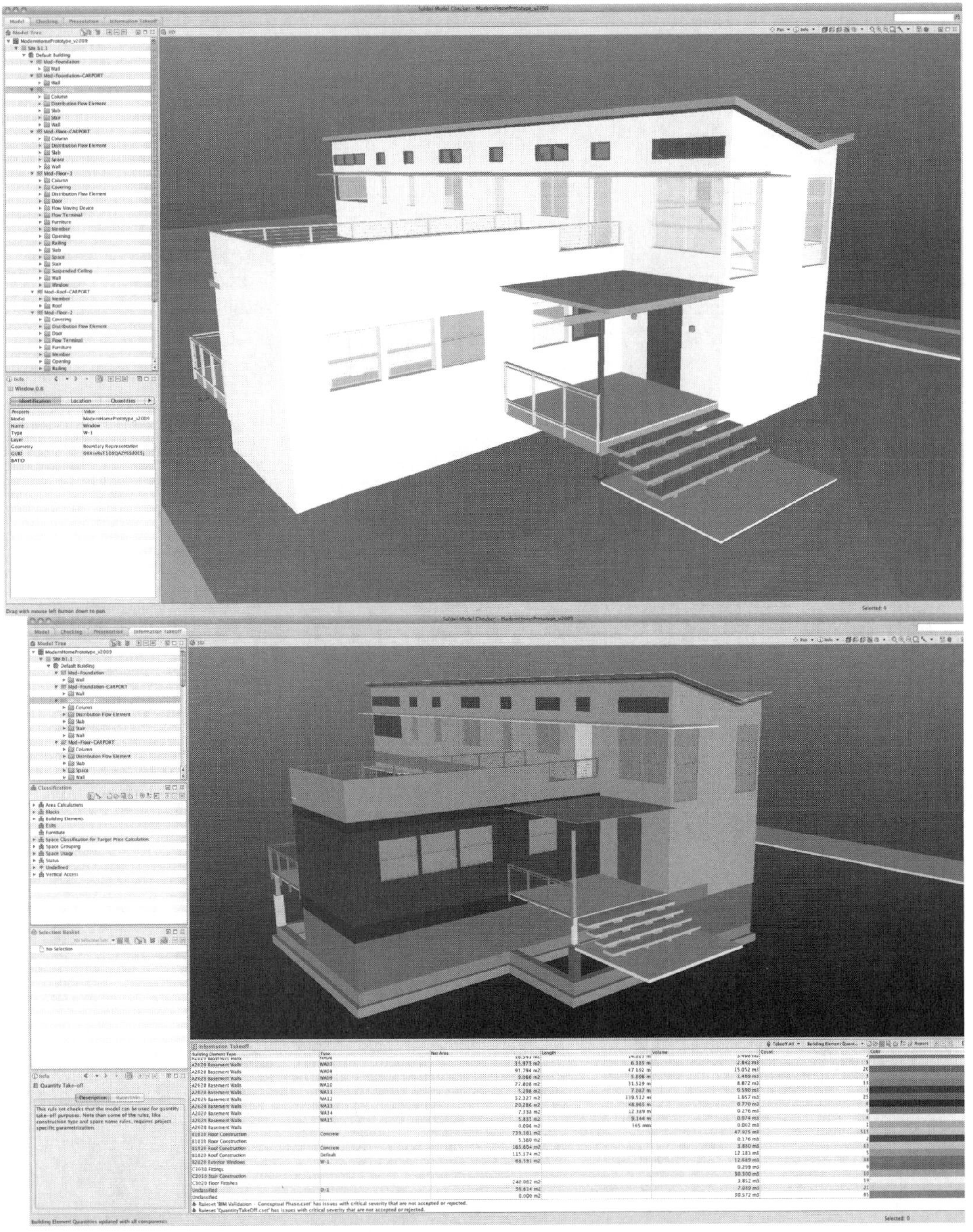

FIGURE 11.10 A BIM model (Vectorworks's Modern Home Prototype) exported as IFC and validated using Solibri Model Checker.

Image ©2011 Nemetschek Vectorworks, Inc.

For energy modeling, IFC is slowly being adopted. The older DOE-2 format is used in well-established and powerful energy simulators (eQuest, Energy-10, Energy Plus); more recent energy modeling software as well as architect-oriented early energy analysis tools like Ecotect and Green Building Studio use gbXML. At the time of this writing, two full-featured energy modelers that can work with IFC are RIUSKA by Granlun and Equa's IDA Indoor Climate and Energy (ICE; Fig. 11.11), both Scandinavian products available in the United States and in English.

PDF

PDF files have become the de facto common medium for communicating 2D drawings:

- between design team members who do not share a common software platform
- in cases where the issuer prefers to distribute uneditable reference drawings
- as a reference companion accompanying other files

When transmitting electronic files such as DWGs to consultants, particularly when exporting to other file formats, it had long been a practice to accompany the drawings with a print set. This served both to verify the completeness of the exported file, and convey the graphic intent of the source. Today, PDF has replaced paper in many practices, and is an essential component of team collaboration (Fig. 11.12).

Some building departments will allow PDFs to be submitted for permitting, and this format may be the most accessible to most small project owners. Sophisticated users of PDFs know that these files may be annotated ("redlined") with simple

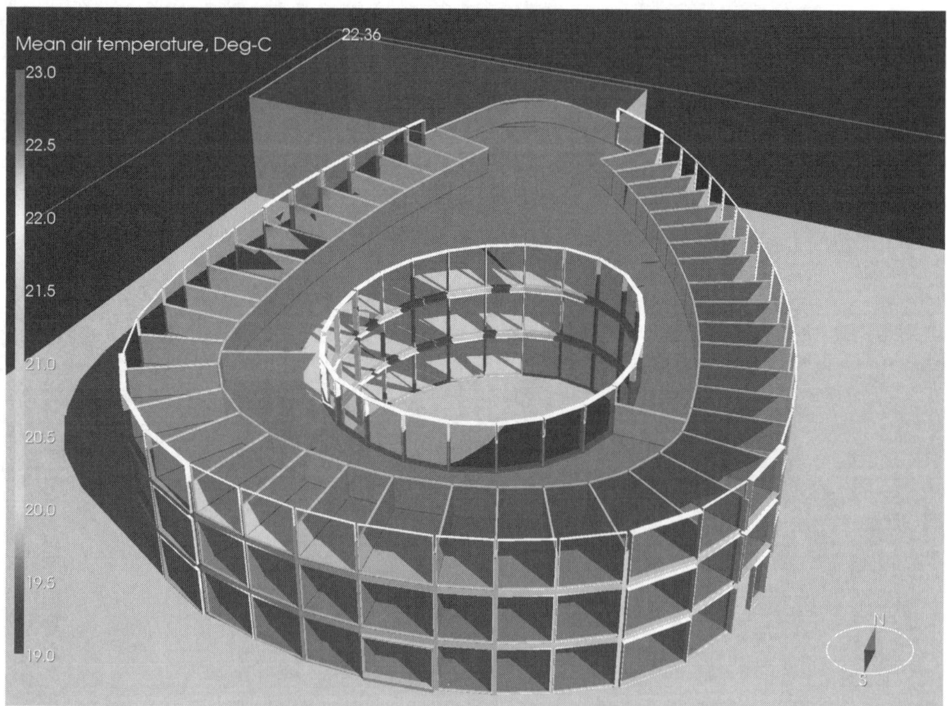

FIGURE 11.11 Equa's IDA ICE is an energy modeler that is able to import IFC data from any IFC-compliant BIM application. This hospital project in Finland was modeled in BIM and then exported via IFC to ICE for further analysis.

©EQUA Simulation AB.

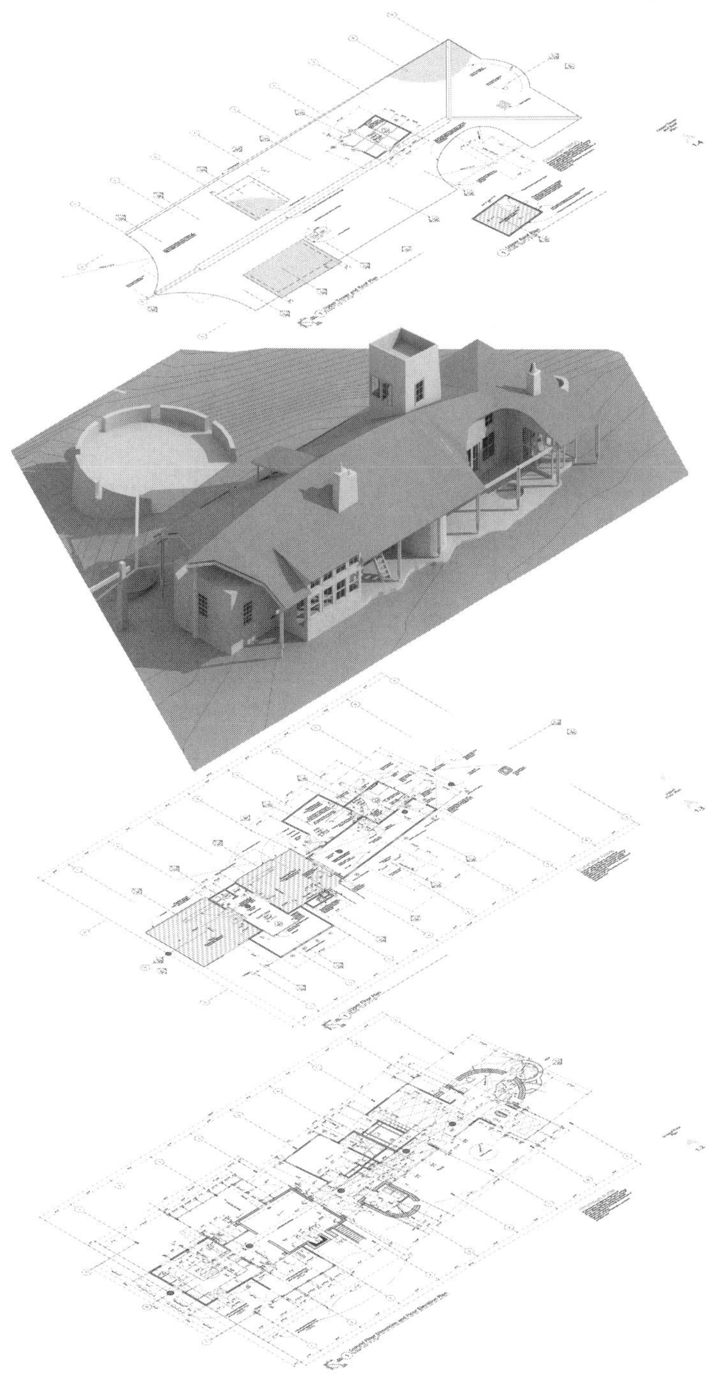

FIGURE 11.12 A BIM model's views may be exported as 2D PDF files (top and lower two), the digital equivalent to printing.

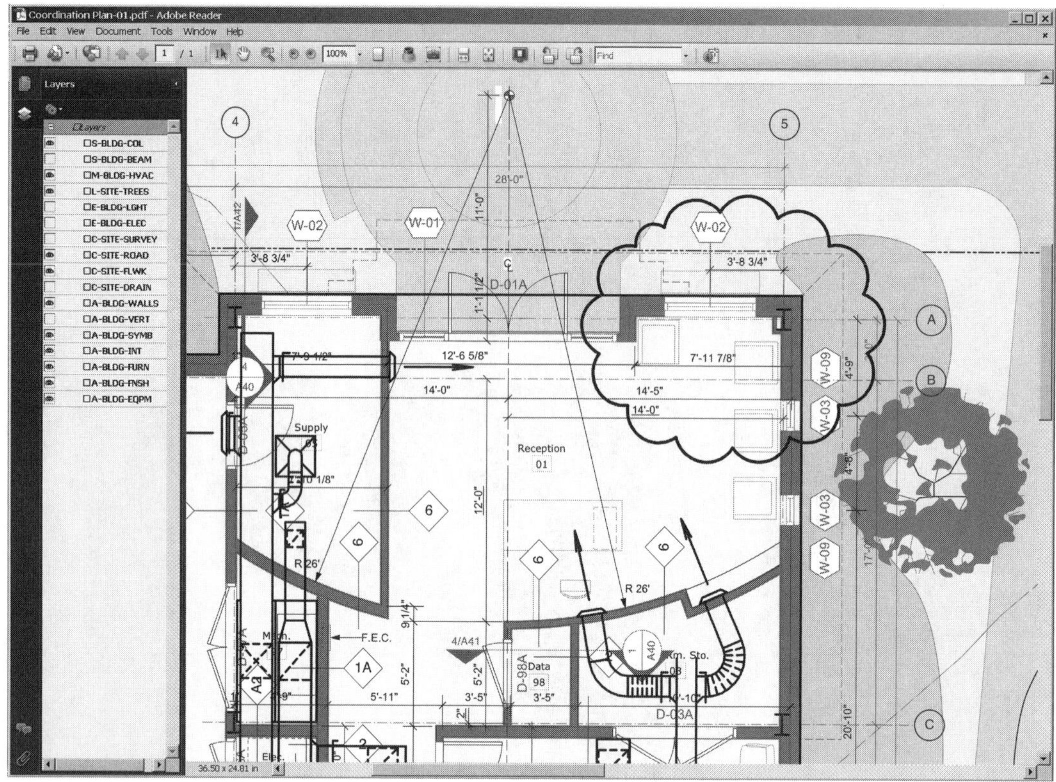

FIGURE 11.13 BIM (or CAD) projects when exported to PDF and viewed in Adobe Acrobat Reader have their layer structure preserved. The viewer may selectively control individual layers.

Image courtesy of Mischa Farrell Architect.

markup tools like text, lines, ovals and rectangles, highlighting, and comment fields. Some authoring applications export PDFs with layer structure and names preserved, which may be useful information for a recipient examining the file using Adobe's free Acrobat PDF viewer (Fig. 11.13; this feature is not supported by the Mac OS Preview viewer application).

PDFs are also "snappable" when imported into in some applications; that is, geometry in the target application can be constrained to the PDF geometry. This is, of course, only true if the PDF was first generated in a vector-based application (a CAD program or Adobe Illustrator, for example). Even then, dimensions may not be exact, so these should be used for dimensionally critical purposes with extreme caution (Fig. 11.14). While this is primarily an "importing" issue, the architect should also consider the uses to which out-going PDF files are put.

There is a solution for those designers who prefer a more conservative approach to data sharing and are concerned about the propagation of PDFs that can be turned back into CAD files. Image software like Photoshop, GIMP, IrfanView or PDF-Xchange Viewer for Windows, Acrobat Pro, or Mac OS X's built-in Preview can open PDFs and save them to a raster format (such as JPG). Some Web sites offer this service as well. Users can then generate accurate PDFs from BIM, saving them "down" to raster files that cannot be snapped to, ungrouped, or turned into editable CAD drawings.

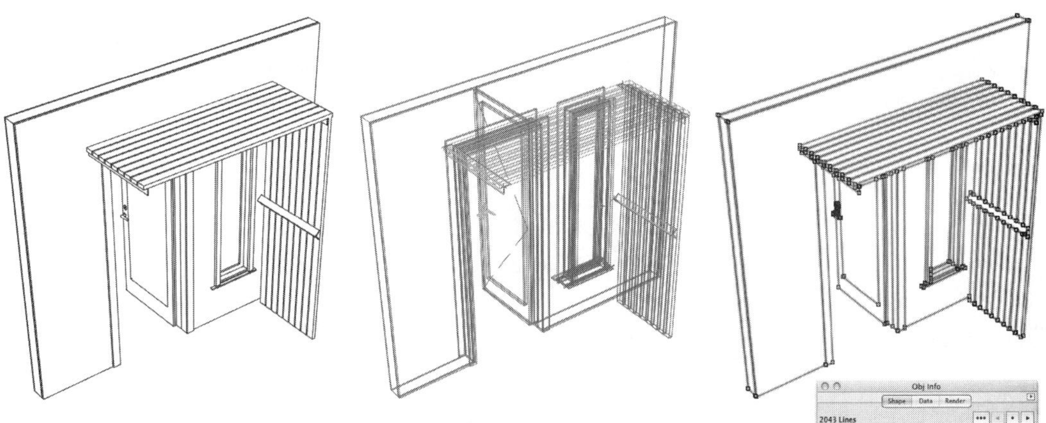

FIGURE 11.14 The resulting geometry from a PDF file once imported and "exploded" in BIM (or CAD) is only a static view, and may be dimensionally slightly inaccurate. The door and window at left are 3D BIM objects in a perspective hidden-line view, as can be seen from the wireframe view at center. The same objects exported to PDF, then re-imported and "exploded" are merely 2D lines, as can be seen from the resulting drawing at right.

3D PDF and 3D viewers

A few years ago, Adobe among others collaborated to develop a universal 3D format, U3D. Acrobat Reader can read U3D files, as well as PDFs with embedded U3D components. These 3D PDFs look like typical PDFs, except that they have embedded within them images of 3D models (Fig. 11.15). The models are drivable, such that the user may rotate and in some cases activate exploded views by dragging the mouse. Most BIM software does not currently export directly to 3D PDF. However, there exists 3D PDF authoring software to which BIM models may be exported as an intermediate step. For example, some third-party SketchUp plug-ins (e.g., RPS 3D Exporter, SimLab 3D PDF Exporter, 3DPaintBrush) export SketchUp models to 3D PDF. Given the popularity of SketchUp, most BIM software exports files to formats SketchUp can read. 3DS is an example of a "bridge" file format exported from BIM and imported to SketchUp.

Apple's QuickTime VR (QTVR) technology (accessible to both Mac and Windows users) also allows exporting the 3D model as either an object (rotated and zoomed by the user) or a panorama (like an interior or site that the user can pan around to get a 360° view; Fig. 11.16). A distinct advantage of QTVR is that file sizes are small and viewable by most modern web browsers. Apple itself has moved away from QTVR in favor of HTML5, and as a result Graphisoft has dropped support for exporting QTVR files from later versions of ArchiCAD, encouraging their users to rely on their proprietary Virtual Building Explorer (VBE) instead. As of this writing, Vectorworks still supports QTVR object and panorama creation. Revit never supported QTVR, but exports to Autodesk's proprietary DWF format, which, like VBE, is not commonly browser supported without additional plugins.

DOE-2

The Department of Energy's energy simulation engine, DOE-2, supports simple 3D geometry as the necessary basis for energy modeling. Advanced energy modelers like eQuest that are DOE-2 based are also able to import DWGs, but only 2D information—3D DWG information is lost. A DWG plan provided to an energy modeling consultant can form the basis of a DOE-2 model, but all the 3D information of the energy model must be reconstructed. Furthermore, most energy simulation tools have very rudimentary physical modeling tools, and some are far from user-friendly. In some cases, modeling in these applications requires that the *xyz* coordinates of each vertex of each plane of the model be

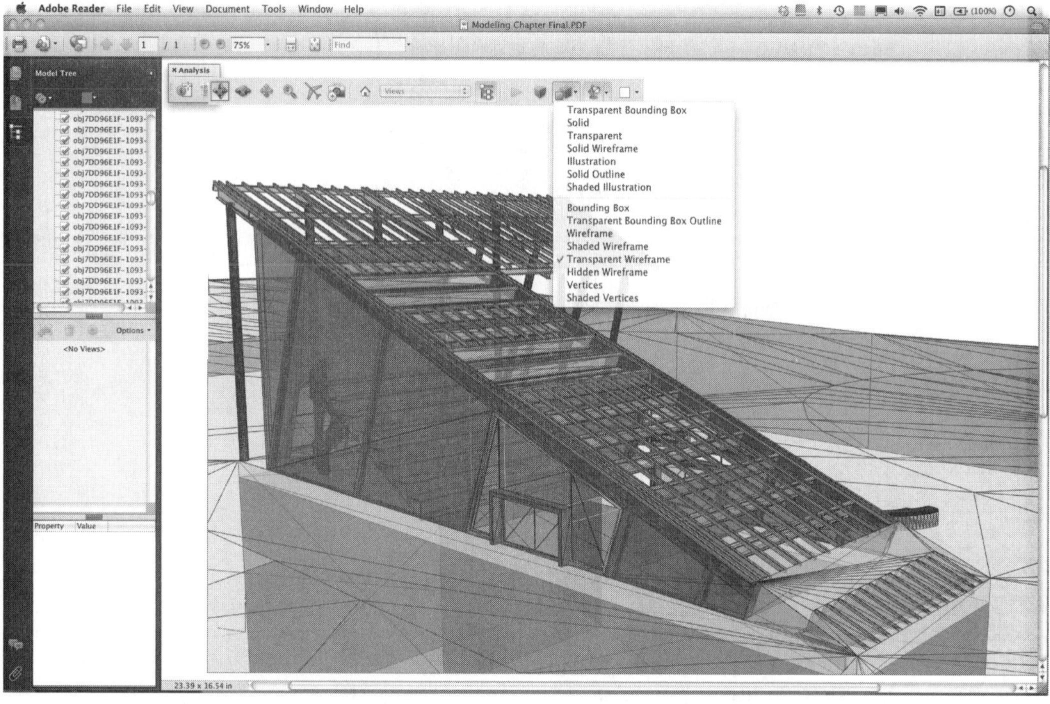

FIGURE 11.15 An ArchiCAD project exported to 3D PDF and opened in Acrobat Reader. The user can pan, zoom, rotate, and translate the model, as well as highlight certain building components or layers from the Model Tree at left, and select from a variety of rendering and lighting modes, all from a free viewer.

Model from the ArchiCAD Training Guide, courtesy of Graphisoft.[1]

FIGURE 11.16 A QuickTime VR interior scene is simply a distorted panorama perspective viewed a portion at a time. A portion of the viewed scene is at left, and the unfurled panorama is at right. As a result, files sizes are small, and the user enjoys some interactive control.

manually input—quite a tedious process for even the simplest geometry. However, energy modelers do not require detailed 3D geometry to be effective; indeed, a simplified model is preferable, as additional surfaces only increase calculation times, with little or no increased accuracy. The energy simulation model may therefore represent walls as planes of no thickness; windows may be modeled as simple rectangles; and so forth. Thermal properties like R-values and solar heat gain coefficient (SHGC) are assigned properties of the geometry and not related to material thickness, so wall thicknesses for example are irrelevant. Any building component that does not affect thermal performance—furnishings, handrails, non-thermally massive structural elements, and so forth—likewise can and should be excluded from the energy simulation (Fig. 11.17).

[1] Training guide available at http://www.graphisoft.com/education/training_guides/.

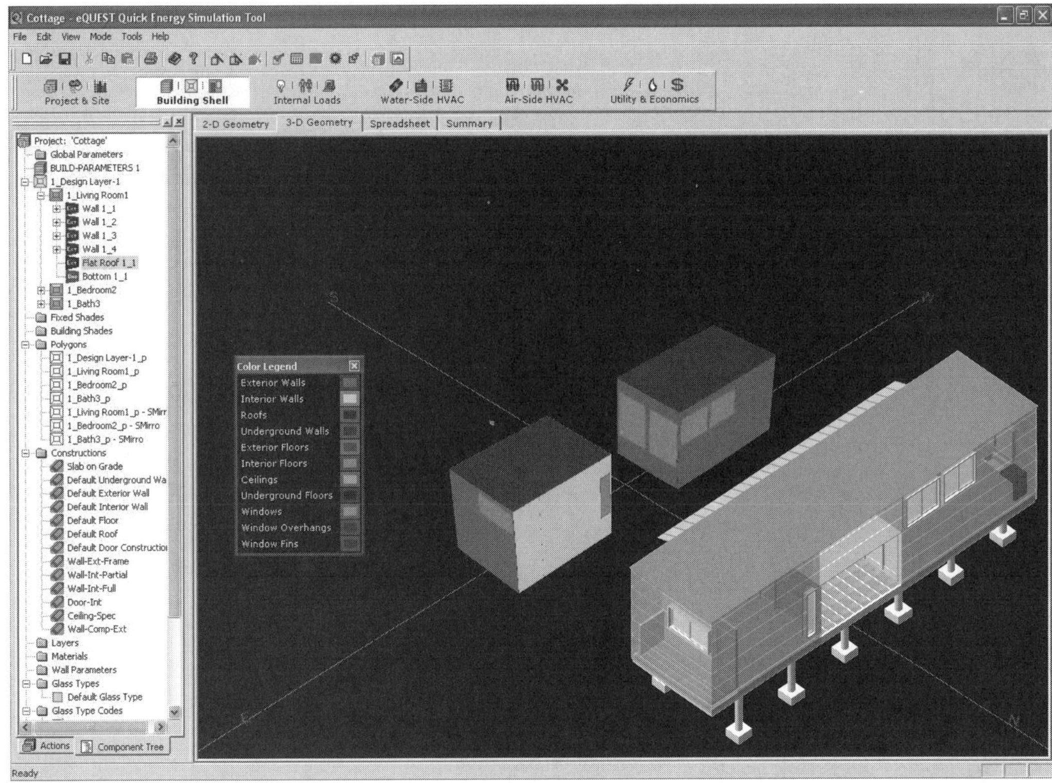

FIGURE 11.17 This simple structure (architectural rendering inset lower right) when exported for energy analysis in eQuest via the DOE-2 format, loses much of its geometry. Only that required for energy analysis is retained: spaces define walls as planes, openings are simple polygons, and the roof and floor are only exported (as planes) in conditioned spaces.

Vectorworks among BIM applications offers a DOE-2 export path. For others wanting detailed energy analysis (with EnergyPlus, eQuest, Energy10, or others), export to gbXML or IFC is ideal. Alternately it is possible to export to DWG (the latter requiring reconstruction of the model as noted above).

gbXML

Green Building eXtensible Markup Language (gbXML) is an open file format intended to encourage interoperability between architectural building modeling software and energy simulators. It is actively supported by BIM applications including Autodesk's Revit, Bentley, and Graphisoft's ArchiCAD (with EcoDesigner or third party extensions). Newer, architect-oriented energy modelers like DesignBuilder, Autodesk Green Building Studio online energy analysis, and Autodesk Ecotect support gbXML file importing, but older modelers like eQuest do not. Such legacy modelers (which tend to be used by engineers) require intermediate translation of the exported BIM model.

Tabular data

Rather than export geometrical data to energy modeling or performance analysis software like Ecotect, the designer may opt to export geometry-driven values from the BIM model and analyze this tabular (numerical) data directly. Number crunching in an external spreadsheet program like Excel, Numbers, Lotus Symphony, or Google Docs is a very effective technique, albeit one that requires a fair amount of setup and preparation. While generally non-graphical and therefore not obviously appealing to architects, spreadsheets can be very powerful parametric design tools when used to explore alternative building scenarios. Indeed, this process is at the heart of much of the approach of sections of this book, which discuss in-BIM analysis using schedules and worksheets at length.

The Passivhaus Institute[2] has assembled an impressive (and perhaps a little daunting) spreadsheet building analysis tool for use by architects and designers in preliminary quantitative design analysis. Their Passive House Planning Package (PHPP) tool calculates (among other things):

- individual assembly U-factors based on user data input and a built-in materials reference
- energy balances
- ventilation rates for comfort and passive cooling
- heat loads (climate data for locations outside of Germany must be provided by the user)

These are calculated based on window, wall, and floor areas and components. The user supplies these values and inputs them manually. However, simple area tabulation schedules or worksheets in the BIM model can greatly simplify the preparation of the building's geometrical data. To that end, Revit and ArchiCAD schedules can be exported in an Excel-compatible format, as can Vectorworks worksheets. A careful study of the PHPP tool (a free demo version is available) will suggest to the user how best to organize the BIM component tabulation schedules.

Models for rendering and visualization

Some practices prefer to export 3D-formatted files from the BIM model for rendering in a dedicated rendering application. There are certain advantages to this: dedicated rendering applications like Artlantis or the freeware Kerkythea, may have better lighting tools and textural controls, as well as environmental modeling (such as ambient light, fog, snow, and so on), and animation options. For photorealistic effects, these may be the best approach. Moreover, dedicated renderers like Piranesi, which deliberately avoid photo-realism in favor of rendering effects associated with hand sketching, offer rendering effects not otherwise possible in BIM without a great deal of post-processing of static images using Photoshop or the freeware GIMP, for example.

On the other hand, rendering within BIM applications themselves is steadily improving, to the point of allowing photorealistic rendering or various nonphotorealistic rendering (NPR) styles within the virtual building application itself. Once the model is exported from BIM, it inevitably loses its parametric and data-rich characteristics. Keeping the model in BIM is particularly of interest if rendering is considered as a *design* tool, rather than a *presentation* or *marketing* tool. The iterative loop from design changes to design impact (modeling to rendering) is potentially very quick, and this fact allows the designer to design more and evaluate more often. It may be tempting to think in terms of the rendering features available on a dedicated rendering program, but the larger issue is one of workflow. While post-processing—whether of a 3D model or a static 2D rendered view—may ultimately be the best way to achieve total rendering control, it must also be redone every time the design is updated or changes.

Of course, this need not be an either/or proposal; the architect may use internal BIM renderings for design evaluation and conceptual communication, and a dedicated rendering process (whether a 3D renderer or 2D post-processing of an exported image) for final or high-quality communication.

Project coordination

A critical function of the architect is that of design coordination, and this is true whether the project delivery method is traditional design-bid-build (DBB), full integrated project delivery (IPD), or something in between. In the role of coordinator, the architect is responsible for detecting conflicts between building systems, which themselves

[2] Professional Web site located at www.passiv.de.

may be the province of other disciplines, and communicating these conflicts to the appropriate subconsultant. As the professional responsible for the architectural intent of the project, the architect is for example responsible for noting potential collisions between structural and mechanical systems, and orchestrating a solution between disciplines.

Since the BIM model is a comprehensive virtual building (albeit with varying degrees of detail, so-called resolution or granularity), it is an excellent medium for clash detection (Fig. 11.18). Indeed, some software automates clash detection, although it can at times be challenging for software to distinguish, for example, a legitimate supply air-branch from the unintended collision between two supply

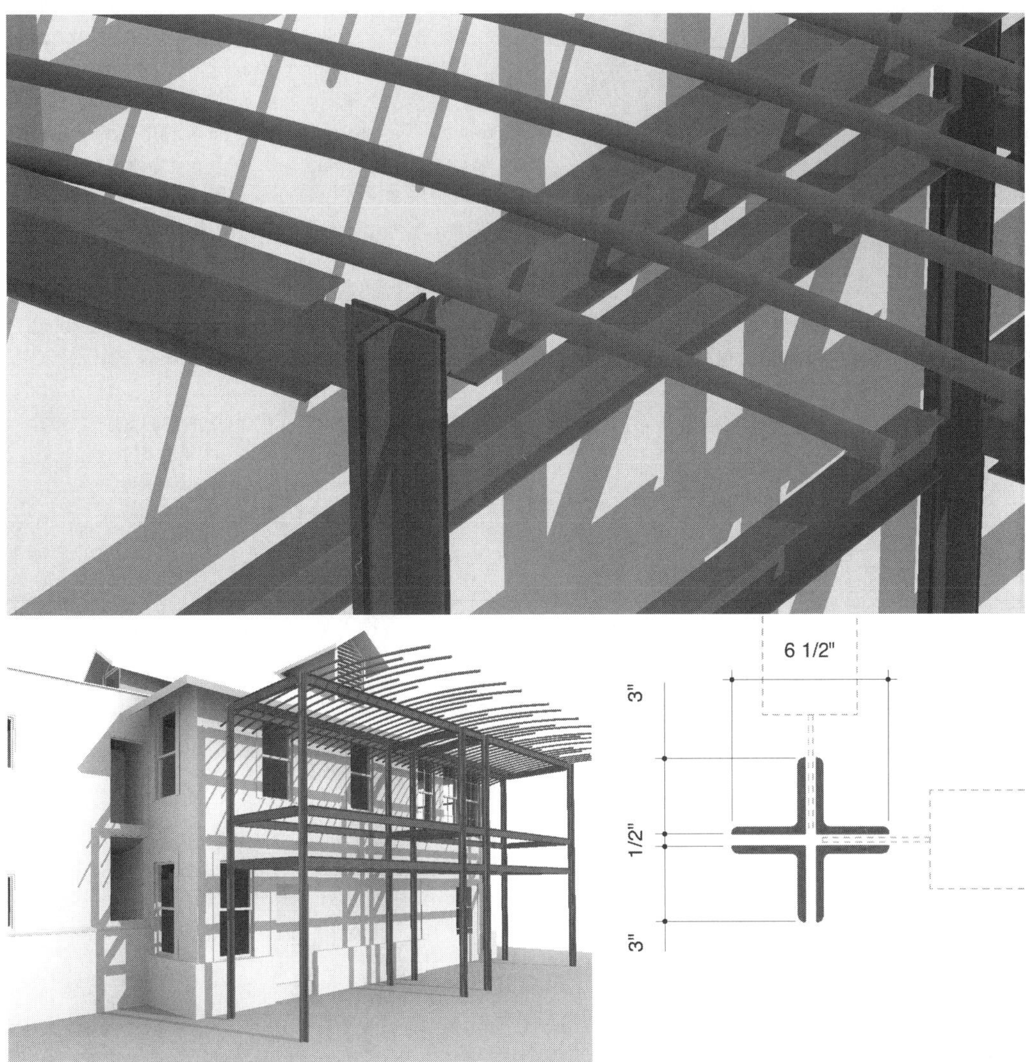

FIGURE 11.18 Some BIM applications automate clash detection, alerting the user when geometry conflicts occur. But clash detection is not infallible, sometimes mistakenly flagging deliberate intersections—like a branching duct or structural connections—as clashes. In those instances, or when automatic clash detection is not available, human intervention is required.

ducts. Furthermore, single elements modeled as two or more separate components may trigger multiple clash alerts when there is only one. Humans, on the other hand, tend to detect fewer clashes but do so more accurately.

With human or automated clash detection, the BIM model serves as the central repository for architect- and engineer-designed building elements. Further on in this chapter we'll address some of the particulars of importing and exporting building information and model parts to and from members of the project team, all of whom will not necessarily be using the same software platform, nor be BIM-capable.

DWG

Thanks to the near-ubiquity of Autodesk's software, by the 1990s AutoCAD's native DWG format had become a frequently required submission format for US federal government building projects. In 1998 several of Autodesk's competitors formed the OpenDWG Alliance, now the Open Design Alliance, to reverse engineer Autodesk's proprietary native format. In this way their respective products could reliably import and export DWG files (and later MicroStation DGN files). With each new release of AutoCAD and the evolution of the DWG format, the Open Drawing Alliance has fairly consistently kept pace, such that competing products can "digest" current or one-revision-old versions of DWG. While the result has been that other software developers' products remain competitive for government projects, DWG has become more firmly entrenched as a standard, albeit a proprietary one.

DWG is therefore a format that every architect working electronically—which is to say nearly every firm—must deal with on a regular basis, whether or not AutoCAD is the software being used, and whether or not the designer is operating in a BIM environment. And while AutoCAD and Revit are both Autodesk products, they have very different origins, such that Revit users have virtually the same issues around DWG as other BIM users.

The DWG format has evolved just as its parent application has, and it can accommodate far more object types than basic 2D shapes: lines, arcs, and polylines (PLines in AutoCAD). The format can handle 3D objects from simple solids to the parametric objects like doors and windows that comprise the modern AutoCAD, as well as schedules and worksheets. As with any transfer of model information across software platforms, however, "smart" objects like parametric building components cease to function parametrically once imported. Objects do retain their geometry in almost every case, whether exporting to DWG or importing files of that format, but the data attached to an object are often lost as well as the ability to easily edit it. An AutoCAD door object when imported into a BIM application—say, ArchiCAD—has its geometry preserved, and may look the same, but it will not be interpreted as an ArchiCAD door object, just a static 3D model. (As discussed further on, the same loss of ready editing of higher-level objects plagues transfer of BIM models via IFC, the BIM transfer format. However, with IFC, an embedded data standard is preserved.)

DWG is therefore an appropriate background medium to reference conditions or designs established by another discipline, but it is not a fully collaborative medium between two firms using different BIM—or even CAD—applications (Fig. 11.19).

When the BIM user is exporting project information for use by a team member, it's frequently preferable for the sender to selectively provide drawings and/or model backgrounds. It's usually not preferred for the entire project to be sent to a consultant, even for small buildings, but just those portions (layers or classes, depending on the terminology of the BIM program of origin) relevant to the recipient. Consider an architect working in BIM who sends architectural design files to a consulting structural engineer working in AutoCAD, primarily in 2D. Since this is a BIM to CAD workflow, the architect is not providing the entire BIM model, but 2D views of it—that is, drawings. The engineer will primarily work in plan, using elevations and sections for reference only. Consequently, the architect might omit interior elevations, details, wall sections, and lighting plans (views), such as they are, providing only DWG plans, building elevations, and sections.

FIGURE 11.19 DWGs exported from the BIM model (above) preserve geometry and layer information, but the resulting objects (below) are not readily editable, and all attached data is lost.

Perhaps the entire drawing set might be transmitted as an accompanying PDF, in the interest of providing as much project context as possible.

BIM + IPD

In design and construction, BIM has been seen as an enabling social framework and technology for integrated project delivery (IPD). IPD methodologies hold the promise of a shift away from jealously guarded fiefdoms carved out of the project scope, and toward an open collaborative where designers, constructors, consultants, and owners have a vested interest in project success. IPD itself is not a technology, but a social structure that makes extensive use of technology to achieve its ends. In the case of IPD, those goals are the reduction of waste, improvement of quality, and maximization of efficiency and value to the project owner. At its heart, IPD is based on collaboration between members of the *project* team (beyond just the design team) and their knowledge sharing, which, in turn, is dependent on communication and trust.

Because IPD is only effective when based on a foundation of communication and trust, it is both conducive to and requires knowledge sharing. The implication is that project information may be shared earlier in the design process, so that all members of the team may inform and influence the design according to their relative expertise. Thus with its emphasis on collaborative project coordination and open communication, IPD finds a ready ally in BIM. The building model encourages coordination with the presence and interaction of interdisciplinary components within a singular model. Architectural, structural and mechanical elements populate the model, increasing the effectiveness of detecting unwanted interactions (clash detection, automated or not). Project team members may submit relevant files for coordination with other disciplines, and may therefore anticipate conflicts earlier in the design process.

BIM can only support IPD, but is not by itself a substitute for it. Conversely, IPD can occur without BIM, but collaborative coordination and knowledge sharing may be hampered by the lack of a robust collective 3D environment. From some perspectives, open collaboration is a fundamental requirement of BIM; without it BIM falls short of its potential for open collaboration and is just a building model environment. BIM without collaboration is just a technology; with the added dimension of collaboration, BIM becomes a social-process enabler.

For the practitioner or firm designing primarily skin-load dominated (or small) projects, a discussion about open BIM might seem beside the point, given that the list of collaborators is short. But even in small projects—and even in those in which IPD agreements may not be in place—open collaboration with the contractor and consultants can yield tangible benefits (Fig. 11.20). As a simple but compelling example, consider construction budgets throughout the project's design. Under the established triumvirate model of Owner-Architect-Contractor, design firms often are reluctant to release quantity material takeoffs to the general contractor for preparation of cost estimates or bids. The most often cited reason is legal liability. On the other hand, a properly constructed BIM model can report accurate takeoffs of a wide variety of materials:

- Net and gross area differentiated for every type of flooring, siding, wallboard, and roofing material
- Bill of materials, by dimensional lumber nominal sizes and lengths of lumber, or number and type of concrete masonry units (CMUs)
- Accurate door and window schedules derived directly from instances inserted in the model
- Total linear values of materials like running and standing trim
- Correct counts of plumbing fixtures, electrical devices, luminaires, and hardware

It's obvious that basing a cost estimate or bid on these reported values should be more accurate and less prone to error than scaling from a printed plan or elevation. Clearly the architect has a vested interest in accurate cost estimating, particularly if those estimates are prepared as early as possible in the design process. Deferring cost estimates until the project design is nearly complete opens the door for redesign (potentially at the architect's cost), or worse yet, project cancellation. Each firm must weigh for itself the benefits of providing early and open project information to potential contractors against the potential for additional legal exposure. However, the traditional practice of leaving general contractors to fend for themselves may seem to "protect" the architects in the short term, only to potentially undermine the project as a whole in the long run.

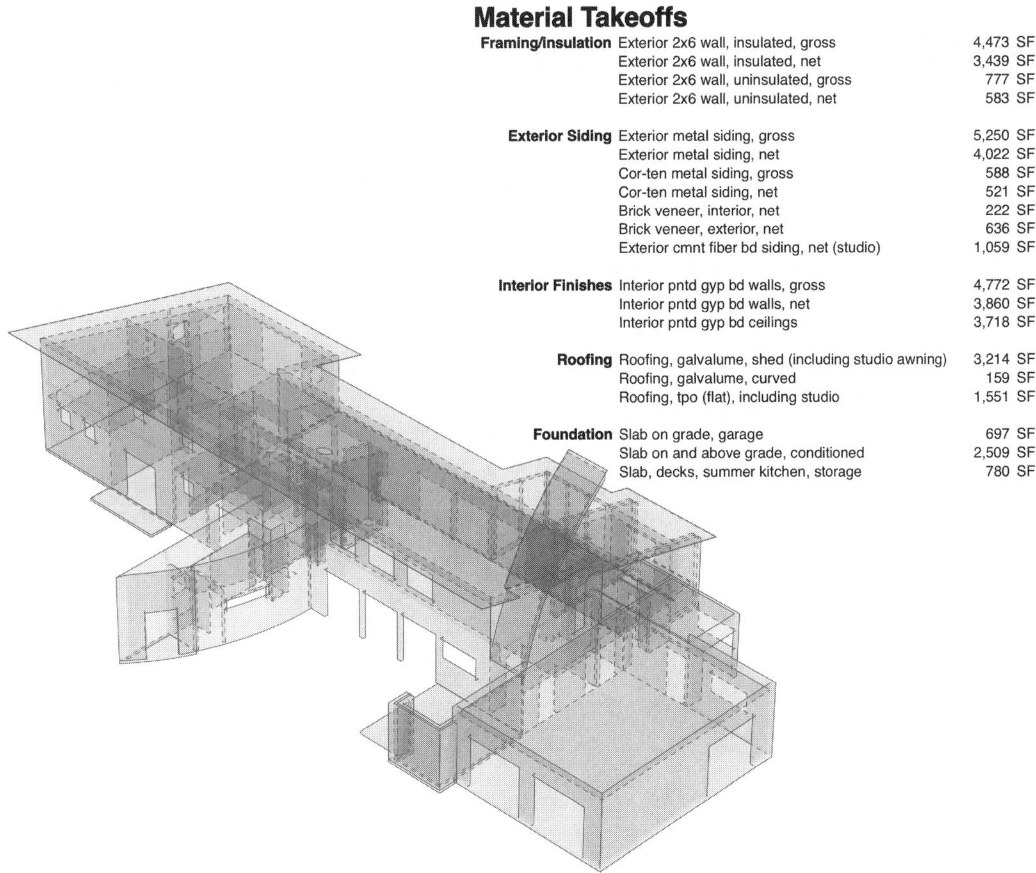

Material Takeoffs

Framing/Insulation	Exterior 2x6 wall, insulated, gross	4,473 SF
	Exterior 2x6 wall, insulated, net	3,439 SF
	Exterior 2x6 wall, uninsulated, gross	777 SF
	Exterior 2x6 wall, uninsulated, net	583 SF
Exterior Siding	Exterior metal siding, gross	5,250 SF
	Exterior metal siding, net	4,022 SF
	Cor-ten metal siding, gross	588 SF
	Cor-ten metal siding, net	521 SF
	Brick veneer, interior, net	222 SF
	Brick veneer, exterior, net	636 SF
	Exterior cmnt fiber bd siding, net (studio)	1,059 SF
Interior Finishes	Interior pntd gyp bd walls, gross	4,772 SF
	Interior pntd gyp bd walls, net	3,860 SF
	Interior pntd gyp bd ceilings	3,718 SF
Roofing	Roofing, galvalume, shed (including studio awning)	3,214 SF
	Roofing, galvalume, curved	159 SF
	Roofing, tpo (flat), including studio	1,551 SF
Foundation	Slab on grade, garage	697 SF
	Slab on and above grade, conditioned	2,509 SF
	Slab, decks, summer kitchen, storage	780 SF

FIGURE 11.20 Tabular data can be reported from the model by virtually any criteria. Here, those parts of the model populating the worksheet are visible; everything else has been turned off (for illustrative purposes only).

As a result, in my practice over a long period of time I have evolved a willingness to share project information from that of erecting a strict firewall behind the construction documents ("refer to the drawings please") to a far more open sharing process, even offering to share read-only files with owners and contractors. Moreover, the AIA has developed a series of evolving contracts that clarify both team member responsibilities and ownership of project information under IPD and BIM. The reader is referred to *Integrated Project Delivery: A Guide* (2007) and other AIA resources for further reading on IPD.

IFC

The Government Services Agency's and other entities' commitment to an open BIM standard, along with other forces, has led to the development of buildingSMART's industry foundation classes (IFC). This file format is critical to the interoperability of BIM, and it is therefore discussed here apart from other import or export files. Unlike DWG, this is an open, non-proprietary file format that is not native to any single application. Rather, a little like Esperanto, it is a "common language" that no one "speaks" natively, but that all can learn and understand (the analogy is loose; in actuality, IFC is not a

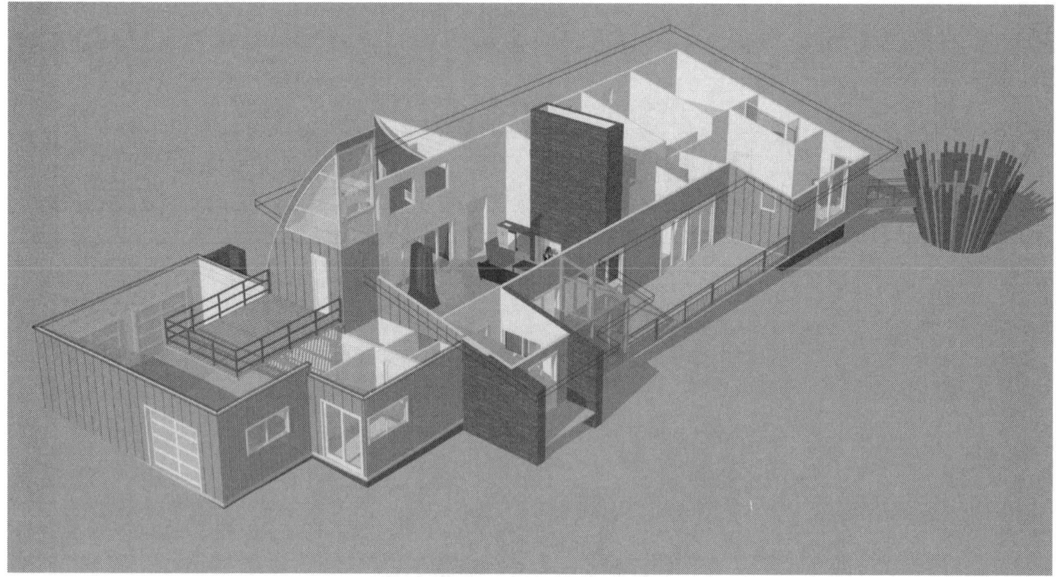

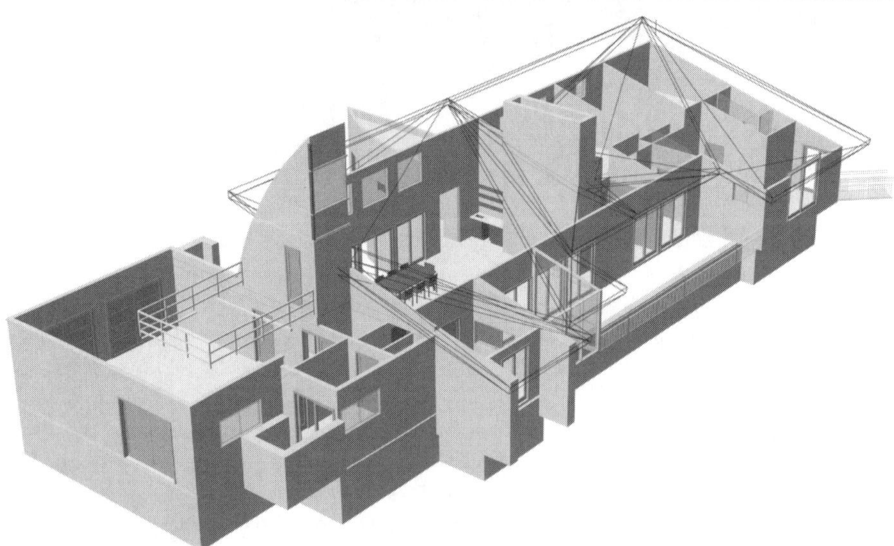

FIGURE 11.21 When exported via IFC, object geometry is preserved, as is attached data (as in Fig. 11.12), but parametric object editing is lost. That is, IFC geometry can still be changed, but by using manual modeling methods. A parametric door exported via IFC retains its geometry and data and can be stretched and changed. If imported into Revit, Vectorworks, or ArchiCAD, however, it is not a door object, like one created with the respective software's door tool.

computer language at all, but a data-rich geometry file format; Fig. 11.21).

BIM can arguably exist without IPD, although increasingly early and pervasive design collaboration and the interoperability it requires are seen as a cornerstone of BIM. IPD, however, entails some medium of architectural communication that captures building geometry and data—BIM is the logical choice. There is therefore a compelling need for a BIM lingua franca, a common file format that all

BIM applications can import and export across all building disciplines. Such a need is even greater for BIM than for CAD, given the former's suitability for collaboration.

IFC-compliant BIM authoring tools (all those discussed in this book) can both import and export this open, neutral format. Unlike other file formats discussed in this chapter, IFC is truly made for BIM. As a standard subject to negotiation and development by many different stakeholders (including software vendors, building owners, architecture and engineering firms, construction companies, and facilities managers), IFC is evolving. Furthermore, it is designed to translate geometry and data, not necessarily object functionality.

Imagine, for example, an architecture firm working in ArchiCAD and a structural engineer using Revit Structure. Both are IFC-compliant. The architect includes an exposed steel W-section in the design, say a W8x35. The object is both parametric (its dimensions and profile may be reshaped in ArchiCAD without being manually redrawn) and data-rich (it identifies itself as a structural member). The engineer receives the IFC file and imports it into Revit. The column geometry is there, and it correctly identifies itself as a structural column. After structural analysis, however, the engineer determines that it is oversized, and suggests a W8x21 instead, a cost and weight savings of 14 pounds per linear foot. The imported structural member is not a Revit column object, however, and is therefore not easily reshaped. Perhaps the engineer will replace it with a Revit column object, or meet with the architect to discuss this and other issues and ask for a refreshed file with a resized W-section. Or, perhaps the architect will want to keep the column roughly 8″ x 8″ for architectural or detailing reasons (Fig. 11.22).

From this example, it is clear that IFC has limitations and benefits. As an inter-operational format specifically designed for BIM, it allows geometry

FIGURE 11.22 A BIM column (left) once exported to IFC (center) can be edited, but not parametrically so (right).

and BIM data to be preserved, assuming that the sender has properly tagged objects. This means that in Figure 11.22 columns must have been identified as structural columns, in addition to having been modeled with the correct dimensions. In many cases the BIM authoring software does this automatically, except for "custom made" objects, which must be manually tagged. On the other hand, the received BIM model is not parametrically editable. While this may seem to be a significant problem with IFC, in fact, this too can be beneficial. Thanks to the relatively static nature of imported IFC geometry, it tends to discourage inadvertent or undisciplined editing of modeled elements of outside authorship. IFC objects, once imported into the BIM model, have their provenance, for the most part, clearly classified as IFC, identifying them as originating in another firm or authored by another discipline.

Case Study: Paisano Senior Housing, El Paso, Texas

By Marianne Bellino
Design firm: Workshop8
Client: Housing Authority of the City of El Paso

Early in 2010 the Housing Authority of the City of El Paso (HACEP) held a national competition for the design of a LEED-platinum, 63-unit, senior housing development (Fig. 11.23). One of the requirements of the competition was that the architectural teams utilize BIM.

For our design team at Workshop8, the adoption of BIM offered a 3D collaborative approach to design. In conjunction with the BIM model generated in Vectorworks, we utilized SketchUp to perform solar analysis and design explorations. On the strength of these technologies we were able to produce a single, multilayered 3D representation that made the design clear and understandable to all parties. In going through this process, we were able to restructure and expedite project delivery. It also offered us an opportunity to resolve problems in the design phase that might arise during construction.

FIGURE 11.23 Workshop8's Paisano Senior Housing Project for the Housing Authority of El Paso is a progressive, sustainable, BIM-developed project consisting of residences organized around interlocking outdoor spaces and a community center. HACEP mandated that projects be developed with BIM, but wisely did not enforce a particular format.

Image courtesy of Workshop8.

In the Paisano Senior Housing Project for HACEP, the use of BIM technologies was critical to the success of the project. With an integrated BIM design process, our team could see the building evolve in 3D, rather than developing the architectural design and then retrofitting the chaos of mechanical, electrical, structural, and other services. As the project evolved, the number of units increased from 63 to 73. We were able to respond to this program change, all the while controlling spatial constraints and building needs, through our use of the integrated building model (Fig. 11.24). We could cut sections through the campus structures with ease, and design with a deeper understanding of interior space and materiality. Key to this design methodology was to have the design team include structural engineers, energy consultants, and landscape designers from the origin of the project.

As a tool to give to the general contractor, the BIM model was also invaluable (Fig. 11.25). During the pricing phase and Bid Negotiation, Workshop8 gave the contractors our model and a brief lesson in how to navigate it. In a very short time (ten to fifteen minutes) they were zooming around on their own. Their excitement was apparent. They immediately realized that the model would greatly help them present the project to their subcontractors and enable the subs to produce more accurate bids, more quickly. The general contractor is looking forward to having the model available during the construction process as it will be the best way to convey information to craftspeople and trades on-site.

FIGURE 11.24 Intimately scaled courtyards are open at one end and lend a humane scale to the housing development. The courtyard's dimensions (contingent on the width and height of adjacent structures) were developed using extensive solar modeling to help ensure passive heating in the winter and adequate shade in the summer.

Image courtesy of Workshop8.

FIGURE 11.25 The Paisano Senior Housing Project's canopy wall was an important component of the project brief. Workshop8's implementation of it serves as a western shade and parking screen, includes onsite energy production, architecturally integrates security and vertical circulation, serves as an edge to the campus, and is an iconic marker for the project.

Image courtesy of Workshop8.

FIGURE 11.26 Like other elements of the project, the Paisano Senior Housing Project's community center envelope was designed using solar studies.

Image courtesy of Workshop8.

We collaboratively exploited BIM as a tool to achieve our goals of designing a project that was economically and programmatically viable. The project will achieve LEED Platinum status, produce sustainable iconic architecture for the Housing Authority of El Paso, and ultimately create an environment that will allow its residents to enjoy a high quality of life (Fig. 11.26).

Afterword

That old curse: we live in interesting times. Within the brief span of my own career (which is hopefully far from over) I have had the peculiar privilege of witnessing the "end" of manual drafting, the rise of CAD, and the sea change of BIM. At each turn, an old guard has decried the loss of a valuable tradition, pitted against evangelists and bleeding-edge early adopters with messianic visions of solving all architectural problems with a new way of working. But by now, we should be suspicious of technological silver bullets that promise to solve all problems—and not just in architecture. Careful consideration of technology—any technology—will lead the thoughtful observer to the conclusion that technological use and change has at least as much a social dimension as a technical one. The word "progress" has become a loaded term. And yet, it truly cannot be stopped. Of the two camps, skeptic and devotee, both are probably somewhat right.

In any technological change, one quality is lost as another is gained, be it a tradition (what a professor of mine called the lore of architecture), a perspective, or an understanding. In the trend away from drawing that BIM undeniably embodies, there is no doubting the loss of a skill set as well as the particular insights that exercising that skill set affords. We take for granted that architects will always draw—like many, I keep a sketch pad by my computer to quickly work out ideas—but perhaps that is just an assumption. And like many of my colleagues, I value beautiful architectural drawings for their own sake. Is that a fetish, I wonder? Is not the business of the architect ultimately the resulting building?

Moreover, the BIM that I practice and advocate in this book offers the designer a path to sustainable design that is more than a last minute band-aid or cosmetic architectural greening. Skin-load dominated buildings can be far more sustainable by applying reliable but simple design guides early in the process, rather than relying on intuition only, or detailed energy modeling too late in the process. As a quantitative design tool, BIM can be a means to such an early sustainable design process.

It has been my goal with this book to help other architects and designers find the tools to create richer, better performing, and yes, more beautiful buildings. It is my position—perhaps fodder for another book—that beauty is found in our human creations when they are most in sympathy with nature. I don't mean that we ought to decorate our artifacts to look "natural," fetishizing organic motifs. Rather, I contend that beauty arises out of a profound understanding of natural systems, their complexity, and their economy. By "economy" I hope to connote both an exchange, and an elegance of effort. In that context, designing for building performance adds another dimension to our creative work: that of conserving energy and securing our children's future. As worthy and critical as designing and living sustainably is, it can be more profound than a mere practical matter of survival, or enjoying a stable standard of living. It can be a way of life and an evolving path to beauty.

As with our societal systems that are adapting to emerging environmental and technological realities, BIM is an evolving process. And it is evolving in at least two directions. One of these is external to the particulars of any one software tool or platform, what some have called big BIM. Here the acronym emphasizes building information model*ing*, and BIM in this sense has larger social ramifications for the way we go about designing as a profession and as individual members of a team. The collaborative creation of an interoperable, open virtual building model shared by building professionals and client is giving rise to (or at least fostering) greater systems of thinking and a more transparent way to design. Of the aspects of BIM, big BIM is perhaps the least understood, the least predictable, and potentially has the greatest unanticipated consequences.

Objecting to these almost frenetically shifting social and technological forces is a voice inside all of us, for some shouting, for others only a whisper: *We designed and drew successfully for centuries without this technological upheaval. Why throw away generations of hard-won design process and wisdom?* But the truth is that change has always been with us; previously it was, at times, slow enough to give us the comforting illusion of permanence. Our methods of designing always changed, and those methods always informed *what* we designed, not just *how*. Process and product are inextricable.

As a practical matter, little BIM, building information model, is also evolving as a software environment. Objects, tools, commands, procedures, features, and capabilities within any given BIM application are being pushed, refined, and made more powerful and robust by software developers and users. As BIM (considered "strictly" as a technology) develops in this sense, methodologies change over time and best practices emerge. (The word *strictly* in the previous sentence is in quotes because it is pure fiction that technology can be divorced from the social forces that deploy it and that technology in turn shapes.) This book seeks to convey those best practices as I understand them from my perspective as a sole practitioner designing sustainable buildings for a demanding climate.

Even on the small time scale of just a few years, many practices are reluctant to adopt new revisions of the software they use every day. Balanced against the promise of greater efficiencies and more powerful tools is the reasonable concern for the disruption in work that new versions may bring. New software often entrains upgrading hardware, which can quickly become a not insignificant investment, in addition to the cost of the application itself. Perhaps, too, there is a nagging fear that the office's legacy library of past projects and details will become inaccessible, or that the new version won't read current project files due to some horrible bug. In addition, new software versions may require retraining, another short-term loss of productivity. Many firms make it a policy to only upgrade every other version for just these reasons. Moreover, even when software is upgraded, there are no assurances that theoretically improved features will be implemented. I've lost track of the number of times I've shown a colleague an established software feature, only to be met with surprise. *When did we get that tool?!*

The decision not to upgrade software is for the most part carefully considered, if at times a bit myopic, and is not simply a case of architects and other design professionals being reactionary. If this is the resistance to adopting new software versions, imagine the opposition to adopting a whole new way of working. The costs of adopting BIM are not inconsiderable and they include software costs, probable hardware costs, training costs, and lost productivity during training. Obviously, the benefits are great, but weighing them against expenses gives some firms justifiable pause.

As an evolving tool, BIM is by definition imperfect and not without its limitations. Software developers must balance market pressures to annually release exciting new features. Moreover, there is the decidedly unglamorous but essential need to make their offerings more stable, robust, and efficient. New features sell, but improvements under the hood keep users on board and support product longevity. And of course the marketing copy must trumpet the new features as breakthroughs without implying that previous versions were inadequate. As conservative as the construction industry may be, it is not immune to social forces, of which BIM is only one exponent. But we also have the power to shape those forces. In the end, we all understand perhaps with a certain sense of unease that change is the norm. Get used to change. Embrace it.

Take what you have read here, understand it, digest it, apply it, and make it your own. Not every chapter will be applicable to every climate, nor to every project you design. For every formula I have offered, every technique I have suggested, there are other approaches available. Be curious. Be a scientist. Explore. More than just a step-by-step primer on quantitative sustainable design, this volume can inspire and encourage you to apply its underlying principles to your own work. Don't hesitate to re-evaluate how you have already been working, and look for ways to add a quantitative dimension to your design process. Don't abandon your architectural processes. Enrich them.

I look forward to hearing from you and especially seeing the extraordinary projects you will design. We live in interesting times indeed.

—Austin, Texas

Bibliography and References

Aksamija, Ajla, and Mir M. Ali. 2008. "Information Technology and Architectural Practice: Knowledge Modeling Approach and BIM." Proceedings of AIA Conference: Breaking New Ground, Moline, IL, November 7–8.

Allen, Edward, and Joseph Iano. 2006. *The Architect's Studio Companion: Rules of Thumb for Preliminary Design*. 4th ed. Hoboken, NJ: John Wiley & Sons.

American Institute of Architects. 2007. *Integrated Project Delivery: A Guide*. Washington, D.C.: American Institute of Architects.

Anderson, Robert. 2010. "An Introduction to the IPD Workflow for Vectorworks BIM Users." Columbia, MD: Nemetschek Vectorworks.

Austin Energy Green Building Program. 2000. *Sustainable Building Sourcebook*. Austin, TX: Austin Energy

Austin Energy Green Building Program. 2011. "Green Building Program Commercial Rating Workbook." Austin, TX: Austin Energy.

Balcomb, Douglas. 1980. *Passive Solar Design Handbook, Vol. 2*. United States Department of Energy.

Bahadoori, Mehdi. 1978. "Passive Cooling Systems in Iranian Architecture." *Scientific American* 238 (2): 144–154.

Battle McCarthy Consulting Engineers. *Wind Towers: Detail in Building*. New York: John Wiley & Sons, 1999.

Bone, Eugenia. 1996. "The House that Max Built." *Metropolis Magazine,* December, 37–42.

Brown, Chris, Jan Gerston, and Stephen Colley. 2005. *The Texas Manual on Rainwater Harvesting*. 3rd ed. Austin: Texas Water Development Board.

Brown, G. Z., and Mark DeKay. 2001. *Sun, Wind & Light: Architectural Design Strategies*. 2nd ed. New York: John Wiley & Sons.

Butti, Ken, and John Perlin. 1980. *A Golden Thread: 2500 Years of Solar Architecture and Technology*. New York: Van Nostrand Reinhold.

Ching, Francis. *Architectural Graphics*. 2002. 4th ed. Hoboken, NJ: John Wiley & Sons.

Ching, Francis. 2008. *Building Construction Illustrated*. 4th ed. Hoboken, NJ: John Wiley & Sons.

Ching, Francis, and Steven R Winkel. 2009. *Building Codes Illustrated*. 3rd ed. Hoboken, NJ: John Wiley & Sons.

Digital Vision Automation. 2010. *Modeling Terrain with Graphisoft ArchiCAD*. Accessed June 2010 from http://www.digitalvis.com/pdfs/support/tipstricks/Terrain%20Modeling.pdf.

Eastman, Chuck, Paul Teicholz, Rafael Sacks, and Kathleen Liston. 2008. *BIM Handbook: A Guide to Building Information Modeling for Owners, Managers, Designers, Engineers, and Contractors*. Hoboken, NJ: John Wiley & Sons.

European Commission. 2010. *EU Energy and Transport in Figures 2010*. Luxembourg: Publications Office of the European Union.

Feenberg, Andrew. 1995. "Subversive Rationalization: Technology, Power, and Democracy." In *Technology and the Politics of Knowledge*, edited by Andrew Feenberg and Alistair Hannay. Bloomington: Indiana University Press.

Fisk, Pliny III, Hal Levin, and Paul Bierman-Lytle. 1992. *Environmental Resource Guide*, Washington, D.C.: The Amercian Institute of Architects.

Fisk, Pliny III. 1983. "Bioregions and Biotechnologies." Presented at *New Perspectives in Planning in the West*. Arizona State University, May.

Franklin, Benjamin. 1758. "Cooling by Evaporation," Letter to John Lining, June 17.

Gleick, Peter H. 2008. "Water Conflict Chronology." In *Data from the Pacific Institute for Studies in Development, Environment, and Security Database on Water and Conflict*

(Water Brief). Pacific Institute for Studies in Development, Environment, and Security, November.

Graedel, T. E., B. R. Allenbry, and P. R. Comrie. 1995. "Matrix Approaches to Abridged Life Cycle Analysis." *Environmental Science & Technology* 29 (3).

Grondzik, Walter T., Alison G. Kwok, Ben Stein, and John S. Reynolds. 2010. *Mechanical and Electrical Equipment for Buildings*. 11th ed. Hoboken, NJ: John Wiley & Sons.

Guzowski, Mary. 1999. *Daylighting for Sustainable Design*. New York: McGraw-Hill.

Heschong, Lisa. 1979. *Thermal Delight in Architecture*. Cambridge, MA: MIT Press.

Hirai, Ken'ichi. 2008. *VW Designs*. Columbia, MD: Nemeteschek North America.

Hughes, Thomas. 1985, "Edison and Electric Light." In *The Social Shaping of Technology*, edited by Donald MacKenzie and Judith Waicman. Berkshire, UK: Open University Press.

International Energy Agency. 2000. *Daylighting in Buildings*. Berkeley, CA: Lawrence Berkeley National Laboratory.

Jansenson, Daniel. 2005. *The Renderworks Recipe Book*. Santa Monica, CA: Imageprops, 2005.

Jansenson, Daniel. 2010. *Remarkable Renderworks: An Introduction to the Basics*. Columbia, MD: Nemetschek North America.

Jernigan, Finith E. 2008. *BIG BIM little bim*. 2nd ed. Sailsbury, MD: 4Site Press.

Khemlani, Lachmi. 2010. "ArchiCAD 14: AECbytes Product Review." Retrieved September 21, 2010, from AECbytes.com.

Krygiel, Eddy, and Brad Nies. 2008. *Green BIM: Successful Sustainable Design with Building Information Modeling*. Indianapolis: Wiley Publishing.

Laiserin, Jerry. 2010. "Designer's BIM: Vectorworks Architect Keeps Design at the Center of BIM Process." Accessed March 2010 from Laiserin.com.

Lechner, Norbert. 2009. *Heating, Cooling, Lighting: Sustainable Design Methods for Architects*. 3rd ed. Hoboken, NJ: John Wiley & Sons,.

Lstiburek, Joseph. 2006. *Builder's Guide to Cold Climates*. Somerville, MA: Building Science Press.

Lyle, John Tillman. 1994. *Regenerative Design for Sustainable Development*. New York: John Wiley & Sons.

McDonough, William. 1996. "Design, Ecology, and the Making of Things." In *Theorizing a New Agenda for Architecture*, edited by Kate Nesbitt. New York: Princeton Architectural Press.

Mekonnen, M. M., and A. Y. Hoekstra. 2010. "The Green, Blue, and Grey Water Footprint of Farm Animals and Animal Products". Delft, Netherlands: UNESCO-IHE Institute for Water Education.

Mendler, Sandra F., William Odell, and Mary Ann Lazarus. 2005. *The HOK Guidebook to Sustainable Design*. 2nd ed. Hoboken, NJ: John Wiley & Sons.

Nelson, M., F. Cattin, M. Rajendran, and L. Hafouda. 2008. "Value-Adding Through Creation of High Diversity Gardens and Ecoscapes in Subsurface Flow Constructed Wetlands: Case Studies in Algeria and Australia of Wastewater Gardens Systems." *11th International Conference on Wetland Systems for Water Pollution Control*. Indore, India: International Water Association, Vikram University, November.

Nye, David. 1994. "The Electrical Sublime." In *American Technological Sublime*. Cambridge, MA: MIT Press.

Nye, David. 1998. *Consuming Power: A Social History of American Energies*. Cambridge, MA: MIT Press.

Olgyay, Victor. 1992. *Design With Climate: A Bioclimatic Approach to Architectural Regionalism*. New York: Van Nostrand Reinhold.

Patterson, Terry. 2001. *Architect's Studio Handbook*. New York: McGraw-Hill Professional Publishing.

Post, Nadine M. 2009. "Digging Into 3D Modeling Unearths Many Worms." *Engineering News Record* 262 (14): 26–27.

Pottmann, Helmut, Andreas Asperl, Michael Hofer, and Axel Kilian. 2007. *Architectural Geometry*. Exton, PA: Bentley Institute Press.

Ramsey, Charles, and George Sleeper. 2007. *Architectural Graphic Standards*. 11th ed. Ed. The American Institute of Architects. Hoboken, NJ: John Wiley & Sons.

Reinhart, C. F., and V. R. M. LoVerso. 2010. "A Rules of Thumb-Based Design Sequence for Diffuse Daylight." *Lighting Research and Technology* 42 (7).

Sheet Metal and Air Conditioning Contractors National Association. 1993. *Architectural Sheet Metal Manual*. 5th ed. Chantilly, VA: Sheet Metal and Air Conditioning Contractors National Association.

Simpson, Grant A., and James B. Atkins. 2005. "Best, Practices in Risk Management: Your Grandfather's Working Drawings." Accessed August 2005 from AIArchitect.com.

Simpson, Grant A., and James B. Atkins. 2005. "Best Practices in Risk Management: Drawing the Line." Accessed September 2005 from AIArchitect.com.

Thayer, Robert. 1996. *Gray World Green Heart: Technology, Nature, and the Sustainable Landscape*. New York: John Wiley & Sons.

Thoo, Sid. 2010. "Graphisoft EcoDesigner: AECbytes Product Review." Accessed February 11, 2010, from AECbytes.com.

Tobey, Ronald. 1994. *Technology as Freedom: The New Deal and the Electronic Modernization of the American Home*. Berkeley, CA: U.C. Press.

U.S. Energy Information Administration. 2009. *Annual Energy Review*. Washington, D.C.: U.S. Energy Information Administration.

U.S. Green Building Council. 2008. *LEED for Homes*. Washington, D.C.: U.S. Green Building Council.

Vliet, Gary C. 1982. *Solar Energy Systems*. Unpublished revision of John R. Howell, Richard B. Bannerot, and Gary C. Vliet, *Solar Thermal Energy Systems Analysis and Design*. New York: McGraw-Hill.

Wing, Eric. 2010. *Revit Architecture 2010: No Experience Required*. Indianapolis: Wiley Publishing.

World Water Council. 2000. *World Water Vision Commission Report: A Water Secure World*. Marseille, France: World Water Council.

Index